BLIZZARD'S DAZZLING WOODEN TOYS

Sterling Publishing Co., Inc. New York

BLIZZARD'S DAZZLING WOODEN TOYS

Richard Blizzard

ACKNOWLEDGEMENTS

When I reach the end of a book I am always very conscious of all the encouragement and practical help I have received from a large number of people from many different professions and all walks of life. So here is a very special 'thank you' to you all, including:

Mervyn Hurford, Peter Farley and Stephanie Banks for their illustrations and drawings;

Jenny Spring who tackled heaps of untidy notes to produce a tidy script;

At BBC Books, Norman Brownsword for the book's design and layout, David Knight who waited so patiently for both script and drawings, and Jennie Allen for taking such care in reading and re-reading the text and for many helpful suggestions;

Andrew Litchfield and Jane Reynolds of Volvo UK for their help in getting the original drawings for Jakob and all the background information that was so necessary before I started making the car.

Allan Williams and Graham Millar for making drawings available for the Volvo 540.

W. D. McCullough, Vice President, Mack Trucks, Pennsylvania, USA who sent drawings and models to help me build the Mack Super Liner.

John Bond for making Jakob's radiator and turned headlights – thank you for a beautiful piece of workmanship.

Peter Westley for his artistic contribution to the design of the models.

The plans for the toys and models were drawn by Peter F. Farley and Mervyn Hurford.

The black and white and color photographs were taken by Michael Michaels.

The running heading and diagrams in the tools section were drawn by Alan Burton.

The guide to building a basic tool kit on pages 210–213 is reproduced by kind permission of Record Marples Tools Ltd.

The photograph on the front cover shows a completed model of a Sopwith Camel and the back cover shows a Volvo dump truck.

Copyright © 1987 by Richard Blizzard
Published in 1989 by Sterling Publishing Co., Inc.
387 Park Avenue South, New York, New York 10016
First published in the U.K. in 1987 by BBC Books, a division of BBC Enterprises, London
Manufactured in the United States of America
All rights reserved
ISBN 0-8069-6614-9

This book was set in 10 key on 11 point Gill by Rowland Phototypesetting Ltd, Bury St Edmunds, Suffolk

Throughout the book metric measurements are given first, followed by imperial measurements in brackets

CONTENTS

Introduction

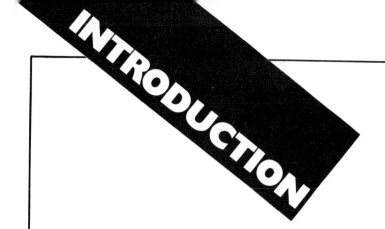

INTRODUCTION

FOREWORD

A tree is a thing both of great beauty and of versatile usefulness. The tree in the Garden of Eden was 'pleasant to the eyes' and 'good for food'. Trees form an integral part of the water cycle, are vital factors in soil conservation and make important habitats. The rich diversity of timbers have an equally legion range of uses – from cradles to rocking chairs. Throughout human life trees are providers – of shade from the summer sun, of furniture for the comfortable home, of handles for the garden tools. What's more, each piece of timber is unique – individually grained.

Wood, because it takes time to grow and to fashion, suggests to me long-term values in a world which is so often pre-occupied only with short-term considerations. Indeed it was the short-term durability of other toys which first prompted Richard Blizzard to begin making sturdy wooden toys for his own children to enjoy. As a natural communicator he found it impossible to keep this to himself, and we are all the richer for his enthusiastic sharing of designs with a wider public, both on television and here again in print.

I appreciate the results of Richard's craftsmanship and his ability to communicate. To those bold enough to embark with saw, hammer and chisel, intent on creating something recognisable and pleasing to children from a raw lump of wood, I commend this excellent book. And to those who simply wish to enjoy the results, buy it for the potential carpenters in your family for whom this book could prove the trigger of a lifetime of creative satisfaction. They'll find working with wood can ward off many a workaday pressure in those precious leisure moments!

I count it a privilege to launch this latest offering from the busy Blizzard pen and to wish cheerful chiselling to beginners and experts alike.

E. John Wibberley
Minchinhampton 1986

INTRODUCTION

This book has been written because you have requested it. I know from thousands of letters and hundreds of phone calls and photographs that you have discovered the 'joy of making'. I know that there are armies of mothers, fathers and grandparents all busily sawing, planing and glueing toys together throughout the length and breadth of the country. Well, here are more toys and models for you to get started on!

I know you like making go-carts, so there is a new self-propelled model that should make youngsters uncatchable across the lawn! I've also included a rocking horse for those who like something a little quieter and, for the younger child, a nutty woodpecker who pecks his way down a tree, knocking off pine cones as he comes!

For those who like to test their skills on large models there is a Mack Super-liner complete with a log trailer – the largest model I have ever built. And if you like cars and built the Silver Ghost from *Blizzard's Wonderful Wooden Toys*, then there's a real challenge in building 'Jakob', the first car Volvo ever made.

It is my hope that this book will bring as much pleasure and enjoyment as the last and that you will continue to follow the words of Robert Bridges, 'I too will something make and joy in the making'.

Richard Blizzard
April 1987

WHIRLY BLOCKS

Young children are always fascinated by movement and colour and this simple pull-along toy provides both. It is easy to build and you will only need the minimum of tools. The base can be made from any timber, but beech is best for the whirly blocks themselves. You can leave these unpainted but the toy is greatly enhanced if spiral shapes are painted in different colours on the top of each, so that, as the wheels turn, the blocks and the spiral patterns turn too. It's all very simple, it won't break and it works well.

1   Cut and shape the base, marking the positions for the axle and dowel rod holes.

2   Drill the axle holes. I advise you to drill the axle holes from both sides of the base and you will need to drill very accurately at 90° in both planes to get them properly aligned. This is a tricky operation and an extra pair of hands and eyes will probably be of great assistance to you.

3   Drill the dowel rod holes directly over the axle rod holes. It doesn't matter if you drill through into them. Glue the dowel rods into the holes. Fit the steel axles into the axle rod holes.

4   Cut your four beech blocks and drill a hole through each of them. These holes need to be slightly larger in diameter than the dowel rods they fit onto, to allow the blocks to turn freely. If you don't have a large enough drill bit, improvise by wrapping a small dowel rod in glasspaper and work this backwards and forwards in the hole to enlarge it. Test each block to see that it rotates freely on the dowel rod. You will find candle wax an excellent lubricant. The edges of the blocks must be gently rounded over with glasspaper since hardwood is sharp and will cut. Paint spiral shapes on the blocks using lead-free paint.

5   Drill a hole at one end of the base to take a nylon towing cord and attach the other end of the cord to a small piece of dowel rod for the pulling handle.

6   Fit the wheels onto the axle rods and slot the painted blocks, when dry, onto the dowel rods. These actually rest on top of the wheels and as the wheels turn round, the blocks revolve.

Cutting list

Base	I off	178 × 89 × 22mm (7 × 3½ × ⅞in)	Timber
	4 off	60mm (2⅜in) × 9mm (⅜in) diam dowelling	
Blocks	2 off	51 × 51 × 41mm (2 × 2 × 1⅝in)	Timber
	2 off	38 × 38 × 41mm (1½ × 1½ × 1⅝in)	Timber
Handle	I off	51mm (2in) × 9mm (⅜in) diam dowelling	
Ancillaries			
	4 off	51mm (2in) diam road wheels	
	2 off	140mm (5½in) long × 6mm (¼in) diam steel axles	
	4 off	9mm (⅜in) i/diam × 6mm (¼in) o/diam × 3mm (⅛in) thick spacers	
	4 off	Spring dome caps to suit 6mm (¼in) diam axles	
	I off	762mm (30in) length nylon pull cord	

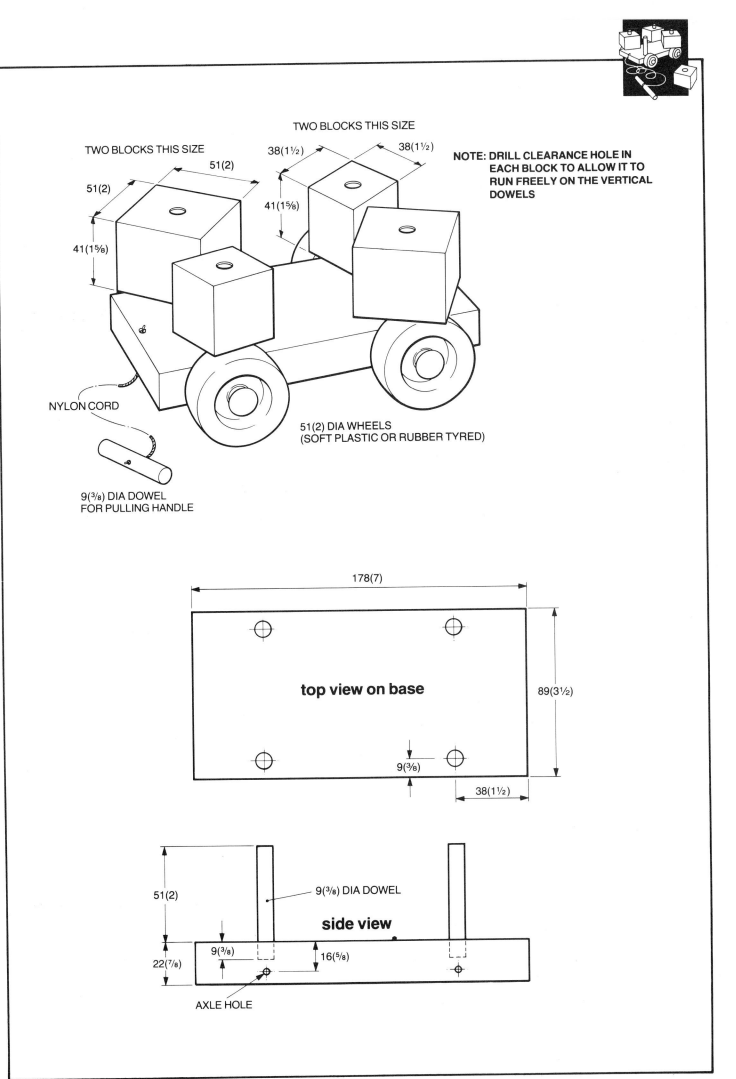

TWO BLOCKS THIS SIZE

TWO BLOCKS THIS SIZE

51(2)

51(2)

41(1⅝)

38(1½)

38(1½)

41(1⅝)

NOTE: DRILL CLEARANCE HOLE IN EACH BLOCK TO ALLOW IT TO RUN FREELY ON THE VERTICAL DOWELS

NYLON CORD

51(2) DIA WHEELS (SOFT PLASTIC OR RUBBER TYRED)

9(⅜) DIA DOWEL FOR PULLING HANDLE

178(7)

top view on base

89(3½)

9(⅜)

38(1½)

51(2)

9(⅜) DIA DOWEL

side view

9(⅜)

16(⅝)

22(⅞)

AXLE HOLE

9

Childrens' toys don't have to be complicated to give many hours of fun. This one is an ideal introduction to wooden toy making, as it is unlikely to 'go wrong' and really any tree or bird shape you care to make will work well. It is also inexpensive since all you need is plywood, a length of dowel rod and offcuts of wood from your wood box.

How it works (I think!)

One end of a length of wire is glued into the bird, the rest is then wound loosely round the dowel rod – trial and error are necessary here to get the right tension. When the tail of the bird is flicked, there is sufficient spring in the wire to make the bird move upwards, thus allowing the coil on the dowel rod to slip down the pole a little, and this cycle repeats itself until the bird can't slip down any further. The beak of the woodpecker must not actually strike the tree or it won't work. Bend the wire a little to get the best setting. Sometimes, for a reason I can't fathom, the pecker goes down the tree in a spiral – funny bird! The clacking of the wire on the rod makes a very realistic woodpecker sound and, to add to the fun, the vibrations start the pine cones falling off the pegs on the tree. The pine cones can be timed to fall off exactly in order as the woodpecker descends, but I have found in trials that it is difficult to give exact dimensions for the pegs in order to achieve this. So, when you fit the dowel pegs into the tree at their slight downward angle, leave them quite long to start with so that you can experiment by cutting pieces off. I have found, however, that cones falling off irregularly and doing the woodpecker an injury has not detracted from the fun of the game with children at all – perhaps the woodpecker should be fitted with a safety helmet!

1 Make the base block for the tree by glueing the two pieces of shaped plywood to the piece of pine. To give the tree stability bore holes through the base and fit lengths of dowel rod through these to prevent any possibility of the tree tipping over. You can make the base any size or shape you wish, but remember it has to be large enough to stop the tree from falling over.

2 Make the tree trunk from a length of dowel rod. Depending on the size of your base, this can be to any practical height.

3 Cut the tree shape out of plywood and glue the tree location block of wood onto the back to take the dowel rod (trunk). Drill the peg holes for the cones in the tree shape.

4 Glue small-diameter dowel rods into the peg holes in the tree. These should be set at a slight downward slant to help the cones slip off. It is also helpful to grease them with candle wax. I found it best to leave the pegs too long to start with and then trim them back once I had got the whole thing working, to achieve the best effect.

5 Shape the cones using a coping saw and remove all rough edges with glasspaper. Drill a peg hole in each one. The cones need to be a very loose fit on the peg, so don't make the peg hole too small.

6 You can make the woodpecker by whittling a block of wood with a knife to achieve a three-dimensional bird. I found this far easier than I had expected, but if you don't feel confident about this cut the shape out of a piece of fairly thick plywood. The wire that attaches it to the trunk does not have to be of any specific gauge; as long as it has a little spring in it, it will work. However, it is vital that the wire is firmly glued into the bird. I used epoxy resin glue for this operation. If there is any looseness here the toy simply won't work.

7 I have suggested a painting scheme for a foreground which you can glue onto the dowel rods in the base assembly, but, of course, you may have ideas of your own. Just be sure that the paint you use is lead-free. I think it is preferable not to glue the trunk into the base and tree, so that the toy can be dismantled for easy storage.

Cutting list

Tree	1 off	457 × 305 × 3mm (18 × 12 × ⅛in)	Plywood
Cone support peg	4 off	20mm (¾in) × 6mm (¼in) diam dowelling	
Tree location block	1 off	152 × 44 × 32mm (6 × 1¾ × 1¼in)	Timber
Cone	4 off	86 × 44 × 12mm (3⅜ × 1¾ × ½in)	Timber
Tree trunk	1 off	1130mm (44½in) × 12mm (½in) diam dowelling	
Base block assembly	1 off	222 × 95 × 44mm (8¾ × 3¾ × 1¾in)	Timber
	2 off	305mm (12in) × 9mm (⅜in) diam dowelling	
Woodpecker	1 off	152 × 64 × 32mm (6 × 2½ × 1¼in)	Timber
Foreground	1 off	254 × 178 × 3mm (10 × 7 × ⅛in)	Plywood

Ancillaries

	1 off	178mm (7in) × 1.5mm (¹⁄₁₆in) diam wire	

25(1) SQUARE GRID

2 HOLES
9(3/8) DIAM

171(6¾)

FOREGROUND 3(1/8) THICK PLYWOOD

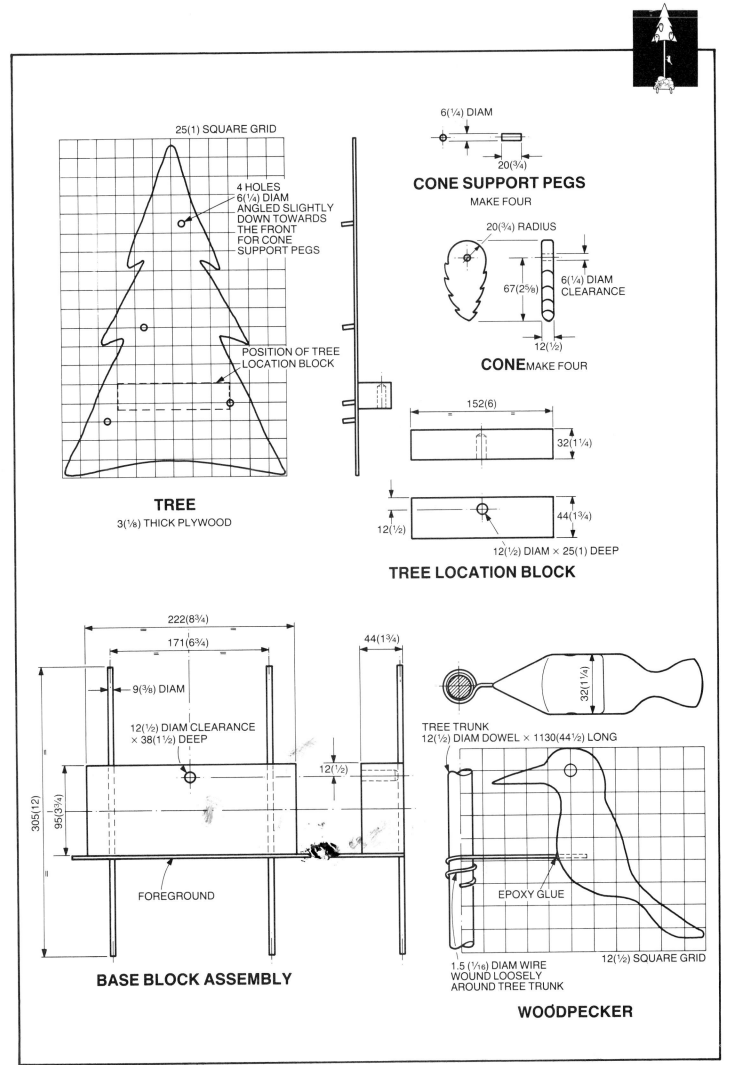

CONE SUPPORT PEGS

6(¼) DIAM

20(¾)

MAKE FOUR

20(¾) RADIUS

67(2⅝)

6(¼) DIAM
CLEARANCE

12(½)

CONE MAKE FOUR

25(1) SQUARE GRID

4 HOLES
6(¼) DIAM
ANGLED SLIGHTLY
DOWN TOWARDS
THE FRONT
FOR CONE
SUPPORT PEGS

POSITION OF TREE
LOCATION BLOCK

TREE

3(⅛) THICK PLYWOOD

152(6)

32(1¼)

12(½)

44(1¾)

12(½) DIAM × 25(1) DEEP

TREE LOCATION BLOCK

222(8¾)

171(6¾)

44(1¾)

9(⅜) DIAM

12(½) DIAM CLEARANCE
× 38(1½) DEEP

12(½)

305(12)

95(3¾)

FOREGROUND

BASE BLOCK ASSEMBLY

32(1¼)

TREE TRUNK
12(½) DIAM DOWEL × 1130(44½) LONG

EPOXY GLUE

12(½) SQUARE GRID

1.5 (1/16) DIAM WIRE
WOUND LOOSELY
AROUND TREE TRUNK

WOODPECKER

CLARENCE THE CLOWN

This sort of action toy is very popular and not only with children!

1 Cut out the basic clown shape from plywood, then carefully work around all the edges with glasspaper, rounding them off.

2 The legs and arms can be held on by a variety of methods:
i dowel rods with wooden stops glued over the ends of the rods;
ii nuts and bolts with washers either side;
iii spring caps with short lengths of steel rod.

Whichever method you choose the joints must move freely, but not too loosely.

3 String the legs and arms together, then attach the finger grip, pull handle and cord.

4 The painting should be done last. It does help to pencil the outline of the clothes on the plywood first. Make sure you use non-toxic paint.

Cutting list

Body	1 off	330 × 203 × 3mm (13 × 8 × ⅛in)	Plywood
Arm	2 off	203 × 102 × 3mm (8 × 4 × ⅛in)	Plywood
Leg	2 off	305 × 152 × 3mm (12 × 6 × ⅛in)	Plywood
Spacer	4 off	25 × 25 × 3mm (1 × 1 × ⅛in)	Plywood
Finger grip	1 off	64 × 38 × 20mm (2½ × 1½ × ¾in)	Timber
Pull handle	1 off	89mm (3½in) × 12mm (½in) diam dowelling	

Ancillaries

	4 off	20mm (¾in) × 5mm (³⁄₁₆in) diam steel pins
	8 off	5mm (³⁄₁₆in) spring dome caps
	1 off	508mm (20in) length of strong pull cord
	1 off	25mm (1in) × no. 6 woodscrew and cup washer

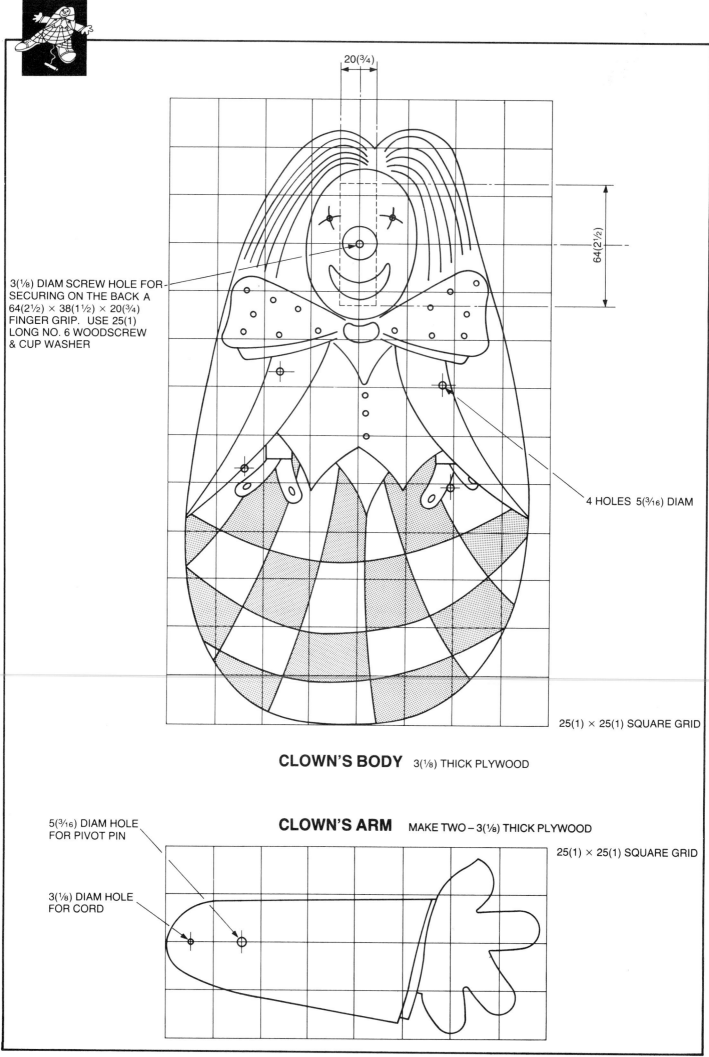

3(⅛) DIAM SCREW HOLE FOR SECURING ON THE BACK A 64(2½) × 38(1½) × 20(¾) FINGER GRIP. USE 25(1) LONG NO. 6 WOODSCREW & CUP WASHER

20(¾)

64(2½)

4 HOLES 5(³⁄₁₆) DIAM

25(1) × 25(1) SQUARE GRID

CLOWN'S BODY 3(⅛) THICK PLYWOOD

CLOWN'S ARM MAKE TWO – 3(⅛) THICK PLYWOOD

25(1) × 25(1) SQUARE GRID

5(³⁄₁₆) DIAM HOLE FOR PIVOT PIN

3(⅛) DIAM HOLE FOR CORD

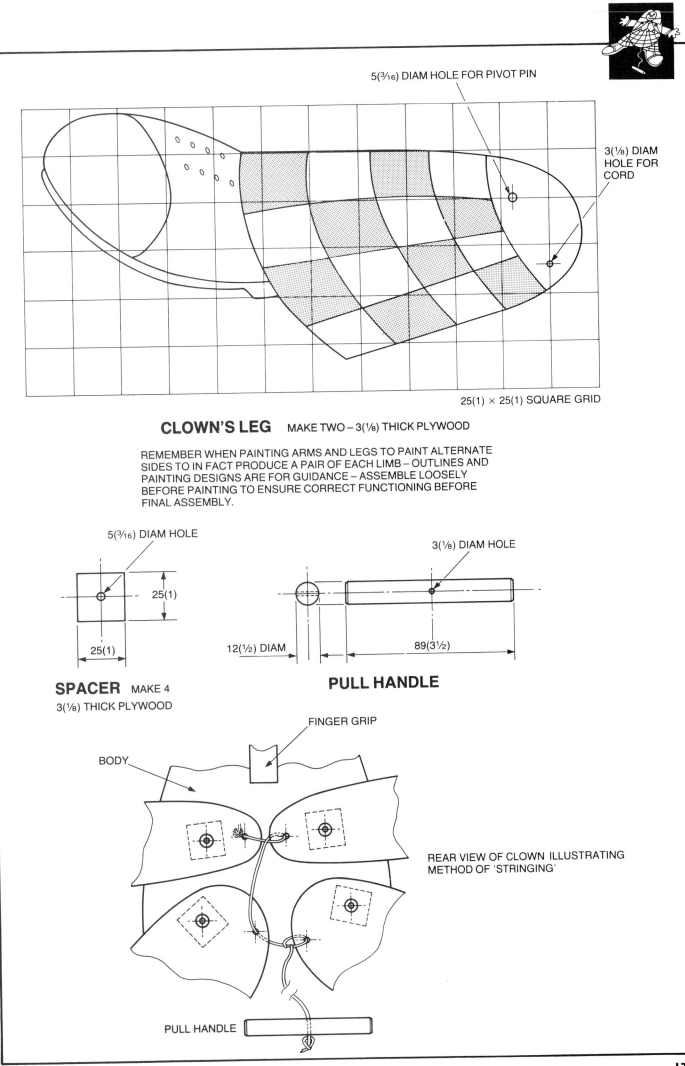

5(³⁄₁₆) DIAM HOLE FOR PIVOT PIN

3(⅛) DIAM
HOLE FOR
CORD

25(1) × 25(1) SQUARE GRID

CLOWN'S LEG MAKE TWO – 3(⅛) THICK PLYWOOD

REMEMBER WHEN PAINTING ARMS AND LEGS TO PAINT ALTERNATE
SIDES TO IN FACT PRODUCE A PAIR OF EACH LIMB – OUTLINES AND
PAINTING DESIGNS ARE FOR GUIDANCE – ASSEMBLE LOOSELY
BEFORE PAINTING TO ENSURE CORRECT FUNCTIONING BEFORE
FINAL ASSEMBLY.

5(³⁄₁₆) DIAM HOLE

25(1)

25(1)

SPACER MAKE 4
3(⅛) THICK PLYWOOD

3(⅛) DIAM HOLE

12(½) DIAM

89(3½)

PULL HANDLE

FINGER GRIP

BODY

REAR VIEW OF CLOWN ILLUSTRATING
METHOD OF 'STRINGING'

PULL HANDLE

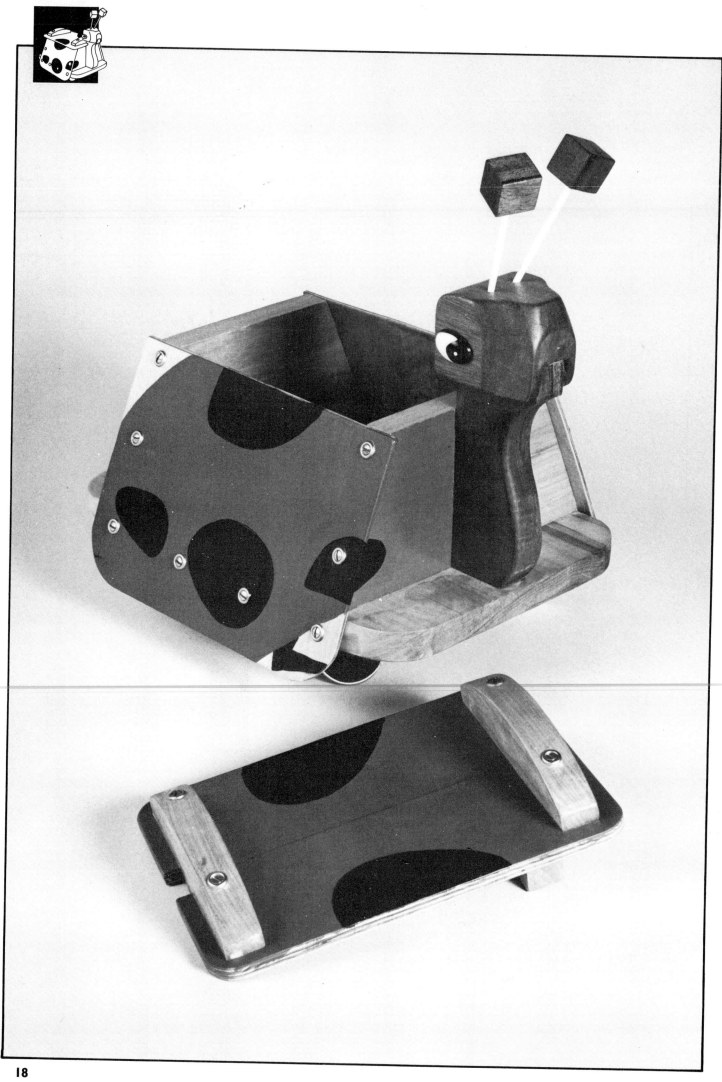

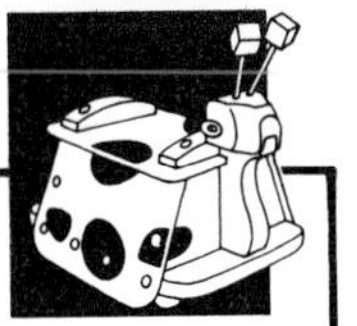

Youngsters love toys on which they can scoot along. This ladybird has the added advantage of a storage compartment for books, paper and felt tips. Not a difficult toy to make, the base and body formers are parana pine, the sides plywood and the head an offcut of mahogany. The four castors are the only expensive items to buy, but they do give the toy tremendous manoeuvrability in small spaces and are well worth fitting.

1 Start by cutting out the base and cutting the housing joints.

2 Make the two body formers (these need to be a tight fit in the base). You will always find that a plane blade needs to be very sharp to cut end grain fibres cleanly. So, before the final shaping of the body former sides, sharpen your plane!

3 The type of castors you buy will determine whether or not you need to drill holes for these in the base since some have a plate that has to be attached with screws. If holes are needed it is best to drill them at this stage of construction.

4 Now shape the neck using a coping saw and make the head. By using mahogany for the head you add a dash of red which sets off the character of this animal. First of all, cut a slot or trench in the block of wood using a tenon saw and chisel. Once the trench has been cut out, offer it up to the top of the neck to make sure you have a tight fit. It is not vital for the head to look the same as mine; use a small gouge, chisel, surform or Stanley knife to produce an interesting shape.

5 The eyes are available from a number of craft or model shops, but if you have difficulty write to 'Wheels' (see page 215). Fixing them securely to the head is of paramount importance. Drill a hole that will take the protruding plastic stub end of the eye – the stub **must** be a tight fit in the hole. Using **epoxy resin glue** (not to be confused with ordinary woodworking glue), glue the eyes in

place. I use a small nail to wipe the glue around the inside of the hole and around the inside of the eye socket. Now push the eye into the hole; ideally the glue should just spill out around the eye. Fixing the eye safely is **very** important since a loose eye could be swallowed by a young child.

6 The antennae are made from plastic-covered wire curtain rail. Glue the large blocks of wood onto them using epoxy resin glue and then drill holes in the head and glue the other ends into the head.
NB The eyes, antennae and blocks should be constantly checked for security. Children love putting things in their mouths and these small items could be dangerous unless they are fixed safely.

7 Now glue the head onto the neck and screw the neck onto the front of the body former. Glue both formers into the housing grooves in the base.

8 Cut and shape the plywood side panels and fit them to the sides of the body formers with no. 8 wood screws.

9 Cut out the pieces for the seat assembly. Cut the notch in the front of the two seat pieces so that they will fit around the neck. Glue and screw two cross members to the top of the seat pieces and the one underneath as shown.

10 I finished the ladybird with polyurethane varnish and painted the spots on afterwards (see Materials and Finishes, page 214).

Cutting list

Base	1 off	330 × 244 × 22mm (13 × 9⅝ × ⅞in)	Timber
Side panel	2 off	244 × 171 × 3mm (9⅝ × 6¾ × ⅛in)	Plywood
Body former	2 off	235 × 121 × 22mm (9¼ × 4¾ × ⅞in)	Timber
Neck	1 off	159 × 67 × 25mm (6¼ × 2⅝ × 1in)	Timber
Seat assembly	1 off	248 × 178 × 9mm (9¾ × 7 × ⅜in)	Plywood
	2 off	152 × 35 × 22mm (6 × 1⅜ × ⅞in)	Timber
	1 off	140 × 28 × 22mm (5½ × 1⅛ × ⅞in)	Timber
Head	1 off	73 × 64 × 60mm (2⅞ × 2½ × 2⅜in)	Timber
Antenna	2 off	25 × 25 × 25mm (1 × 1 × 1in)	Timber
Ancillaries			
	4 off	51mm (2in) diam castoring wheels	
	2 off	102mm (4in) × 5mm (³⁄₁₆in) diam plastic-covered coiled wire	
	2 off	Eyes	

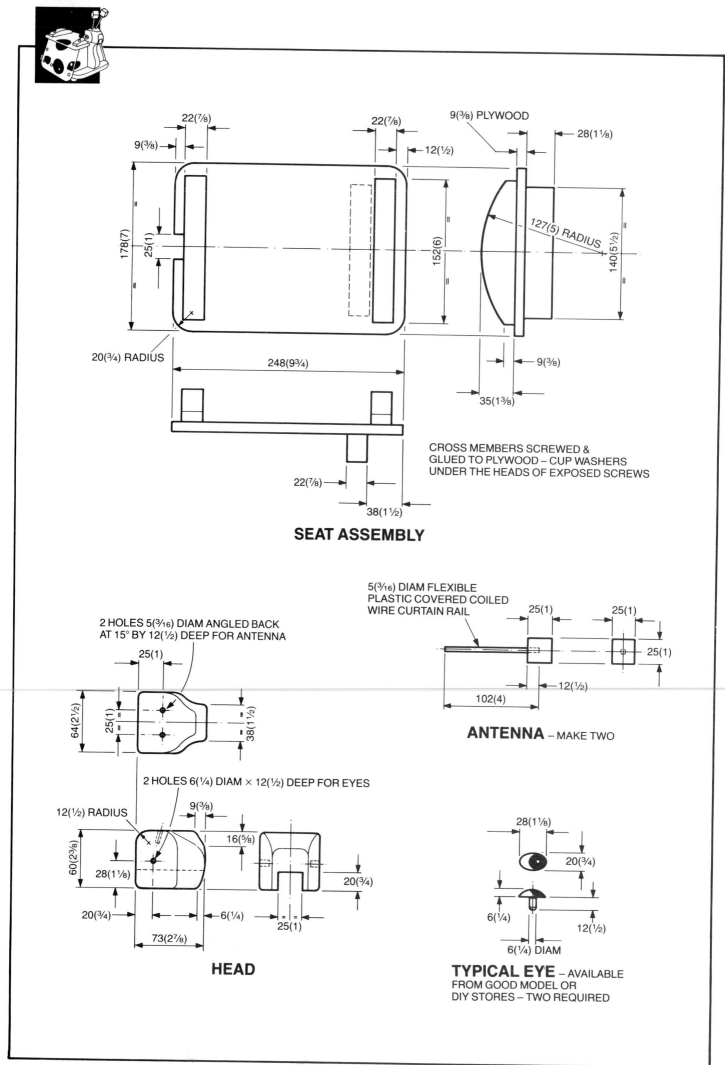

22(⅞)

9(⅜)

22(⅞)

9(⅜) PLYWOOD

28(1⅛)

12(½)

127(5) RADIUS

178(7)

25(1)

152(6)

140(5½)

20(¾) RADIUS

248(9¾)

9(⅜)

35(1⅜)

CROSS MEMBERS SCREWED &
GLUED TO PLYWOOD – CUP WASHERS
UNDER THE HEADS OF EXPOSED SCREWS

22(⅞)

38(1½)

SEAT ASSEMBLY

5(³⁄₁₆) DIAM FLEXIBLE
PLASTIC COVERED COILED
WIRE CURTAIN RAIL

2 HOLES 5(³⁄₁₆) DIAM ANGLED BACK
AT 15° BY 12(½) DEEP FOR ANTENNA

25(1)

25(1)

25(1)

25(1)

64(2½)

38(1½)

12(½)

102(4)

ANTENNA – MAKE TWO

2 HOLES 6(¼) DIAM × 12(½) DEEP FOR EYES

12(½) RADIUS

9(⅜)

16(⅝)

28(1⅛)

60(2⅜)

28(1⅛)

20(¾)

20(¾)

20(¾)

6(¼)

6(¼)

12(½)

6(¼)

25(1)

73(2⅞)

6(¼) DIAM

HEAD

TYPICAL EYE – AVAILABLE
FROM GOOD MODEL OR
DIY STORES – TWO REQUIRED

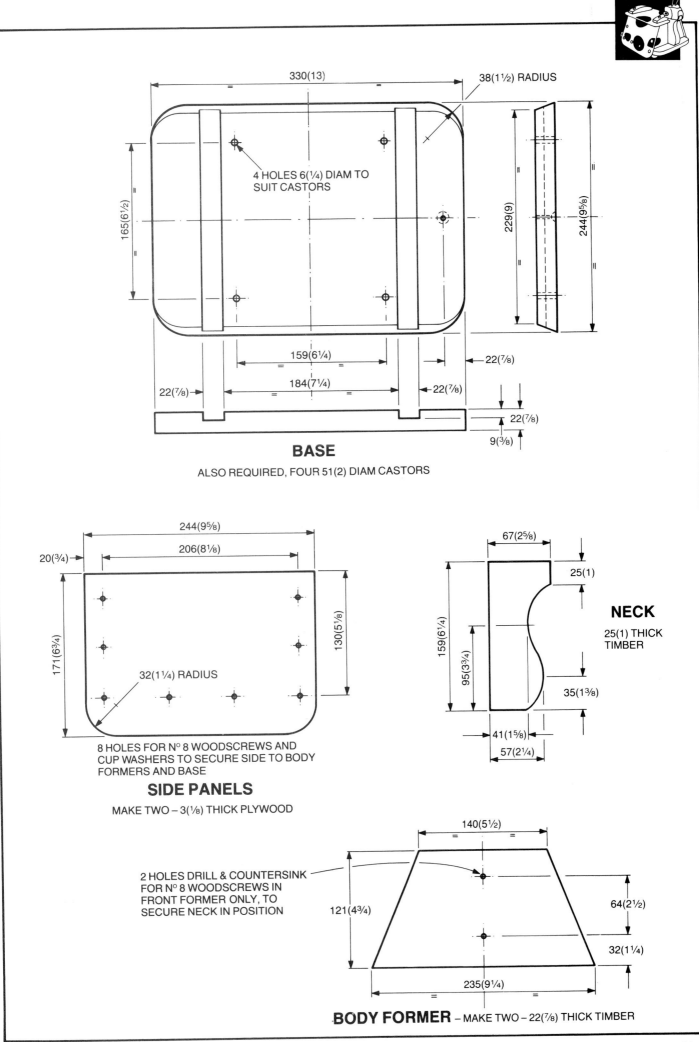

330(13)

38(1½) RADIUS

165(6½)

229(9)

244(9⅝)

4 HOLES 6(¼) DIAM TO SUIT CASTORS

159(6¼)

184(7¼)

22(⅞)

22(⅞)

22(⅞)

22(⅞)

9(⅜)

BASE

ALSO REQUIRED, FOUR 51(2) DIAM CASTORS

244(9⅝)

206(8⅛)

20(¾)

171(6¾)

130(5⅛)

32(1¼) RADIUS

8 HOLES FOR N° 8 WOODSCREWS AND CUP WASHERS TO SECURE SIDE TO BODY FORMERS AND BASE

SIDE PANELS

MAKE TWO – 3(⅛) THICK PLYWOOD

67(2⅝)

25(1)

159(6¼)

95(3¾)

35(1⅜)

41(1⅝)

57(2¼)

NECK

25(1) THICK TIMBER

2 HOLES DRILL & COUNTERSINK FOR N° 8 WOODSCREWS IN FRONT FORMER ONLY, TO SECURE NECK IN POSITION

140(5½)

121(4¾)

64(2½)

32(1¼)

235(9¼)

BODY FORMER – MAKE TWO – 22(⅞) THICK TIMBER

DRAGON

Children are usually fascinated by stories of dragons and 'knights of old'. This dragon looks fairly harmless and does not require too much skill to make.

1   From the squared grid given mark out the dragon shape onto a piece of wood. The timber I used was parana pine which is available from most builders' merchants. You can, of course, use plywood, but if you do you will not get the lovely natural grain markings that are such a feature of parana pine.

2   Cut out the dragon using a coping saw which is ideal for cutting around all the curves. (However, a jigsaw will obviously do the job much quicker.)

3   Now cut out the pieces around the head and the wings. The eyes and nose can be made from offcuts.

4   Perhaps the most time-consuming job on this toy is removing the rough saw cuts from all the intricate internal cuts. I used a sanding sheet made from steel, which lasts much longer than glasspaper, wrapped around a dowel rod.

5   Glue on all the details and fit the tail by cutting slots in the body and glueing in a piece of leather.

6   Now fit the wheels. You can either make wooden wheels or use blow-moulded plastic ones, as I have, and paint the centres.

7   A dragon is incomplete without a long red tongue. Leather is best for this (a good source is a shoe repair shop) or you could use a piece of red felt. Cut two or three strips and glue them into the mouth.

8   Make sure you have smoothed off all sharp edges before final varnishing.

Cutting list

Body	I off	533 × 356 × 22mm (21 × 14 × ⅞in)	Timber
Axle block	2 off	279 × 38 × 22mm (11 × 1½ × ⅞in)	Timber
Inner wing block	2 off	203 × 152 × 22mm (8 × 6 × ⅞in)	Timber
Outer wing block	2 off	140 × 102 × 22mm (5½ × 4 × ⅞in)	Timber
Mane block	2 off	165 × 152 × 22mm (6½ × 6 × ⅞in)	Timber
Eye	2 off	51 × 38 × 9mm (2 × 1½ × ⅜in)	Timber
Nostril	2 off	38 × 25 × 9mm (1½ × 1 × ⅜in)	Timber
Ancillaries			
	4 off	108mm (4¼in) diam road wheels	
	2 off	146mm (5¾in) × 6mm (¼in) diam steel axles	
	4 off	6mm (¼in) diam spring dome caps	
	I off	152mm (6in) × 102mm (4in) soft leather	

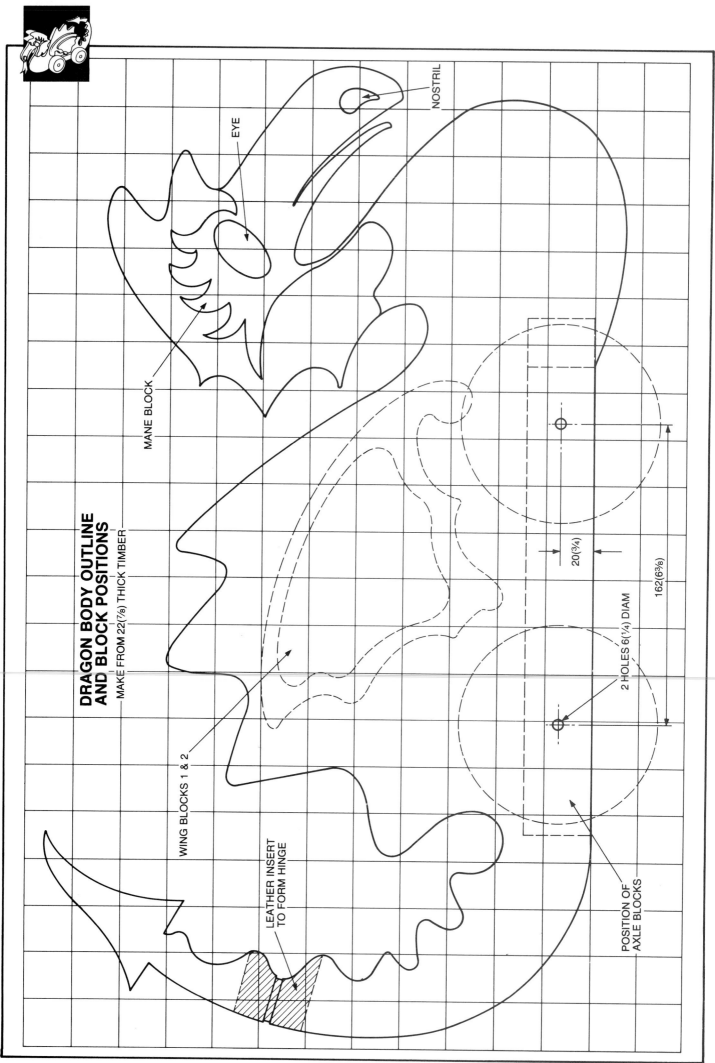

DRAGON BODY OUTLINE AND BLOCK POSITIONS

— MAKE FROM 22(7/8) THICK TIMBER

EYE

NOSTRIL

MANE BLOCK

WING BLOCKS 1 & 2

LEATHER INSERT TO FORM HINGE

POSITION OF AXLE BLOCKS

2 HOLES 6(1/4) DIAM

20(3/4)

162(63/8)

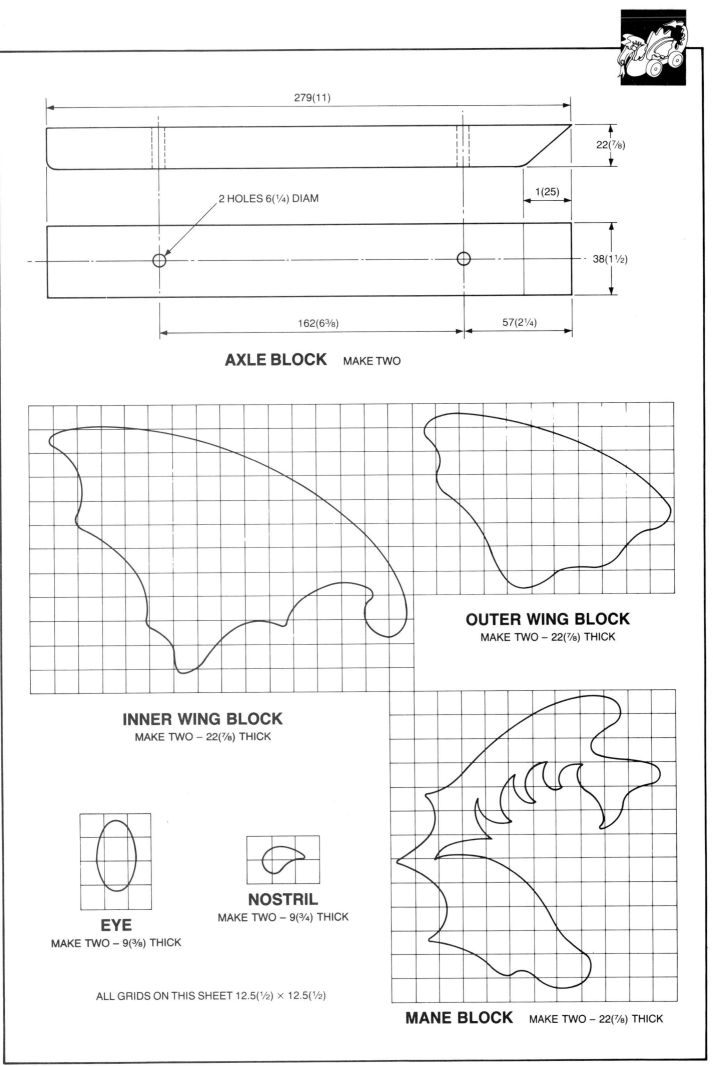

279(11)

22(⁷⁄₈)

1(25)

2 HOLES 6(¼) DIAM

38(1½)

162(6³⁄₈)

57(2¼)

AXLE BLOCK MAKE TWO

OUTER WING BLOCK

MAKE TWO – 22(⁷⁄₈) THICK

INNER WING BLOCK

MAKE TWO – 22(⁷⁄₈) THICK

EYE

MAKE TWO – 9(³⁄₈) THICK

NOSTRIL

MAKE TWO – 9(¾) THICK

ALL GRIDS ON THIS SHEET 12.5(½) × 12.5(½)

MANE BLOCK MAKE TWO – 22(⁷⁄₈) THICK

These two pull-along toys have their trolley in common, and both are activated by a cam which rotates on the front axle. They are not difficult to make and only require basic cutting out of wooden shapes. If you are considering making your first wooden toy, then perhaps the rabbit would be a good one to try. A coping saw, hand drill, tenon saw and screwdriver are the tools you will need. I made these toys from parana pine (easily available from builders' merchants), but the squirrel's tail was made from an offcut of mahogany.

Rabbit

1   From the grid given, mark out a paper template for the rabbit's body, and then use it to pencil the shape onto the wood. You can make the rabbit any size you like depending on the size of the squares you decide to use.

2   Drill the hole that will hold the legs in place and provide the pivot point for the body. Now cut around the shape with a coping saw and remove the saw marks with glasspaper.

3   Mark and cut out the two halves of the tail, the ears and the eyes. Glue these into place on the body.

4   Cut out the legs, but before final shaping tape them both together with masking tape and drill the pivot hole through both. Cut the dowel rod, onto which they must be fixed, to length and make sure it does not 'bind' in the body. If it does, glasspaper it and rub it with candle wax. When you are sure the body will move up and down freely, assemble the rod, body and legs and glue the legs onto the ends of the rod.

Squirrel

1   As with the rabbit, the squirrel body should be marked out using the grid provided and the size of the finished animal will depend on the size of the squares you decide to use. Drill the pivot hole.

2   Use a coping saw to cut out the body, eyes, ears, legs and nut. Once the cutting out has been done, glasspaper the rough saw marks smooth. Tape the legs together and drill the pivot hole.

3   The tail takes a little more effort. Cut out the basic shape and then reduce the thickness of the wood at the root of the tail to match that of the body. Rounding and shaping the top part of the tail will take a little time. This shape can be carved, but there are also Surform or Trimtool rasps that will do the job just as well. The Surform tools have dozens of small sharp teeth that are punched out of a metal plate. They are available in a variety of shapes and are very useful in all shaping work. Once the tail has been shaped, glue it onto the body.

4   Glue the eyes, ears and nut onto the body.

5   As with the rabbit, cut the dowel rod to length, glasspaper it smooth and, when you are happy with how it fits in the body, assemble the rod, body and legs and glue the legs onto the rod.

Trolley

The trolley is identical for both animals.

1   Cut out the platform on which the animal will sit. Cut a long slot in the front to accommodate the wooden cam.

2   Cut out the two strips of wood that hold the wheels to the platform. Tape them together and drill the holes to take the axle rods. The holes in the front in particular must allow the axle to turn freely. Separate the two strips and attach them to the platform with screws.

3   Mark out the cam onto a piece of wood and cut out the shape. Very carefully, glasspaper away all rough surfaces. This is very important as with both animals part of their bodies will be in direct contact with the cam at all times.

4   Fit the back wheels and attach the spring caps to the axles. If this is the first time you have used spring caps then you will need to know that you have to file a chamfer onto the axle ends to allow the spring caps to fit.

5   The front axle and wheels are the same in size but they function entirely differently. This is because the cam is also fixed to the axle and turns as the wheels turn, making the animal resting on top move up and down. The simplest way to achieve this is to clean both the axle and the inside of the wheels with methylated spirit to remove all traces of grease. Now thread the axle through the wheels, trolley and cam and, using epoxy resin glue, glue the cam to the axle (being careful to position it correctly in the middle of the slot). Then glue the wheels to the ends of the axle, and fit spring caps. The front wheels will now turn the cam around and activate the animal, while the back wheels just turn freely on the axle rod.

6   Finally, glue the rabbit or squirrel onto the trolley.

Cutting list

Common Trolley

Chassis assembly	I off	267 × 86 × 22mm (10½ × 3⅜ × ⅞in)	Timber
	2 off	267 × 22 × 20mm (10½ × ⅞ × ¾in)	Timber
	I off	86 × 22 × 12mm (3⅜ × ⅞ × ½in)	Timber
Handle	I off	76mm (3in) × 22mm (⅞in) diam dowelling	
Cam	I off	64 × 44 × 22mm (2½ × 1¾ × ⅞in)	Timber

Ancillaries

	4 off	76mm (3in) diam road wheels
	2 off	137mm (5⅜in) × 6mm (¼in) diam steel axles
	4 off	Spring dome caps to suit 6 mm (¼in) diam axles
	4 off	Washers for 6mm (¼in) diam axles
	I off	610mm (24in) length of nylon pull cord

Rabbit

Body	I off	286 × 159 × 22mm (11¼ × 6¼ × ⅞in)	Timber
Tail	2 off	67 × 38 × 22mm (2⅝ × 1½ × ⅞in)	Timber
Leg	2 off	124 × 105 × 22mm (4⅞ × 4⅛ × ⅞in)	Timber
Ear	2 off	114 × 47 × 22mm (4½ × 1⅞ × ⅞in)	Timber
Eye	2 off	38 × 25 × 6mm (1½ × 1 × ¼in)	Timber
Pivot spindle	I off	73mm (2⅞in) × 12mm (½in) diam dowelling	

Squirrel

Body	I off	210 × 200 × 22mm (8¼ × 7⅞ × ⅞in)	Timber
Tail	I off	257 × 102 × 44mm (10⅛ × 4 × 1¾in)	Timber
Leg	2 off	162 × 133 × 22mm (6⅜ × 5¼ × ⅞in)	Timber
Ear	2 off	47 × 38 × 9mm (1⅞ × 1½ × ⅜in)	Timber
Eye	2 off	38 × 25 × 6mm (1½ × 1 × ¼in)	Timber
Nut	I off	25 × 16 × 16mm (1 × ⅝ × ⅝in)	Timber
Pivot spindle	I off	73mm (2⅞in) × 12mm (½in) diam dowelling	

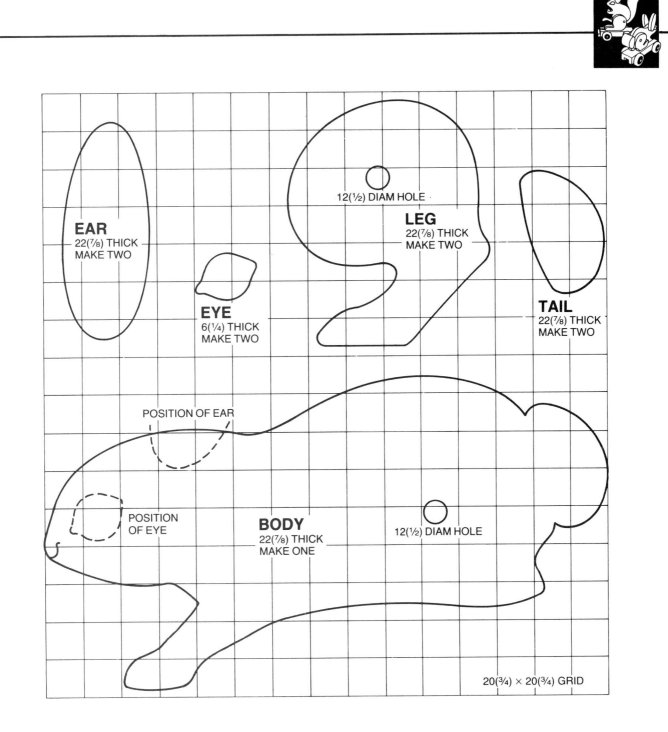

EAR
22(⅞) THICK
MAKE TWO

EYE
6(¼) THICK
MAKE TWO

12(½) DIAM HOLE

LEG
22(⅞) THICK
MAKE TWO

TAIL
22(⅞) THICK
MAKE TWO

POSITION OF EAR

POSITION
OF EYE

BODY
22(⅞) THICK
MAKE ONE

12(½) DIAM HOLE

20(¾) × 20(¾) GRID

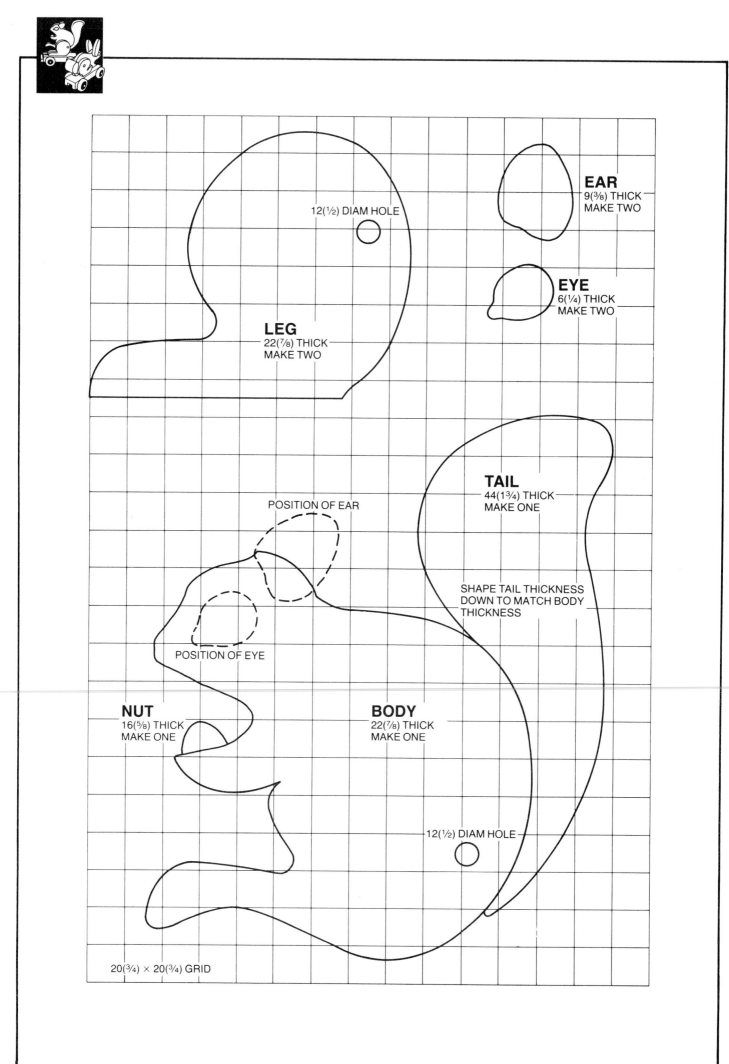

EAR
9(³⁄₈) THICK
MAKE TWO

12(½) DIAM HOLE

EYE
6(¼) THICK
MAKE TWO

LEG
22(⅞) THICK
MAKE TWO

TAIL
44(1¾) THICK
MAKE ONE

POSITION OF EAR

SHAPE TAIL THICKNESS
DOWN TO MATCH BODY
THICKNESS

POSITION OF EYE

NUT
16(⅝) THICK
MAKE ONE

BODY
22(⅞) THICK
MAKE ONE

12(½) DIAM HOLE

20(¾) × 20(¾) GRID

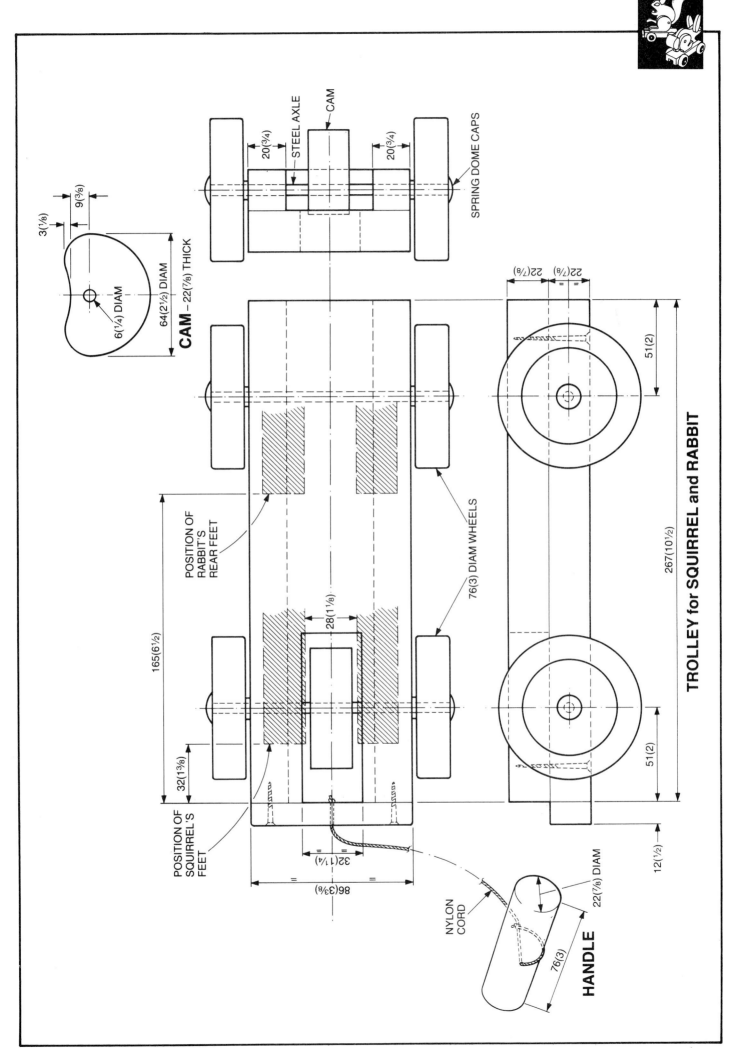

CAM – 22(⁷⁄₈) THICK

64(2½) DIAM

6(¼) DIAM

3(⅛)

9(³⁄₈)

STEEL AXLE

CAM

SPRING DOME CAPS

20(³⁄₄)

20(³⁄₄)

POSITION OF RABBIT'S REAR FEET

76(3) DIAM WHEELS

POSITION OF SQUIRREL'S FEET

165(6½)

32(1³⁄₈)

28(1⅛)

32(1¼)

86(3³⁄₈)

22(⁷⁄₈)

22(⁷⁄₈)

51(2)

51(2)

267(10½)

12(½)

NYLON CORD

22(⁷⁄₈) DIAM

76(3)

HANDLE

TROLLEY for SQUIRREL and RABBIT

31

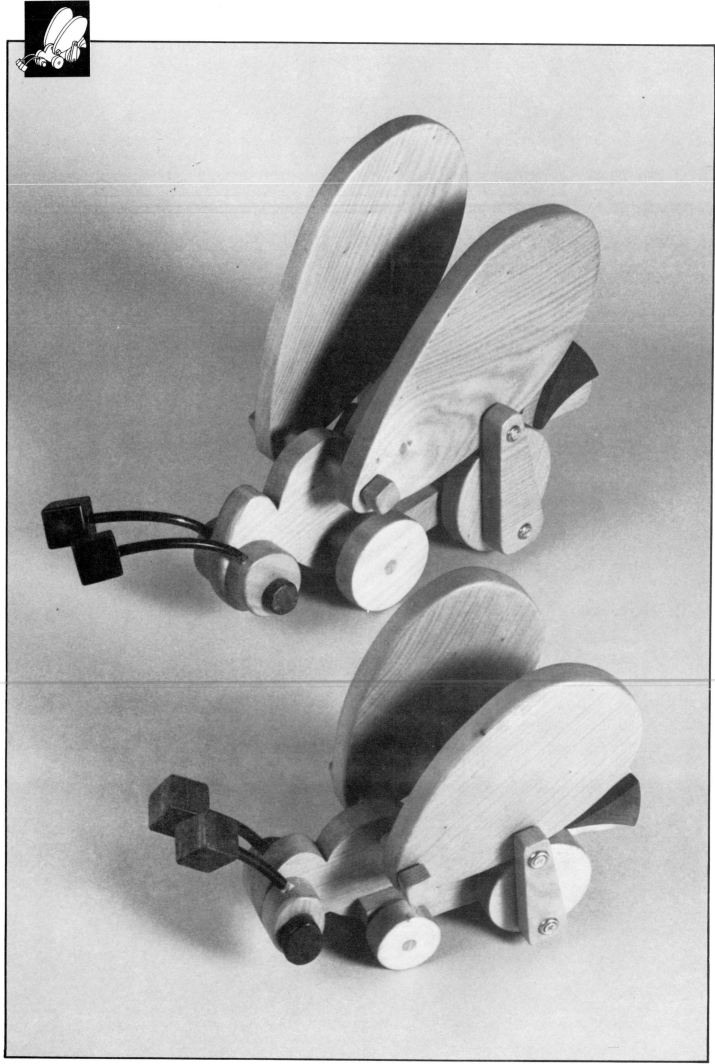

FIREFLY

The essential ingredient for a successful pull-along toy is plenty of action as it moves. This firefly is an inquisitive insect that will give young children lots of fun. I made two fireflies as I felt that a small one trailing behind mum would add to the enjoyment.

1 Make paper templates using the grid given in the plans. The size of each firefly is determined by the size of the squares the shape is drawn over. If you decide therefore to make the second one half the size of the first reduce the size of squares used by 50%. Haberdashers often sell squared paper for dress patterns and I have found this very useful when preparing paper templates.

2 Mark out the body by drawing around the template. Then cut out the shape using a coping saw or jigsaw. Remove all the saw cuts from the edges with glasspaper.

3 Glue the two reinforcing strips onto the body and, after the glue has dried, drill the holes to take the axles (dowel rods). Make sure you drill the holes carefully keeping them at 90° to the body in both planes.

4 Now make the wheels. I found it easier to bore the axle holes in the wheels before cutting them out. Wheels are not the easiest of things to make, and it is fairly critical that you cut to the pencil line marked. I found that a coping saw did a good job and if, at the end, the wheels are not 100% round you will probably find that this does not prevent them working quite satisfactorily.

5 Push the dowel rod axles through the body and glue the wheels onto the ends on one side only. It is critical to get the dowel rods to turn smoothly in the body. To achieve this, keep glasspapering the axle rods until they are really smooth and then rub candle wax on them. Work the wax well into the rods and keep trying them in the body until the wheels and axles turn smoothly without 'snatching'. Now glue the wheels onto the axles on the other side.

6 Glue the shapes of wood onto the body. I used mahogany as it contrasts well with the honey-coloured parana pine. You don't have to use these two woods but I think it is important to choose woods that contrast attractively.

7 Before fixing the eye pieces in place, drill a small hole in each to take the plastic-covered wires that represent the antennae. Fix these wires into the holes with epoxy resin glue; fix a cube onto the end of each antenna in the same way. (As young children give their toys a tough time it is vital to use epoxy resin glue to hold these pieces in place.) Glue the shaded 'pupil' onto each eye, then glue the eyes onto the head.

8 Mark out and cut the wings to shape. Bore a hole at the front end of each wing to take the dowel rod that runs through the front of the body. To keep the wings at the correct distance from the side of the body use plastic tube spacers (see plans). Glue small square pieces of wood onto the ends of the dowel rod to prevent the wings from coming off.

9 The wings are moved (cranked) up and down by a leg on each side which is attached in two places: at the top to the wing and at the bottom to the rear wheel. Drill holes in each leg that will allow the screws used to turn freely. Behind each screw head fit a screw cup washer which will prevent the head from binding in the wood. The important thing is to get the screws holding each leg to rotate freely around the screw head and shank.

10 It is important when fitting the legs to the wheels to make sure that you arrange for one wing to be at the top while the other is at the bottom. This creates a cranking effect and it is essential if the toy is to work properly.

11 Finally drill a hole in the top of the head and attach a length of cord. An off-cut of dowel rod can be used for the pulling handle.

Cutting list

Body	1 off	381 × 133 × 20mm (15 × 5¼ × ¾in)	Timber
Reinforcing strip	2 off	152 × 32 × 20mm (6 × 1¼ × ¾in)	Timber
Bands	Make from 229 × 102 × 9mm (9 × 4 × ⅜in)		Timber
Wing	2 off	267 × 152 × 20mm (10½ × 6 × ¾in)	Timber
Wing pivot shaft	1 off	140mm (5½in) × 12mm (½in) diam dowelling	
Shaft end blocks	2 off	22 × 22 × 16mm (⅞ × ⅞ × ⅝in)	Timber
Rear wheel	2 off	20mm (¾in) × 102mm (4in) diam dowelling	
Front wheel	2 off	20mm (¾in) × 76mm (3in) diam dowelling	
Axle	2 off	111mm (4⅜in) × 12mm (½in) diam dowelling	
Leg	2 off	121 × 44 × 20mm (4¾ × 1¾ × ¾in)	Timber
Antenna	2 off	28 × 28 × 28mm (1⅛ × 1⅛ × 1⅛in)	Timber
Eye	2 off	64 × 47 × 20mm (2½ × 1⅞ × ¾in)	Timber
	2 off	28 × 22 × 9mm (1⅛ × ⅞ × ⅜in)	Timber

Ancillaries

	2 off	20mm (¾in) o/diam × 12mm (½in) i/diam × 25mm (1in) long plastic spacer
	2 off	127mm (5in) × 6mm (¼in) diam plastic-covered coiled wire

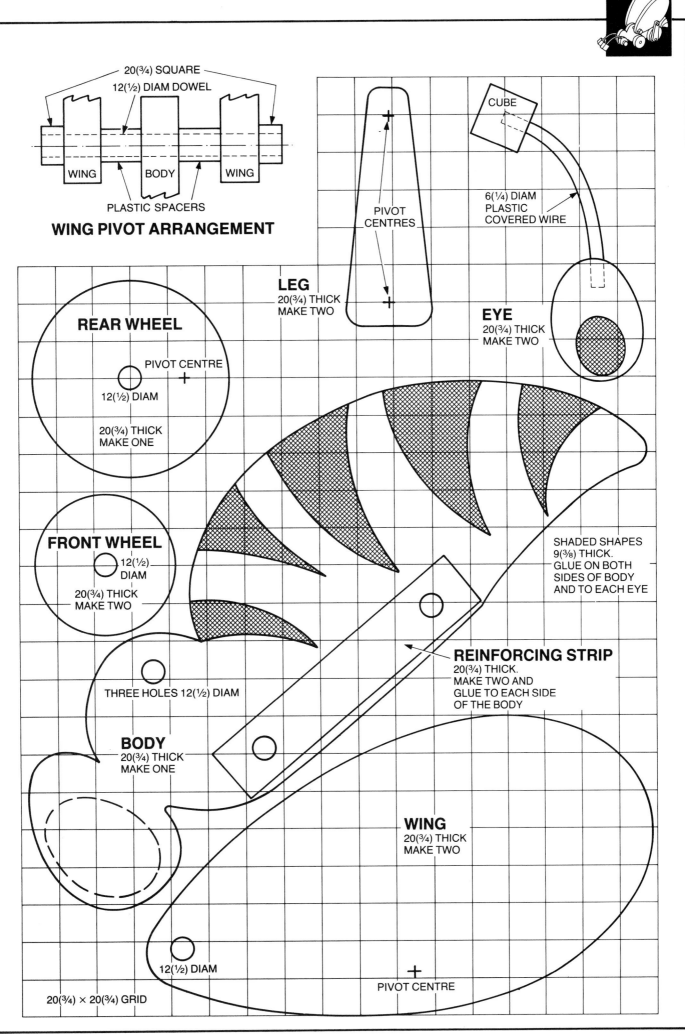

WING PIVOT ARRANGEMENT

20(¾) SQUARE
12(½) DIAM DOWEL
WING
BODY
WING
PLASTIC SPACERS

LEG
20(¾) THICK
MAKE TWO

PIVOT
CENTRES

CUBE

6(¼) DIAM
PLASTIC
COVERED
WIRE

EYE
20(¾) THICK
MAKE TWO

REAR WHEEL
PIVOT CENTRE
12(½) DIAM
20(¾) THICK
MAKE ONE

FRONT WHEEL
12(½) DIAM
20(¾) THICK
MAKE TWO

SHADED SHAPES
9(⅜) THICK.
GLUE ON BOTH
SIDES OF BODY
AND TO EACH EYE

THREE HOLES 12(½) DIAM

REINFORCING STRIP
20(¾) THICK.
MAKE TWO AND
GLUE TO EACH SIDE
OF THE BODY

BODY
20(¾) THICK
MAKE ONE

WING
20(¾) THICK
MAKE TWO

12(½) DIAM

PIVOT CENTRE

20(¾) × 20(¾) GRID

35

BORIS THE TANK ENGINE

Perhaps no-one will ever be able to express exactly what it is that attracts so many people to steam engines. This one, which I have christened Boris, is designed to give years of trouble-free running and is constructed in the simplest way possible. Extensive use of screws has eliminated the mastery of joints. Therefore, to prevent the somewhat ugly appearance of screw heads all over the engine and its train, I have made extensive use of the plug cutter. If you do not have one of these useful tools then now is your chance to buy one and put it to good use! The engine and its train are constructed entirely of beech using ramin dowel rods for chimneys etc. Other hardwoods would be equally suitable (see page 214).

Engine and tender

1 Cut out the bed plate, and prepare and drill the holes that take the tender and side wall. Cut, drill and shape the two lower side members (treat them as a pair, taped together, for drilling operations). All the screw holes have to be counterbored – a process that allows the screw head to drop just below the surface of the wood (see plan) without impairing its strength. My method is to drill the small pilot hole first, then change the drill bit for a larger one that will allow the screw head to fit easily in the hole bored. As there are many drilling operations employed in all forms of woodworking, do consider buying a vertical drill stand – it does make things easier.

2 Cut and shape the running boards. These boards make it possible for the engine driver to put his feet somewhere when he is being towed along (by Grandfather, of course!). As the screws will show on the running boards, counterbore the holes, cut plugs and glue these over the screw heads. When the glue is dry, cut off the excess wood with a chisel and glasspaper to remove any rough edges.

3 Mark out the engine and tender side walls as a pair and, using a coping saw, cut out the access points for the driver and fireman.

4 The two sides are fixed together by the boiler front piece and the tender rear wall. Before fixing the boiler front, drill a large hole in this and the boiler rear face to take a length of plastic pipe to simulate the boiler. For this you will need to have a set of tank hole cutters as you cannot use an ordinary bit. (These cutters are useful and can also be used for making small wooden wheels.) Now fix the engine and tender side walls together using screws and glue. Once again counterbore the screw holes and cover them with wood plugs.

5 Cut and shape the two cab side walls and fix them to the engine sides with glue, screws and wood plugs.

6 Cut the roof to size and counterbore the three fixing holes. I felt that the cab roof needed a bit of shape. This is not difficult to achieve, but if you don't feel confident about using a plane or spokeshave then just leave it flat. If you are happy to have a go, pencil a gentle curve on the back and front edges, and then, holding the roof in a vice, use a sharp smoothing plane or spokeshave to remove the excess wood. Finish off with glasspaper.

7 The cab front wall has two 'port hole' windows which will need to be cut out with a tank cutter. To add a touch of character and realism I cut two circular surrounds of wood (also with the tank cutter) which I glued onto the outside of the cab wall, making sure that they lined up properly with the windows. You can also make the interior of the cab more interesting by cutting out dials and gauges and glueing these on. You could paint them different colours too.

8 Now make and shape the boiler top and drill holes in it for the chimney and pressure dome.

9 The chimney can be beautifully shaped if you have a lathe. However, I assumed that most people won't have one and decided to do the best I could with a length of hoe handle. Using the tank cutter I cut a thick disc which I glued on the top and further shaped with glasspaper. I then fitted a small piece of brass strip round this using panel pins. The steam dome came from the same hoe handle and I rounded the top off using a chisel. It obviously makes good sense to buy the hoe handle before drilling holes in the boiler to make sure it will fit!

10 Fix the boiler top onto the sides using screws, glue and wood plugs, then fix on the cab front wall assembly, followed by the cab roof. The wood plugs will all need cutting off and glasspapering when the glue has dried.

11 Shape and fix on the tender top/seat.

12 Cut and shape the front and rear buffer beams and bore a large centre hole in the front one to take a cord for towing the engine. I made the buffers themselves by cutting off lengths of hoe handle and simply glueing them to the beams. Fix the assembled buffers to the

bed plate with screws, glue and plugs. The rear buffer beam has a recess cut in it to accommodate the hitch pin which should be screwed very securely into the bed plate.

13 I have always found that children like to be able to open up things and find out how they work. For this reason I felt that adding a boiler and boiler access door was a good idea. A piece of sink waste pipe makes an ideal boiler, and you will need the tank cutter again to make the door. Cut a rebate in the door to take a small piece of wood, onto which the two brass hinges should be fixed. Screw the hinges to the boiler front and fix on the little screw eye and hook which complete the door. If you like, you could cut some extra wooden plugs, store them in the tender and use them as fuel.

14 The axles and wheels should be fitted last after all the varnishing has been done.

Carriage, truck and guard's van
All railways need a mixed set of rolling stock. I have therefore designed a truck, a carriage and a guard's van. However, these have a common factor in that all the chassis are the same.

Chassis
Start by cutting the base to shape. Then tape together the two side frames which will hold the wheels and drill the holes for the axles. Now drill the counterbore holes for the screws that will allow the side frames to be fixed to the underside of the base. Make the two end cross

members and cut a notch in each to take the hitches. Screw the cross members into place and, again, use wood pegs to hide the screws. This is the basic chassis for all the rolling stock.

Open top truck
Cut the two sides and two ends to length. Glue and screw the pieces together, and fit the wood plugs over the screw heads. The sides of the open truck are fixed onto the basic chassis by screws that pass through from the underside of the chassis. The top edges of the truck will need rounding off to prevent children being cut by any sharp edges.

Passenger carriage
1 Mark out carefully the shapes of the sides and, with a coping saw or jigsaw, cut them out. (If you use a coping saw you will have to move the blade around in the frame to allow clearance between the saw back and the carriage side.) Once the shapes have been cut out, careful shaping of the curves is necessary to remove the saw marks and the rough edges.

2 Fix the end walls to the sides using screws, glue and wood plugs. Glue in the seats – no need to use screws here – but do make sure that each one is carefully shaped and glasspapered before fixing it into its final position.

3 Attach the sides to the chassis with screws that must pass up through the underneath of the chassis.

4 Now fit the carriage roof on, once again using screws, glue and wood plugs.

This will also need to be rounded off at all edges.

Guard's van
Glue, screw and plug the two side walls to the front wall. Shape the rear wall. Screw all the walls to the chassis. Shape the roof and attach it in exactly the same way as for the carriage.

Links
All the rolling stock should be fitted with dowel rod hitches which make them fully interchangeable. I made the links which hold them all together from beech. It is a good idea to make the holes in the links slightly oversize as this will help 'the guard' couple and uncouple the rolling stock very quickly. The link method prevents the trucks from becoming accidentally uncoupled when negotiating dips in paths and door sills. However, it has one drawback in that it makes it quite difficult to go into reverse!

Finishing
I used matt polyurethane varnish throughout to finish off the train (see page 214).

Tool notes
Plug cutters and counterbore drills can be purchased as a set. The tank cutter has a series of circular blades that are most useful for cutting holes in a variety of sizes. They will, however, only work well when driven by an electric drill.

Cutting list

Bed plate	1 off	508 × 168 × 22mm (20 × 6⅝ × ⅞in)	Timber
Lower side member	2 off	508 × 35 × 22mm (20 × 1⅜ × ⅞in)	Timber
Running board	2 off	235 × 32 × 22mm (9¼ × 1¼ × ⅞in)	Timber
Front buffer assembly	1 off	197 × 35 × 22mm (7¾ × 1⅜ × ⅞in)	Timber
	2 off	6mm (¼in) × 25mm (1in) diam dowelling	
Rear buffer assembly	1 off	197 × 44 × 22mm (7¾ × 1¾ × ⅞in)	Timber
	2 off	6mm (¼in) × 25mm (1in) diam dowelling	
Tender hitch pin	1 off	124 × 35 × 22mm (4⅞ × 1⅜ × ⅞in)	Timber
	1 off	51mm (2in) × 12mm (½in) diam dowelling	
Engine and tender side wall	2 off	435 × 89 × 22mm (17⅛ × 3½ × ⅞in)	Timber
Tender rear wall	1 off	168 × 89 × 20mm (6⅝ × 3½ × ¾in)	Timber
Tender top/seat	1 off	168 × 143 × 22mm (6⅝ × 5⅝ × ⅞in)	Timber
Cab side wall	2 off	194 × 89 × 20mm (7⅝ × 3½ × ¾in)	Timber
Cab roof	1 off	181 × 127 × 20mm (7⅛ × 5 × ¾in)	Timber
Cab front wall assembly	1 off	162 × 83 × 20mm (6⅜ × 3¼ × ¾in)	Timber
	2 off	6mm (¼in) × 38mm (1½in) diam dowelling	
	2 off	6mm (¼in) × 20mm (¾in) diam dowelling	

Boiler top	1 off	235 × 168 × 20mm (9¼ × 6⅝ × ¾in)	Timber
Funnel	1 off	133mm (5¼in) × 25mm (1in) diam dowelling	
	1 off	20mm (¾in) × 32mm (1¼in) diam dowelling	
Pressure dome	1 off	32mm (1¼in) × 25mm (1in) diam dowelling	
Boiler rear face	1 off	89 × 79 × 20mm (3½ × 3⅛ × ¾in)	Timber
Boiler front	1 off	168 × 89 × 20mm (6⅝ × 3½ × ¾in)	Timber
Boiler access door	1 off	86 × 86 × 20mm (3⅜ × 3⅜ × ¾in)	Timber
	1 off	73 × 32 × 9mm (2⅞ × 1¼ × ⅜in)	Timber

Ancillaries

4 off	108mm (4¼in) diam road wheels	
2 off	222mm (8¾in) × 6mm (¼in) diam steel axles	
4 off	Spring dome caps to suit 6mm (¼in) diam axles	
4 off	6mm (¼in) washers	
1 off	229mm (9in) × 44mm (1¾in) o/diam plastic tube for dummy boiler	
1 off	203 × 9 × 1.5mm (8 × ⅜ × 1/16) brass strip	
1 off	Screwed eye and hook	
2 off	25mm (1in) brass hinges	

Cutting list

Common Chassis

Chassis bed	1 off	254 × 165 × 20mm (10 × 6½ × ¾in)	Timber
Side frame	2 off	254 × 35 × 20mm (10 × 1⅜ × ¾in)	Timber
End cross member	2 off	203 × 41 × 20mm (8 × 1⅝ × ¾in)	Timber
Hitch	2 off	102 × 35 × 20mm (4 × 1⅜ × ¾in)	Timber
	2 off	51mm (2in) × 12mm (½in) diam dowelling	
Link	1 off	95 × 35 × 20mm (3¾ × 1⅜ × ¾in)	Timber

Ancillaries

4 off	83mm (3¾in) diameter road wheels	
2 off	222mm (8¾in) × 6mm (¼in) diam steel axles	
4 off	Spring dome caps to suit 6mm (¼in) diam axles	

Open Top Truck Body

Side	2 off	292 × 89 × 20mm (11½ × 3½ × ¾in)	Timber
End	2 off	165 × 89 × 20mm (6½ × 3½ × ¾in)	Timber

Passenger Carriage Body

Side wall	2 off	292 × 187 × 20mm (11½ × 7⅜ × ¾in)	Timber
Roof	1 off	318 × 222 × 20mm (12½ × 8¾ × ¾in)	Timber
End wall	2 off	165 × 95 × 20mm (6½ × 3¾ × ¾in)	Timber
Seat	2 off	165 × 44 × 20mm (6½ × 1¾ × ¾in)	Timber

Guard's Van Body

Side wall	2 off	203 × 187 × 20mm (8 × 7⅜ × ¾in)	Timber
Front wall	1 off	187 × 127 × 20mm (7⅜ × 5 × ¾in)	Timber
Rear wall	1 off	127 × 86 × 20mm (5 × 3⅜ × ¾in)	Timber
Roof	1 off	318 × 216 × 20mm (12½ × 8½ × ¾in)	Timber

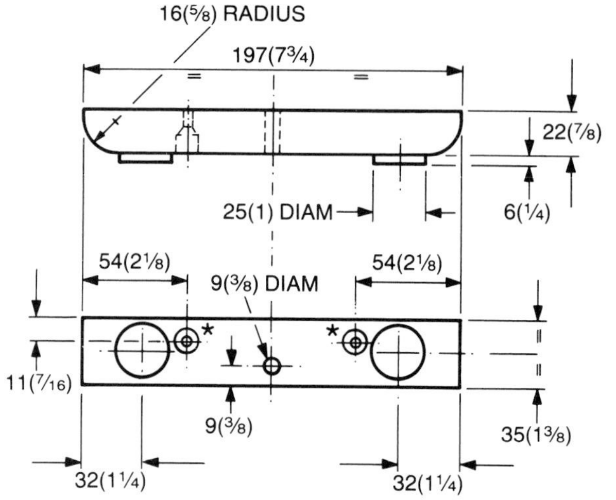

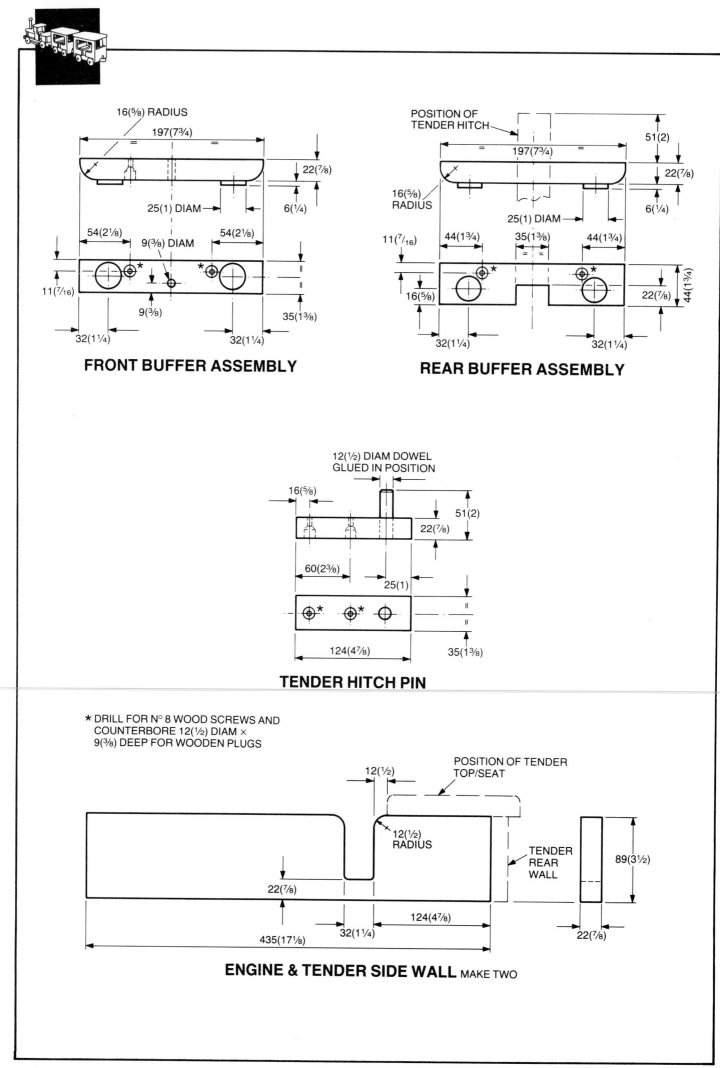

16(5/8) RADIUS
197(7 3/4)
22(7/8)
6(1/4)
25(1) DIAM
54(2 1/8)
9(3/8) DIAM
54(2 1/8)
11(7/16)
9(3/8)
35(1 3/8)
32(1 1/4)
32(1 1/4)

FRONT BUFFER ASSEMBLY

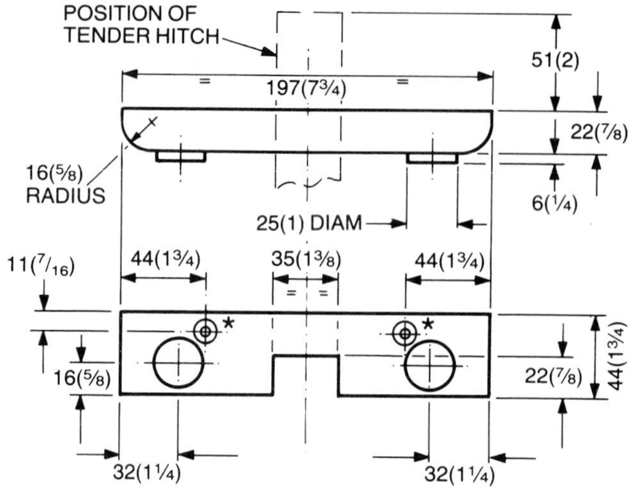

POSITION OF TENDER HITCH
197(7 3/4)
51(2)
22(7/8)
16(5/8) RADIUS
6(1/4)
25(1) DIAM
11(7/16)
44(1 3/4)
35(1 3/8)
44(1 3/4)
16(5/8)
22(7/8)
44(1 3/4)
32(1 1/4)
32(1 1/4)

REAR BUFFER ASSEMBLY

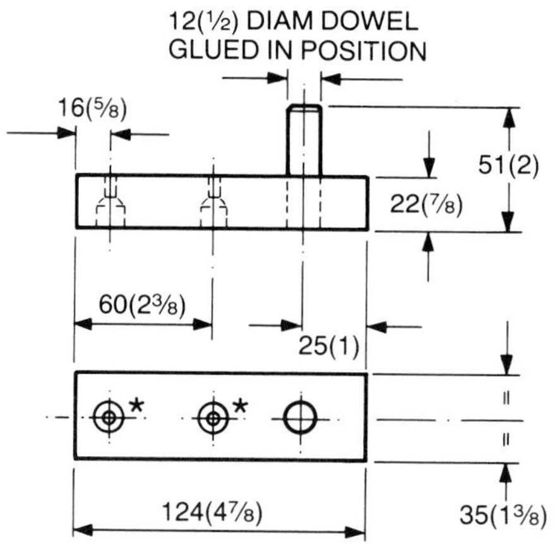

12(1/2) DIAM DOWEL
GLUED IN POSITION
16(5/8)
51(2)
22(7/8)
60(2 3/8)
25(1)
124(4 7/8)
35(1 3/8)

TENDER HITCH PIN

* DRILL FOR N° 8 WOOD SCREWS AND COUNTERBORE 12(1/2) DIAM × 9(3/8) DEEP FOR WOODEN PLUGS

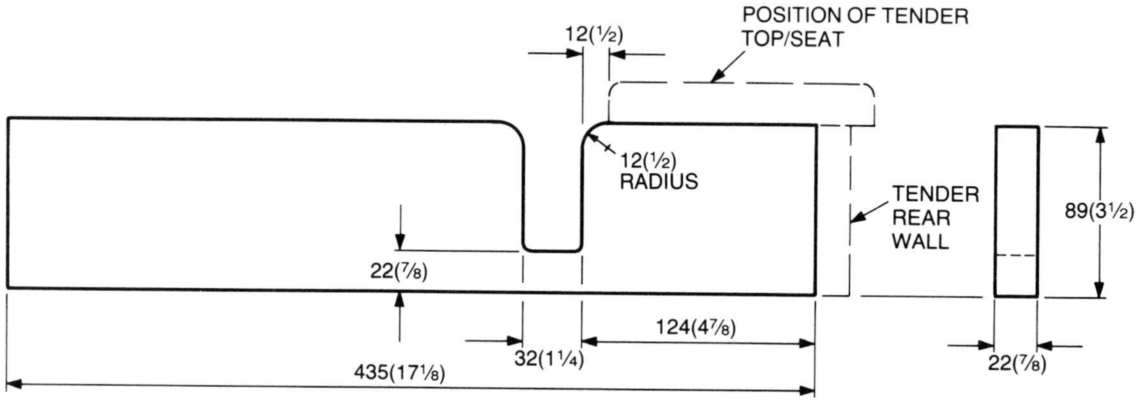

12(1/2)
POSITION OF TENDER
TOP/SEAT
12(1/2)
RADIUS
TENDER
REAR
WALL
89(3 1/2)
22(7/8)
124(4 7/8)
32(1 1/4)
435(17 1/8)
22(7/8)

ENGINE & TENDER SIDE WALL MAKE TWO

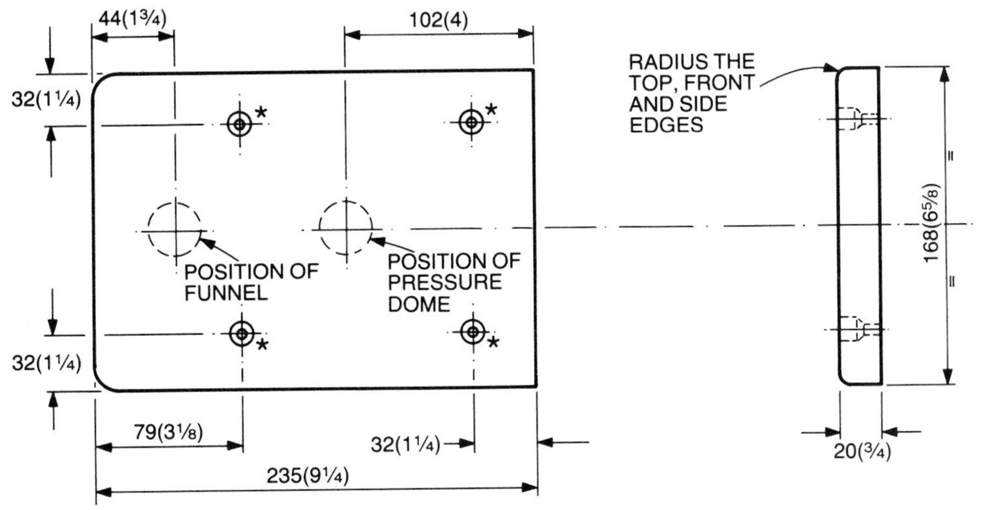
44(1¾)
102(4)
32(1¼)
RADIUS THE TOP, FRONT AND SIDE EDGES
POSITION OF FUNNEL
POSITION OF PRESSURE DOME
32(1¼)
168(6⅝)
79(3⅛)
32(1¼)
235(9¼)
20(¾)

BOILER TOP

* DRILL FOR N° 8 WOOD SCREWS AND COUNTERBORE 12(½) DIAM × 9(⅜) DEEP FOR WOODEN PLUGS

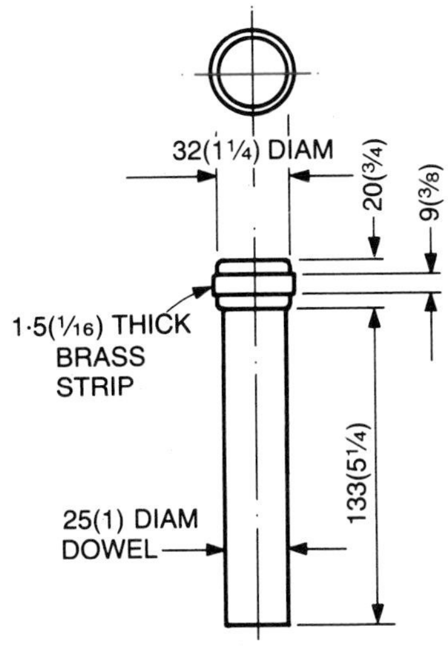
32(1¼) DIAM
20(¾)
9(⅜)
1·5(1/16) THICK BRASS STRIP
133(5¼)
25(1) DIAM DOWEL

FUNNEL

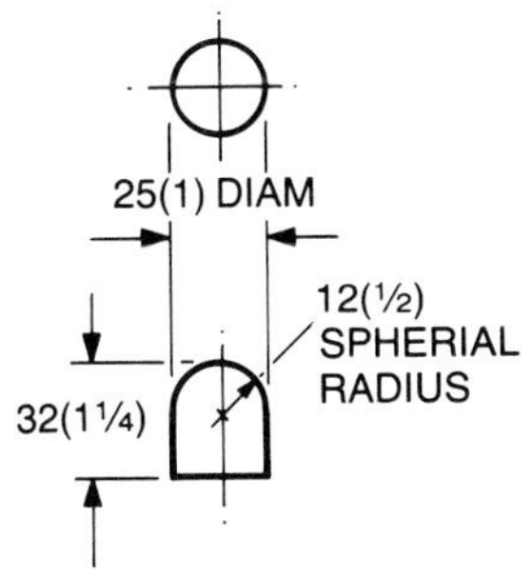
25(1) DIAM
12(½) SPHERIAL RADIUS
32(1¼)

PRESSURE DOME

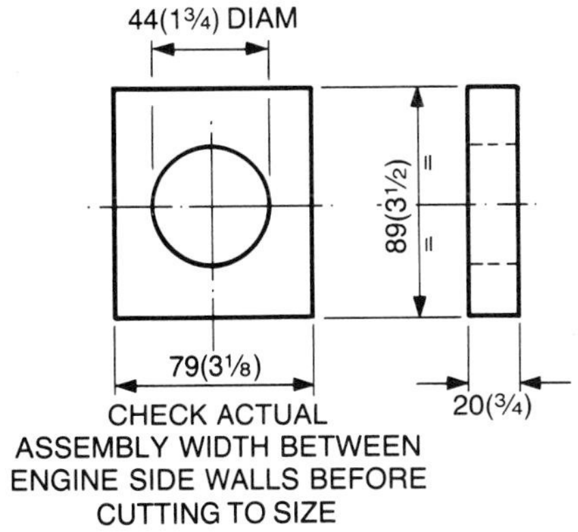
44(1¾) DIAM
89(3½)
79(3⅛)
20(¾)
CHECK ACTUAL ASSEMBLY WIDTH BETWEEN ENGINE SIDE WALLS BEFORE CUTTING TO SIZE

BOILER REAR FACE

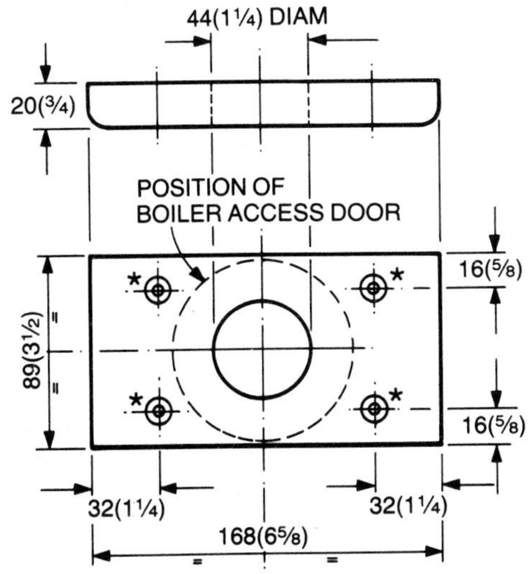
44(1¼) DIAM
20(¾)
POSITION OF BOILER ACCESS DOOR
16(⅝)
89(3½)
16(⅝)
32(1¼)
32(1¼)
168(6⅝)

BOILER FRONT

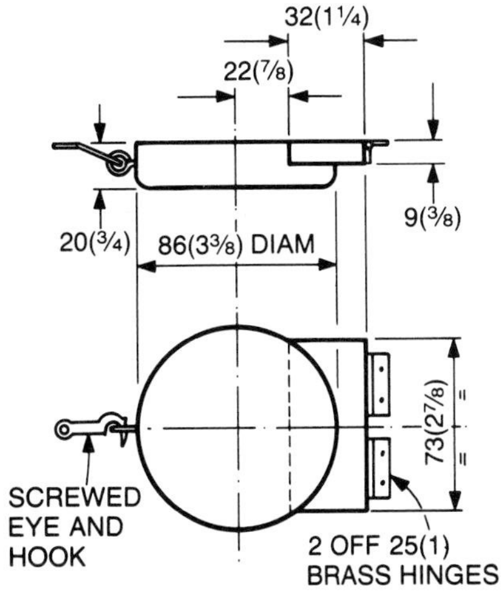
32(1¼)
22(⅞)
20(¾)
86(3⅜) DIAM
9(⅜)
73(2⅞)
SCREWED EYE AND HOOK
2 OFF 25(1) BRASS HINGES

BOILER ACCESS DOOR ASSEMBLY

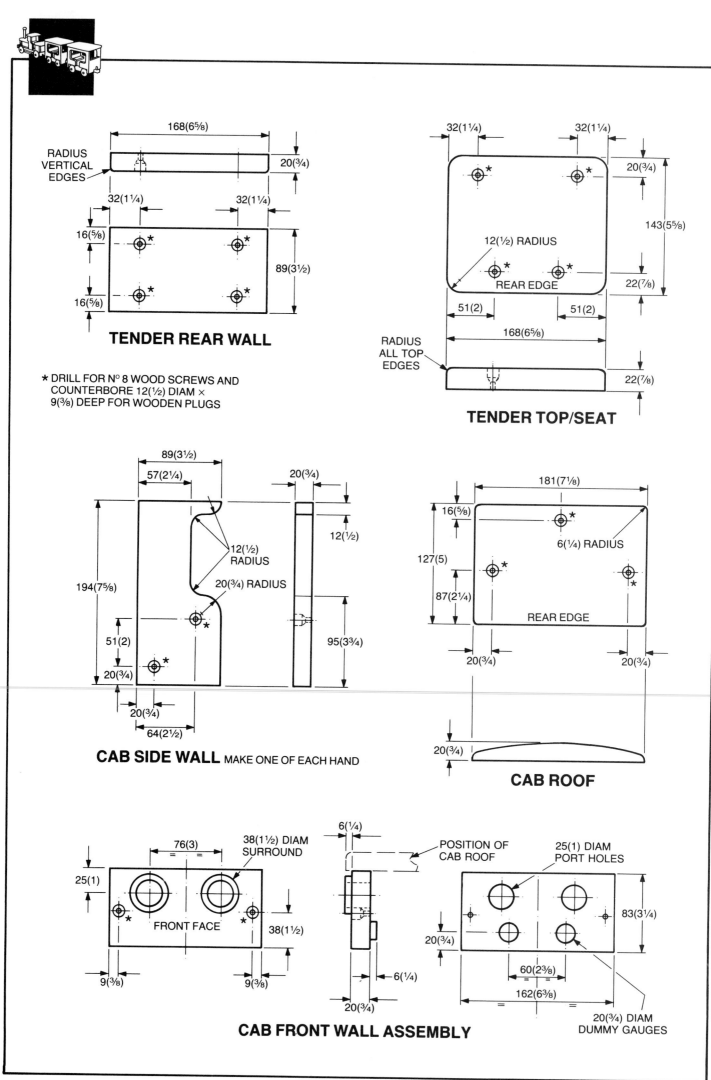

TENDER REAR WALL

★ DRILL FOR N° 8 WOOD SCREWS AND
COUNTERBORE 12(½) DIAM ×
9(⅜) DEEP FOR WOODEN PLUGS

TENDER TOP/SEAT

CAB SIDE WALL MAKE ONE OF EACH HAND

CAB ROOF

CAB FRONT WALL ASSEMBLY

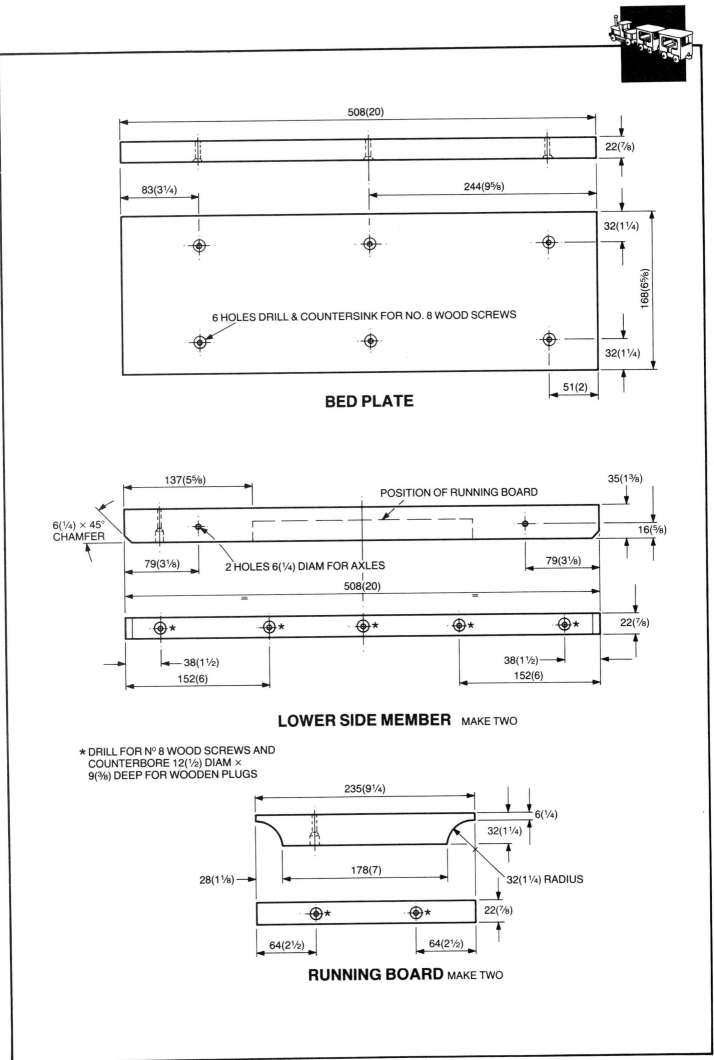

508(20)

22(⅞)

83(3¼)

244(9⅝)

32(1¼)

168(6⅝)

6 HOLES DRILL & COUNTERSINK FOR NO. 8 WOOD SCREWS

32(1¼)

51(2)

BED PLATE

137(5⅝)

POSITION OF RUNNING BOARD

35(1⅜)

6(¼) × 45°
CHAMFER

16(⅝)

79(3⅛)

2 HOLES 6(¼) DIAM FOR AXLES

79(3⅛)

508(20)

22(⅞)

38(1½)

38(1½)

152(6)

152(6)

LOWER SIDE MEMBER MAKE TWO

★ DRILL FOR N° 8 WOOD SCREWS AND
COUNTERBORE 12(½) DIAM ×
9(⅜) DEEP FOR WOODEN PLUGS

235(9¼)

6(¼)

32(1¼)

28(1⅛)

178(7)

32(1¼) RADIUS

22(⅞)

64(2½)

64(2½)

RUNNING BOARD MAKE TWO

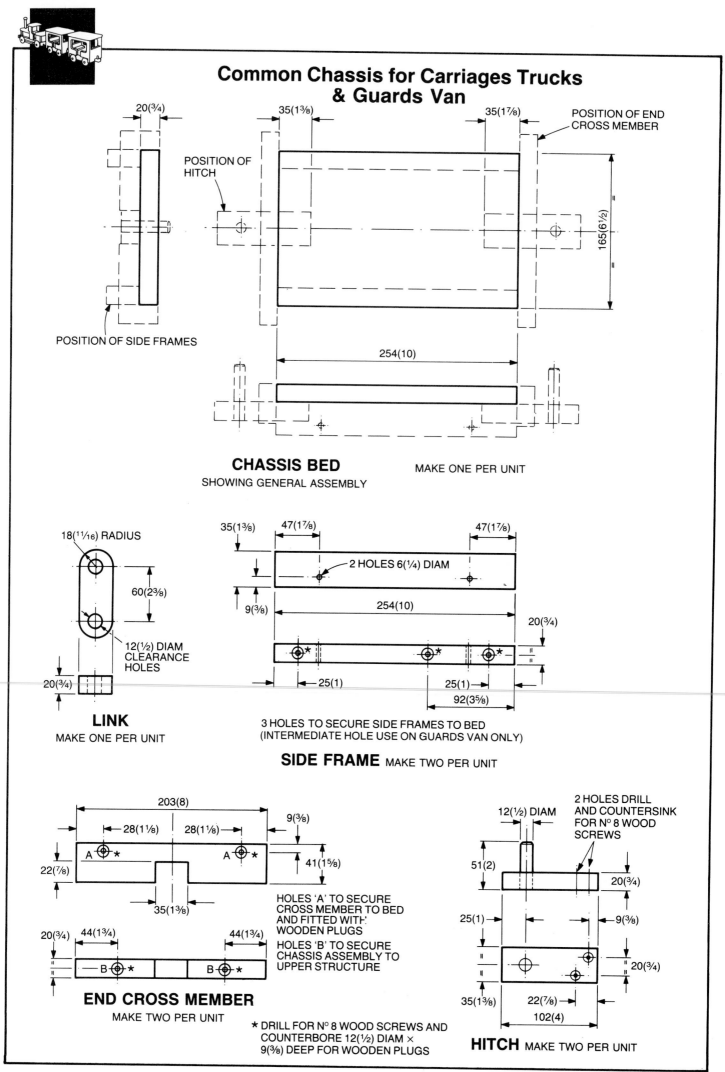

Common Chassis for Carriages Trucks & Guards Van

20(¾)

35(1⅜)

35(1⅞)

POSITION OF END
CROSS MEMBER

POSITION OF
HITCH

165(6½)

POSITION OF SIDE FRAMES

254(10)

CHASSIS BED   MAKE ONE PER UNIT

SHOWING GENERAL ASSEMBLY

18(¹¹/₁₆) RADIUS

60(2⅜)

12(½) DIAM
CLEARANCE
HOLES

20(¾)

LINK

MAKE ONE PER UNIT

35(1⅜)   47(1⅞)   47(1⅞)

2 HOLES 6(¼) DIAM

9(⅜)

254(10)

20(¾)

25(1)   25(1)

92(3⅝)

3 HOLES TO SECURE SIDE FRAMES TO BED
(INTERMEDIATE HOLE USE ON GUARDS VAN ONLY)

SIDE FRAME MAKE TWO PER UNIT

203(8)

28(1⅛)   28(1⅛)   9(⅜)

A   A   41(1⅝)

22(⅞)

35(1⅜)

HOLES 'A' TO SECURE
CROSS MEMBER TO BED
AND FITTED WITH
WOODEN PLUGS

20(¾)   44(1¾)   44(1¾)

B   B

HOLES 'B' TO SECURE
CHASSIS ASSEMBLY TO
UPPER STRUCTURE

END CROSS MEMBER

MAKE TWO PER UNIT

* DRILL FOR Nº 8 WOOD SCREWS AND
COUNTERBORE 12(½) DIAM ×
9(⅜) DEEP FOR WOODEN PLUGS

2 HOLES DRILL
AND COUNTERSINK
FOR Nº 8 WOOD
SCREWS

12(½) DIAM

51(2)

20(¾)

25(1)   9(⅜)

20(¾)

35(1⅜)   22(⅞)

102(4)

HITCH MAKE TWO PER UNIT

Open Top Truck

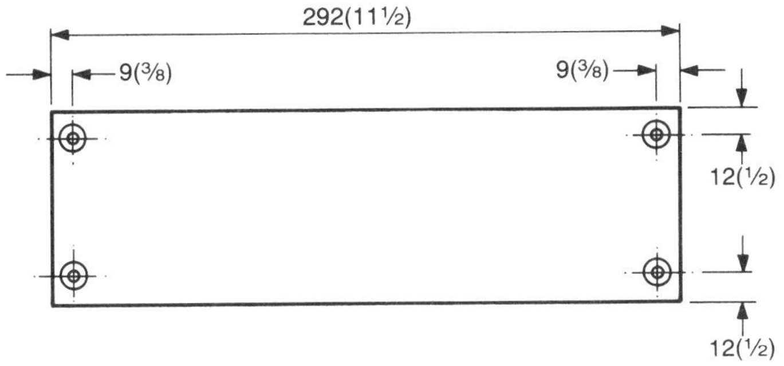

292(11½)
9(⅜)
9(⅜)
12(½)
12(½)

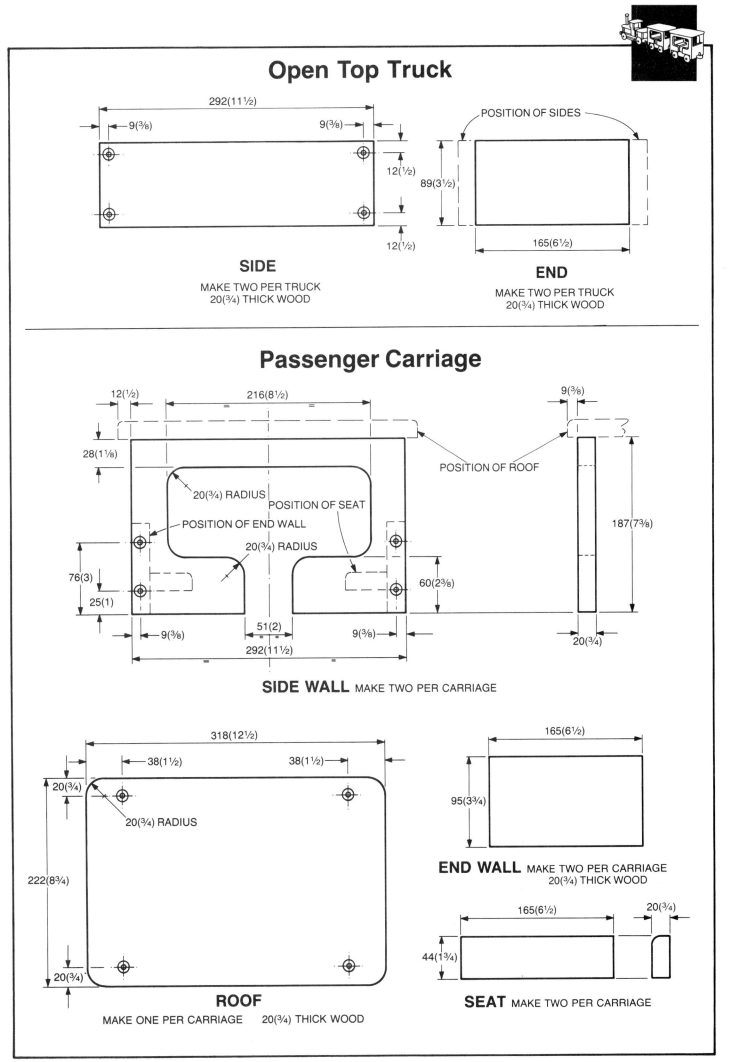

SIDE

MAKE TWO PER TRUCK
20(¾) THICK WOOD

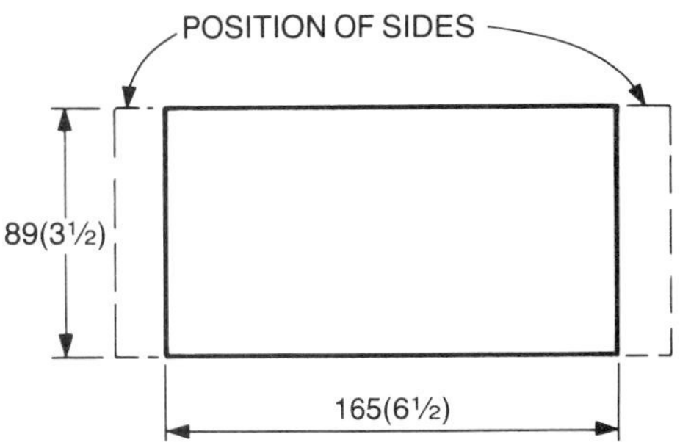

POSITION OF SIDES
89(3½)
165(6½)

END

MAKE TWO PER TRUCK
20(¾) THICK WOOD

Passenger Carriage

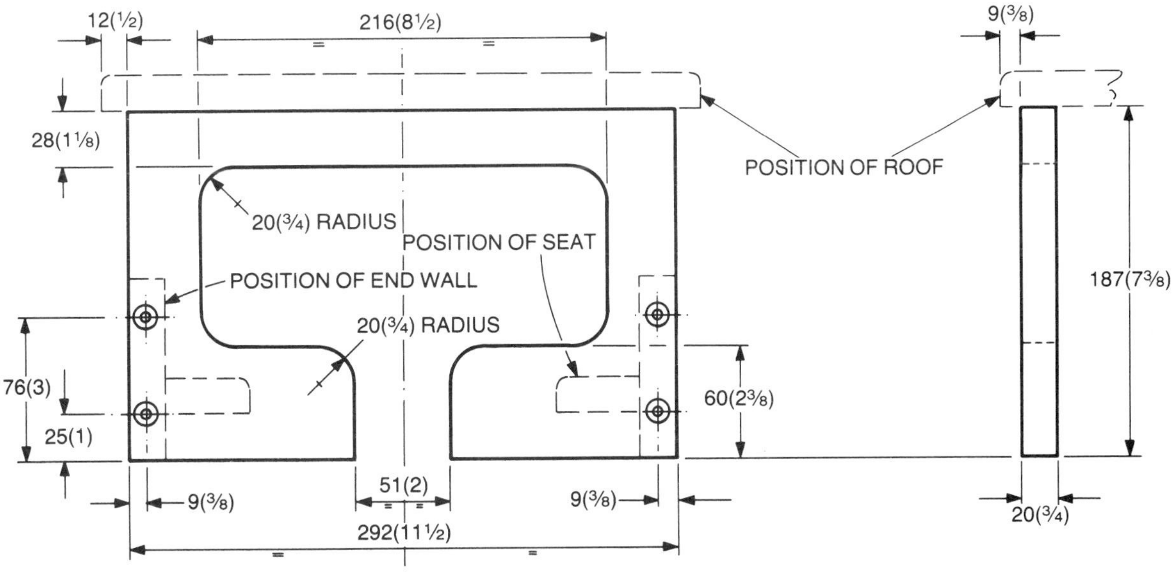

12(½)
216(8½)
9(⅜)
28(1⅛)
POSITION OF ROOF
20(¾) RADIUS
POSITION OF SEAT
POSITION OF END WALL
187(7⅜)
20(¾) RADIUS
76(3)
60(2⅜)
25(1)
9(⅜)
51(2)
9(⅜)
292(11½)
20(¾)

SIDE WALL MAKE TWO PER CARRIAGE

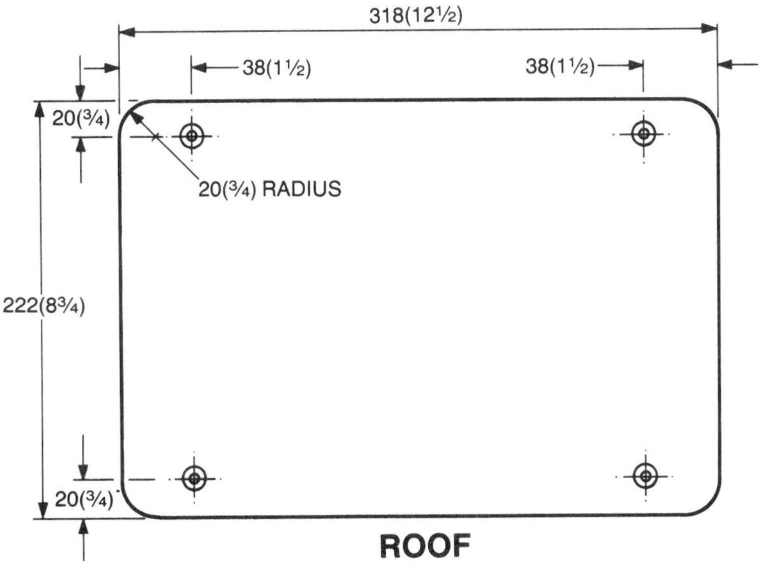

318(12½)
38(1½)
38(1½)
20(¾)
20(¾) RADIUS
222(8¾)
20(¾)

ROOF

MAKE ONE PER CARRIAGE 20(¾) THICK WOOD

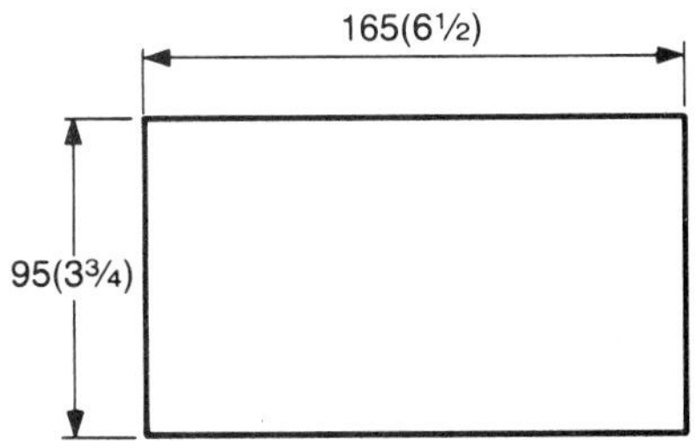

165(6½)
95(3¾)

END WALL MAKE TWO PER CARRIAGE
20(¾) THICK WOOD

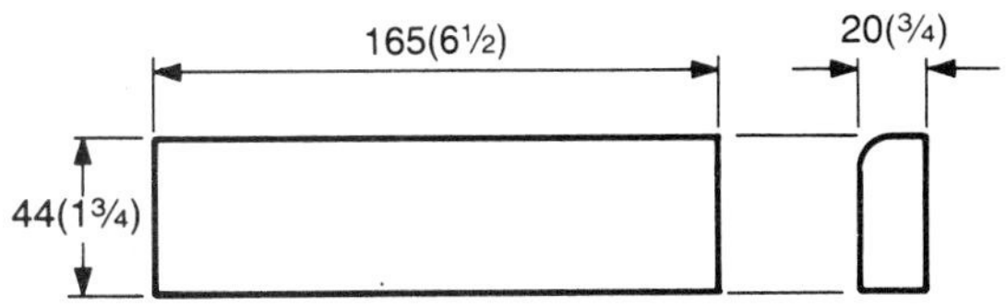

165(6½)
20(¾)
44(1¾)

SEAT MAKE TWO PER CARRIAGE

GUARDS VAN

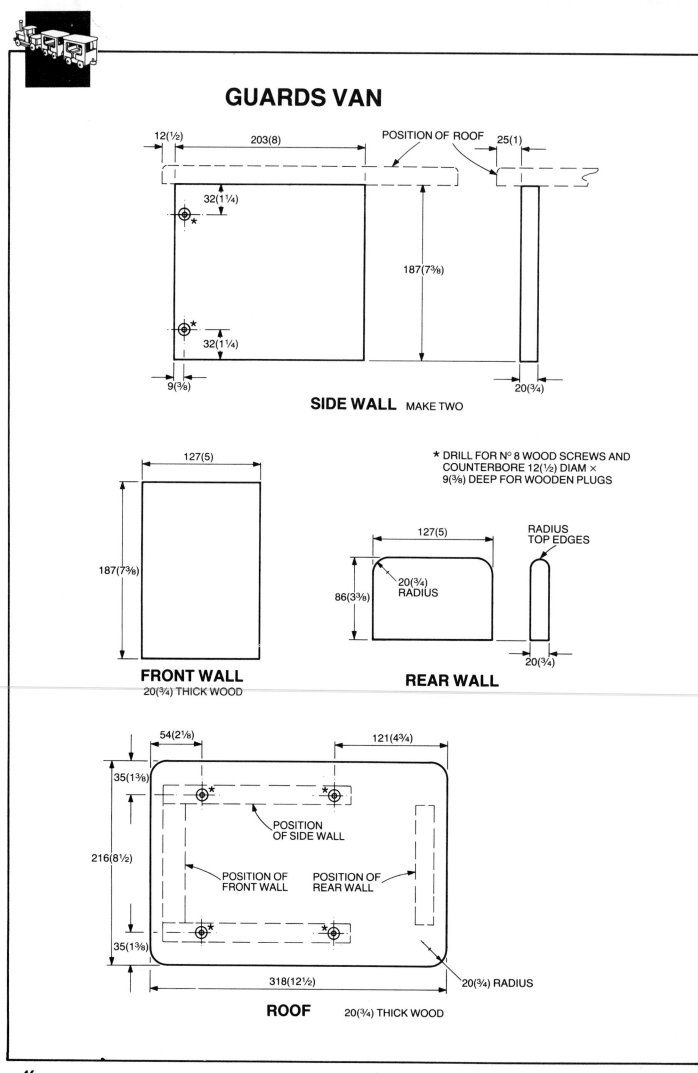

SIDE WALL MAKE TWO

12(½) 203(8) POSITION OF ROOF 25(1)

32(1¼)

187(7⅜)

32(1¼)

9(⅜) 20(¾)

127(5)

187(7⅜)

FRONT WALL
20(¾) THICK WOOD

* DRILL FOR N° 8 WOOD SCREWS AND
COUNTERBORE 12(½) DIAM ×
9(⅜) DEEP FOR WOODEN PLUGS

127(5) RADIUS TOP EDGES

86(3⅜) 20(¾) RADIUS

20(¾)

REAR WALL

54(2⅛) 121(4¾)

35(1⅜)

POSITION OF SIDE WALL

216(8½)

POSITION OF FRONT WALL POSITION OF REAR WALL

35(1⅜)

318(12½) 20(¾) RADIUS

ROOF 20(¾) THICK WOOD

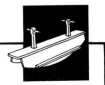

INDOOR ROCKER

This rocker is designed to be used by two or four children and its construction is simple but very sturdy. Playgroups are always looking for strong toys that have a lot of 'playability' and will withstand the rough and tumble of many dozens of youngsters; this would certainly fit the bill. The timber used for the sides is parana pine (readily available from most builders' merchants). The reason for using this wood is that it can easily be obtained in boards of sufficient width for the rocker sides to be made without the added complication of jointing boards.

1 Start by marking out the two rocker sides as a pair. Draw the curve for the rockers and pencil in the three stopped housing joints which take the webs that will hold the sides together.

2 Prepare to cut the grooves for the stopped housing joints. There are two methods that can be used for making these:

i The traditional way would be to attach a rocker side firmly to the bench and cut out a small oblong hole at one end of the groove with a chisel. Cut the hole to the correct width and depth. Use a tenon saw to cut along both pencil lines to the other end of the groove. Then chisel out the wood in the middle to the correct width and depth. Cutting the waste wood out with a chisel to an even depth on the bottom is not easy, so make sure you only remove small quantities of chippings at a time. If you don't make all the grooves to a uniform depth, the two sides will not line up when you come to fit the webs. Traditionally, you would use a hand router to finish off the bottom of the groove, but this is a specialist tool and rather costly compared with an electric router.

ii Electric routers have become more and more popular in the past five years and in many cases have made it possible for the novice to do some extremely skilled work with the minimum of practice. With an electric router all that is necessary to make the grooves for the webs is to select a cutter of the same width as the plywood, fix a fence to guide the router and off you go. The advantage of such a tool is that it can be used in many different woodworking processes and undoubtedly has made it possible for many amateur DIY enthusiasts to carry out woodworking processes that previously would have been impossible.

3 Drill the holes for the footplates and then, using a bow saw or coping saw, cut out the rocker shapes. An electric jigsaw will naturally speed up this process.

4 Once the curves of the rockers have been cut out, they will need to be smoothed. Place both rockers as a pair in the vice and, using a spokeshave, remove the saw cuts and any slight 'flats' on the curved surface. It is worth taking some

care over this and I always find that if I run my fingers along the curve I can feel a flat spot more easily than I can see one. Naturally the 'flat spots' will spoil the rocking action so it is important to remove them. When this task has been completed, slightly chamfer the edges of the rockers, otherwise there will be a tendency for them to cut into the floor-covering when heavily laden with four youngsters doing a 100 mph!

5 Cut out the foot plates – these are essential to prevent children trapping their feet under the rockers. Drill holes for the screws, then screw the footplates to the rockers from the inside. As a precaution I glued as well as screwed the foot plates to the sides since they will get a great deal of wear.

6 The plywood webs should now be cut and shaped. The two outer ones must be drilled to take no. 10 screws which provide the 'anchorage' places for the handles.

7 Assemble the webs in the grooves before glueing anything. It is at this point that discrepancies in the 'trenches' of the housing joints will show up and it may be necessary to adjust things before you can go on. Once you are satisfied, glue the webs into the sides. Because of the angle of the sides cramping is difficult, and it is a good idea to place heavy weights on the sides while the glue is drying. If you possess and decide to use sash cramps, cut angle blocks to fit under the cramp heads.

8 Now shape the handles and fit the dowel rod cross-pieces. An ideal substitute for large diameter dowel rod is a broom handle, but whatever you use, do make sure that it is both glued and screwed in place. Screw the handles to the webs.

9 Now you can fit the seat. I used parana pine for this although other timbers would be equally suitable. Cut the plank into three pieces and cut notches to accommodate the handles. Care should be taken to get a good tight fit at this point. The planks are screwed onto the top of the rockers. To improve the appearance I counterbored the holes and fitted wooden plugs over the tops of the screws. This is not essential but does add greatly to the look of the finished article.

10 Particular care should now be given to all the edges since careful rounding off and smoothing of all surfaces is essential if splinters are to be avoided. Polyurethane varnish is probably the best type of finish to apply (see page 214).

Cutting list

Rocker	2 off	1473 × 295 × 20mm (58 × 11⅝ × ¾in)	Timber
Foot plate	2 off	1154 × 67 × 25mm (45½ × 2⅝ × 1in)	Timber
Web	3 off	295 × 178 × 9mm (11⅝ × 7 × ⅜in)	Timber
Handle	2 off	533 × 70 × 38mm (21 × 2¾ × 1½in)	Timber
	2 off	305mm (12in) × 25mm (1in) diam dowelling	
Seat	1 off	1625 × 238 × 20mm (64 × 9⅜ × ¾in)	Timber

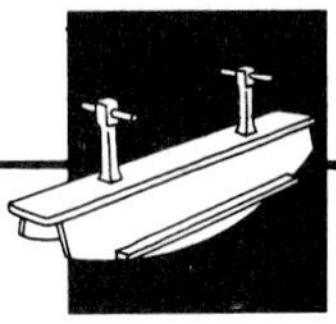

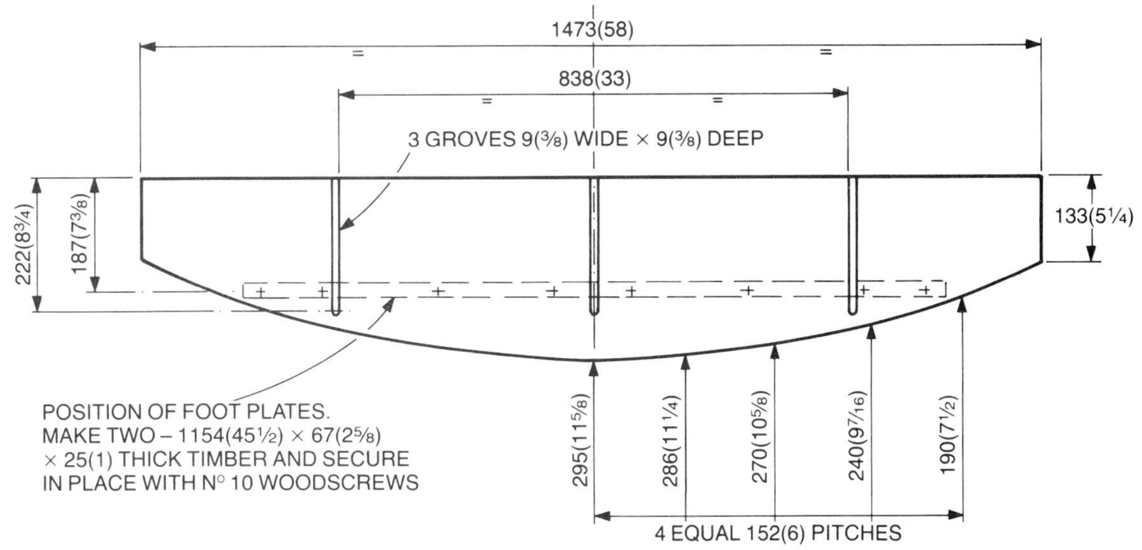

1473(58)
838(33)
3 GROVES 9(⅜) WIDE × 9(⅜) DEEP
222(8¾)
187(7⅜)
133(5¼)
POSITION OF FOOT PLATES.
MAKE TWO – 1154(45½) × 67(2⅝)
× 25(1) THICK TIMBER AND SECURE
IN PLACE WITH N° 10 WOODSCREWS
295(11⅝)
286(11¼)
270(10⅝)
240(9 7/16)
190(7½)
4 EQUAL 152(6) PITCHES

ROCKER – MAKE TWO – 20(¾) THICK TIMBER

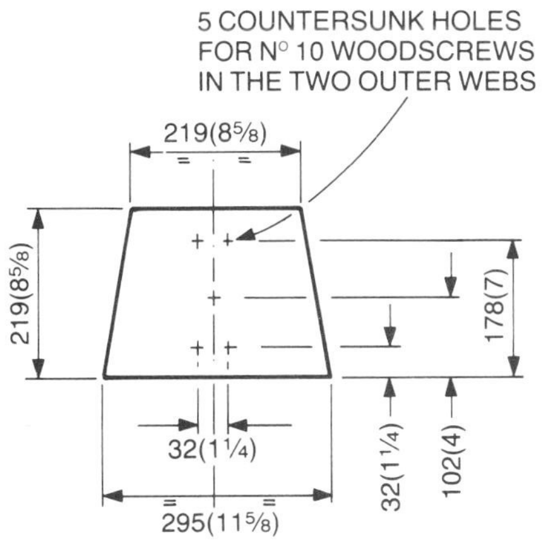

5 COUNTERSUNK HOLES
FOR N° 10 WOODSCREWS
IN THE TWO OUTER WEBS
219(8⅝)
219(8⅝)
178(7)
32(1¼)
32(1¼)
102(4)
295(11⅝)

WEB – MAKE THREE – 9(⅜) THICK PLYWOOD

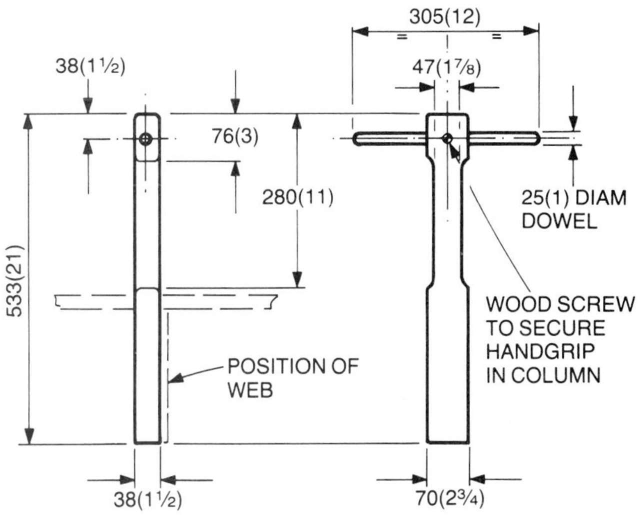

305(12)
38(1½)
47(1⅞)
76(3)
280(11)
25(1) DIAM
DOWEL
533(21)
WOOD SCREW
TO SECURE
HANDGRIP
IN COLUMN
POSITION OF
WEB
38(1½)
70(2¾)

HANDLE – MAKE TWO
HANDLE SECURED TO INNER
FACE OF OUTER RIBS

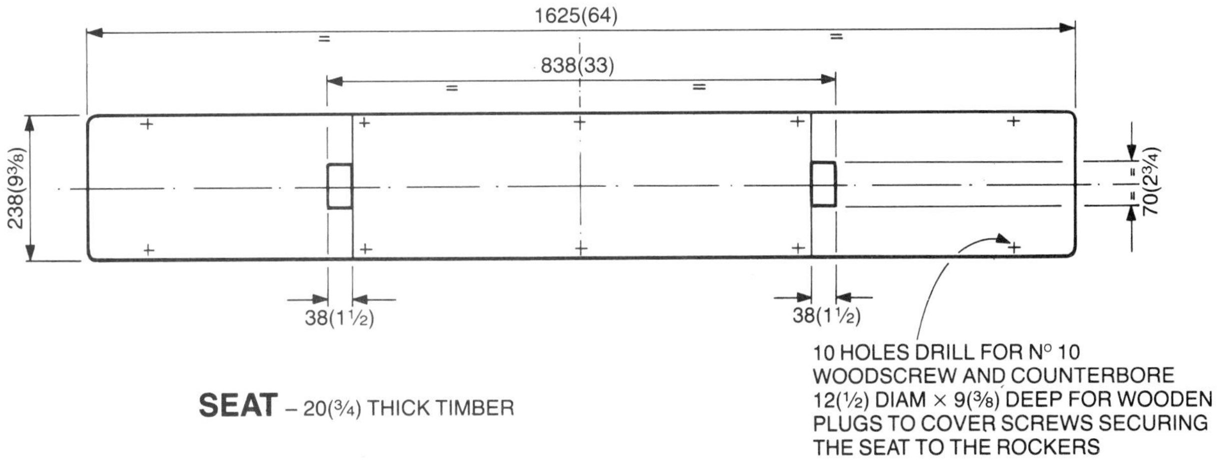

1625(64)
838(33)
238(9⅜)
70(2¾)
38(1½)
38(1½)
10 HOLES DRILL FOR N° 10
WOODSCREW AND COUNTERBORE
12(½) DIAM × 9(⅜) DEEP FOR WOODEN
PLUGS TO COVER SCREWS SECURING
THE SEAT TO THE ROCKERS

SEAT – 20(¾) THICK TIMBER

SOPWITH CAMEL

A good project for the beginner

Youngsters enjoy toys that they can sit on and 'scoot' along. This bi-plane is extremely sturdy and is designed to be 'flown' in the average house. The tail wheel is supported by an industrial castor which makes it possible for the machine to be turned round in its own length, and thus the toy is very manoeuvrable. The big chunky wheels add greatly to its charm. Most of the parts are made in beech, but the engine cowl and propellor are mahogany. (A number of 'red' African hardwoods would do equally as well.) To add a dash of colour I painted the 'dished' sections of the wheels and the front axle red. The 'stringing' between the wings is simply nylon cord.

1 Start by making the fuselage (body) and cutting out the recesses for the wing and tailplane/seat. Drill the hole for the machine gun handle and, from scrap wood, glue a 'boss' onto the side of the fuselage. The purpose of this is to increase the 'bearing' area and allow the handle for the machine gun to be turned smoothly.

2 The radial engine cowl, which is in two parts, is best glued onto the front of the fuselage before final shaping takes place. Once the glue has dried cut and trim until you have a smooth circle.

3 The propellor is an interesting exercise in wood whittling. Start by cutting the basic shape and drilling the hole to take the centre screw. Using a sharp knife (Stanley or spokeshave) begin to reduce the thickness on the sides of the propellor. It is best to work at each end alternately, aiming to reduce the amount of wood evenly at both ends and on both sides. This does add realism to the front of the aeroplane and can be a very interesting talking point for a young child who wants to know how a propellor works.

Fixing the propellor to the front of the radial engine cowl is best done at the very end, but it is a good idea at this stage to start searching for a 'cup' washer which will make the propellor rotate smoothly. As the propellor screw is going into 'end grain' a fairly long screw should be used, eg gauge no. 8 or 10, 5cm (2in) long. Don't forget to drill a pilot hole for the screw to prevent splitting the front of the fuselage.

4 Now start work on the tailplane, undercarriage and tail fin. The tailplane doubles up as a seat and to prevent a young child from falling off backwards I fitted a back (or, rather, bottom) rest to the tailplane. This is held in place by screws from the underside of the seat.

Drill holes on the underside of the tailplane to take the dowel rods that will attach it to the rear undercarriage. The simplest method of doing this is to tape the rear undercarriage and tailplane together with masking tape. Drill the dowel rod holes from the underside of the undercarriage into the tailplane. I stopped the drill before it 'broke' through

the top of the tailplane so that when the unit was assembled no dowel rods would show from the top side. This is only a detail but it does improve the overall finish of the toy. If you don't have a vertical drill stand you may find it difficult to drill these four holes accurately.

Once the drilling is complete and you are sure that all the dowel rods will line up when they are passed through the undercarriage into the tailplane you can separate the two pieces. Drill the hole to take the rear castor (tail wheel) in the undercarriage. Glue the fin onto the seat back and fit and glue all the dowel rods in place. The whole assembly is attached to the fuselage by two large screws (gauge no. 8 or 10). I counterbored the screw holes and fitted wooden plugs over the top – it improves the look of the finished toy.

5 The wings are made from two identical lengths of timber, the only difference being the 'cut out' in the top wing. As with the tail assembly, the easiest method of drilling the dowel rod and rigging holes is to tape both wings together and mark the positions of all the dowel rods and holes for the rigging. Then drill all the holes right through the wood and finally separate the two wings and 'shape up' the edges. Always remember that rounded edges are essential with all wooden toys – hardwoods can have very sharp edges that can give nasty cuts.

Cut the four dowel rods which will hold the wings together to *exactly* the same length. Glue the rods into the bottom wing using a hammer and waste block of wood to tap them through until the ends are just proud of the underside of the wing. Chamfer the four projecting rod ends slightly. Now apply glue to the ends of the rods and gently ease the top wing onto them. Using your scrap of wood and hammer, tap the top wing evenly down the rods until the top of the rods are just proud of the top of the wing. This whole operation needs care, but should be carried out as quickly as possible, otherwise the glue setting around the dowel rods will make it extremely difficult to get the rods into the right position. (If the telephone rings, don't answer it!) The wings are fitted to the fuselage by two large screws (gauge no. 10 or 12, 5 cm (2in) long).

6 The undercarriage needs to be very substantial as it will have to take a large number of bad landings! Make the top, bottom and ends. Drill the axle holes in the end pieces and cut rebates on the top and bottom pieces. (Rebates can be cut with a chisel, but it is a good idea to invest in a rebate plane.) Glue the undercarriage together and, when it has set, attach it to the underside of the wing with three large screws (gauge no. 10 or 12).

7 A prominent feature of this type of aeroplane used to be the 'rigging' of the wings. I threaded nylon cord through the holes from the underside, tying the knots on the top wing as I think this is preferable to loops of nylon showing on the top wing surface. The nylon cord has to be stretched very tight before you tie the knot to ensure it remains taut and looks 'workmanlike'.

8 The machine gun barrels are made from two lengths of dowel rod, drilled at one end to accept two smaller diameter dowels. I planed the underneath of the larger dowels to flatten the surface slightly and increase the glueing area. Glue both barrels onto the top of the fuselage. You could also paint them as I have done.

But children like guns to make a noise so I have devised a clicker mechanism. Mark out a complete circle carefully with a compass and cut it out. Now cut out teeth using a fine-toothed saw. Make the clicker handle and fit it through the side of the fuselage. (Rubbing some candle wax on it will help it to rotate smoothly.) Glue the clicker wheel on to the end of the rod. Make the clicker lever and attach one end to the fuselage with a screw so that the other end rests on the wheel. As the handle is turned, this arrangement will produce a realistic rattling noise. If you feel strongly about guns on children's toys, you don't need to make this part of the aeroplane. With or without the armament it still looks good.

9 Glasspaper down all edges and make sure that there are no sharp corners. Check also that there are no steel 'splinters' on the screw heads that could possibly get into children's fingers. Before finally attaching the wheels, propeller etc., carry out the varnishing processes (see page 214).

Cutting list

Wing	2 off	508 × 124 × 20mm (20 × 4⅞ × ¾in)	Timber
Strut	4 off	197mm (7¾in) × 12mm (½in) diam dowelling	
Main undercarriage	1 off	248 × 86 × 20mm (9¾ × 3⅜ × ¾in)	Timber
	2 off	98 × 86 × 20mm (3⅞ × 3⅜ × ¾in)	Timber
	2 off	248 × 20 × 20mm (9¾ × ¾ × ¾in)	Timber
Fuselage	1 off	540 × 117 × 20mm (2¼ × 4⅝ × ¾in)	Timber
	1 off	38 × 38 × 20mm (1½ × 1½ × ¾in)	Timber
Radial engine cowl	2 off	121 × 60 × 28mm (4¾ × 2⅜ × 1⅛in)	Timber
Propeller	1 off	280 × 44 × 16mm (11 × 1¾ × ⅝in)	Timber
Machine gun	2 off	98mm (3⅞in) × 25mm (1in) diam dowelling	
Tailplane/seat	1 off	203 × 137 × 20mm (8 × 5⅜ × ¾in)	Timber
Seat back	1 off	191 × 165 × 20mm (7½ × 6½ × ¾in)	Timber
Rear undercarriage	1 off	178 × 64 × 20mm (7 × 2½ × ¾in)	Timber
	4 off	127mm (5in) × 12mm (½in) diam dowelling	
Tail fin	1 off	140 × 89 × 20mm (5½ × 3½ × ¾in)	Timber
Clicker wheel	1 off	57 × 57 × 20mm (2¼ × 2¼ × ¾in)	Timber
Clicker lever	1 off	137 × 20 × 12mm (5⅜ × ¾ × ½in)	Timber
Clicker handle	1 off	44 × 20 × 20mm (1¾ × ¾ × ¾in)	Timber
		Make from 165mm (6½in) × 12mm (½in) diam dowelling	

Ancillaries

	2 off	143mm (5⅝in) diam × 62mm (2½in) wide wheels	
	1 off	362mm (14¼in) × 9mm (⅜in) diam steel axles	
	2 off	Spring dome caps to suit 9mm (⅜in) diam axles	
	1 off	1220mm (48in) fine nylon cord for stringing the wings	
	1 off	51mm (2in) diam castor wheel assembly, nut and washer	

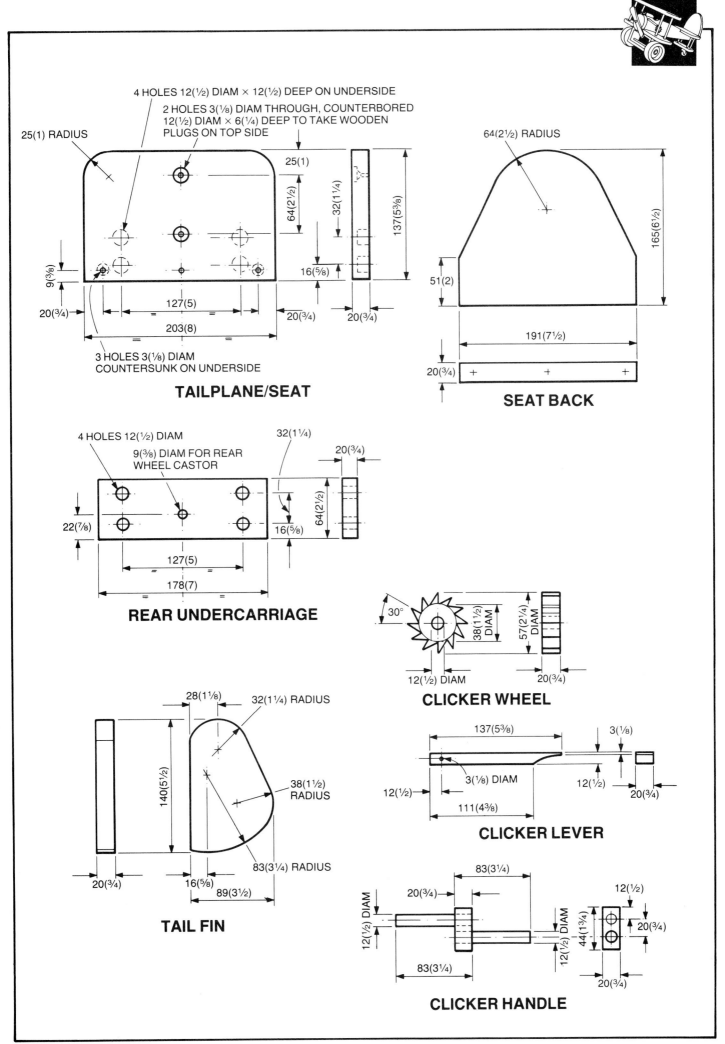

4 HOLES 12(½) DIAM × 12(½) DEEP ON UNDERSIDE

2 HOLES 3(⅛) DIAM THROUGH, COUNTERBORED
12(½) DIAM × 6(¼) DEEP TO TAKE WOODEN
PLUGS ON TOP SIDE

25(1) RADIUS

64(2½) RADIUS

25(1)

64(2½)

32(1¼)

137(5⅜)

9(⅜)

16(⅝)

20(¾)

127(5)

20(¾)

20(¾)

203(8)

3 HOLES 3(⅛) DIAM
COUNTERSUNK ON UNDERSIDE

TAILPLANE/SEAT

165(6½)

51(2)

191(7½)

20(¾)

SEAT BACK

4 HOLES 12(½) DIAM

9(⅜) DIAM FOR REAR
WHEEL CASTOR

32(1¼)

20(¾)

22(⅞)

64(2½)

16(⅝)

127(5)

178(7)

REAR UNDERCARRIAGE

30°

38(1½) DIAM

57(2¼) DIAM

12(½) DIAM

20(¾)

CLICKER WHEEL

137(5⅜)

3(⅛)

3(⅛) DIAM

12(½)

12(½)

20(¾)

111(4⅜)

CLICKER LEVER

28(1⅛)

32(1¼) RADIUS

140(5½)

38(1½)
RADIUS

83(3¼) RADIUS

20(¾)

16(⅝)

89(3½)

TAIL FIN

83(3¼)

20(¾)

12(½)

12(½) DIAM

12(½) DIAM

44(1¾)

20(¾)

12(½)

83(3¼)

20(¾)

CLICKER HANDLE

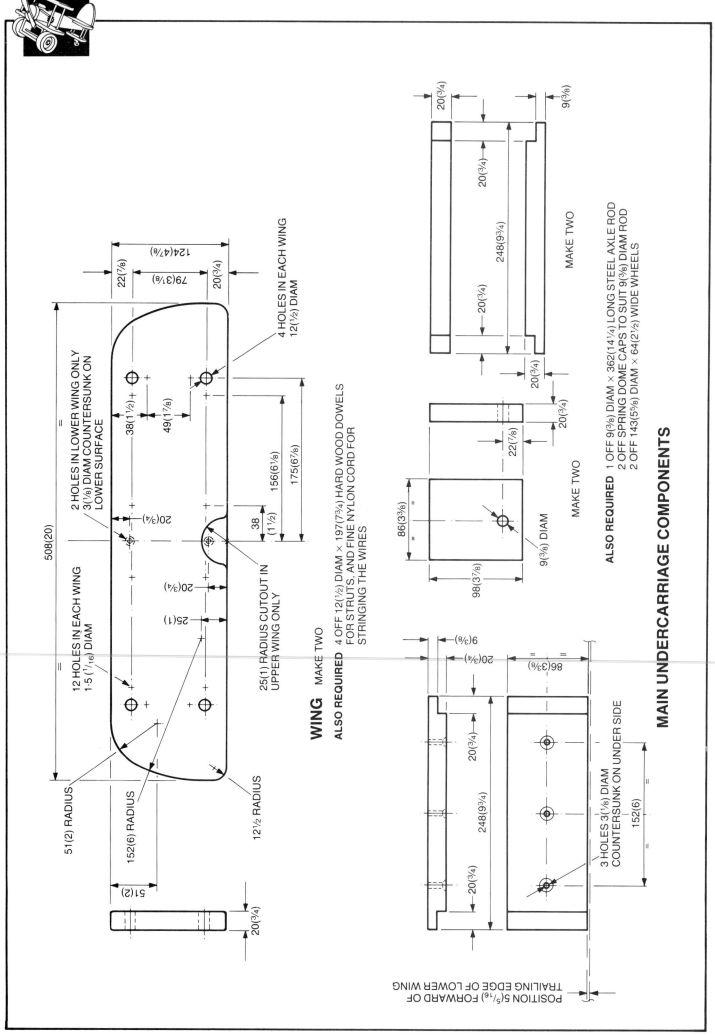

WING MAKE TWO

ALSO REQUIRED 4 OFF 12(½) DIAM × 197(7¾) HARD WOOD DOWELS FOR STRUTS, AND FINE NYLON CORD FOR STRINGING THE WIRES

2 HOLES IN LOWER WING ONLY 3(⅛) DIAM COUNTERSUNK ON LOWER SURFACE

4 HOLES IN EACH WING 12(½) DIAM

12 HOLES IN EACH WING 1·5 (¹/₁₆) DIAM

25(1) RADIUS CUTOUT IN UPPER WING ONLY

51(2) RADIUS

152(6) RADIUS

12½ RADIUS

508(20)

124(4⅞)

22(⅞)

79(3⅛)

20(¾)

38(1½)

49(1⅞)

156(6⅛)

175(6⅞)

38 (1½)

20(¾)

20(¾)

25(1)

51(2)

20(¾)

MAIN UNDERCARRIAGE COMPONENTS

ALSO REQUIRED 1 OFF 9(⅜) DIAM × 362(14¼) LONG STEEL AXLE ROD
2 OFF SPRING DOME CAPS TO SUIT 9(⅜) DIAM ROD
2 OFF 143(5⅝) DIAM × 64(2½) WIDE WHEELS

MAKE TWO

MAKE TWO

20(¾)

9(⅜)

20(¾)

20(¾)

248(9¾)

20(¾)

22(⅞)

20(¾)

86(3⅜)

98(3⅞)

9(⅜) DIAM

3 HOLES 3(⅛) DIAM COUNTERSUNK ON UNDER SIDE

9(⅜)

20(¾)

86(3⅜)

20(¾)

248(9¾)

20(¾)

152(6)

POSITION 5(⁵/₁₆) FORWARD OF TRAILING EDGE OF LOWER WING

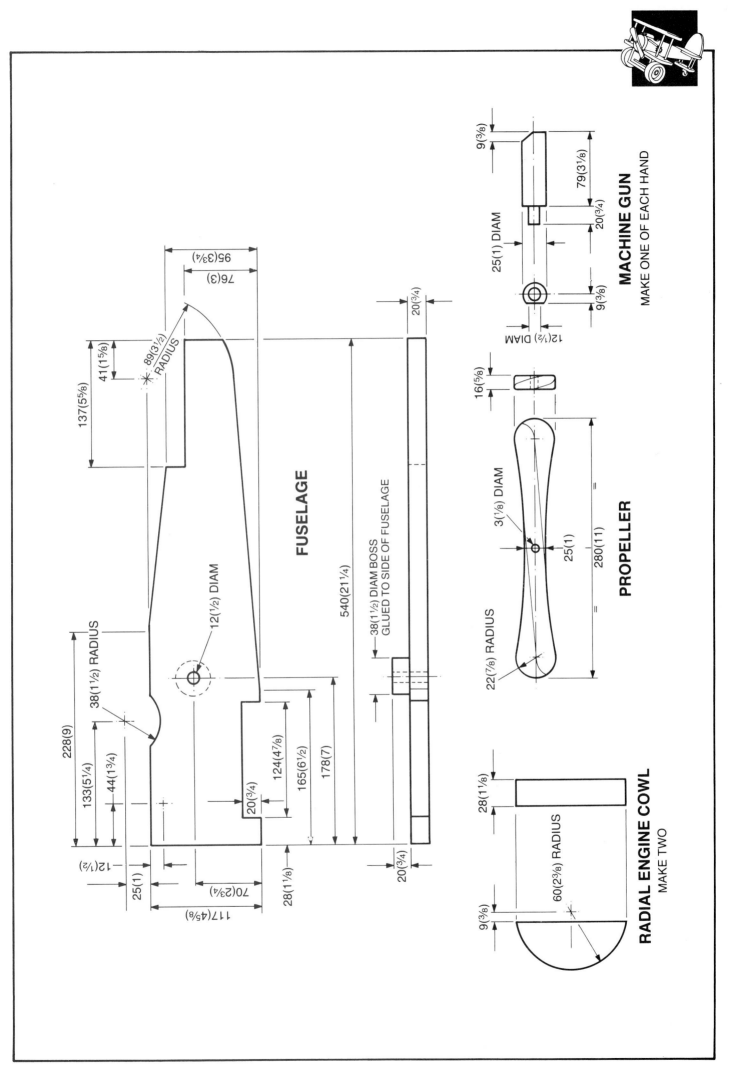

FUSELAGE

MACHINE GUN
MAKE ONE OF EACH HAND

PROPELLER

RADIAL ENGINE COWL
MAKE TWO

This traditional toy always gives youngsters great fun and encourages them to get outside for a gallop to let off steam. It is a toy that can be made with the minimum of tools and time.

1 If you look at the plans for the rocking horse (page 61) you will see that the shape of the hobby horse's head is exactly the same. Mark and cut it out as described on page 59.

2 Cut the stick to the required length. Drill the axle hole at the bottom and then cut out the slot for the wheel.

3 Very carefully mark the slot at the top of the stick which will take the plywood head (a marking gauge would be useful here). Cut out the slot with a coping saw, making sure that the head is a tight fit. Now glue the head into the stick. Once the glue has dried, bore a hole through the head and stick to take the dowel rod that forms the handle.

Dowel rods in wooden toys often work loose so to prevent this, drive in two panel pins from the underside of the stick. The panel pins will go right through the dowel rod into the wood on the other side, securing it firmly.

4 Fit the axle and wheel into the bottom of the stock. The axle is held in place by a spring cap on either side.

5 Make and fit the harness and mane as described for the rocking horse on pages 59–60.

Cutting list

Head	1 off	406 × 330 × 9mm (16 × 13 × 3/8in)	Plywood
Stick	1 off	978 × 73 × 22mm (38½ × 2⅞ × ⅞in)	Timber
Hand hold rod	1 off	229mm (9in) × 16mm (⅝in) diam dowelling	
Ancillaries			
	1 off	106mm (4³/₁₆in) diam road wheel	
	1 off	57mm (2¼in) × 6mm (¼in) diam steel axle	
	2 off	6mm (¼in) spring dome caps	
	2 off	Stick-on eyes	
	1 off	381mm (15in) × 76mm (3in) artificial fur fabric	

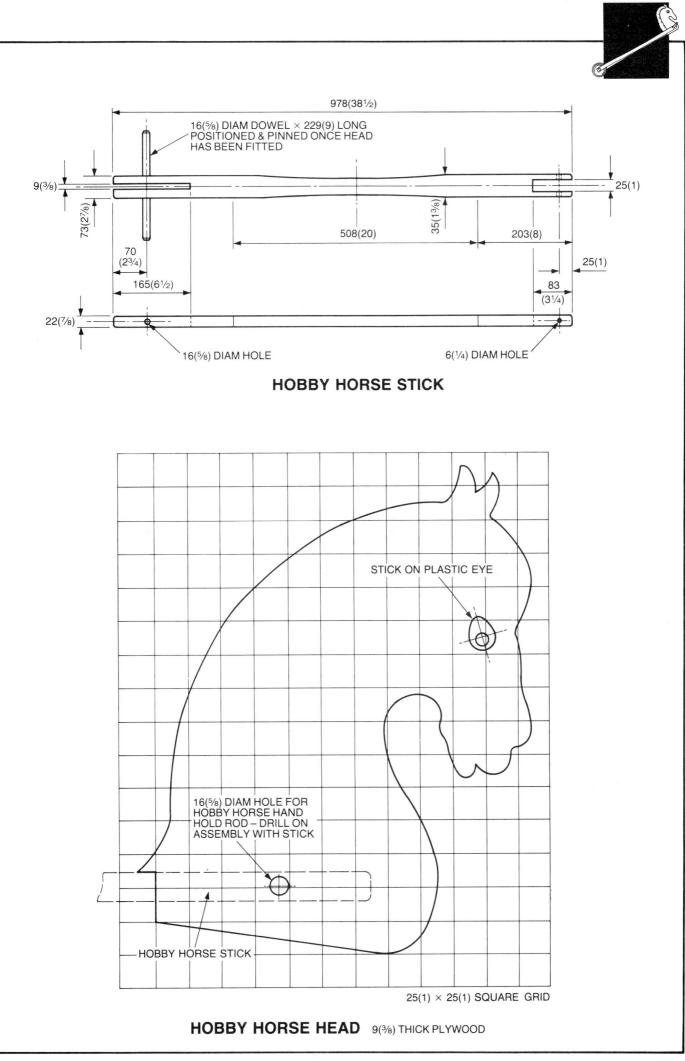

978(38½)

16(⅝) DIAM DOWEL × 229(9) LONG
POSITIONED & PINNED ONCE HEAD
HAS BEEN FITTED

9(⅜)

73(2⅞)

70
(2¾)

165(6½)

508(20)

35(1⅜)

203(8)

25(1)

25(1)

83
(3¼)

22(⅞)

16(⅝) DIAM HOLE

6(¼) DIAM HOLE

HOBBY HORSE STICK

STICK ON PLASTIC EYE

16(⅝) DIAM HOLE FOR
HOBBY HORSE HAND
HOLD ROD – DRILL ON
ASSEMBLY WITH STICK

HOBBY HORSE STICK

25(1) × 25(1) SQUARE GRID

HOBBY HORSE HEAD 9(⅜) THICK PLYWOOD

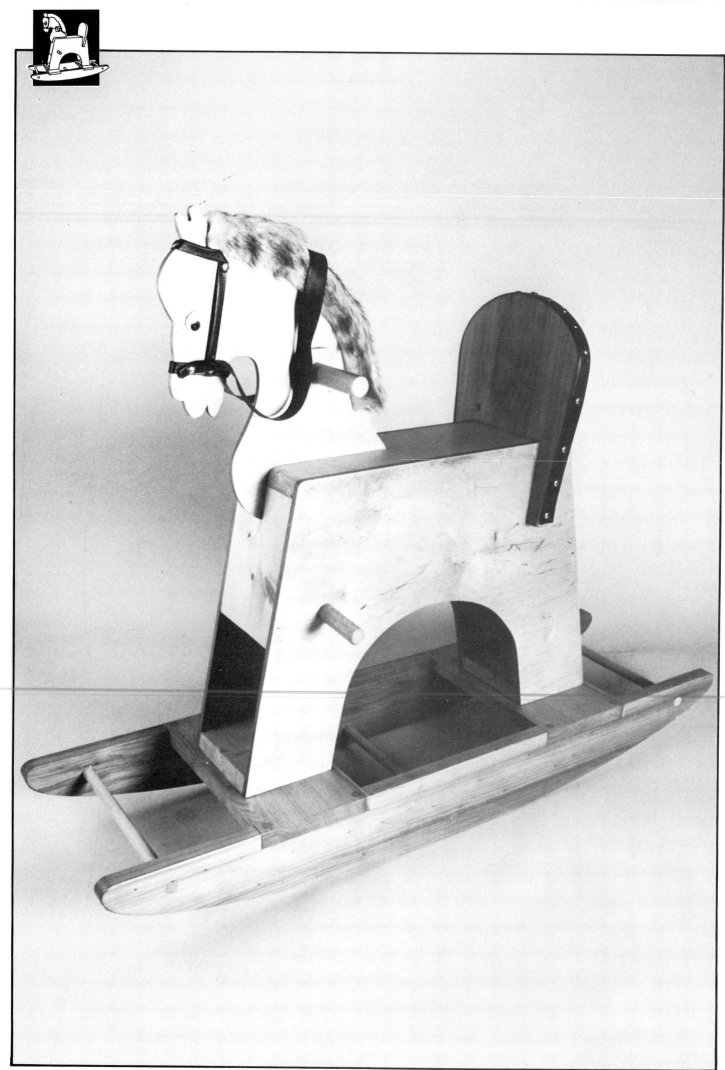

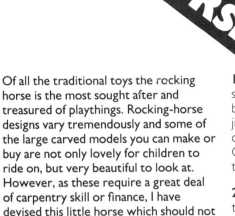

Of all the traditional toys the rocking horse is the most sought after and treasured of playthings. Rocking-horse designs vary tremendously and some of the large carved models you can make or buy are not only lovely for children to ride on, but very beautiful to look at. However, as these require a great deal of carpentry skill or finance, I have devised this little horse which should not overtax either.

1 Start by cutting out the two plywood side panels of the horse. The large curve between the legs needs to be cut with a jigsaw as there is not sufficient frame clearance to cut it with a coping saw. Clamp or tape the sides together and drill the holes for the foot rest.

2 The sides are fixed together with a total of five spacers: two at the bottom for the feet, one forming the seat or 'back' and the other two forming the 'breast' and 'rump' of the horse. Cut out these spacers. Drill a hole in the rump spacer and thread and knot a piece of plaited cord through it for the tail. (You could also use rope.) Cut the slots in the seat and breast spacers for the plywood head. (This needs to be a tight fit.)

3 Using cramps, assemble the spacers and the two sides. If everything fits properly, glue the sides onto the spacers. You will find that if you use cramps to hold everything together while the glue is setting the glue tends to make the pieces move about. To overcome this problem I fastened the sides to the spacers with long panel pins (38mm/1½in) as well as glue. Fix one side first, then turn the body over and check that both sides line up, paying particular attention to the position of the slots for the head. If all is well, panel pin the other side in. I found this method easier than using cramps.

If you follow this method it is a good idea to use a nail punch on each pin head and thump them below the surface. Then fill the little pin hole with beeswax or Brummer stopping. This sounds rather fiddly but is important both from the point of view of safety and the look of the finished toy.

4 Using the grid provided in the plans, mark out the shape of the head on plywood and cut it out. You will find that the finest-toothed blade available is best for plywood, and if you use a jigsaw, fit it with a metal-cutting blade as this will stop plywood 'spilches'. Drill a hole to take the head handle.

5 Now fit the head into the slots on the breast spacer and seat. If the head is too tight a fit, *very carefully* file away the slots to make them larger. Once you have a good fit, glue the head into the body.

The rocker
If you have difficulty in finding a board of sufficient width for the rocker then parana pine, readily available from builders' merchants, is a good choice for this job.

1 Make a cardboard template for the rockers using the grid and curve coordinates provided. Place the card template on the wood, mark around and cut out. A coping saw will manage this job (make sure you have a few spare blades before you start), but obviously it takes a little longer than with a jigsaw, which is probably the best tool to use. Cut out the second rocker, then tape or cramp the two rockers together for final shaping.

The traditional tool used for this sort of shaping is a spokeshave, but there are others that can do the task just as well, eg a sandplate file (see page 210). It is important when shaping the underside of the rocker to make sure you obtain a constant curve with no flat spots, which may take a little bit of patience.

2 With the rockers still taped together, drill holes for the three dowel rods and mark out recesses or 'halving joints' where the two cross-pieces will fit. Place the two rockers in a vice and cut down the sides of each halving joint. Remove the waste in the middle with a coping saw, then chisel out the bottom of the joints and get them flat.

3 Before assembling the rockers, smooth down all edges with a sandplate file. When this is done, glue one end of each dowel rod into one of the rockers. Chamfer the other ends of the rods slightly to help you assemble the other rocker onto them. Once the dowel rods have been fitted, glue the cross-pieces into the halving joints on the top of the rockers.

Trimmings
It is always the little details which give toy animals characters, so it's worth putting in extra effort here. Eyes can be bought from shops that sell materials for soft toy making as can the mane (imitation fur for a coat collar) and the harness (leather binding tape for frayed cuffs).

1 Glue the eyes and the mane onto the head using Evo-stick impact adhesive or a similar product. Do make sure that the eyes are very, very secure – children will swallow anything!

2 Fit the harness to the head with brass upholstery nails. These have domed heads like drawing pins.

3 Glue the head handle into place and also the two small circular discs on either side of the head which will give extra strength to the handle and prevent it working loose after the first gallop!

4 The high-backed 'saddle' is a safety measure. Small children are naturally inquisitive and will love climbing onto this horse. I therefore felt it necessary to prevent them falling off backwards by designing this high back rest. Cut out and shape the back rest, then glue it onto the body of the horse. More leather trimming fitted with brass upholstery nails adds extra decoration and looks fairly realistic.

Finally, attach the horse to the rocker assembly by screwing two large screws from the underside of each rocker cross-pieces into each foot spacer.

Cutting list

Head	1 off	406 × 330 × 9mm (16 × 13 × ⅜in)	Plywood
Side panel	2 off	584 × 406 × 9mm (23 × 16 × ⅜in)	Plywood
Back rest	1 off	305 × 229 × 22mm (12 × 9 × ⅞in)	Timber
Rump and breast spacer	2 off	191 × 127 × 22mm (7½ × 5 × ⅞in)	Timber
Foot spacer	2 off	127 × 127 × 22mm (5 × 5 × ⅞in)	Timber
Foot rest	1 off	298mm (11¾in) × 22mm (⅞in) diam dowelling	
Seat	1 off	441 × 127 × 22mm (17⅜ × 5 × ⅞in)	Timber
Rocker assembly	2 off	1041 × 127 × 22mm (41 × 5 × ⅞in)	Timber
	2 off	305 × 159 × 22mm (12 × 6¼ × ⅞in)	Timber
	3 off	305mm (12in) × 16mm (⅝in) diam dowelling	
Hand hold rod	1 off	216mm (8½in) × 25mm (1in) diam dowelling	
Hand hold rod reinforcing plate	2 off	64 × 64 × 9mm (2½ × 2½ × ⅜in)	Plywood
Ancillaries			
	1 off	381mm (15in) × 76mm (3in) artificial fur fabric	
	1 off	2134mm (84in) length of 25mm (1in) wide coat cuff leather trimming	
	25 off	6mm (¼in) domed brass upholstery nails	
	1 off	2000mm (78in) nylon cord for plaiting	
	2 off	Stick-on eyes	

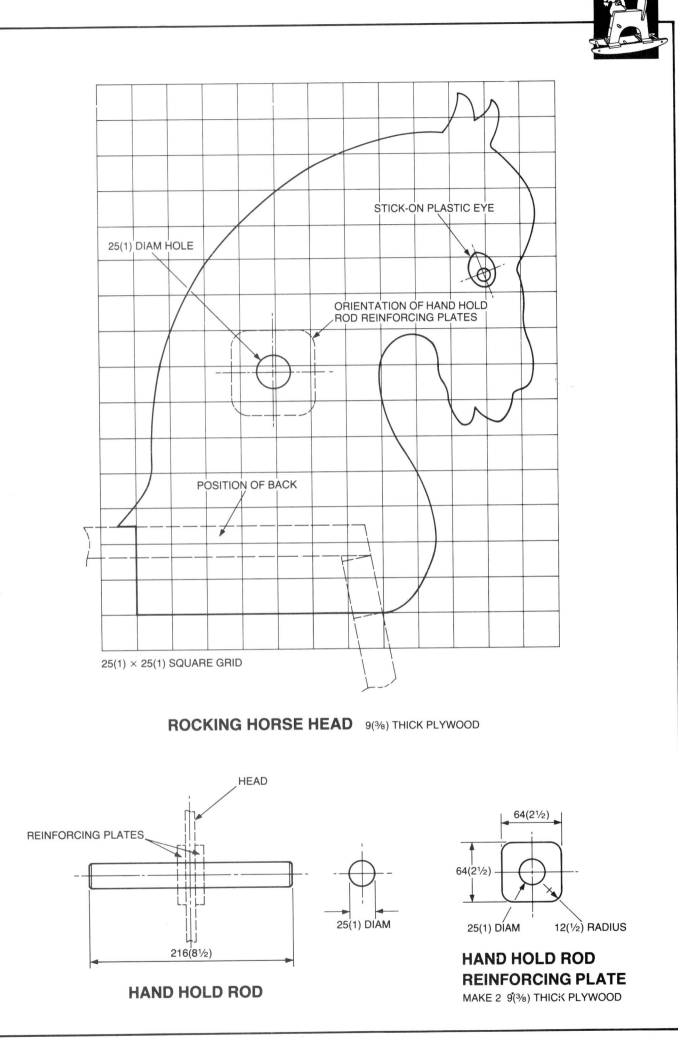

STICK-ON PLASTIC EYE

25(1) DIAM HOLE

ORIENTATION OF HAND HOLD
ROD REINFORCING PLATES

POSITION OF BACK

25(1) × 25(1) SQUARE GRID

ROCKING HORSE HEAD 9(⅜) THICK PLYWOOD

HEAD

REINFORCING PLATES

216(8½)

HAND HOLD ROD

25(1) DIAM

64(2½)

64(2½)

25(1) DIAM   12(½) RADIUS

**HAND HOLD ROD
REINFORCING PLATE**
MAKE 2 9(⅜) THICK PLYWOOD

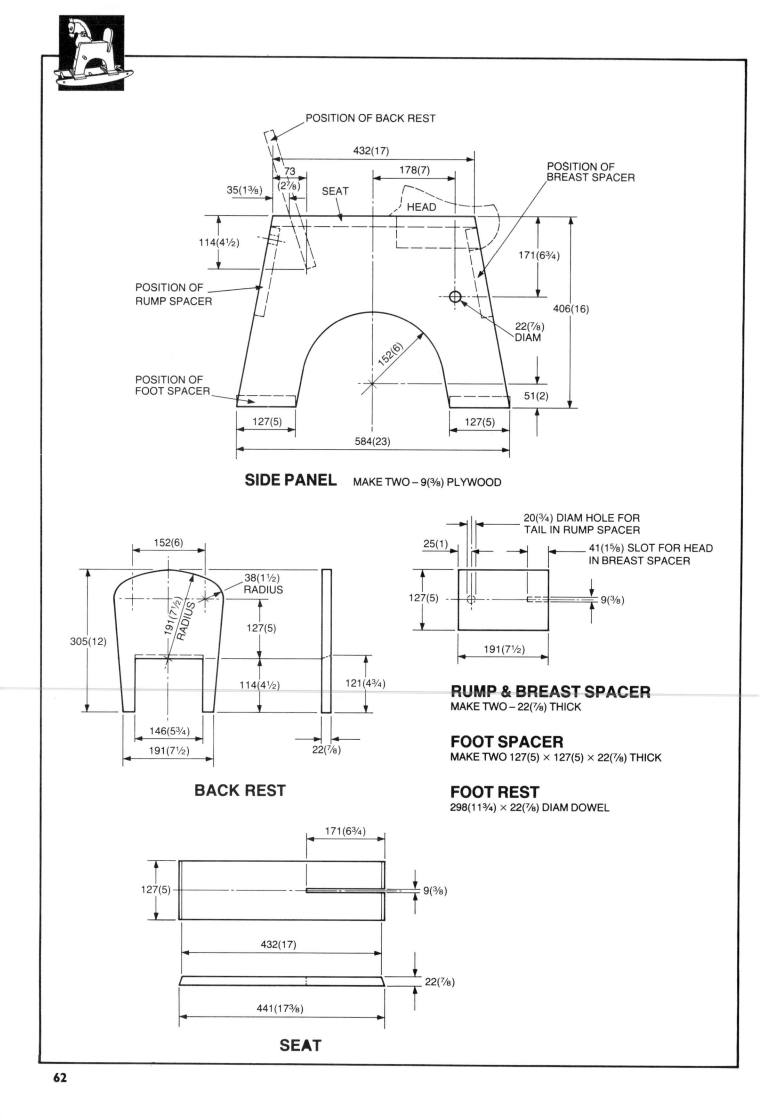

SIDE PANEL MAKE TWO – 9(⅜) PLYWOOD

BACK REST

RUMP & BREAST SPACER
MAKE TWO – 22(⅞) THICK

FOOT SPACER
MAKE TWO 127(5) × 127(5) × 22(⅞) THICK

FOOT REST
298(11¾) × 22(⅞) DIAM DOWEL

SEAT

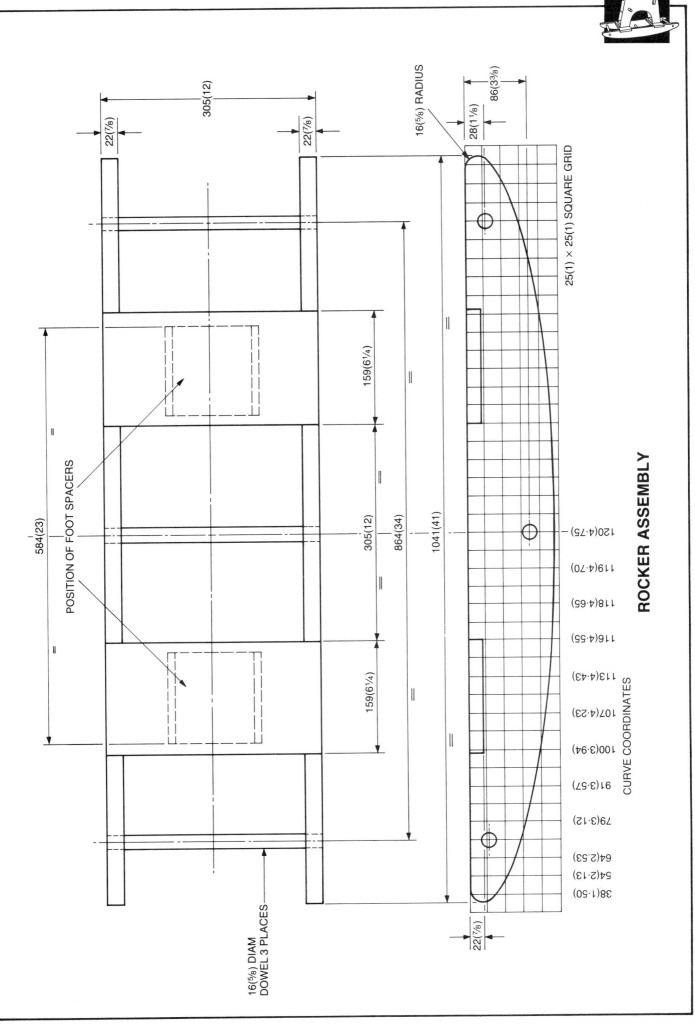

ROCKER ASSEMBLY

POSITION OF FOOT SPACERS

16(⅝) DIAM
DOWEL 3 PLACES

305(12)

22(⅞)

22(⅞)

584(23)

159(6¼)

305(12)

159(6¼)

864(34)

1041(41)

16(⅝) RADIUS

28(1⅛)

86(3⅜)

25(1) × 25(1) SQUARE GRID

22(⅞)

CURVE COORDINATES

38(1·50)
54(2·13)
64(2·53)
79(3·12)
91(3·57)
100(3·94)
107(4·23)
113(4·43)
116(4·55)
118(4·65)
119(4·70)
120(4·75)

WORKBENCH

I know that there are many people throughout the country who do all their woodwork on the kitchen table! Finding space to work in is always a problem and those of us who have a shed or garage should probably count ourselves lucky. Wherever you work though, if you're going to do a lot of DIY a good solid work table is essential, particularly as a base to which timber can be clamped firmly for sawing and planing.

I made the legs and stretcher rails for this workbench from joinery quality pine, the top and sides (known as aprons) from beech. It is not essential to use a hardwood for the top, but beech is far more durable to work on than pine.

The vice used is made by Record Marples (see page 215) and is constructed of beech throughout. The great advantage of this vice is that it is approximately half the price of a cast iron equivalent.

The bench incorporates overhangs at the ends to allow for clamping and the small wooden bench stop is fully adjustable. The bench has been deliberately designed without a 'well' as it is intended for general handicrafts and not woodworking specifically. The use of coach bolts is necessary for stability if you are going to do a lot of sawing, planing and morticing work, otherwise wooden dowel pegs would be adequate to hold the bench together for light art work.

1 Start by marking out the legs and cross members – you need two identical pairs of each. Because of the width of the legs you will need to join them to the cross members using twin stub mortice and tenon joints. It is well worth the effort to make a good joint here since this method should ensure that your bench will last a lifetime (barring accidents!).

Do all the marking out together, then you will be certain of everything lining up once the joints are cut. Ideally you should use a mallet and sash mortice chisel to cut the mortices, and a tenon and coping saw to cut the tenons – and if you have to work at these joints in anything less than perfect conditions (such as on the garage floor) at least you can be spurred on by the thought that when the task is completed you will never have to do so again! When you have cut all the pieces and joints, assemble the two sets of legs. Ensure they are square, then glue and cramp them up.

2 Now for the top. I made this from two beech planks fixed together with a rebate joint. The planks should then be cramped together and four cross members of hardwood screwed to the underside in order to brace the top. The legs have to fit in between the cross members, so it is a good idea to use one of the legs as a 'spacer' to get the right width before screwing the cross members down. The woodscrews should be counterbored in all four cross members.

3 Cut out the aprons (I made these from beech) and screw them on to the top. As I did not want the screws to show I lightly counterbored the holes and, after I had fixed the aprons, I glued wood pegs over the screw heads, trimming them flush with the bench aprons when the glue was dry.

4 Now cut the hole for the bench stop. This needs great care and has to be done from both sides of the bench top. First mark out the position for the stop in pencil and, from the underside, start chopping with a large firmer or bevel-edged chisel. Remove the wood chips to approximately half the depth of the final hole. Now turn the top over and chop from the top side until the hole is complete. Tidy up the hole and carefully plane a wood stop to fit smoothly into it. Drill a long slot in the block to take the coach bolt. This slot allows the block to be raised or lowered and the bolt allows the block to be firmly fixed to one of the end cross members.

5 Now bolt the tie members on to the assembled legs using coach bolts and then bolt the top on to the legs through the aprons.

6 Now fit the wood vice. This is provided with two countersunk screw holes, but I drilled an extra two just to make sure of a good fixing on the side of the bench. If you use a different vice you may have to mount it in some other way

7 As this is to be a general 'work-horse' I finished it off with clear polyurethane varnish.

Cutting list

Bench leg	4 off	838 × 95 × 44mm (33 × 3¾ × 1¾in)	Timber
Cross member	4 off	406 × 95 × 44mm (16 × 3¾ × 1¾in)	Timber
Tie member	2 off	750 × 44 × 44mm (29½ × 1¾ × 1¾in)	Timber
Bench top assembly	2 off	914 × 229 × 25mm (36 × 9 × 1in)	Timber
Apron	2 off	914 × 140 × 25mm (36 × 5½ × 1in)	Timber
Cross member	4 off	445 × 57 × 32mm (17½ × 2¼ × 1½in)	Timber
Bench stop	1 off	121 × 54 × 44mm (4¾ × 2⅛ × 1¾in)	Timber
Ancillaries			
	1 off	305mm (12in) Record 61 wooden vice	
	4 off	102mm (4in) × 12mm (½in) diam coach bolts, washers and wing nuts	
	1 off	102mm (4in) × 9mm (⅜in) diam coach bolt, washer and wing nut for bench stop	

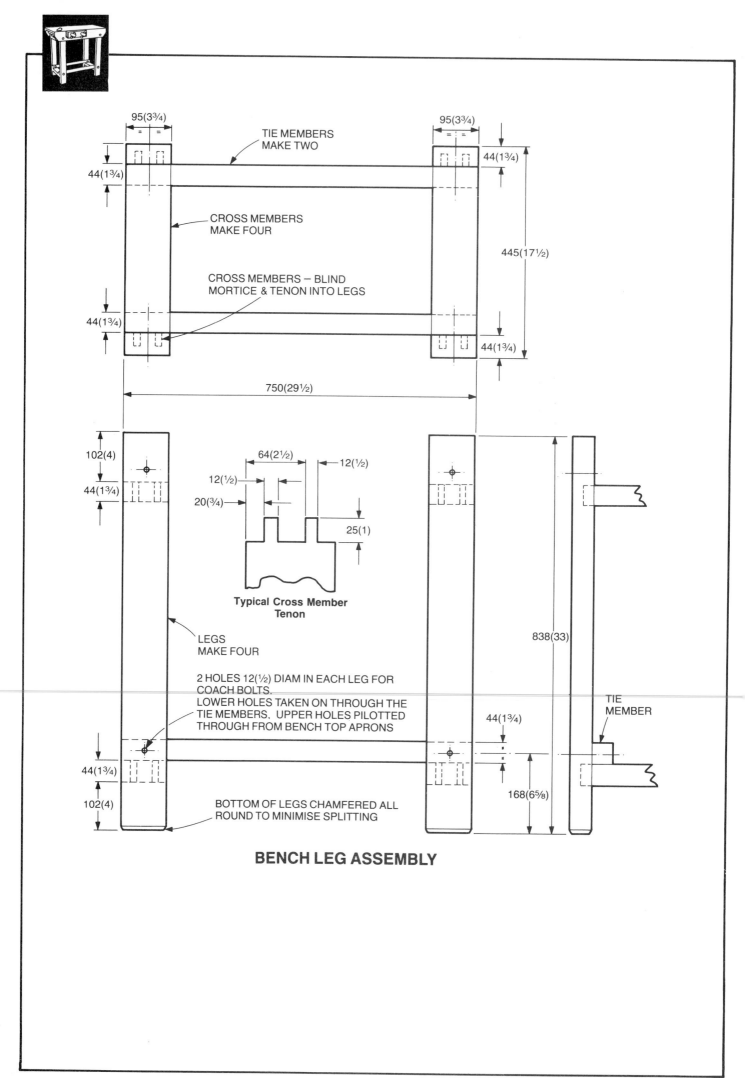

95(3¾)

TIE MEMBERS
MAKE TWO

95(3¾)

44(1¾)

44(1¾)

CROSS MEMBERS
MAKE FOUR

445(17½)

CROSS MEMBERS — BLIND
MORTICE & TENON INTO LEGS

44(1¾)

44(1¾)

750(29½)

102(4)

64(2½)

12(½)

44(1¾)

12(½)

20(¾)

25(1)

**Typical Cross Member
Tenon**

838(33)

LEGS
MAKE FOUR

2 HOLES 12(½) DIAM IN EACH LEG FOR
COACH BOLTS.
LOWER HOLES TAKEN ON THROUGH THE
TIE MEMBERS, UPPER HOLES PILOTTED
THROUGH FROM BENCH TOP APRONS

TIE
MEMBER

44(1¾)

44(1¾)

102(4)

BOTTOM OF LEGS CHAMFERED ALL
ROUND TO MINIMISE SPLITTING

168(6⅝)

BENCH LEG ASSEMBLY

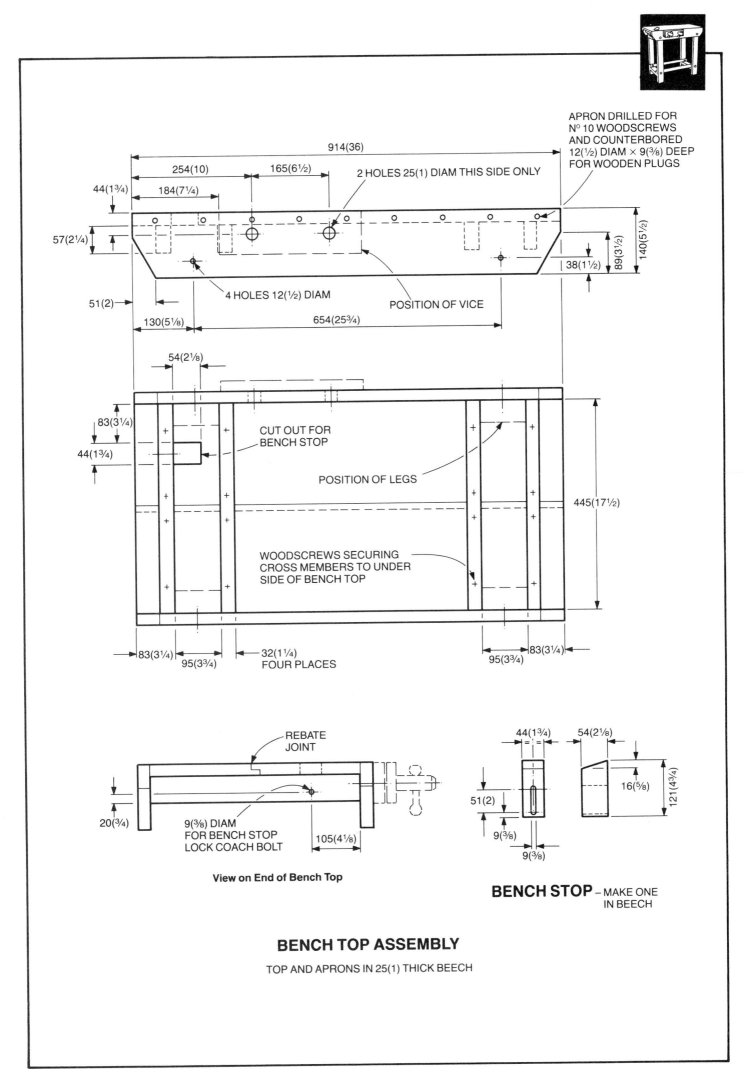

APRON DRILLED FOR
Nº 10 WOODSCREWS
AND COUNTERBORED
12(½) DIAM × 9(⅜) DEEP
FOR WOODEN PLUGS

914(36)

254(10)

184(7¼)

165(6½)

2 HOLES 25(1) DIAM THIS SIDE ONLY

44(1¾)

57(2¼)

140(5½)

89(3½)

38(1½)

51(2)

4 HOLES 12(½) DIAM

POSITION OF VICE

130(5⅛)

654(25¾)

54(2⅛)

83(3¼)

44(1¾)

CUT OUT FOR
BENCH STOP

POSITION OF LEGS

445(17½)

WOODSCREWS SECURING
CROSS MEMBERS TO UNDER
SIDE OF BENCH TOP

83(3¼)

95(3¾)

32(1¼)
FOUR PLACES

95(3¾)

83(3¼)

REBATE
JOINT

20(¾)

9(⅜) DIAM
FOR BENCH STOP
LOCK COACH BOLT

105(4⅛)

View on End of Bench Top

44(1¾)

54(2⅛)

51(2)

16(⅝)

121(4¾)

9(⅜)

9(⅜)

BENCH STOP – MAKE ONE
IN BEECH

BENCH TOP ASSEMBLY

TOP AND APRONS IN 25(1) THICK BEECH

GARDEN SLIDE

Perhaps the most daunting task for most practical householders is not how to make a slide but where to keep it when it's made! I have therefore designed the climbing frame for this slide to fold absolutely flat by using 'lift off' hinges; yet the whole structure can be assembled in a few minutes. The timber used is pine (joinery quality available from all builders' merchants) and the wood preservative I used is Sandolin (mahogany-coloured) though there are many others on the market.

1 A glance at the working drawings will show you that the climbing apparatus is basically a framework constructed using mortice and tenon joints. Start by marking and cutting out the four upright and eight cross-pieces for the two side frames. Then mark and cut out the mortice holes in the uprights. Make sure that you take into account the differences between the left-hand side and the shop side. Assemble these two frames and check the joints fit well. When you are satisfied with the fit, glue and cramp them.

2 Follow the same procedure for the rear frame which allows access on to the top of the slide. The two inner uprights at the top should be drilled to take coach bolts that will also pass through the ladder sides.

3 Now make the front frame. This takes the slide and, like the rear frame, has holes to accommodate coach bolts to fix the slide securely.

4 The top decking is made from three boards that drop into place over the framework sides. Besides providing the floor for the tower, these side pieces also give rigidity to the structure. When you have cut the boards to length, screw a guide piece of wood to both ends of each one to hold them in position on the frame.

5 The sides of the ladder are made from the same wood as the frame, but the rungs are sturdy dowel rods, which saves a great deal of time. To drill the holes for the rungs, tape the two ladder sides together, then use a flat bit to drill as many holes as you want rungs. Garden centres are a good source of supply for large diameter dowel rod.

6 Now make the slide itself. This again uses mortice and tenon joints for the underframe, and the slide itself (a piece of plywood) is attached to this frame with screws. The side walls should be drilled with holes to take coach bolts and then screwed to the underframe. Finally you need to make the lower leg assembly to support the slide at the bottom using mortice and tenon joints once more. Chamfer the ends that rest on the ground to minimise splitting and drill

holes in the other ends to take coach bolts. The leg assembly should then be bolted on to the bottom of the slide underframe.

7 I felt that a shop or 'ticket office' could easily be accommodated and would greatly increase the pleasure children derived from this 'play structure'. Screw the counter flap on to the second lowest cross-piece of the right-hand side frame using back flap hinges.

Make the frame for the awning. I made the awning itself from a length of deck chair canvas available from really good hardware and major department stores. The two support stays are dowel rods which fit into holes bored in the awning frame and counter. The counter is supported on both sides by nylon cord. The whole shop tucks away into the frame and does not prevent the main framework folding up.

8 The final stage is to fit all the hinges to the frames. Folding structures are inevitably not as rigid as glued and framed structures. I therefore feel it is advisable to fit two casement catches for corners B and D (see 'plan view on assembled structure'). These catches tie the structure together and give greater rigidity to the framework.

Cutting list

Side frame	4 off	1588 × 44 × 44mm (62½ × 1¾ × 1¾in)	Timber
	8 off	775 × 44 × 44mm (30½ × 1¾ × 1¾in)	Timber
Rear frame	2 off	1588 × 44 × 44mm (62½ × 1¾ × 1¾in)	Timber
	3 off	775 × 44 × 44mm (30½ × 1¾ × 1¾in)	Timber
	2 off	495 × 44 × 44mm (19½ × 1¾ × 1¾in)	Timber
	2 off	235 × 44 × 44mm (9¼ × 1¾ × 1¾in)	Timber
	1 off	552 × 44 × 44mm (21¾ × 1¾ × 1¾in)	Timber
Front frame	2 off	1588 × 44 × 44mm (62½ × 1¾ × 1¾in)	Timber
	3 off	775 × 44 × 44mm (30½ × 1¾ × 1¾in)	Timber
	1 off	552 × 44 × 44mm (21¾ × 1¾ × 1¾in)	Timber
	1 off	324 × 44 × 44mm (12¾ × 1¾ × 1¾in)	Timber
	1 off	400 × 44 × 44mm (15¾ × 1¾ × 1¾in)	Timber
Decking	3 off	1003 × 225 × 22mm (39½ × 8⅞ × ⅞in)	Timber
	6 off	225 × 44 × 44mm (8⅞ × 1¾ × 1¾in)	Timber
Slide bed assembly	2 off	1651 × 51 × 44mm (65 × 2 × 1¾in)	Timber
	5 off	241 × 51 × 44mm (9½ × 2 × 1¾in)	Timber
	1 off	1829 × 305 × 9mm (72 × 12 × ⅜in)	Plywood
Slide side wall	2 off	1880 × 187 × 22mm (74 × 7⅜ × ⅞in)	Timber
Ladder	2 off	1524 × 44 × 32mm (60 × 1¾ × 1¼in)	Timber
	5 off	225mm (8⅞in) × 25mm (1in) diam dowelling	
Slide lower leg	2 off	435 × 44 × 44mm (17⅛ × 1¾ × 1¾in)	Timber
	2 off	152 × 44 × 44mm (6 × 1¾ × 1¾in)	Timber
Counter flap	1 off	730 × 222 × 22mm (28¾ × 8¾ × ⅞in)	Timber
Awning frame	1 off	686 × 44 × 44mm (27 × 1¾ × 1¾in)	Timber
	2 off	276 × 44 × 44mm (10⅞ × 1¾ × 1¾in)	Timber
Support stay	2 off	476mm (18¾in) × 16mm (⅝in) diam dowelling	
Ancillaries			
	6 off	51mm (2in) conventional hinges	
	4 off	Lift-off hinges	
	2 off	Casement catches	
	4 off	Screwed eyes	
	2 off	300mm (12in) nylon cord	
	1 off	431 × 1086mm (17 × 42¾in) canvas	
	2 off	89mm (3½in) × 6mm (¼in) diam coach bolts, washers and wing nuts for ladder attachment	
	2 off	102mm (4in) × 9mm (⅜in) diam coach bolts, washers and wing nuts for awning frame attachment	
	2 off	76mm (3in) × 6mm (¼in) diam coach bolts, washers and wing nuts for slide attachments	
	2 off	127mm (5in) × 9mm (⅜in) diam coach bolts, washers and lock nuts to secure leg to slide frame	

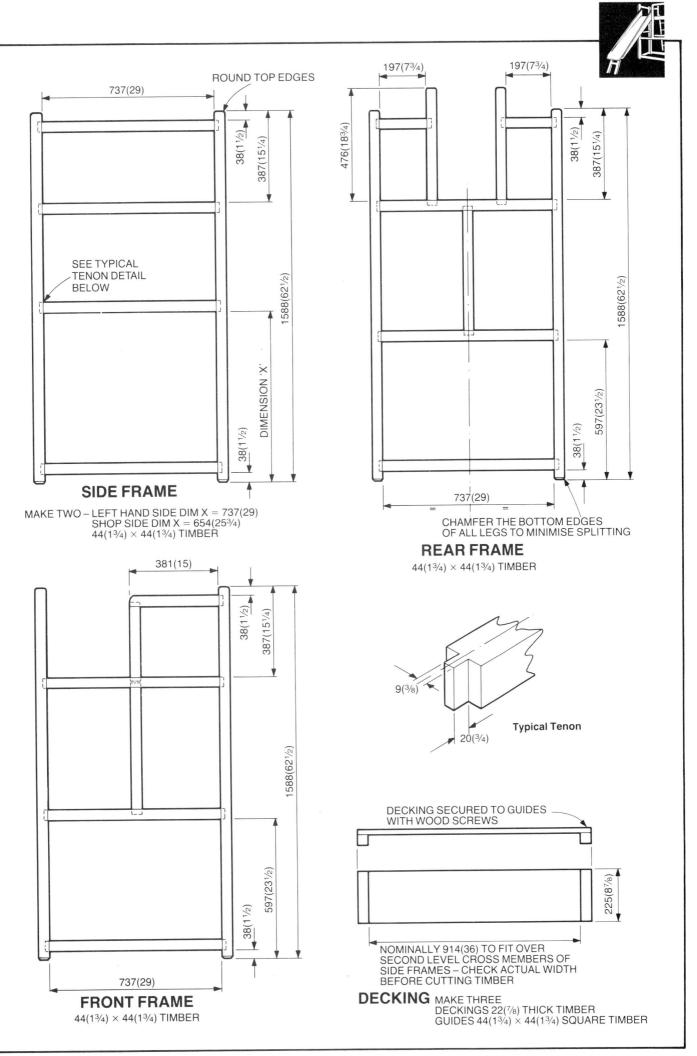

SIDE FRAME

ROUND TOP EDGES

737(29)

38(1½)
387(15¼)

SEE TYPICAL
TENON DETAIL
BELOW

DIMENSION 'X'

1588(62½)

38(1½)

MAKE TWO – LEFT HAND SIDE DIM X = 737(29)
SHOP SIDE DIM X = 654(25¾)
44(1¾) × 44(1¾) TIMBER

REAR FRAME

197(7¾)   197(7¾)

476(18¾)

38(1½)
387(15¼)

1588(62½)

597(23½)

38(1½)

737(29)

CHAMFER THE BOTTOM EDGES
OF ALL LEGS TO MINIMISE SPLITTING

44(1¾) × 44(1¾) TIMBER

FRONT FRAME

381(15)

38(1½)
387(15¼)

1588(62½)

597(23½)

38(1½)

737(29)

44(1¾) × 44(1¾) TIMBER

9(⅜)

Typical Tenon

20(¾)

DECKING

DECKING SECURED TO GUIDES
WITH WOOD SCREWS

225(8⅞)

NOMINALLY 914(36) TO FIT OVER
SECOND LEVEL CROSS MEMBERS OF
SIDE FRAMES – CHECK ACTUAL WIDTH
BEFORE CUTTING TIMBER

MAKE THREE
DECKINGS 22(⅞) THICK TIMBER
GUIDES 44(1¾) × 44(1¾) SQUARE TIMBER

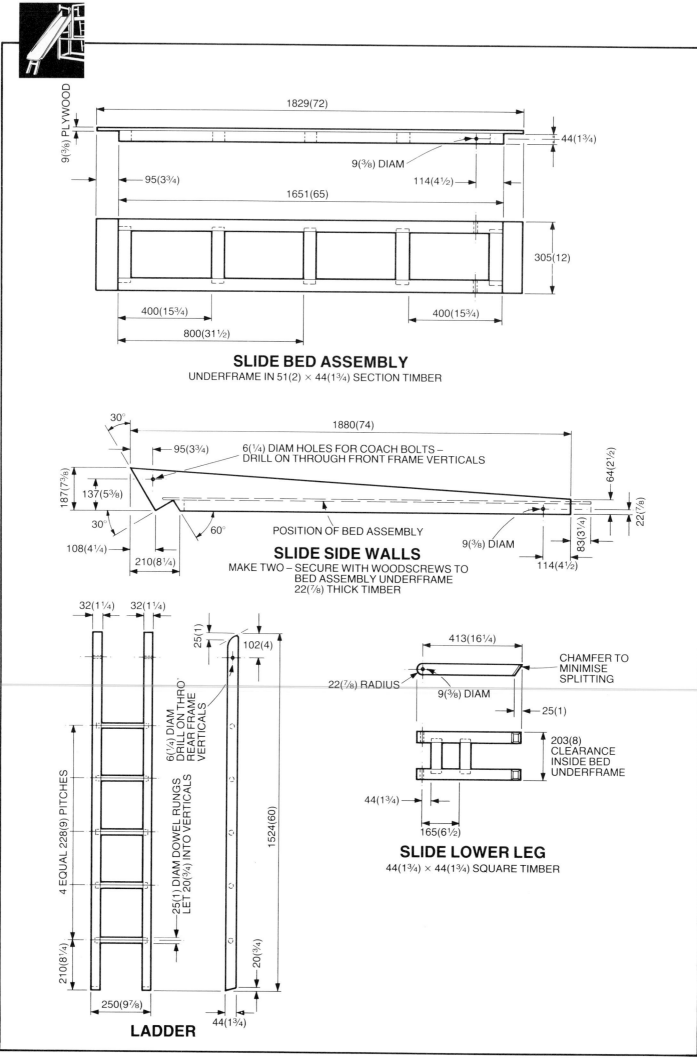

SLIDE BED ASSEMBLY
UNDERFRAME IN 51(2) × 44(1¾) SECTION TIMBER

1829(72)
9(⅜) PLYWOOD
44(1¾)
9(⅜) DIAM
95(3¾)
114(4½)
1651(65)
305(12)
400(15¾)
400(15¾)
800(31½)

SLIDE SIDE WALLS
MAKE TWO – SECURE WITH WOODSCREWS TO
BED ASSEMBLY UNDERFRAME
22(⅞) THICK TIMBER

30°
1880(74)
95(3¾)
6(¼) DIAM HOLES FOR COACH BOLTS –
DRILL ON THROUGH FRONT FRAME VERTICALS
64(2½)
187(7⅜)
137(5⅜)
22(⅞)
30°
60°
POSITION OF BED ASSEMBLY
9(⅜) DIAM
83(3¼)
108(4¼)
210(8¼)
114(4½)

LADDER

32(1¼)
32(1¼)
25(1)
102(4)
6(¼) DIAM DRILL ON THRO' REAR FRAME VERTICALS
1524(60)
4 EQUAL 228(9) PITCHES
25(1) DIAM DOWEL RUNGS LET 20(¾) INTO VERTICALS
210(8¼)
20(¾)
250(9⅞)
44(1¾)

SLIDE LOWER LEG
44(1¾) × 44(1¾) SQUARE TIMBER

413(16¼)
CHAMFER TO MINIMISE SPLITTING
22(⅞) RADIUS
9(⅜) DIAM
25(1)
203(8) CLEARANCE INSIDE BED UNDERFRAME
44(1¾)
165(6½)

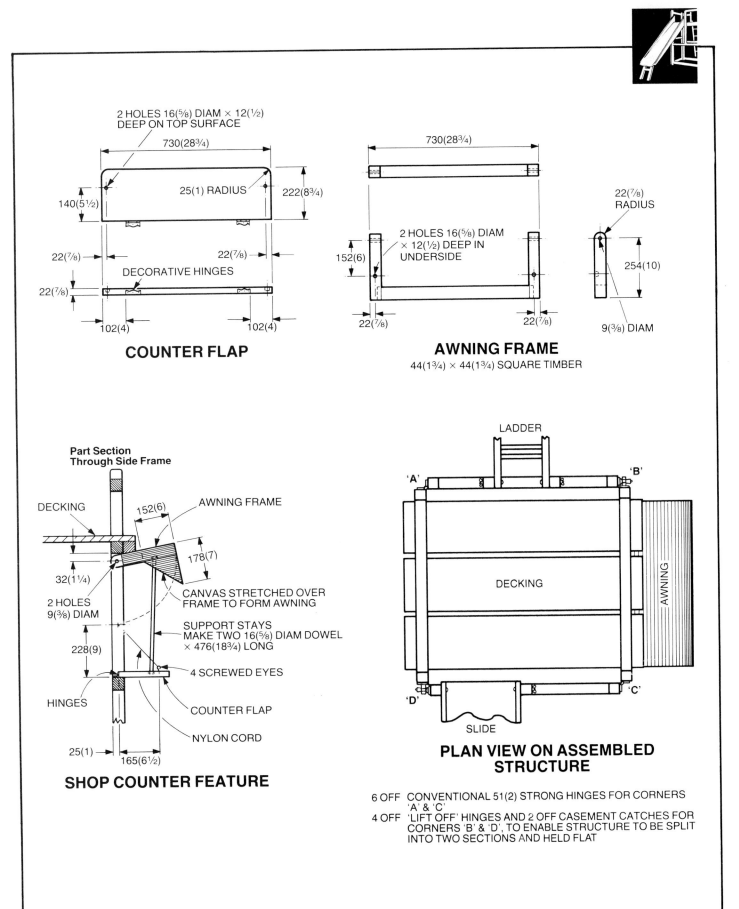

2 HOLES 16(5/8) DIAM × 12(1/2) DEEP ON TOP SURFACE

730(28¾)

25(1) RADIUS

222(8¾)

140(5½)

22(⅞)   22(⅞)

DECORATIVE HINGES

22(⅞)

102(4)   102(4)

COUNTER FLAP

730(28¾)

2 HOLES 16(⅝) DIAM × 12(½) DEEP IN UNDERSIDE

152(6)

22(⅞)   22(⅞)

AWNING FRAME
44(1¾) × 44(1¾) SQUARE TIMBER

22(⅞) RADIUS

254(10)

9(⅜) DIAM

**Part Section
Through Side Frame**

DECKING

AWNING FRAME

152(6)

178(7)

32(1¼)

2 HOLES
9(⅜) DIAM

CANVAS STRETCHED OVER FRAME TO FORM AWNING

SUPPORT STAYS
MAKE TWO 16(⅝) DIAM DOWEL × 476(18¾) LONG

228(9)

4 SCREWED EYES

HINGES

COUNTER FLAP

NYLON CORD

25(1)

165(6½)

SHOP COUNTER FEATURE

LADDER

'A'   'B'

DECKING

AWNING

'D'   'C'

SLIDE

**PLAN VIEW ON ASSEMBLED
STRUCTURE**

6 OFF   CONVENTIONAL 51(2) STRONG HINGES FOR CORNERS 'A' & 'C'
4 OFF   'LIFT OFF' HINGES AND 2 OFF CASEMENT CATCHES FOR CORNERS 'B' & 'D', TO ENABLE STRUCTURE TO BE SPLIT INTO TWO SECTIONS AND HELD FLAT

GO CART

Since I built my first pedal car it has been my ambition to make a self-propelled go cart. The success of the first go cart (see *Blizzard's Wonderful Wooden Toys*) and the tremendous amount of correspondence I have received have confirmed my feelings that you also would like to build a machine that does not require you to keep pushing and pulling your youngsters around the garden. So I have created one, and the prototype works well. However, be warned that you will need a basic understanding of how bearings and cranks work in order to construct the cart without problems. This model has been designed for the seven-to-ten year olds: a younger child may have difficulty in cranking and steering the machine, though you can obviously alter the dimensions to make it suitable.

Braking The cranking handle is the brake, and when the cart is travelling down slopes the handle must be held very firmly and under no circumstances be allowed to go free. *Both hands* must firmly hold the handle. Do make sure your children can drive safely before you let them go far afield in the cart.

Some children may have difficulty in both steering and cranking themselves along at the same time: it's therefore a good idea to tighten the bolt on the steering mechanism so that, to start with, the cart only goes backwards and forwards – just until the driver gains some experience.

The child will also need to learn that there are 'dead centres' on the crank and a push start will be necessary to get under way. In its present form the cart will not climb steep banks, and if this is tried it will just go into reverse. This sort of machine is a compromise and if you get more handle movement you have more power – or a lower gear – but the amount of handle movement is then too great and can almost knock the child off the seat. Nevertheless it's interesting to alter pivot points and see how much variation you can achieve.

I have kept the design of the go cart as simple as possible and you don't even have to make the steel crank yourself, since a kit of parts, bearings, crank and so on is available from me (see Accessories, page 215).

1 The chassis consists of six pieces: two longitudinal battens that run the full length, onto which are screwed four extra battens of the same size. Two of these are attached at the back – giving a wide area for the crankshaft bearings – and the other two are screwed at the front to give extra width and rigidity to the chassis. Mark and cut out all six pieces, then glue and screw the three pieces for each side together.

2 Clamp the chassis halves together, mark the position for the rear axles and then drill the holes. It is important that this is done accurately. Separate the two chassis halves and insert the relevant bronze bearings into the axle holes, one on each side of each chassis member. Glue the bearings into the holes with epoxy resin to prevent them 'creeping' out. It does not matter that there is a gap in the middle between the two bearings in each half of the chassis. The most important thing is that the crankshaft is supported by four bearings. I used lubra bronze bearings on this cart – once these have been oiled, the oil penetrates them and will go on lubricating the axles and shafts for a very long time. However, six-monthly oiling sessions are recommended. Be careful when handling the bearings not to damage their surfaces.

When inserting the bearings in each half of the chassis it is a good idea also to insert the axle intended for that side, as this will help to keep the bearings aligned while the epoxy resin is setting. Accurate alignment of bearings is obviously essential for smooth running. These are the only bearings that I feel it necessary to glue into place: all the rest (fitted later) are a tight push fit.

3 Cut out the rear cross member. Assemble the axles in the rear of the chassis and also the crank mechanism. When all is correctly in place, glue and screw the rear cross member in place.

4 The front axle beam consists of a length of timber onto which two stub axles are glued and screwed. To add strength to the joint between the front axle beam and the stub axles, cut out halving joints in the stub axles (and drill the axle holes) and then glue and screw them onto the axle beam. Cut off the tops of the stub axles at an angle to provide good foot rests for steering the cart. To add further strength and to keep the driver's feet off the front wheels, glue and screw mudguards into the sides. These also give strength to the front axle beam and should ensure that the stub axles are not torn off when the cart is traversing rough ground.

Cut a front spoiler from plywood and glue it onto the front axle beam. Fix the front axle beam in place by fitting the front cross member beneath the chassis. Pass a large coach bolt right through the front axle beam and through the front cross member. Make sure to add a washer before doing up the bolt.

5 To keep the cart simple I used large-diameter dowel rods to hold the seat in place. It is best to buy the dowel before you drill the holes in case you can't get the exact diameter specified. Bore four holes to take the dowels in the top side of the chassis and on the under side of the plywood seat. The holes should be slightly larger than the diameter of the dowel. Now cut the dowel rods to length, the back ones being longer than those at the front.

Glue and screw the seat together as shown on the plans and, when it has set, fit the dowel rods and seat on to the chassis. You will find that the over-size holes allow the seat to be fitted at an angle and that when the rods are glued into place the whole unit becomes very rigid. This is the simplest method of angling the seat.

The rear spoiler is a 'bolt-on' extra and is detachable. It is held in place by two dowel rods that fit into the blocks on the back of the seat.

6 Mark and cut out the cranking handle. Drill the holes for the dowel rod grip, the pivot rod and the crank bar rod before shaping the shaft and cutting out the slot in the bottom that will take the crank bar. Now cut out the two support blocks that go either side of the crank handle. Clamp these together and drill the holes for the pivot rod. Insert a bearing into each block.

7 Mark and cut out the crank bar. Drill the hole at the front for the steel rod that

will link the bar to the crank handle. The connection between the crank bar and crank itself is slightly more complex. Following the plan, first drill a hole in the rear of the bar to the outside diameter of the single large bearing. Now cut away a section of the bar as shown on the plan and carefully drill the two holes specified in both the bar and the cut-away piece.

The large bearing now has to be cut in half in order to go around the crank shaft. Oil the bearing and clamp it up in place with the crank bar and cut-away section. Insert the two screws and tighten them until the bearing is clamped. Don't over-tighten – as the bearing 'settles in' it may be necessary to tighten the two screws just a fraction more. If, on the other hand, you find that the screws clamp the bearing too tightly, insert a small piece of packing between the crank bar and cut-away section. It's a case of trial and error. To prevent the bearing

slipping out cut two circles of plastic tube, slit each through on one side only and slip them over the crank shaft on either side of the crank bar.

At the front end the crank bar is fitted in the slot provided. Insert a bearing in the hole and one in the holes on either side of the crank handle. Oil the bearings well. Now very carefully insert the steel rod and hold it in place by clipping two spring caps on either end.

Now insert the bearings in the pivot hole of the cranking handle – oil them well and insert the pivot rod from one side. Fit a piece of plastic tubing on either side of the crank handle to keep the bearings in and to keep the handle in the middle of the support blocks. Pushing the rod into position and dropping the plastic tube in place is a fiddly job because there is so little room to get your fingers in. Once this is done, clip spring caps onto the ends of the steel bar.

7 Clean the rear axle ends and the inside of the crank where the axle ends go. I find that methylated spirit is excellent for the removal of any grease. Don't touch the metal surfaces with your fingers after cleaning, otherwise there will be small deposits that will prevent a good bond. Apply Loctite 601 engineering adhesive liberally to the axle ends and assemble. Follow the glue maker's directions as to setting times.

8 Push the front axle rod into the pre-drilled holes in the stub axles (having first chamfered the axle on both ends), slip the wheels on and push the spring clips in place.

9 It's a good idea to paint the cart with an exterior-grade paint as it will tend to spend most of its time out in the garden. Ensure that all paints used are non-toxic (see page 215).

Cutting list

Chassis	2 off	737 × 47 × 47mm (29 × 1⅞ × 1⅞in)	Timber
	2 off	432 × 47 × 47mm (17 × 1⅞ × 1⅞in)	Timber
	2 off	229 × 47 × 47mm (9 × 1⅞ × 1⅞in)	Timber
Front cross member	1 off	171 × 47 × 47mm (6¾ × 1⅞ × 1⅞in)	Timber
Rear cross member	1 off	362 × 47 × 47mm (14¼ × 1⅞ × 1⅞in)	Timber
Crank handle support blocks	2 off	159 × 70 × 47mm (6¼ × 2¾ × 1⅞in)	Timber
Cranking handle	1 off	552 × 64 × 47mm (21¾ × 2½ × 1⅞in)	Timber
	1 off	267mm (10½in) × 9mm (⅜in) diam dowelling	
Crank bar	1 off	597 × 57 × 25mm (23½ × 2¼ × 1in)	Timber
Front axle beam	1 off	381 × 47 × 47mm (15 × 1⅞ × 1⅞in)	Timber
	2 off	197 × 47 × 47mm (7¾ × 1⅞ × 1⅞in)	Timber
Front wheel mudguards	2 off	216 × 152 × 12mm (8½ × 6 × ½in)	Plywood
Front spoiler	1 off	381 × 133 × 12mm (15 × 5¼ × ½in)	Plywood
Rear spoiler	1 off	432 × 127 × 12mm (17 × 5 × ½in)	Plywood
	2 off	127mm (5in) × 12mm (½in) diam dowelling	
Seat	1 off	349 × 305 × 12mm (13¾ × 12 × ½in)	Plywood
	1 off	349 × 114 × 12mm (13¾ × 4½ × ½in)	Plywood
	2 off	114 × 102 × 12mm (4½ × 4 × ½in)	Plywood
	2 off	95 × 47 × 47mm (3¾ × 1⅞ × 1⅞in)	Timber
Seat support pillar	2 off	143mm (5⅝in) × 20mm (¾in) diam dowelling	
	2 off	114mm (4½in) × 20mm (¾in) diam dowelling	

Ancillaries

	2 off	248mm (9¾in) diam road wheels	
	2 off	12mm (½in) diam spring dome caps	
	2 off	28mm (1⅛in) o/diam × 22mm (⅞in) i/diam × 5mm (³⁄₁₆in) thick spacers	
	2 off	210mm (8¼in) diam road wheels	
	2 off	114mm (4½in) × 9mm (⅜in) diam steel axles	
	4 off	9mm (⅜in) diam spring dome caps	
	1 off	127mm (5in) long × 9mm (⅜in) diam coach bolt, nut and washer	

	9 off	20mm (¾in) o/diam × 12mm (½in) i/diam × 25mm (1in) long plain bronze bearings
	2 off	20mm (¾in) o/diam × 12mm (½in) i/diam × 16mm (⅝in) long plain bronze bearings
	1 off	25mm (1in) o/diam × 22mm (⅞in) i/diam × 25mm (1in) long plain bronze bearing
	1 off	184mm (7¼in) × 12mm (½in) diam steel pin
	1 off	76mm (3in) × 12mm (½in) diam steel pin
	4 off	12mm (½in) diam spring dome caps
Crank	2 off	210mm (8¼in) × 12mm (½in) diam steel rod
	2 off	20mm (¾in) o/diam × 12mm (½in) i/diam × 54mm (2⅛in) long steel tubes
	1 off	57mm (2¼in) × 22mm (⅞in) diam steel rod
	2 off	64 × 25 × 9mm (2½ × 1 × ⅜in) steel strips

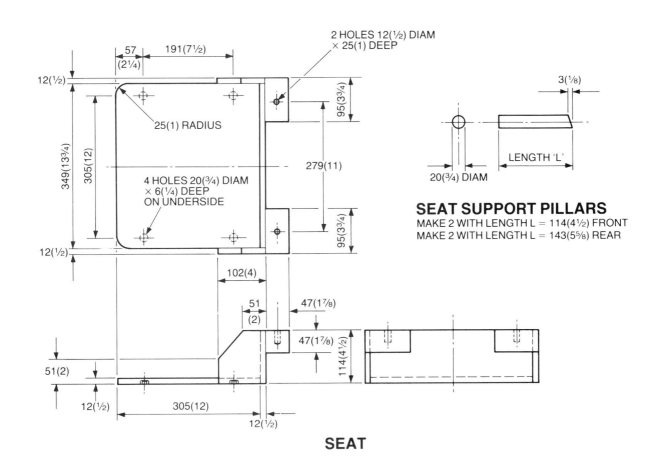

SEAT SUPPORT PILLARS
MAKE 2 WITH LENGTH L = 114(4½) FRONT
MAKE 2 WITH LENGTH L = 143(5⅝) REAR

SEAT

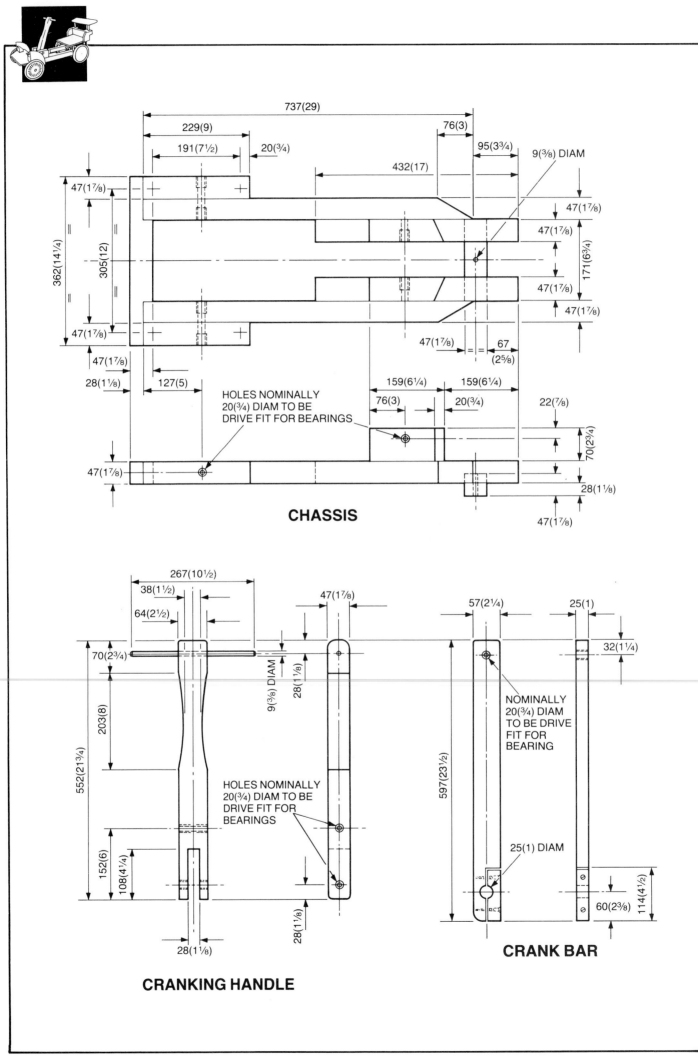

CHASSIS

HOLES NOMINALLY 20(¾) DIAM TO BE DRIVE FIT FOR BEARINGS

HOLES NOMINALLY 20(¾) DIAM TO BE DRIVE FIT FOR BEARINGS

CRANKING HANDLE

NOMINALLY 20(¾) DIAM TO BE DRIVE FIT FOR BEARING

CRANK BAR

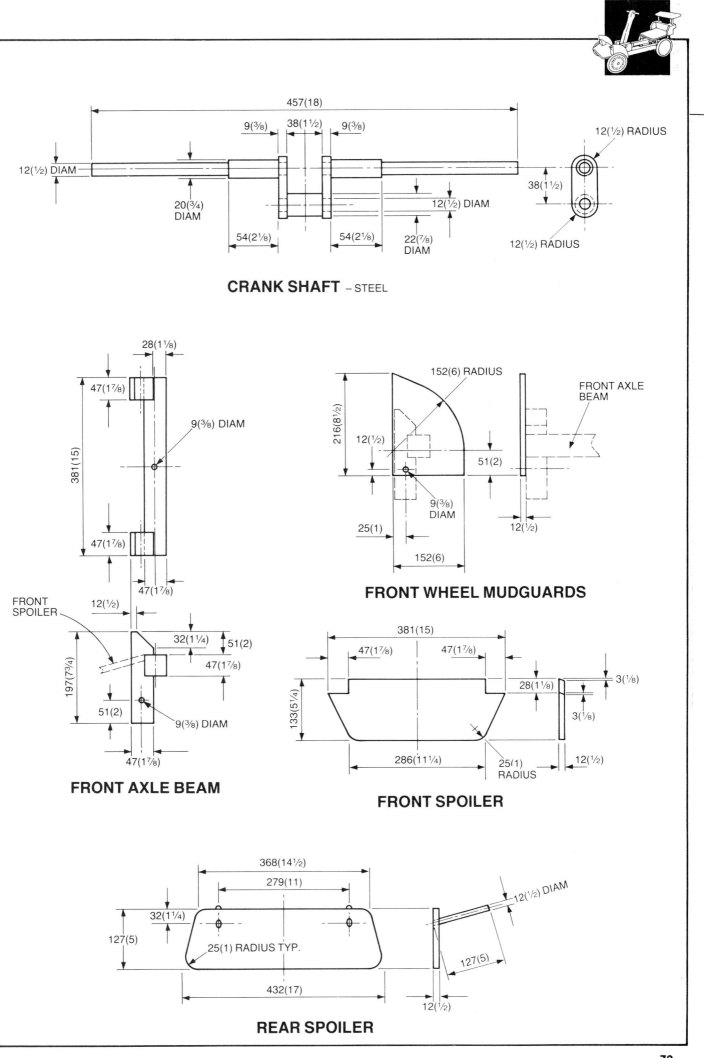

CRANK SHAFT – STEEL

457(18)

9(³/₈) 38(1¹/₂) 9(³/₈)

12(¹/₂) DIAM

20(³/₄) DIAM

54(2¹/₈) 54(2¹/₈)

12(¹/₂) DIAM

22(⁷/₈) DIAM

12(¹/₂) RADIUS

38(1¹/₂)

12(¹/₂) RADIUS

28(1¹/₈)

47(1⁷/₈)

381(15)

9(³/₈) DIAM

47(1⁷/₈)

47(1⁷/₈)

FRONT SPOILER

12(¹/₂)

32(1¹/₄) 51(2)

47(1⁷/₈)

197(7³/₄)

51(2)

9(³/₈) DIAM

47(1⁷/₈)

FRONT AXLE BEAM

152(6) RADIUS

FRONT AXLE BEAM

216(8¹/₂)

12(¹/₂)

51(2)

9(³/₈) DIAM

25(1)

152(6)

12(¹/₂)

FRONT WHEEL MUDGUARDS

381(15)

47(1⁷/₈) 47(1⁷/₈)

28(1¹/₈)

3(¹/₈)

133(5¹/₄)

3(¹/₈)

286(11¹/₄)

25(1) RADIUS

12(¹/₂)

FRONT SPOILER

368(14¹/₂)

279(11)

32(1¹/₄)

12(¹/₂) DIAM

127(5)

25(1) RADIUS TYP.

127(5)

432(17)

12(¹/₂)

REAR SPOILER

79

AIRPORT

Good strong nursery toys do seem to be rather expensive if you buy wooden ones – and the blow-moulded plastic bubble toys very quickly look scruffy. These airport toys are relatively simple to make requiring only a minimum of hand tools. You can obviously make as many aeroplanes, helicopters and baggage-handling tractors as you like.

Jet airliner

1 Start by cutting the fuselage (body) of the aeroplane to shape. Use a coping saw to cut the curved section at the nose and remove saw cuts with a small plane, spokeshave or sandplate (see page 210).

2 Cut the wings, fin and tailplane from plywood, again using a coping saw. Glue the fin, tailplane and wing onto the fuselage.

3 Now cut out the undercarriage, drill the axle holes and glue the undercarriage onto the underside of the wing. Push steel axles through the holes, chamfer the ends of the axles and fit the wheels and spring caps (see Accessories, page 215).

4 I glued a length of dowel rod beneath each wing to represent the engine nacelles. In order to increase the glueing area for these, plane 'flats' on each dowel rod before fixing them onto the underside of the wing. Screw an eye onto the fuselage so that the aeroplane can be towed by the towing tractor.

5 You can either paint the aeroplane completely, or just paint colour lines on the wings, fin and tailplane, and finish it off with a coat of clear varnish.

Helicopter

1 Before you start shaping the block of wood from which the helicopter fuselage is made, drill the axle hole and the hole to take the main rotor blades on top. Then, using a coping saw, rough out the shape and glasspaper off all the saw cut marks. Drill the hole for the tail rotor.

2 Make the rotor blades and cut a very small halving joint in one of them. Glue them together and, when the glue is dry, drill a hole through the middle. To get the blades to spin freely place a washer under them when you screw them to the fuselage and use a screw cup washer on top.

3 Make the tiny tail rotor and screw it onto the fuselage, again using a cup washer.

Towing tractor

1 Shape up a block of wood, planing a taper at the back. Drill holes to take the axle rods and another hole in the top to take the steering wheel column (dowel rod).

2 Make the steering wheel by drilling a hole in a large piece of dowel rod, and then cutting off a short length and glueing it onto the steering column. Glue the steering column into the tractor.

3 Fit the axles, wheels and spring caps.

Large towing tractor

1 Cut the two pieces of wood to shape and drill the holes for the steering wheel and axle rods. Glue the two pieces together.

2 Repeat the same process described above for making and fitting the steering wheel.

3 Screw an eye into the back of the tractor which will couple up with the hooks on the baggage cars and also fit neatly into the recessed hole on the underside of the petrol tanker.

Baggage cars

1 These are all made in exactly the same way, so if you intend to make, say, 4 it's a good idea to mark all the chassis out on a single length of timber, drill all the axle holes and then cut it up into individual cars. This method speeds up the making process.

2 To prevent the suitcases falling off, glue small pieces of plywood onto the back and front of each car, but before doing so, drill the holes for the linking cord.

3 Fit the axles, wheels and spring caps. Attach the cars to each other with lengths of nylon cord, knotted at each end. Screw a hook onto the end car so that it can couple up with the tractor.

Petrol tanker

1 Start by shaping the tanker chassis. Drill holes for the axles, the larger diameter hole to accommodate the 'hook eye' for towing and the small hole to take a short length of dowel that will keep the tanker level when the large towing tractor is uncoupled.

2 Make the tank itself from a piece of plastic waste pipe and glue pieces of dowel rod into the ends to seal it. Cut, shape and glue the two pieces of plywood for the tank cradle on top of the chassis.

3 Glue in the dowel rod and fit the axles, wheels and spring caps.

Airport buildings

1 Cut out all the walls and roofs of the various buildings and use a coping saw to cut out the doors and windows. Drill the holes for the railings on the departure building roof.

2 Assemble the buildings by glueing and panel pinning the edges together. Use a pin punch to drive the pins below the surface.

3 To make the railings around the roof of the departure building, drill holes in eleven lengths of dowel. This is a tricky job as you tend to get lots of splinters when the drill breaks through so you will need to exercise patience and care. Glue the dowels in position and thread soft wire through the holes.

4 The heliport roof has a helipad made by glueing a circular piece of plywood to a small support block. Glue this and the awning to the roof as shown.

5 The control building has a radar scanner which I made by glueing a piece of dowel into the shaped piece of timber that represents the 'dish'. I lined the dish with the type of aluminium mesh used to repair car wings. Drill a hole in the mounting block at a 15° angle to take the support, then glue everything in place.

Painting
These sort of toys are much more interesting if a little colour is added. I outlined the edges of the buildings and the windows and doors in yellow or red, and also painted the steering wheels on the tow tractors and around the plywood edges of the baggage cars. You could also paint the insides of the wheels to add further interest. Whatever you decide to do, please remember to use non-toxic varnish and paints (see page 215).

Cutting list

Airliner

Fuselage	1 off	318 × 44 × 35mm (12½ × 1¾ × 1⅜in)	Timber
Wing	1 off	318 × 114 × 9mm (12½ × 4½ × ⅜in)	Plywood
Tail plane	1 off	152 × 38 × 9mm (6 × 1½ × ⅜in)	Plywood
Fin	1 off	133 × 60 × 9mm (5¼ × 2⅜ × ⅜in)	Plywood
Engine nacelles	2 off	64mm (2½in) × 12mm (½in) diam dowelling	
Undercarriage	1 off	114 × 32 × 22mm (4½ × 1¼ × ⅞in)	Timber

Ancillaries

	4 off	28mm (1⅛in) diam wheels
	2 off	70mm (2¾in) × 5mm (³⁄₁₆in) diam steel axles
	4 off	5mm (³⁄₁₆in) spring dome caps
	1 off	9mm (⅜in) screwed eye

Helicopter

Fuselage	1 off	152 × 44 × 32mm (6 × 1¾ × 1¼in)	Timber
Main rotor blade	2 off	171 × 16 × 9mm (6¾ × ⅝ × ⅜in)	Timber
Tail rotor	1 off	32 × 11 × 5mm (1¼ × ⁷⁄₁₆ × ³⁄₁₆in)	Plywood

Ancillaries

	2 off	28mm (1⅛in) diam wheels
	1 off	70 mm (2¾in) × 5mm (³⁄₁₆in) diam steel axle
	2 off	5 mm (³⁄₁₆in) spring dome caps
	1 off	25mm (1in) no. 6 wood screw
	1 off	20mm (¾in) no. 6 wood screw
	3 off	Cup washers

Towing Tractor

Body	1 off	92 × 32 × 25mm (3⅝ × 1¼ × 1in)	Timber
Steering wheel	1 off	3mm (⅛in) × 16mm (⅝in) diam dowelling	
Steering column	1 off	22mm (⅞in) × 6mm (¼in) diam dowelling	

Ancillaries

	4 off	28mm (1⅛in) diam road wheels
	2 off	67mm (2⅝in) × 5mm (³⁄₁₆in) diam steel axles
	4 off	5mm (³⁄₁₆in) spring dome caps
	1 off	12mm (½in) screwed hook

Baggage Cars

Chassis	1 off	76 × 38 × 25mm (3 × 1½ × 1in)	Timber
Ends	2 off	38 × 38 × 3mm (1½ × 1½ × ⅛in)	Plywood

Ancillaries

	4 off	28mm (1⅛in) diam road wheels
	2 off	76mm (3in) × 5mm (³⁄₁₆in) diam steel axles
	4 off	5mm (³⁄₁₆in) spring dome caps
	1 off	12mm (½in) screwed hook
	1 off	76mm (3in) length of nylon cord

Large Towing Tractor

Body	1 off	102 × 35 × 25mm (4 × 1⅜ × 1in)	Timber
	1 off	51 × 35 × 25mm (2 × 1⅜ × 1in)	Timber
Steering wheel	1 off	3mm (⅛in) × 16mm (⅝in) diam dowelling	
Steering column	1 off	25mm (1in) × 6mm (¼in) diam dowelling	

Ancillaries

	4 off	28mm (1⅛in) diam road wheels
	2 off	73mm (2⅞in) × 5mm (³⁄₁₆in) diam steel axles
	4 off	5mm (³⁄₁₆in) spring dome caps
	1 off	9mm (⅜in) screwed eye

Petrol Tanker

Chassis	1 off	165 × 38 × 35mm (6½ × 1½ × 1⅜in)	Timber
	1 off	25mm (1in) × 6mm (¼in) diam dowelling	
Tank ends	2 off	6mm (¼in) × 32mm (1¼in) diam dowelling (to suit i/diam of tank)	
Cradle	2 off	32 × 12 × 9mm (1¼ × ½ × ⅜in)	Timber

Ancillaries

	4 off	28mm (1⅛in) diam road wheels
	2 off	73mm (2⅞in) × 5mm (³⁄₁₆in) diam steel axles
	4 off	5mm (³⁄₁₆in) spring dome caps
	1 off	38mm (1½in) o/diam × 32mm (1¼in) i/diam × 162mm (6⅜in) long plastic tube

Departure Building

Roof	1 off	413 × 178 × 9mm (16¼ × 7 × ⅜in)	Plywood
Front and rear walls	2 off	381 × 127 × 9mm (15 × 5 × ⅜in)	Plywood
End walls	2 off	152 × 127 × 9mm (6 × 5 × ⅜in)	Plywood
Hand rail posts	Make from 419mm (16½in) × 6mm (¼in) diam dowelling		

Ancillaries

	1 off	660mm (26in) × 1.5mm (¹⁄₁₆in) diam soft wire

Heliport

Roof	1 off	476 × 152 × 9mm (18¾ × 6 × ⅜in)	Plywood
Awning	1 off	400 × 38 × 9mm (15¾ × 1½ × ⅜in)	Plywood
Front and rear walls	2 off	381 × 127 × 9mm (15 × 5 × ⅜in)	Plywood
End walls	2 off	152 × 127 × 9mm (6 × 5 × ⅜in)	Plywood
Platform	1 off	203 × 203 × 9mm (8 × 8 × ⅜in)	Plywood
Platform support	1 off	76 × 38 × 25mm (3 × 1½ × 1in)	Timber

Control Tower

Control room roof	1 off	292 × 152 × 9mm (11½ × 6 × ⅜in)	Plywood
Control room front and rear walls	2 off	152 × 89 × 9mm (6 × 3½ × ⅜in)	Plywood

Control room end walls	2 off	146 × 89 × 9mm (5¾ × 3½ × ⅜in)	Plywood
Control building roof	1 off	305 × 267 × 9mm (12 × 10½ × ⅜in)	Plywood
Control building front and rear walls	2 off	279 × 152 × 9mm (11 × 6 × ⅜in)	Plywood
Control building end walls	2 off	203 × 152 × 9mm (8 × 6 × ⅜in)	Plywood
Radar scanner	1 off	152 × 76 × 44mm (6 × 3 × 1¾in)	Timber
	1 off	140mm (5½in) × 12mm (½in) diam dowelling	
Radar scanner mounting block	1 off	76 × 32 × 25mm (3 × 1¼ × 1in)	Timber
Ancillaries			
	1 off	229mm (9in) × 44mm (1¾in) × 1.5mm (1/16in) aluminium mesh	

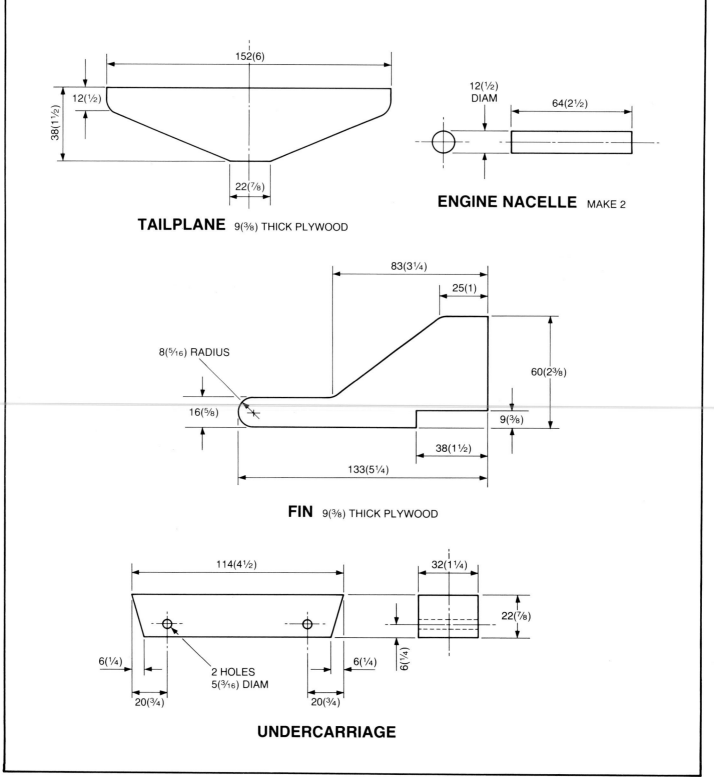

TAILPLANE 9(⅜) THICK PLYWOOD

ENGINE NACELLE MAKE 2

FIN 9(⅜) THICK PLYWOOD

UNDERCARRIAGE

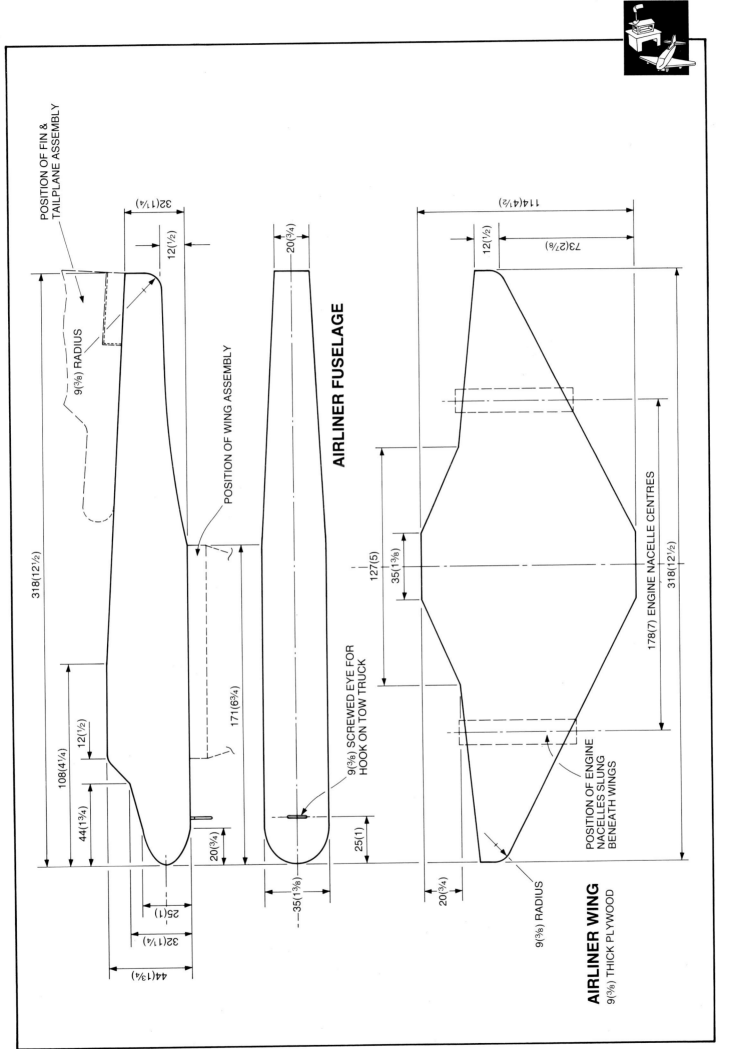

AIRLINER FUSELAGE

POSITION OF FIN & TAILPLANE ASSEMBLY

POSITION OF WING ASSEMBLY

9(³⁄₈) RADIUS

318(12½)

32(1¼)

12(½)

108(4¼)

12(½)

44(1¾)

20(¾)

25(1)

32(1¼)

44(1¾)

171(6¾)

20(¾)

9(³⁄₈) SCREWED EYE FOR HOOK ON TOW TRUCK

35(1³⁄₈)

25(1)

AIRLINER WING
9(³⁄₈) THICK PLYWOOD

114(4½)

73(2⁷⁄₈)

12(½)

127(5)

35(1³⁄₈)

178(7) ENGINE NACELLE CENTRES

318(12½)

POSITION OF ENGINE NACELLES SLUNG BENEATH WINGS

9(³⁄₈) RADIUS

20(¾)

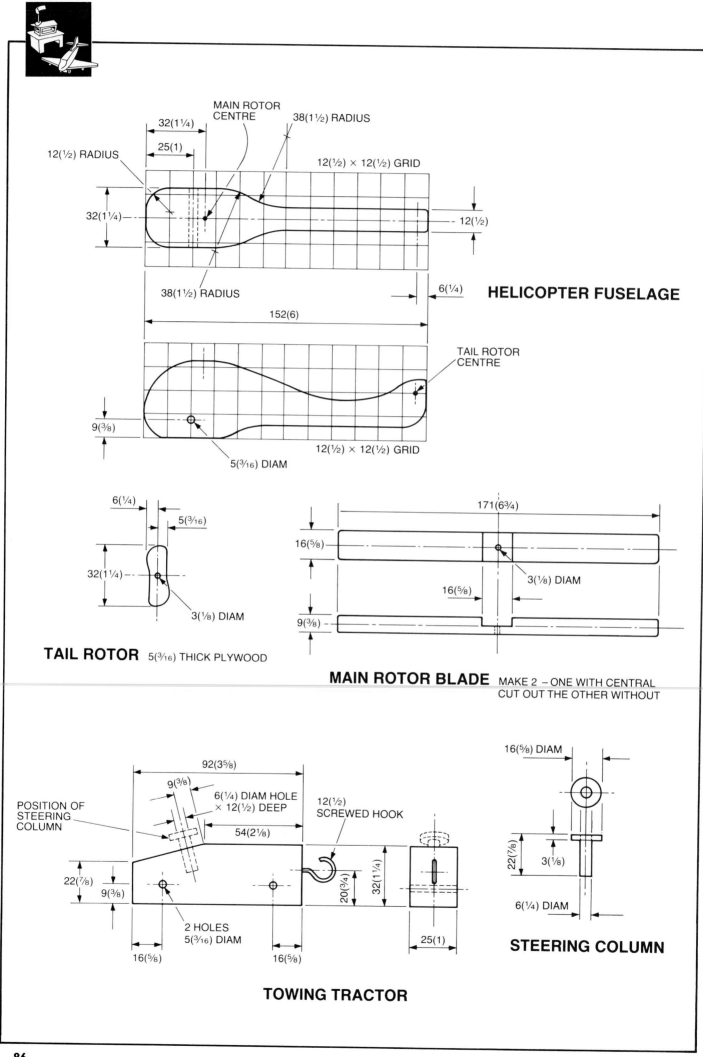

12(½) RADIUS

32(1¼)

MAIN ROTOR CENTRE

38(1½) RADIUS

32(1¼)

25(1)

12(½) × 12(½) GRID

12(½)

38(1½) RADIUS

6(¼)

152(6)

HELICOPTER FUSELAGE

TAIL ROTOR CENTRE

9(⅜)

12(½) × 12(½) GRID

5(³⁄₁₆) DIAM

6(¼)

5(³⁄₁₆)

32(1¼)

3(⅛) DIAM

TAIL ROTOR 5(³⁄₁₆) THICK PLYWOOD

171(6¾)

16(⅝)

3(⅛) DIAM

16(⅝)

9(⅜)

MAIN ROTOR BLADE MAKE 2 – ONE WITH CENTRAL CUT OUT THE OTHER WITHOUT

92(3⅝)

9(⅜)

6(¼) DIAM HOLE × 12(½) DEEP

12(½) SCREWED HOOK

POSITION OF STEERING COLUMN

54(2⅛)

22(⅞)

9(⅜)

20(¾)

32(1¼)

2 HOLES 5(³⁄₁₆) DIAM

16(⅝)

16(⅝)

25(1)

TOWING TRACTOR

16(⅝) DIAM

22(⅞)

3(⅛)

6(¼) DIAM

STEERING COLUMN

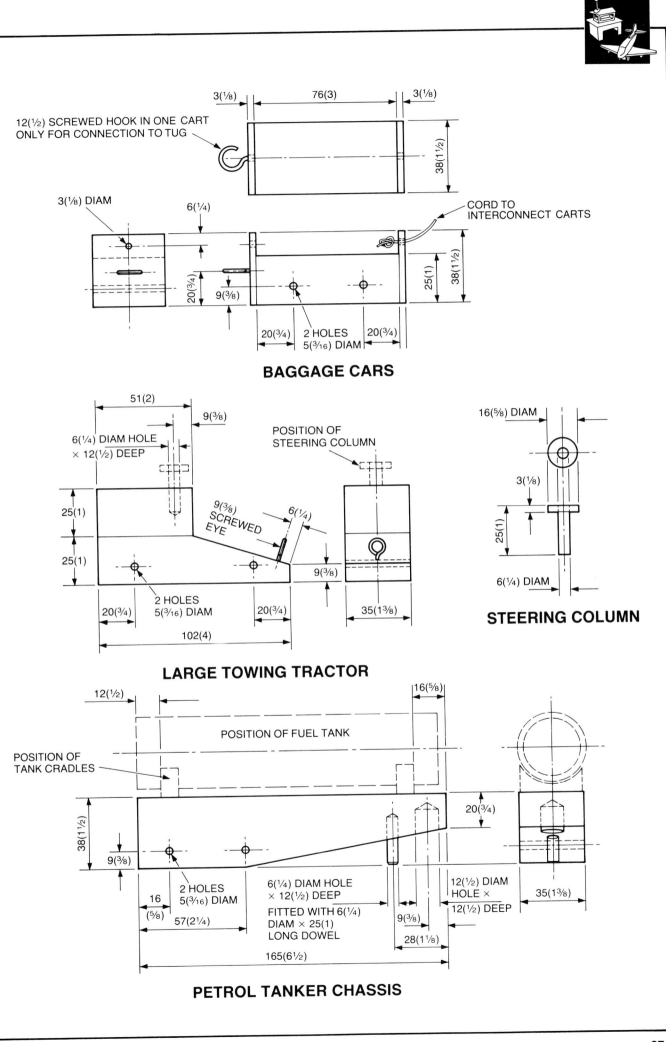

12(½) SCREWED HOOK IN ONE CART
ONLY FOR CONNECTION TO TUG

3(⅛) DIAM

6(¼)

20(¾)

9(⅜)

20(¾)   2 HOLES
        5(³⁄₁₆) DIAM   20(¾)

3(⅛)   76(3)   3(⅛)

38(1½)

CORD TO
INTERCONNECT CARTS

25(1)   38(1½)

BAGGAGE CARS

51(2)

9(⅜)

6(¼) DIAM HOLE
× 12(½) DEEP

25(1)

25(1)

9(⅜)
SCREWED
EYE

6(¼)

9(⅜)

POSITION OF
STEERING COLUMN

20(¾)   2 HOLES
        5(³⁄₁₆) DIAM   20(¾)

102(4)

35(1⅜)

LARGE TOWING TRACTOR

16(⅝) DIAM

3(⅛)

25(1)

6(¼) DIAM

STEERING COLUMN

12(½)   16(⅝)

POSITION OF FUEL TANK

POSITION OF
TANK CRADLES

38(1½)

9(⅜)

2 HOLES
5(³⁄₁₆) DIAM

16
(⅝)

57(2¼)

6(¼) DIAM HOLE
× 12(½) DEEP

FITTED WITH 6(¼)
DIAM × 25(1)
LONG DOWEL

9(⅜)

28(1⅛)

20(¾)

12(½) DIAM
HOLE ×
12(½) DEEP

35(1⅜)

165(6½)

PETROL TANKER CHASSIS

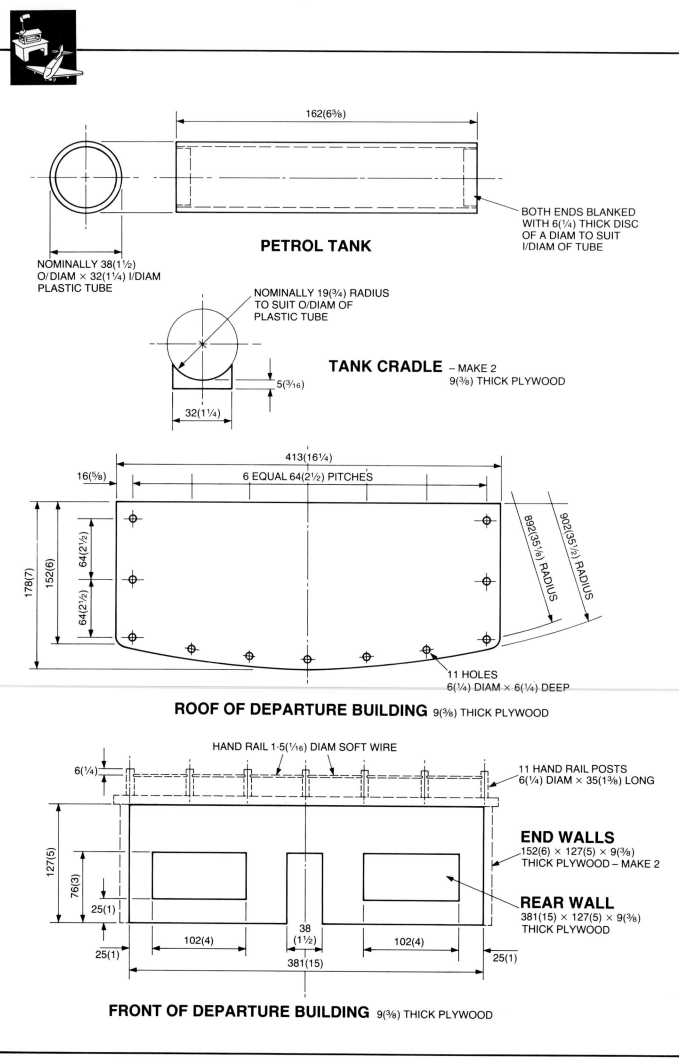

162(6⅜)

PETROL TANK

BOTH ENDS BLANKED
WITH 6(¼) THICK DISC
OF A DIAM TO SUIT
I/DIAM OF TUBE

NOMINALLY 38(1½)
O/DIAM × 32(1¼) I/DIAM
PLASTIC TUBE

NOMINALLY 19(¾) RADIUS
TO SUIT O/DIAM OF
PLASTIC TUBE

TANK CRADLE – MAKE 2
9(⅜) THICK PLYWOOD

5(³/₁₆)

32(1¼)

413(16¼)

16(⅝)

6 EQUAL 64(2½) PITCHES

178(7)

152(6)

64(2½)

64(2½)

892(35⅛) RADIUS

902(35½) RADIUS

11 HOLES
6(¼) DIAM × 6(¼) DEEP

ROOF OF DEPARTURE BUILDING 9(⅜) THICK PLYWOOD

HAND RAIL 1·5(¹/₁₆) DIAM SOFT WIRE

6(¼)

11 HAND RAIL POSTS
6(¼) DIAM × 35(1⅜) LONG

END WALLS
152(6) × 127(5) × 9(⅜)
THICK PLYWOOD – MAKE 2

REAR WALL
381(15) × 127(5) × 9(⅜)
THICK PLYWOOD

127(5)

76(3)

25(1)

102(4)

38
(1½)

102(4)

25(1)

25(1)

381(15)

25(1)

FRONT OF DEPARTURE BUILDING 9(⅜) THICK PLYWOOD

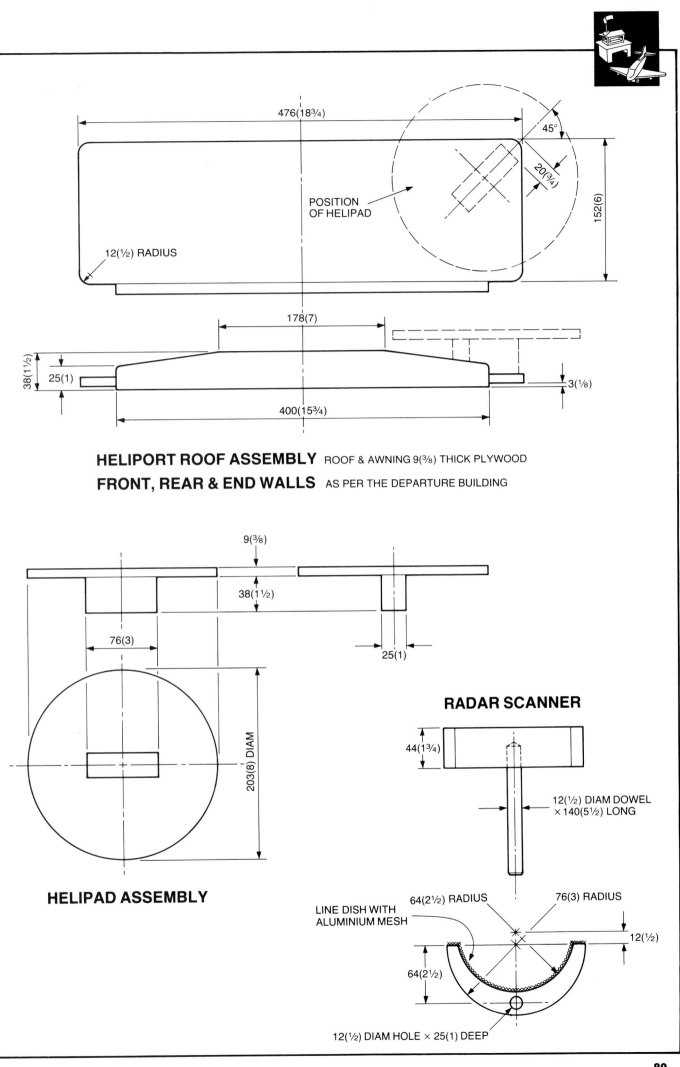

476(18¾)

45°

20(¾)

152(6)

POSITION
OF HELIPAD

12(½) RADIUS

178(7)

38(1½)

25(1)

3(⅛)

400(15¾)

HELIPORT ROOF ASSEMBLY ROOF & AWNING 9(⅜) THICK PLYWOOD
FRONT, REAR & END WALLS AS PER THE DEPARTURE BUILDING

9(⅜)

38(1½)

76(3)

25(1)

203(8) DIAM

HELIPAD ASSEMBLY

RADAR SCANNER

44(1¾)

12(½) DIAM DOWEL
× 140(5½) LONG

64(2½) RADIUS

76(3) RADIUS

12(½)

LINE DISH WITH
ALUMINIUM MESH

64(2½)

12(½) DIAM HOLE × 25(1) DEEP

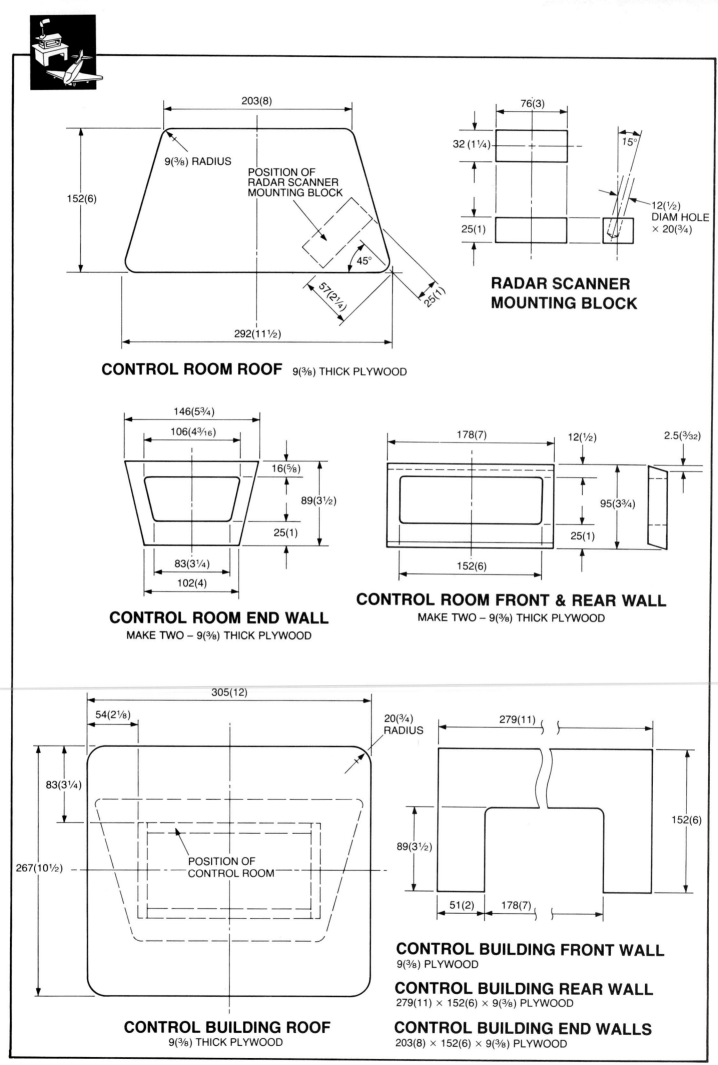

203(8)

9(⅜) RADIUS

152(6)

POSITION OF
RADAR SCANNER
MOUNTING BLOCK

45°

57(2¼)

25(1)

292(11½)

CONTROL ROOM ROOF 9(⅜) THICK PLYWOOD

76(3)

32(1¼)

25(1)

15°

12(½)
DIAM HOLE
× 20(¾)

**RADAR SCANNER
MOUNTING BLOCK**

146(5¾)

106(4³⁄₁₆)

16(⅝)

89(3½)

25(1)

83(3¼)

102(4)

CONTROL ROOM END WALL

MAKE TWO – 9(⅜) THICK PLYWOOD

178(7)

12(½)

2.5(³⁄₃₂)

95(3¾)

25(1)

152(6)

CONTROL ROOM FRONT & REAR WALL

MAKE TWO – 9(⅜) THICK PLYWOOD

305(12)

54(2⅛)

20(¾)
RADIUS

83(3¼)

POSITION OF
CONTROL ROOM

267(10½)

CONTROL BUILDING ROOF

9(⅜) THICK PLYWOOD

279(11)

152(6)

89(3½)

51(2)

178(7)

CONTROL BUILDING FRONT WALL

9(⅜) PLYWOOD

CONTROL BUILDING REAR WALL

279(11) × 152(6) × 9(⅜) PLYWOOD

CONTROL BUILDING END WALLS

203(8) × 152(6) × 9(⅜) PLYWOOD

DOCKYARD

The ideal plaything should lend itself to many different uses and should be capable of being arranged and re-arranged in a multiplicity of ways. This sort of toy allows a child's imagination plenty of scope and gives him or her the opportunity of being one moment the captain of a merchant ship and the next the driver of a lorry leaving the docks with a full load of blocks.

Instructions are given here to make a sufficient number of playthings for a **small** group of children; but obviously, if the dockyard is to be used in a playgroup, any number of cranes, lorries and ships can be added.

The dockyard can be made from any clean-grained (knot-free) hardwood or softwood. The thickness of timber used is not critical, so to a certain extent you can be guided by what your timber yard is able to supply.

Crane and Dock

1   Start by making the crane base board. To give the children maximum scope with the cranes I drilled holes along the front to allow the cranes to be positioned at the most convenient places for off-loading the ships. The holes for the base board are best drilled with a flat bit fitted in an electric drill. Using a plane, remove all the sharp edges and corners of the base board – little fingers are easily cut and bruised.

2   The cranes I kept as simple as possible. You can if you wish fit winding mechanisms, ratchets, and so on (see *Blizzard's Wonderful Wooden Toys*). However, I felt that the ability to load and off-load quickly and efficiently was the most important consideration in this case, so I decided to use a simple pivoted arm holding a magnet on a length of nylon cord.

Start by making the crane mast. Before carrying out any shaping, carefully drill the hole at the bottom to take the dowel rod that locates in the holes in the base board. Drill the holes to take the two dowel rods at the top of the mast and the centre pivot hole for the crane jib. The purpose of the two dowel rods at the top is to limit the travel of the jib.

3   Cut to shape and plane the crane jib. Drill two small pilot holes at either end to take the screw eyes through which the nylon cord runs. Attach the jib to the crane mast either with a length of steel rod with spring caps on each end or by a small nut and bolt.

4   Attach a horseshoe magnet to the end of the cord. The magnets used need to be fairly strong, otherwise they will not lift the blocks from the ships. There are alternatives to magnets – for instance, hooks and eyes – but these tend to spoil the stacking capabilities of the blocks, and they are a little fiddly for small fingers. It is best to use a fairly large-diameter nylon cord (coloured if possible) for it will far outlast string and is less likely to tangle or become knotted.

5   The dockyard looks more workmanlike if a couple of extra wharfs (platforms) are built, providing somewhere to tie up ships waiting to off-load – this also makes for some very interesting dockyard variations.

Barge

1   There are no joints in the barge and all that is required is careful shaping and glueing together. Begin by cutting the hull to length and then marking out the shape of the prow. The prow is built up with an extra piece of wood: cut this and glue it onto the front of the hull. The final shaping of the prow is best left until the glue is dry and both pieces can be placed in the vice and shaped together.

2   Make a small block to form the bridge assembly. After cutting and shaping, drill the hole – at a slight angle – to take the funnel. If you are not confident about drilling a hole off-set, drill a 90° hole but slightly bigger than is required, put plenty of glue in it and you will then be able to set the funnel at an angle in the glue. Once this is completed, glue the bridge onto the hull.

3   When the bridge is in place, glue on the two small side panels. These prevent the 'cargo' of blocks from falling overboard.

Articulated lorry

1   The lorries are quite simple to construct and, being made from solid pieces of wood, are very strong. No joints are used and, as with the barges, it is simply a case of cutting to size and glueing together.

Make the lorry chassis first and drill holes in it to take the axles. Drilling holes accurately through fairly thick timber requires the skill to keep the drill at 90° in both planes. A great deal of frustration is avoided if you buy a vertical drill stand in which to mount your electric drill. This extra piece of equipment is of tremendous value in a small workshop and will make all drilling operations safer and very much more accurate.

2   Having drilled the axle holes in the lorry chassis, cut to size and shape the cab assembly. Remember that, if shaping is required, it is far easier to do this before glueing. Take care over shaping the cab assembly and, when you are satisfied with it, glue it onto the chassis.

3   Cut out the trailer chassis and drill the axle holes with the same accuracy as those of the lorry, then carry out the final shaping. The wedge shape of the trailer allows the lorry to turn fairly sharply without its rear wheels rubbing on the trailer chassis.

4 Glue the bed onto the trailer chassis, along with the head and tail board that stop the 'cargo' of blocks slipping. Fit lengths of chain along the outside edges of the bed.

5 Varnish the completed lorry and fit the wheels and spring caps.

Cargo-handling gantry
This piece of equipment allows an infinite variety of handling operations to be carried out and thus greatly increases the dockyard's potential as a plaything.

Gantry
1 No joints are used, all the pieces being held together by screws and glue. Start by shaping the four support legs, then cut and fit the two overhead longitudinal members. It is best both to glue and screw these onto the legs. Now fix the two sides together with the overhead cross members, again glueing and screwing them into place.

2 The trolley that runs backwards and forwards on the gantry is guided by plastic channel – the type sold by large DIY stores and certain electrical shops as housing for electric cable. Glue the plastic channel onto the overhead longitudinal members with impact adhesive glue. This type of glue is applied in two stages: spread a coat onto the top of each member and onto the underside of each plastic channel; leave for about ten minutes (check the maker's instructions); then join the two surfaces together. It is best to glue the channel into place as the use of panel pins or even countersunk screw heads would affect the smooth running of the trolley wheels in the channel.

Overhead trolley
1 Start by making the trolley chassis. Mark out the centre area, which has to be cut out. Drill a small hole in one of the corners and, using a coping saw, cut the middle out. For those of you who have a jigsaw, this job is quickly done; however, the coping saw is quite capable of doing the job, even if it does take a few minutes longer.

2 Prepare two strips of wood with holes drilled for axles to fit on the chassis underside. Glue these into place.

3 Make two identical pieces to fit onto the top side of the chassis. It will help if you hold these together with tape before you drill the holes for the winch handles.

4 Now cut and shape the two winch handles. Assemble the handle sides and the spindle and glue them onto the chassis of the trolley. Turn the winch handles to ensure that everything is free before the glue dries. Drill a small hole in the centre of the spindle for a screwed eye which makes an anchorage point for the cord. Then fit the axles and wheels.

Blocks
For the magnets to get a good grip on the wood blocks it is necessary to fit each block with a steel wood screw. The screw needs to have a fairly large head: a no. 10 or 12 gauge is ideal. To prevent the possibility of their injuring the user, countersink the screws (a special tool called a countersink bit is used for this job), then drive the screw heads into the blocks, but allow them to stand slightly proud of the wood. Do check that after the screw has been driven into the block there are no steel splinters on the head – these occur quite often and can be very painful if they stick into little fingers.

NB Wheeled toys When attempting to fit spring caps, it is vitally important that you file a small chamfer onto the ends of the steel axles. The chamfer allows the spring claws to clip onto the axle rod.

Wheels and magnets See Accessories, page 215.

Cutting list

Crane and dock

Base board	1 off	610 × 162 × 38mm (24 × 6⅜ × 1½in)	Timber
Jib	1 off	387 × 54 × 20mm (15¼ × 2⅛ × ¾in)	Timber
Mast	1 off	305 × 47 × 38mm (12 × 1⅞ × 1½in)	Timber
	1 off	86mm (3⅜in) × 16mm (⅝in) diam dowelling	
	2 off	51mm (2in) × 9mm (⅜in) diam dowelling	

Ancillaries

	1 off	60mm (2⅜in) × 6mm (¼in) diam steel pin	
	2 off	6mm (¼in) spring dome caps	
	2 off	12mm (½in) diam screwed eyes	
	1 off	610mm (24in) length of cord	
	1 off	Horseshoe magnet	

Note – Jib, mast and ancillaries are numbers required per tower crane

Barge

Hull	1 off	305 × 70 × 20mm (12 × 2⅜ × ¾in)	Timber
Prow	1 off	70 × 70 × 20mm (2⅜ × 2⅜ × ¾in)	Timber
Side panel	2 off	191 × 20 × 6mm (7½ × ¾ × ¼in)	Timber
Bridge	1 off	70 × 57 × 38mm (2¾ × 2¼ × 1½in)	Timber
Funnel	1 off	76mm (3in) × 16mm (⅝in) diam dowelling	

Wharf side

Deck	1 off	381 × 114 × 20mm (15 × 4½ × ¾in)	Timber
Support	2 off	114 × 22 × 20mm (4½ × ⅞ × ¾in)	Timber

Articulated lorry

Chassis	1 off	152 × 64 × 38mm (6 × 2½ × 1½in)	Timber
	1 off	38mm (1½in) × 9mm (⅜in) diam dowelling	
Cab	1 off	105 × 102 × 20mm (4⅛ × 4 × ¾in)	Timber
	1 off	89 × 64 × 38mm (3½ × 2½ × 1½in)	Timber

Ancillaries

	4 off	51mm (2in) diam road wheels	
	2 off	114mm (4½in) × 6mm (¼in) diam steel axles	
	4 off	6mm (¼in) diam spring dome caps	

Trailer

Bed	1 off	305 × 102 × 20mm (12 × 4 × ¾in)	Timber
Head and tail board	2 off	102 × 20 × 20mm (4 × ¾ × ¾in)	Timber
Chassis	1 off	248 × 64 × 38mm (9¾ × 2½ × 1½in)	Timber

Ancillaries

	4 off	51mm (2in) diam road wheels
	2 off	114mm (4½in) × 6mm (¼in) diam steel axles
	4 off	6mm (¼in) diam spring dome caps
	1 off	610mm (24in) length of lightweight chain

Cargo-handling Gantry

Overhead longitudinal member	2 off	660 × 38 × 20mm (26 × 1½ × ¾in)	Timber
Overhead cross member	2 off	191 × 44 × 20mm (7½ × 1¾ × ¾in)	Timber
Support leg	4 off	295 × 51 × 20mm (11⅝ × 2 × ¾in)	Timber

Ancillaries

	2 off	20mm (¾in) × 12mm (½in) × 572mm (22½in) lengths of plastic channel section

Overhead Trolley

Chassis	1 off	114 × 89 × 20mm (4½ × 3½ × ¾in)	Timber
Side piece	2 off	89 × 44 × 20mm (3½ × 1¾ × ¾in)	Timber
	2 off	89 × 25 × 20mm (3½ × 1 × ¾in)	Timber
Winch handle	2 off	44 × 25 × 20mm (1¾ × 1 × ¾in)	Timber
	1 off	167mm (6½in) × 9mm (⅜in) diam dowelling	
	2 off	51mm (2in) × 9mm (⅜in) diam dowelling	

Ancillaries

	4 off	41mm (1⅝in) diam road wheels
	2 off	162mm (6⅜in) × 5mm (³⁄₁₆in) diam steel axles
	4 off	5mm (³⁄₁₆in) diam spring dome caps
	1 off	12mm (½in) diam screwed eye
	1 off	610mm (24in) length of cord
	1 off	Bar magnet
	2 off	12mm (½in) o/diam × 9mm (⅜in) i/diam × 5mm (³⁄₁₆in) tubular spacers
Cargo containers	Make from	56mm (2³⁄₁₆in) × 44mm (1¾in) section timber offcuts
	As req'd	38mm (1½in) × no. 8 wood screws

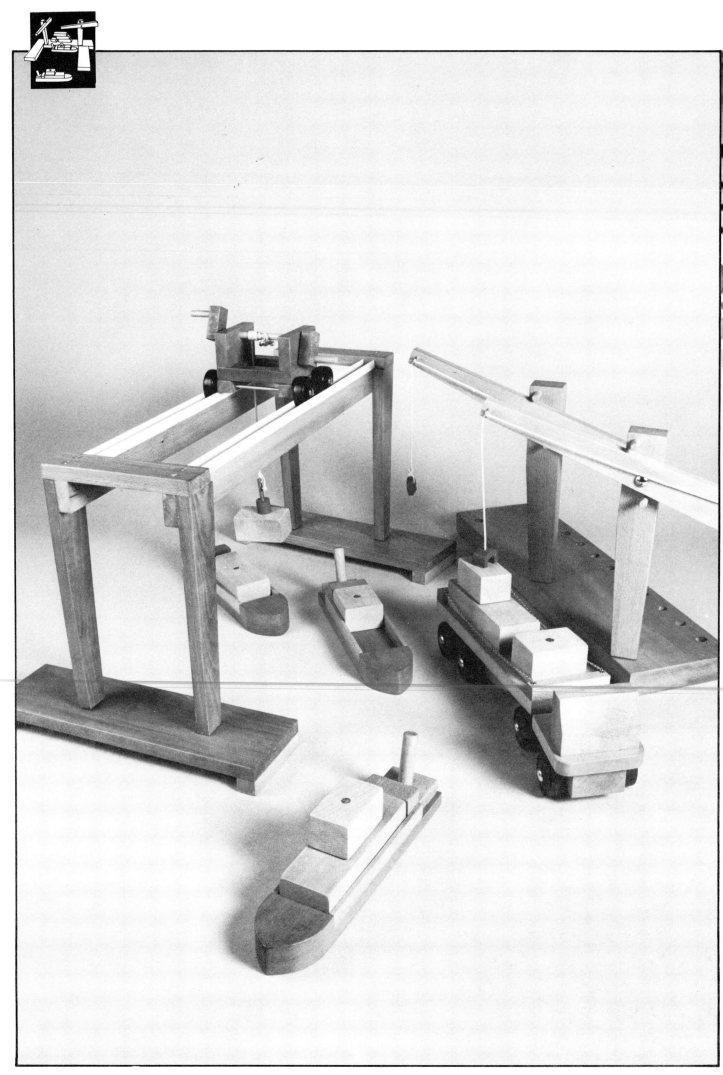

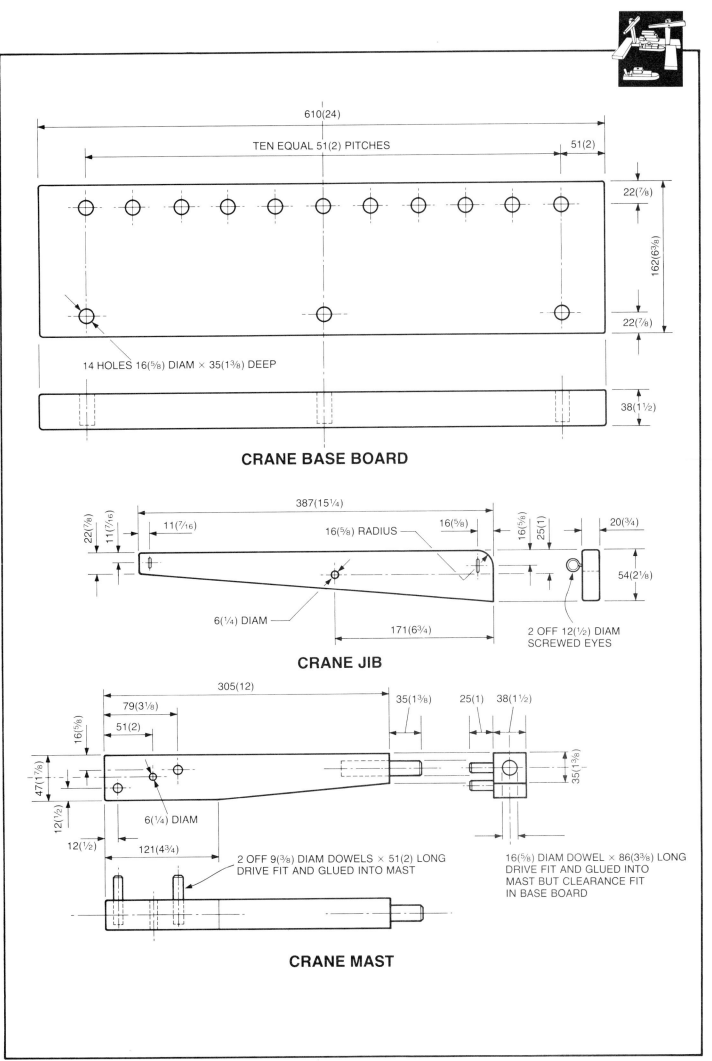

610(24)

TEN EQUAL 51(2) PITCHES

51(2)

22(⁷⁄₈)

162(6³⁄₈)

22(⁷⁄₈)

14 HOLES 16(⁵⁄₈) DIAM × 35(1³⁄₈) DEEP

38(1½)

CRANE BASE BOARD

387(15¼)

22(⁷⁄₈)

11(⁷⁄₁₆)

11(⁷⁄₁₆)

16(⁵⁄₈) RADIUS

16(⁵⁄₈)

16(⁵⁄₈)

25(1)

20(¾)

54(2⅛)

6(¼) DIAM

171(6¾)

2 OFF 12(½) DIAM SCREWED EYES

CRANE JIB

305(12)

79(3⅛)

51(2)

35(1³⁄₈)

25(1)

38(1½)

16(⁵⁄₈)

35(1³⁄₈)

47(1⁷⁄₈)

12(½)

6(¼) DIAM

12(½)

121(4¾)

2 OFF 9(³⁄₈) DIAM DOWELS × 51(2) LONG DRIVE FIT AND GLUED INTO MAST

16(⁵⁄₈) DIAM DOWEL × 86(3³⁄₈) LONG DRIVE FIT AND GLUED INTO MAST BUT CLEARANCE FIT IN BASE BOARD

CRANE MAST

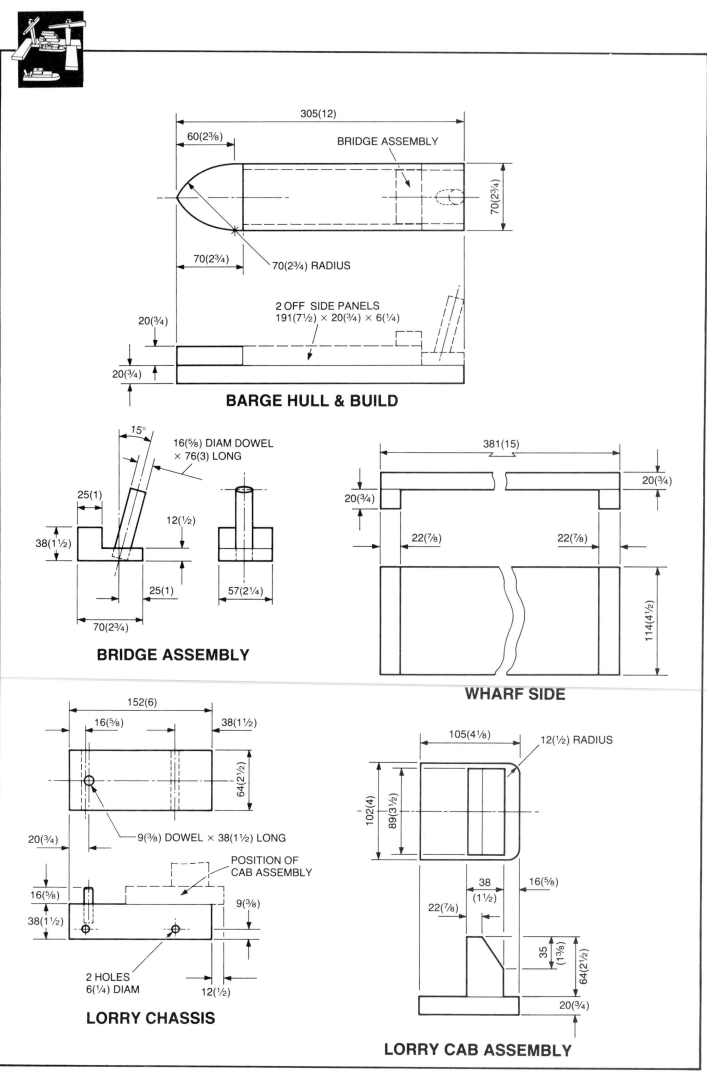

305(12)

60(2⅜)

BRIDGE ASSEMBLY

70(2¾)

70(2¾) RADIUS

70(2¾)

20(¾)

2 OFF SIDE PANELS
191(7½) × 20(¾) × 6(¼)

20(¾)

BARGE HULL & BUILD

15°

16(⅝) DIAM DOWEL
× 76(3) LONG

25(1)

12(½)

38(1½)

25(1)

57(2¼)

70(2¾)

BRIDGE ASSEMBLY

381(15)

20(¾)

20(¾)

22(⅞)

22(⅞)

114(4½)

WHARF SIDE

152(6)

16(⅝)

38(1½)

64(2½)

9(⅜) DOWEL × 38(1½) LONG

20(¾)

POSITION OF
CAB ASSEMBLY

16(⅝)

9(⅜)

38(1½)

2 HOLES
6(¼) DIAM

12(½)

LORRY CHASSIS

105(4⅛)

12(½) RADIUS

102(4)

89(3½)

38
(1½)

16(⅝)

22(⅞)

35
(1⅜)

64(2½)

20(¾)

LORRY CAB ASSEMBLY

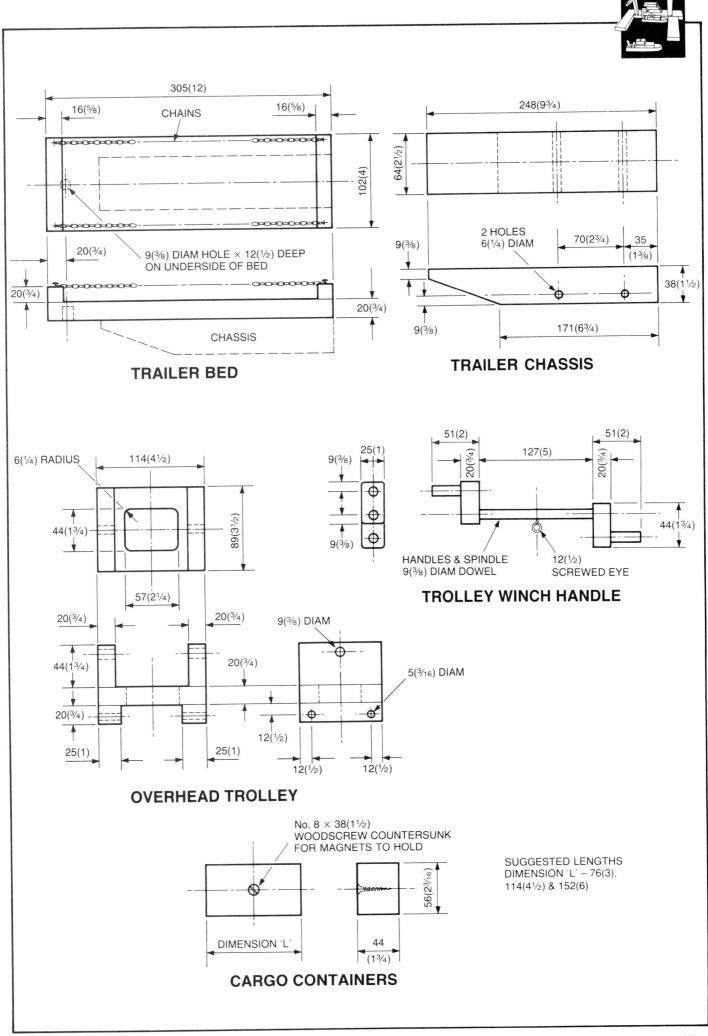

TRAILER BED

305(12)

16(5/8) CHAINS 16(5/8)

102(4)

20(3/4)

9(3/8) DIAM HOLE × 12(1/2) DEEP
ON UNDERSIDE OF BED

20(3/4)

20(3/4)

CHASSIS

TRAILER CHASSIS

248(9¾)

64(2½)

9(3/8)

2 HOLES
6(¼) DIAM

70(2¾) 35 (1⅜)

38(1½)

9(3/8)

171(6¾)

OVERHEAD TROLLEY

6(¼) RADIUS 114(4½)

44(1¾) 89(3½)

57(2¼)

20(3/4) 20(3/4)

44(1¾) 20(3/4)

20(3/4)

25(1) 25(1)

25(1)

12(1/2)

12(1/2) 12(1/2)

9(3/8) DIAM

5(3/16) DIAM

25(1)

9(3/8)

9(3/8)

HANDLES & SPINDLE
9(3/8) DIAM DOWEL

TROLLEY WINCH HANDLE

51(2) 127(5) 51(2)

20(3/4) 20(3/4)

44(1¾)

12(1/2)
SCREWED EYE

CARGO CONTAINERS

No. 8 × 38(1½)
WOODSCREW COUNTERSUNK
FOR MAGNETS TO HOLD

56(2³/₁₆)

DIMENSION 'L'

44
(1¾)

SUGGESTED LENGTHS
DIMENSION 'L' – 76(3),
114(4½) & 152(6)

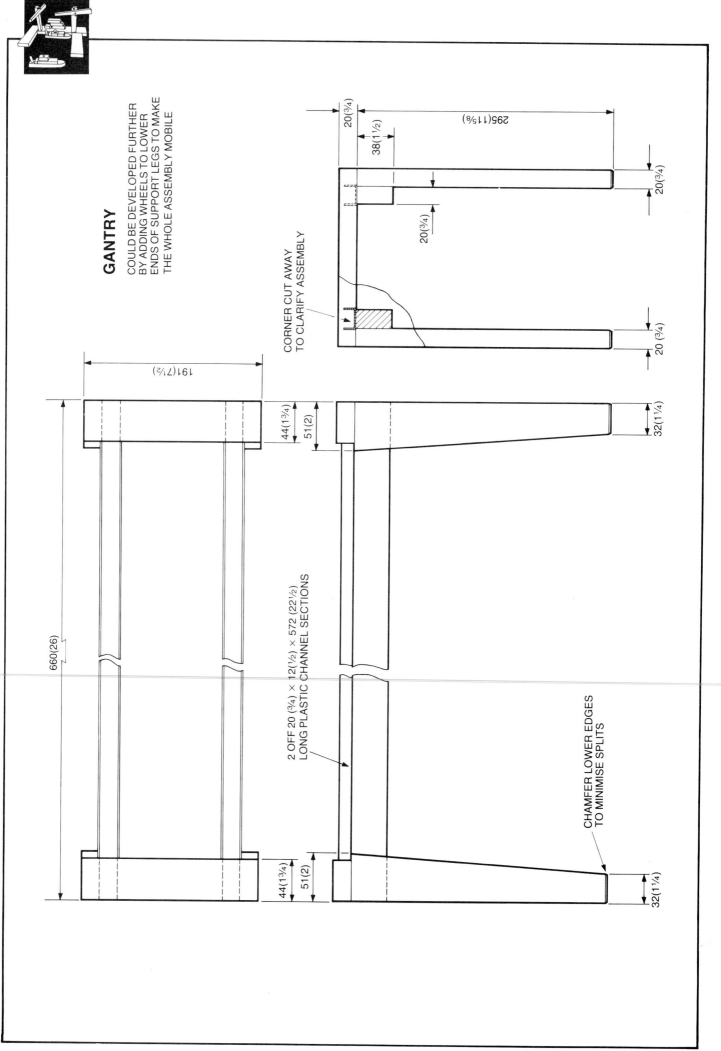

GANTRY

COULD BE DEVELOPED FURTHER
BY ADDING WHEELS TO LOWER
ENDS OF SUPPORT LEGS TO MAKE
THE WHOLE ASSEMBLY MOBILE

CORNER CUT AWAY
TO CLARIFY ASSEMBLY

20(¾)

38(1½)

295(11⅝)

20(¾)

20(¾)

20 (¾)

191(7½)

44(1¾)

51(2)

32(1¼)

660(26)

2 OFF 20 (¾) × 12(½) × 572 (22½)
LONG PLASTIC CHANNEL SECTIONS

CHAMFER LOWER EDGES
TO MINIMISE SPLITS

44(1¾)

51(2)

32(1¼)

DOLLS' HOUSE

This is always a tremendously popular project and from other dolls' houses I have designed I know that all the family get involved in making and playing with it. I felt that as this is such a popular toy I should design it so that it could be made by someone with a minimum of tools and woodworking skills. I have even simplified the front door so that there are no hinges to fit. The house can be constructed mainly from plywood and covered with a brick-patterned paper.

1 The two side walls of the dolls' house are joined together by battens. These battens have the dual function of holding the floors up and keeping the sides together. It is best to tape both sides together and mark out in pencil the six cutouts. With both sides still together fix them in the vice and cut down the sides of the notches with a tenon saw. The waste is now best removed with a coping saw. The coping saw is a very versatile tool and it is not difficult to turn its narrow blade at an angle of 90° at the bottom of the notch to remove the piece of waste plywood in the middle.

2 Separate the two side walls and plane slight bevels on the top of each wall to allow the roof to be fitted. Glue the cross battens into place.

3 Now make the three floors and cut out the stair well areas. Glue the floors in place.

4 The stairs are made from a strip of wood with 'notches' cut out for the treads. These would not pass the building regulations but I think they are rather nice and it does avoid complications. Glue them in place.

5 Cut out the roof pieces and glue them on.

6 Make the front and rear walls and cut out the holes for the windows and door. Cutting out holes in the middle of plywood sheets always causes problems. Unless you take great care at this stage large splinters will break out and completely spoil the look of the walls so I

suggest you use the following system:
i Mark out in pencil, using a try square and ruler, the exact position of the windows on both sides of each wall.
ii Now, with a large sharp chisel, cut along the pencil line. Don't try to cut all the way through from one side. Turn the wall over and repeat the cutting operation from the other side.
iii Turn the wall over once again and cut around the edges of the window once more, and the plywood should come away without a shower of splinters. Do remember to do this part of the work on a firm surface. All the windows and the door should be cut out in this way.

7 Glue the rear wall in place and fit the front wall using magnetic catches. These catches are available at all DIY stores.

8 Now glue the house onto the base. Also glue on small strips of wood to form walls around the house.

9 The next stage is to glue brick-patterned paper onto the walls. I then used a tile pattern for the roof. Once the paper is fixed and has dried you can fit the windows (see Accessories, page 215).

10 Cut out the chimney pieces. I covered the bottom half of the chimney stack with brick paper and painted the top half red. Glue the two pieces together and glue the chimney to the roof.

11 Finally, to avoid the paper becoming scuffed it is advisable to varnish the house all over (see Materials and Finishes, page 214).

Front and rear wall	2 off	600 × 300 × 6mm (23⅝ × 11⅞ × ¼in)	Plywood
Side wall	2 off	505 × 200 × 6mm (19⅞ × 7⅞ × ¼in)	Plywood
Floor assembly	3 off	288 × 200 × 6mm (11⅜ × 7⅞ × ¼in)	Plywood
	6 off	300 × 16 × 12mm (11⅞ × ⅝ × ½in)	Timber
Roof	2 off	254 × 210 × 6mm (10 × 8¼ × ¼in)	Plywood
Roof supports		Make from 381 × 16 × 12mm (15 × ⅝ × ½in)	Timber
Side wall fixing blocks		Make from 140 × 16 × 12mm (5½ × ⅝ × ½in)	Timber
Chimney	1 off	76 × 32 × 20mm (3 × 1¼ × ¾in)	Timber
Stairs	3 off	130 × 73 × 16mm (5⅛ × 2⅞ × ⅝in)	Timber
Base	1 off	470 × 254 × 6mm (18½ × 10 × ¼in)	Plywood
Fence		Make from 660 × 16 × 12mm (26 × ⅝ × ½in)	Timber

Ancillaries

1 off	Door assembly
3 off	Triple light windows and shutters
4 off	Single light windows and shutters
1 off	Chimney pot
2 off	Magnetic catches and plates
	Various brick and tile papers

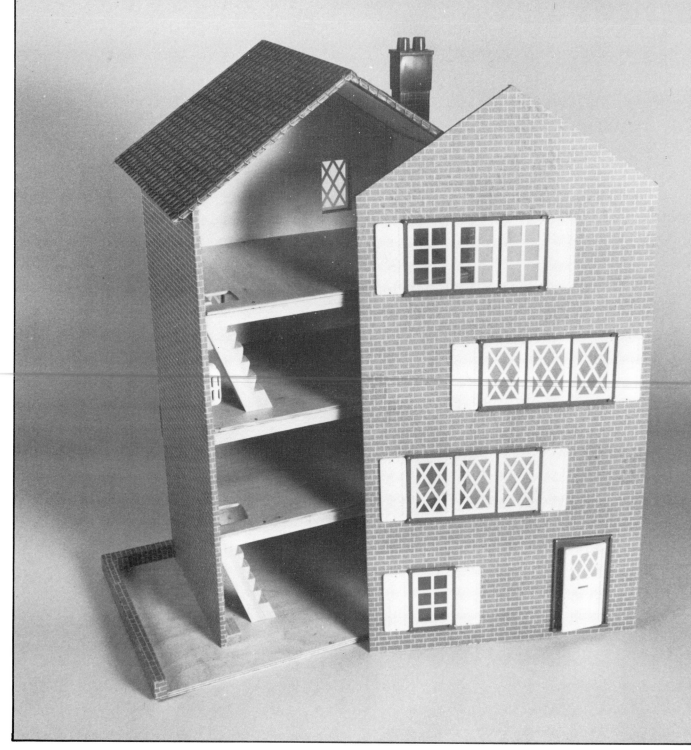

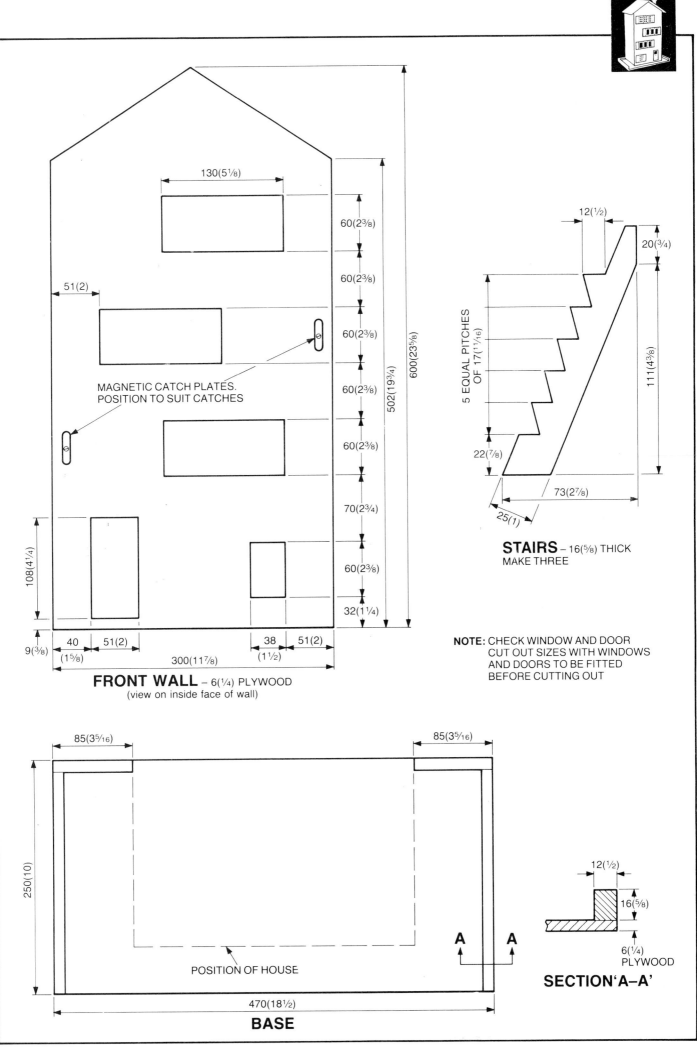

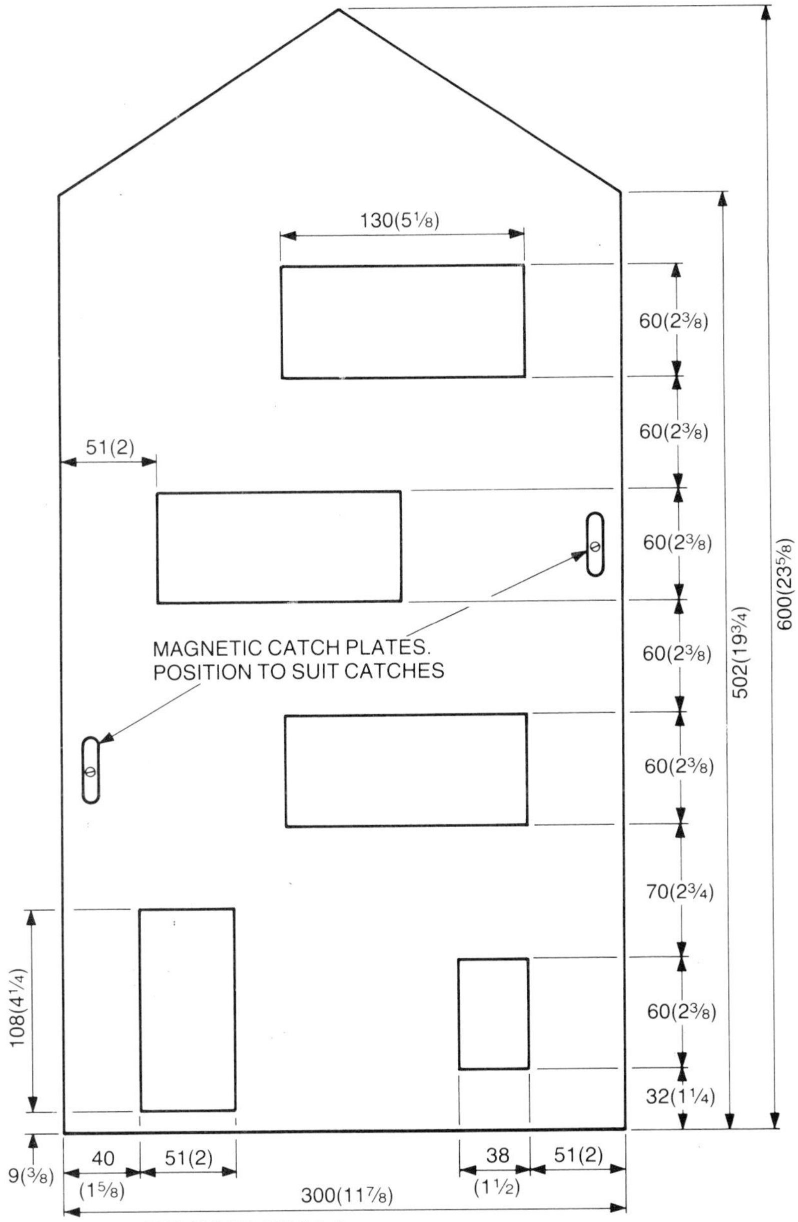
130(5 1/8)
60(2 3/8)
60(2 3/8)
51(2)
60(2 3/8)
MAGNETIC CATCH PLATES.
POSITION TO SUIT CATCHES
60(2 3/8)
502(19 3/4)
600(23 5/8)
60(2 3/8)
70(2 3/4)
108(4 1/4)
60(2 3/8)
32(1 1/4)
9(3/8)
40
(1 5/8)
51(2)
38
(1 1/2)
51(2)
300(11 7/8)

FRONT WALL – 6(1/4) PLYWOOD
(view on inside face of wall)

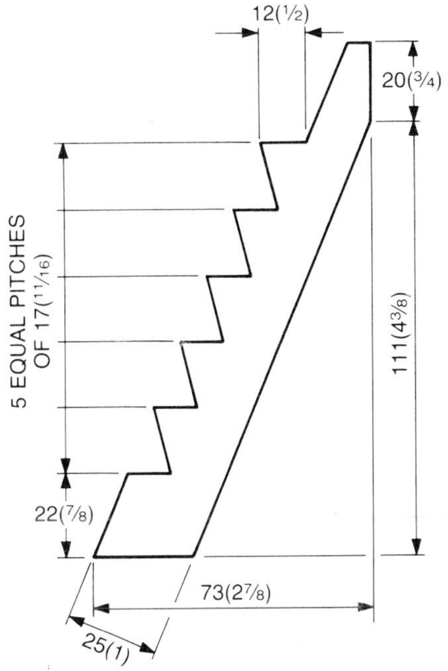
12(1/2)
20(3/4)
5 EQUAL PITCHES
OF 17(11/16)
111(4 3/8)
22(7/8)
73(2 7/8)
25(1)

STAIRS – 16(5/8) THICK
MAKE THREE

NOTE: CHECK WINDOW AND DOOR CUT OUT SIZES WITH WINDOWS AND DOORS TO BE FITTED BEFORE CUTTING OUT

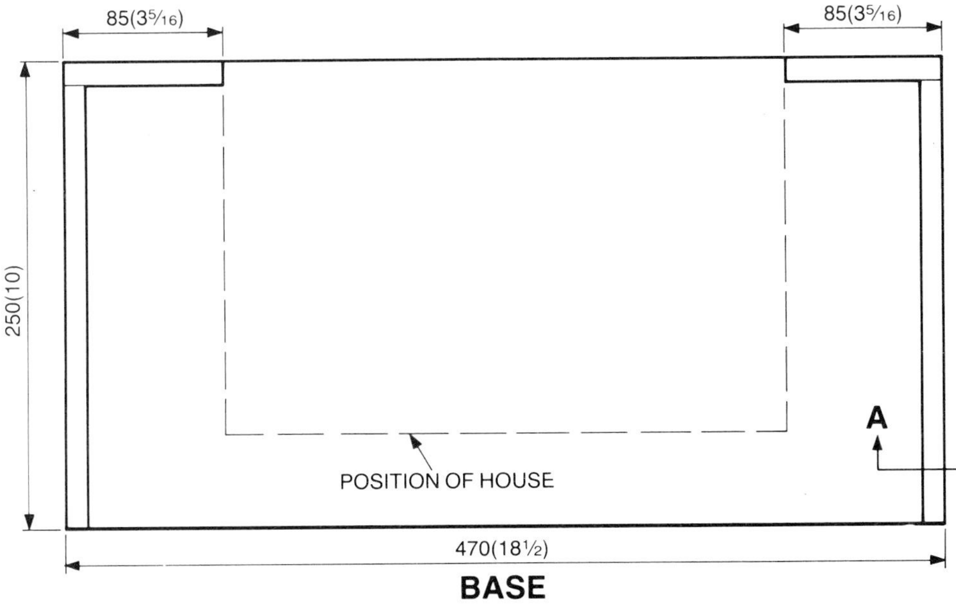
85(3 5/16)
85(3 5/16)
250(10)
A
A
POSITION OF HOUSE
470(18 1/2)

BASE

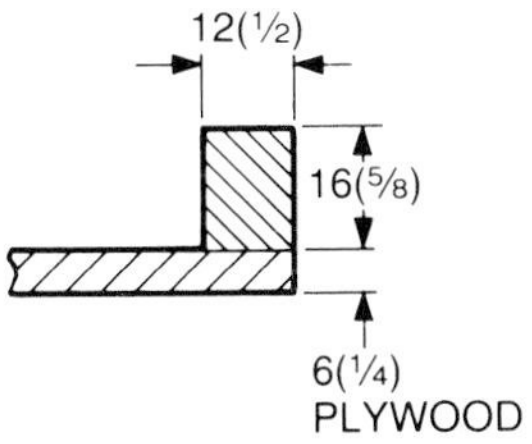
12(1/2)
16(5/8)
6(1/4)
PLYWOOD

SECTION 'A–A'

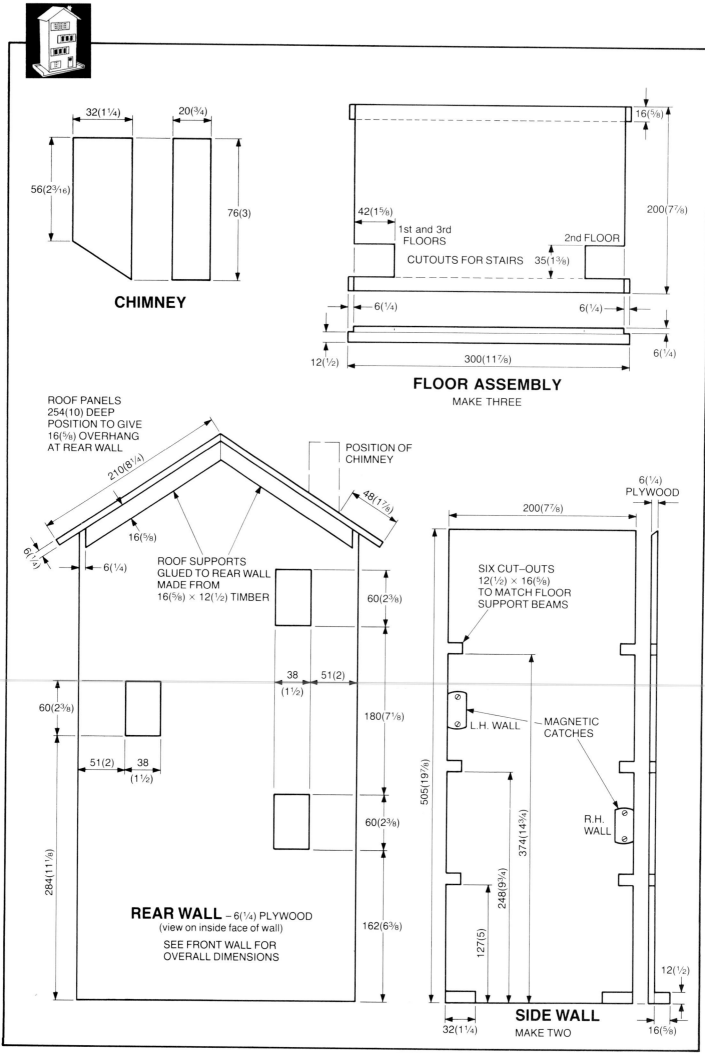

32(1¼) 20(¾)

56(2³⁄₁₆)   76(3)

CHIMNEY

16(⁵⁄₈)

200(7⁷⁄₈)

42(1⁵⁄₈)

1st and 3rd FLOORS

2nd FLOOR   35(1³⁄₈)

CUTOUTS FOR STAIRS

6(¼)   6(¼)   6(¼)

12(½)   300(11⁷⁄₈)

FLOOR ASSEMBLY
MAKE THREE

ROOF PANELS
254(10) DEEP
POSITION TO GIVE
16(⁵⁄₈) OVERHANG
AT REAR WALL

210(8¼)

POSITION OF
CHIMNEY

48(1⁷⁄₈)

16(⁵⁄₈)

6(¼)

6(¼)

ROOF SUPPORTS
GLUED TO REAR WALL
MADE FROM
16(⁵⁄₈) × 12(½) TIMBER

60(2³⁄₈)

38   51(2)
(1½)

180(7⅛)

6(¼)
PLYWOOD

200(7⁷⁄₈)

SIX CUT-OUTS
12(½) × 16(⁵⁄₈)
TO MATCH FLOOR
SUPPORT BEAMS

60(2³⁄₈)

51(2)   38
(1½)

284(11⅛)

REAR WALL – 6(¼) PLYWOOD
(view on inside face of wall)

SEE FRONT WALL FOR
OVERALL DIMENSIONS

60(2³⁄₈)

162(6³⁄₈)

L.H. WALL

MAGNETIC
CATCHES

R.H.
WALL

505(19⁷⁄₈)

374(14¾)

248(9¾)

127(5)

32(1¼)

SIDE WALL
MAKE TWO

12(½)

16(⁵⁄₈)

CASTLE

Children get a great deal of enjoyment from playing with castles and this castle is scaled to suit both the plastic and die-cast soldiers that are available in toy shops.

As space in any child's bedroom is usually at a premium the inside of the castle mound could be used as a storage space for the tower walls etc. and the ramp is fitted with a hinged end to hold the soldiers so there's no excuse for not tidying things away after the game!

1 The construction is not difficult and only really requires the basic skill of cutting all the plywood pieces out carefully. Plywood is a very useful man-made board but it can cause great frustration since it tends to develop nasty long 'spilches' on the underside when it is cut. The secret of successful cutting is to:
i use a very fine-tooth blade in a coping saw, or a metal-cutting blade if you have a jigsaw;
ii tape over the area to be cut beforehand.
Cutting the castellations needed is rather a tedious job but it is vital to get neat 'square' edges and corners. This is the procedure I suggest you follow:
i cut all the vertical lines with a tenon saw;
ii cut all horizontal lines with a coping saw;
iii tidy up any slight roughness with a sandplate or glasspaper block.

2 When all the pieces are ready for assembly they have to be glued together as shown on the plans. It does help to use panel pins too since the pins not only hold the pieces together while the glue dries, but also add to the strength of the castle. Use a pin punch to drive the little pin heads well into the plywood, then fill the holes prior to painting or varnishing.

3 All the towers, walls and the keep are free-standing so that the castle-builder can arrange and re-arrange them in a variety of different ways. Once you have mastered the basic technique of construction you can build an unlimited variety of outer walls, turrets, and so on.

4 The drawbridge and keep doors are fixed in place with hinges, as is the end of the ramp. I used hooks and screwed eyes to keep the end of the ramp closed.

5 The drawbridge tower front and side walls must be drilled with holes for the drawbridge chains and the winding shaft respectively. When you assemble this section, remember to pass the shaft through the sides first, then fix the end stop in place and attach the chains to the winding shaft. Thread the other ends of the chains through the holes in the front of the tower and then glue and pin all the tower walls together. Finally, attach the drawbridge to the tower base with hinges and fit the ends of the chains onto the drawbridge.

6 To add realism I covered the whole castle with a natural stone paper (see Accessories, page 215) and, when the glue had dried (I used wood glue), I varnished all the paper to strengthen it and also make the colour look more realistic.

Cutting list

Castle mound assembly	Top	1 off	445 × 381 × 6mm (17½ × 15 × ¼in)	Plywood
	Sides	2 off	445 × 222 × 6mm (17½ × 8¾ × ¼in)	Plywood
	Front and rear	2 off	445 × 231 × 6mm (17½ × 9⅛ × ¼in)	Plywood
Ramp assembly	Top	1 off	127 × 83 × 6mm (5 × 3¼ × ¼in)	Plywood
	Ramp	1 off	406 × 127 × 6mm (16 × 5 × ¼in)	Plywood
	Sides	2 off	425 × 216 × 6mm (16¾ × 8½ × ¼in)	Plywood
	Base	1 off	425 × 127 × 6mm (16¾ × 5 × ¼in)	Plywood
	Hinged end	1 off	216 × 127 × 6mm (8½ × 5 × ¼in)	Plywood
	Fixed end	1 off	127 × 20 × 6mm (5 × ¾ × ¼in)	Plywood
Keep assembly	Tower – Front and rear	2 off	356 × 225 × 6mm (14 × 9 × ¼in)	Plywood
	Tower – Sides	2 off	356 × 114 × 6mm (14 × 4½ × ¼in)	Plywood
	Tower – Upper floor	1 off	213 × 114 × 6mm (8½ × 4½ × ¼in)	Plywood
	Door	2 off	113 × 49 × 6mm (4⁷⁄₁₆ × 1¹⁵⁄₁₆ × ¼in)	Timber
		1 off	113 × 20 × 6mm (4⁷⁄₁₆ × ¾ × ¼in)	Timber

	Balcony – Front	1 off	325 × 67 × 6mm (13 × 2⅝ × ¼in)	Plywood
	Balcony – Sides	2 off	165 × 67 × 6mm (6½ × 2⅝ × ¼in)	Plywood
	Balcony – Rear	2 off	67 × 50 × 6mm (2⅝ × 2 × ¼in)	Plywood
	Balcony – Floor	1 off	313 × 165 × 6mm (12½ × 6½ × ¼in)	Plywood
Small tower assembly	Front and rear	2 off	152 × 99 × 6mm (6 × 4 × ¼in)	Plywood
	Sides	2 off	152 × 75 × 6mm (6 × 3 × ¼in)	Plywood
	Upper floor	1 off	87 × 75 × 6mm (3½ × 3 × ¼in)	Plywood
Side wall assembly	Wall	1 off	165 × 124 × 6mm (6½ × 4⅞ × ¼in)	Plywood
	Walkway	1 off	165 × 25 × 6mm (6½ × 1 × ¼in)	Timber
	Base	1 off	165 × 25 × 12mm (6½ × 1 × ½in)	Timber
Rear wall assembly	Wall	1 off	125 × 124 × 6mm (5 × 4⅞ × ¼in)	Plywood
	Walkway	1 off	125 × 25 × 6mm (5 × 1 × ¼in)	Timber
	Base	1 off	125 × 25 × 12mm (5 × 1 × ½in)	Timber
Front corner wall assembly				
	Front wall	1 off	225 × 165 × 6mm (9 × 6½ × ¼in)	Plywood
	Side wall	1 off	245 × 165 × 6mm (9¾ × 6½ × ¼in)	Plywood
	Front walkway	1 off	175 × 44 × 12mm (7 × 1¾ × ½in)	Timber
	Side walkway	1 off	245 × 44 × 12mm (9¾ × 1¾ × ½in)	Timber
Drawbridge tower assembly				
	Tower – Front and rear	2 off	229 × 200 × 6mm (9 × 8 × ¼in)	Plywood
	Tower – Sides	2 off	229 × 100 × 6mm (9 × 4 × ¼in)	Plywood
	Tower – Upper floor	1 off	200 × 88 × 6mm (8 × 3½ × ¼in)	Plywood
	Tower – Base	1 off	212 × 114 × 6mm (8½ × 4½ × ¼in)	Plywood
	Drawbridge	1 off	127 × 73 × 6mm (5 × 2⅞ × ¼in)	Plywood
		1 off	127 × 20 × 6mm (5 × ¾ × ¼in)	Timber
	Balcony – Front	1 off	100 × 64 × 6mm (4 × 2½ × ¼in)	Plywood
	Balcony – Sides	2 off	64 × 50 × 6mm (2½ × 2 × ¼in)	Plywood
	Balcony – Floor	1 off	100 × 44 × 6mm (4 × 1¾ × ¼in)	Plywood
	Winding assembly	1 off	248 (9¾in) × 9mm (⅜in) diam dowelling	
		1 off	51mm (2in) × 9mm (⅜in) diam dowelling	
		1 off	51 × 16 × 16mm (2 × ⅝ × ⅝in)	Timber
		1 off	16 × 16 × 12mm (⅝ × ⅝ × ½in)	Timber
Rampart assembly	Front wall	1 off	275 × 114 × 6mm (11 × 4½ × ¼in)	Plywood
	Side walls	2 off	114 × 88 × 6mm (4½ × 3½ × ¼in)	Plywood
	Upper floor	1 off	267 × 88 × 6mm (10½ × 3½ × ¼in)	Plywood

Ancillaries

4 off	25mm (1in) brass hinges (ramp and drawbridge)	
4 off	20mm (¾in) brass hinges (keep door)	
2 off	Hooks and screwed eyes (ramp)	
1 off	600mm (24in) length of 3mm (⅛in) pitch chain (drawbridge)	

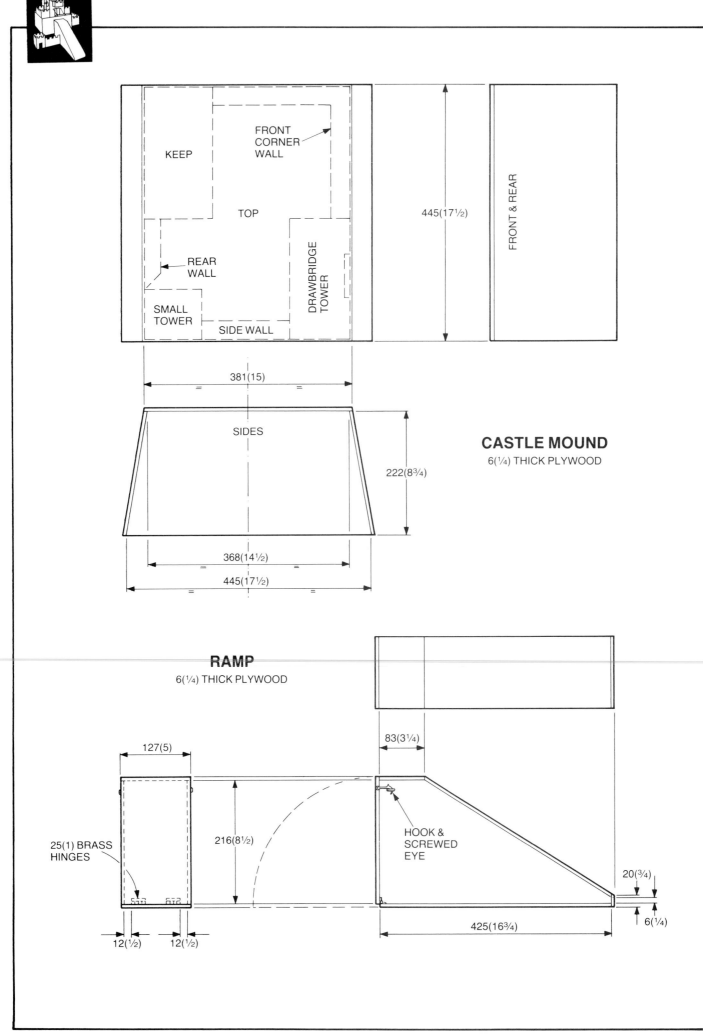

KEEP

FRONT CORNER WALL

TOP

REAR WALL

SMALL TOWER

SIDE WALL

DRAWBRIDGE TOWER

FRONT & REAR

445(17½)

381(15)

SIDES

222(8¾)

368(14½)

445(17½)

CASTLE MOUND
6(¼) THICK PLYWOOD

RAMP
6(¼) THICK PLYWOOD

83(3¼)

127(5)

216(8½)

25(1) BRASS HINGES

HOOK & SCREWED EYE

20(¾)

6(¼)

12(½)   12(½)

425(16¾)

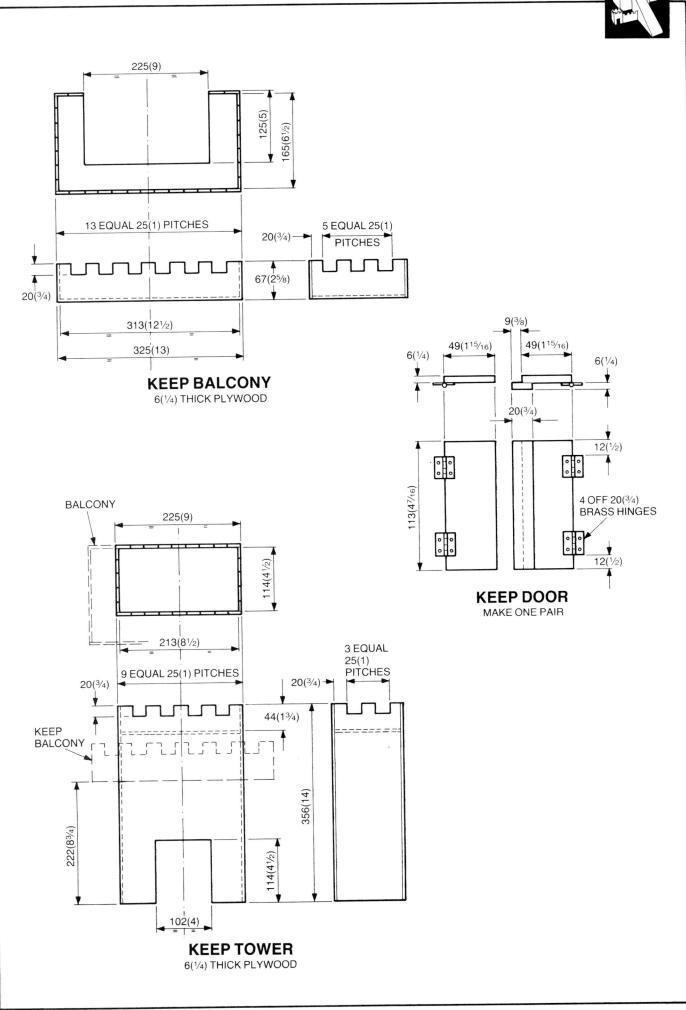

225(9)

125(5)

165(6½)

13 EQUAL 25(1) PITCHES

5 EQUAL 25(1) PITCHES

20(¾)

20(¾)

67(2⅝)

313(12½)

325(13)

KEEP BALCONY
6(¼) THICK PLYWOOD

9(⅜)

49(1¹⁵/₁₆) 49(1¹⁵/₁₆)

6(¼)

6(¼)

20(¾)

12(½)

113(4⁷/₁₆)

4 OFF 20(¾)
BRASS HINGES

12(½)

KEEP DOOR
MAKE ONE PAIR

BALCONY

225(9)

114(4½)

213(8½)

9 EQUAL 25(1) PITCHES

3 EQUAL
25(1)
PITCHES

20(¾)

20(¾)

KEEP
BALCONY

44(1¾)

356(14)

222(8¾)

114(4½)

102(4)

KEEP TOWER
6(¼) THICK PLYWOOD

107

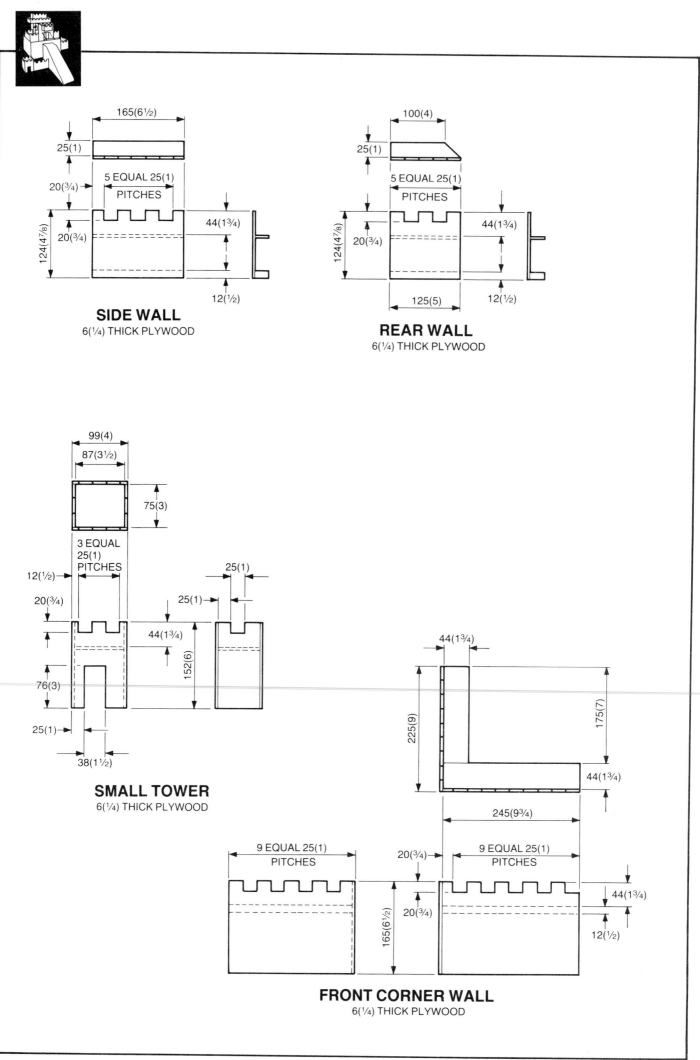

SIDE WALL
6(¼) THICK PLYWOOD

165(6½)
25(1)
20(¾)
124(4⅞)
20(¾)
44(1¾)
12(½)
5 EQUAL 25(1) PITCHES

REAR WALL
6(¼) THICK PLYWOOD

100(4)
25(1)
124(4⅞)
20(¾)
44(1¾)
125(5)
12(½)
5 EQUAL 25(1) PITCHES

SMALL TOWER
6(¼) THICK PLYWOOD

99(4)
87(3½)
75(3)
3 EQUAL 25(1) PITCHES
12(½)
20(¾)
44(1¾)
76(3)
25(1)
38(1½)
152(6)
25(1)
25(1)

FRONT CORNER WALL
6(¼) THICK PLYWOOD

44(1¾)
225(9)
175(7)
44(1¾)
245(9¾)
9 EQUAL 25(1) PITCHES
20(¾)
9 EQUAL 25(1) PITCHES
20(¾)
165(6½)
44(1¾)
12(½)

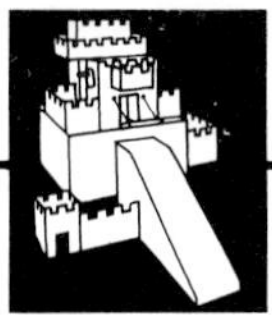

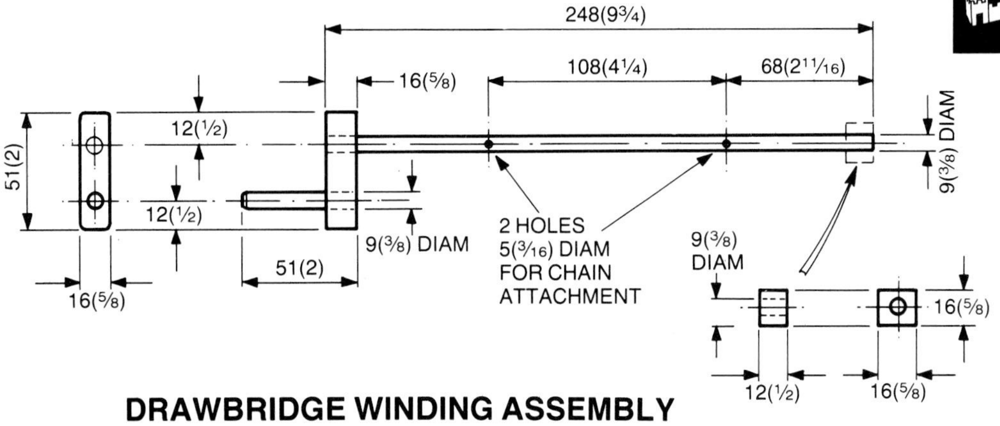

248(9 3/4)
16(5/8)
108(4 1/4)
68(2 11/16)
12(1/2)
51(2)
12(1/2)
9(3/8) DIAM
9(3/8) DIAM
51(2)
16(5/8)
2 HOLES
5(3/16) DIAM
FOR CHAIN
ATTACHMENT
9(3/8)
DIAM
16(5/8)
12(1/2)
16(5/8)

DRAWBRIDGE WINDING ASSEMBLY

END STOP TO BE PINNED IN POSITION ONCE THE TOWER IS ASSEMBLED

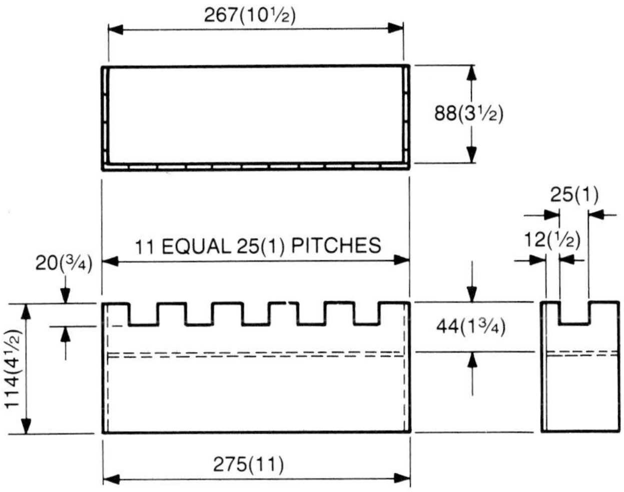

267(10 1/2)
88(3 1/2)
25(1)
12(1/2)
11 EQUAL 25(1) PITCHES
20(3/4)
44(1 3/4)
114(4 1/2)
275(11)

RAMPART 6(1/4) THICK PLYWOOD

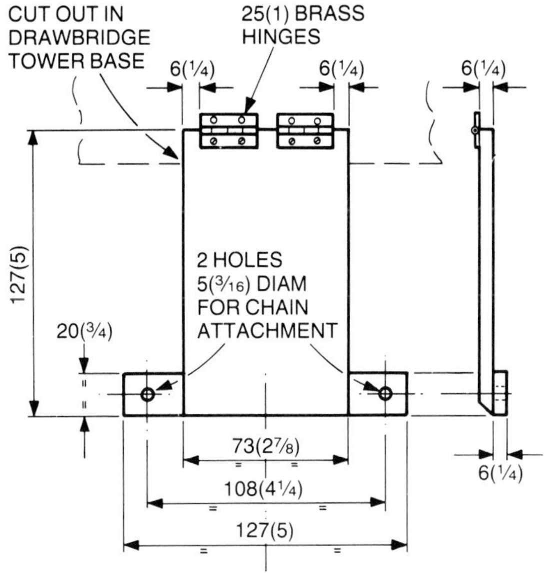

CUT OUT IN
DRAWBRIDGE
TOWER BASE
25(1) BRASS
HINGES
6(1/4)
6(1/4)
6(1/4)
127(5)
2 HOLES
5(3/16) DIAM
FOR CHAIN
ATTACHMENT
20(3/4)
73(2 7/8)
108(4 1/4)
127(5)
6(1/4)

DRAWBRIDGE

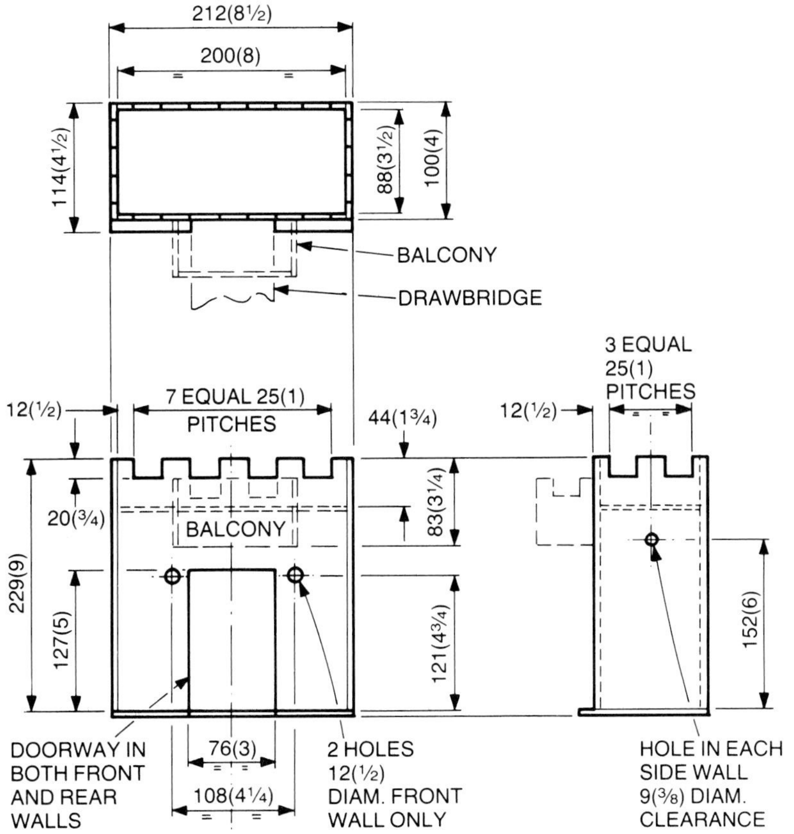

212(8 1/2)
200(8)
114(4 1/2)
88(3 1/2)
100(4)
BALCONY
DRAWBRIDGE
3 EQUAL
25(1)
PITCHES
12(1/2)
7 EQUAL 25(1)
PITCHES
44(1 3/4)
12(1/2)
229(9)
20(3/4)
BALCONY
83(3 1/4)
127(5)
121(4 3/4)
152(6)
DOORWAY IN
BOTH FRONT
AND REAR
WALLS
76(3)
108(4 1/4)
2 HOLES
12(1/2)
DIAM. FRONT
WALL ONLY
HOLE IN EACH
SIDE WALL
9(3/8) DIAM.
CLEARANCE

DRAWBRIDGE TOWER 6(1/4) THICK PLYWOOD

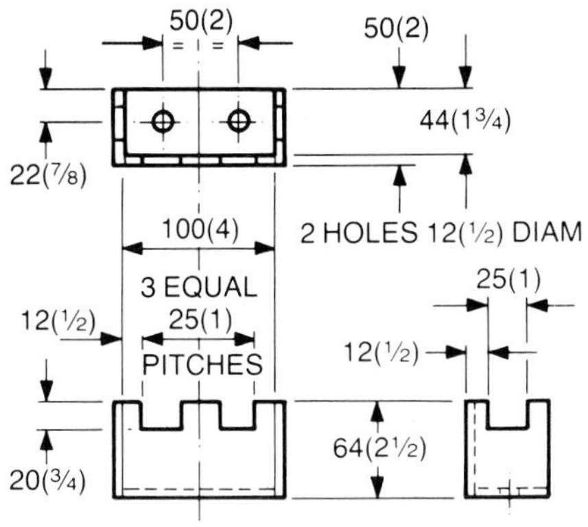

50(2)
50(2)
44(1 3/4)
22(7/8)
100(4)
2 HOLES 12(1/2) DIAM
3 EQUAL
25(1)
PITCHES
12(1/2)
25(1)
12(1/2)
64(2 1/2)
20(3/4)

DRAWBRIDGE TOWER BALCONY

6(1/4) THICK PLYWOOD

Playing with a toy farmyard gives a child so much scope for imagination. The pigs have to be moved, the cows milked and the sheep are always getting out. Today there are some really superb model animals available. In my last toy book I gave all the necessary instruction for making farm buildings – I now feel it's time that we had a tractor and trailer. I admit that, from a practical point of view, these ones are out of scale with my farm, but I haven't found that this has spoilt the pleasure of any young farmers I know!

The inspiration to build this model came from watching a David Brown tractor working a headland in Cornwall. Sadly the machine is no longer in production, but it is surprising how many of them can still be found doing a good day's work. Transfers for the sides are not available so I made mine by using rub-on lettering which is available from major stationers. The woods used were beech and elm but any good hardwood would be suitable.

1 Mark and cut out the chassis. Drill the holes for the counter balance weight pin. The counter balance weights on the front of a tractor are, so I am reliably told, necessary to counter balance the heavy implements such as the plough, which are mounted at the rear. Make a counter balance weight pin and two weights from dowel rod.

2 Cut out the halving joints on the underside of the chassis. As I felt it was necessary to have some means of steering, the sides of the halving joint at the front end have to be cut at angles to allow for front axle steerage.

3 Drill a hole at the rear end of the chassis for the hitch pin.

4 Cut out the cab floor which will hold the rear axle. Carefully mark the position of the axle hole from both sides and then, holding the floor in a vice and taking great care to hold the drill at 90°, drill approximately half way through from both sides until the hole is complete.

5 Mark and cut out the front axle frame. Drill the axle holes using the same method as described above. (I have always found it easier to do all the drilling first and then remove the waste wood.) Attach the front axle frame to the underside of the chassis using a small coach bolt (easily obtainable from hardware shops) and, just to make sure it stays secure, use a spring star washer under the nut.

6 The engine block is basically a solid piece of wood but, to add some interest and to try and make it *look* like an engine, I cut a variety of small pieces of wood and glued these onto the sides. It's not vital exactly where they go or how many you cut, but they do make the final toy look more realistic. Make the radiator grille in the same way. Drill the hole for the steering wheel at a 45° angle and bore a small hole on the underside of the block to allow the coach bolt head room.

7 Make the exhaust stack by carefully planing a piece of dowel rod to shape. Fit the two smaller pieces of dowel on either end. In the interests of safety it is a good idea to fit a piece of flexible rubber tube, available from motor accessory shops, to the top of the exhaust stack.

8 Make the steering wheel and glue it into the hole in the engine block.

9 The seat is an interesting exercise in wood shaping and whittling. Rough the basic shape out with a coping saw, then use a small gouge, a chisel and a wood-carving knife to finish it off.

10 Cut out the cab front bulkhead and side walls. The cab bulkhead, in particular, has to be very carefully marked out so as to fit snugly around the engine block.

11 Now cut out the windows using a coping saw. Perhaps the most time-consuming part of making this model is tidying up these windows. I find a variety of things helpful, especially using different diameter dowel rods with glasspaper wrapped around them to get into awkward places. I also found that the tractor cab looked better if a slight chamfer was applied to all the outside edges of the windows. This 'tidying-up' is one of those fiddly jobs that is irksome but if not done spoils the entire look of the finished toy. Do not fit the plastic for the windscreen until all the shaping *and* varnishing has been done.

12 Cut and shape the cab roof, mudguards and the steps.

13 Once all the pieces have been cut and the shaping and glasspapering completed, assemble the parts 'dry' to check that everything fits. When you are satisfied that all is well glue the parts together.

14 After the glue has dried, apply the rub-on lettering and fit the axles, wheels and spring caps (see Accessories, page 215).

Cutting list

Chassis	I off	305 × 54 × 22mm (12 × 2⅛ × ⅞in)	Timber
Cab floor	I off	108 × 92 × 20mm (4¼ × 3⅝ × ¾in)	Timber
Counter balance weight pin	I off	38mm (1½in) × 12mm (½in) diam dowelling	
	I off	67mm (2⅝in) × 6mm (¼in) diam dowelling	
Counter balance weight	2 off	51 × 16 × 12mm (2 × ⅝ × ½in)	Timber
Front axle frame	I off	108 × 51 × 22mm (4¼ × 2 × ⅞in)	Timber
Steps	2 off	38 × 22 × 12mm (1½ × ⅞ × ½in)	Timber
Engine block	I off	165 × 60 × 35mm (6½ × 2⅜ × 1⅜in)	Timber
	2 off	152 × 12 × 6mm (6 × ½ × ¼in)	Timber
	2 off	47 × 32 × 6mm (1⅞ × 1¼ × ¼in)	Timber
	I off	76mm (3in) × 6mm (¼in) diam dowelling	
	I off	67mm (2⅝in) × 12mm (½in) diam dowelling	
Radiator	Make from	83 × 5 × 1·5mm (3¼ × ³⁄₁₆ × ¹⁄₁₆in)	Timber
Exhaust stack	I off	57mm (2¼in) × 20mm (¾in) diam dowelling	
	2 off	38mm (1½in) × 9mm (⅜in) diam dowelling	
Cab side wall	2 off	152 × 127 × 16mm (6 × 5 × ⅝in)	Timber
Cab roof	I off	133 × 108 × 16mm (5¼ × 4¼ × ⅝in)	Timber
Steering wheel	I off	6mm (¼in) × 32mm (1¼in) diam dowelling	
	I off	54mm (2⅛in) × 6mm (¼in) diam dowelling	
Cab front bulkhead	I off	152 × 92 × 9mm (6 × 3⅝ × ⅜in)	Timber
Mudguard	2 off	76 × 25 × 16mm (3 × 1 × ⅝in)	Timber
Seat	I off	70 × 38 × 38mm (2¾ × 1½ × 1½in)	Timber
Hitch pin	I off	57mm (2¼in) × 8mm (⁵⁄₁₆in) diam dowelling	
Ancillaries			
	2 off	102mm (4in) diam road wheels	
	2 off	51mm (2in) diam road wheels	
	I off	159mm (6¼in) × 6mm (¼in) diam steel axle	
	I off	152mm (6in) × 6mm (¼in) diam steel axle	
	4 off	Spring dome caps to suit 6mm (¼in) diam axle	
	I off	51mm (2in) × 6mm (¼in) diam coach bolt, spring washer and nuts	
	I off	102mm (4in) length of chain	
	I off	73 × 51 × 1·5mm (2⅞ × 2 × ¹⁄₁₆in) clear plastic	

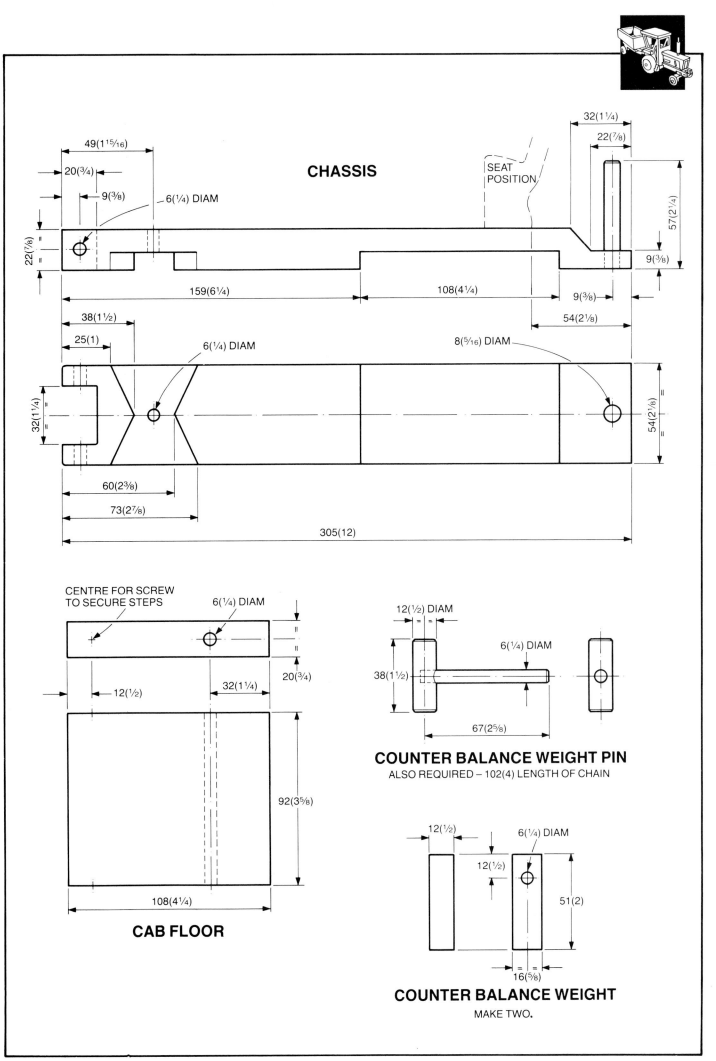

CHASSIS

SEAT POSITION

49(1¹⁵⁄₁₆)

20(³⁄₄)

9(³⁄₈)

6(¹⁄₄) DIAM

22(⁷⁄₈)

32(1¹⁄₄)

22(⁷⁄₈)

57(2¹⁄₄)

9(³⁄₈)

159(6¹⁄₄)

108(4¹⁄₄)

9(³⁄₈)

54(2¹⁄₈)

38(1¹⁄₂)

25(1)

6(¹⁄₄) DIAM

8(⁵⁄₁₆) DIAM

32(1¹⁄₄)

54(2¹⁄₈)

60(2³⁄₈)

73(2⁷⁄₈)

305(12)

CENTRE FOR SCREW
TO SECURE STEPS

6(¹⁄₄) DIAM

20(³⁄₄)

12(¹⁄₂)

32(1¹⁄₄)

92(3⁵⁄₈)

108(4¹⁄₄)

CAB FLOOR

12(¹⁄₂) DIAM

6(¹⁄₄) DIAM

38(1¹⁄₂)

67(2⁵⁄₈)

COUNTER BALANCE WEIGHT PIN

ALSO REQUIRED – 102(4) LENGTH OF CHAIN

12(¹⁄₂)

6(¹⁄₄) DIAM

12(¹⁄₂)

51(2)

16(⁵⁄₈)

COUNTER BALANCE WEIGHT

MAKE TWO.

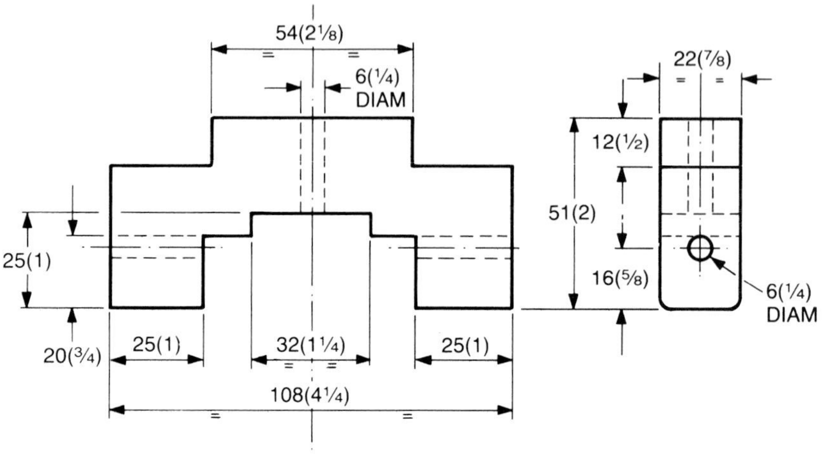
54(2 1/8)
6(1/4) DIAM
25(1)
20(3/4)
25(1)
32(1 1/4)
25(1)
108(4 1/4)
22(7/8)
12(1/2)
51(2)
16(5/8)
6(1/4) DIAM

FRONT AXLE FRAME

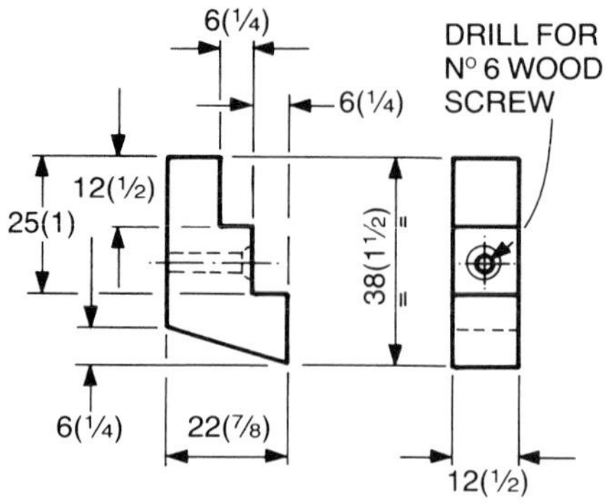
6(1/4)
6(1/4)
DRILL FOR N° 6 WOOD SCREW
12(1/2)
25(1)
38(1 1/2)
6(1/4)
22(7/8)
12(1/2)

STEPS – MAKE TWO

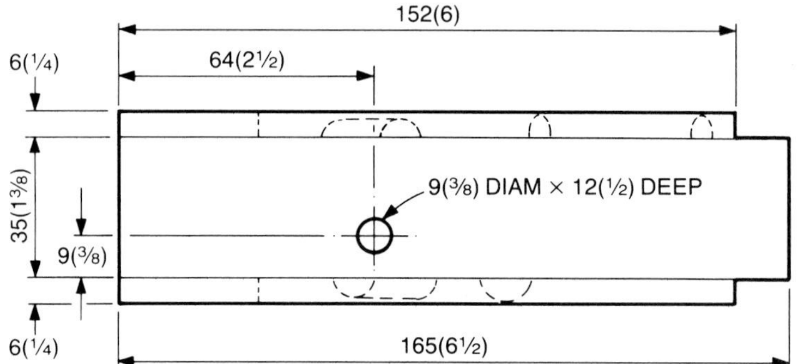
152(6)
64(2 1/2)
6(1/4)
35(1 3/8)
9(3/8) DIAM × 12(1/2) DEEP
9(3/8)
6(1/4)

ENGINE BLOCK

LOCALLY RELIEVE UNDERSIDE OF BLOCK FOR THE HEAD OF THE FRONT AXLE COACH BOLT

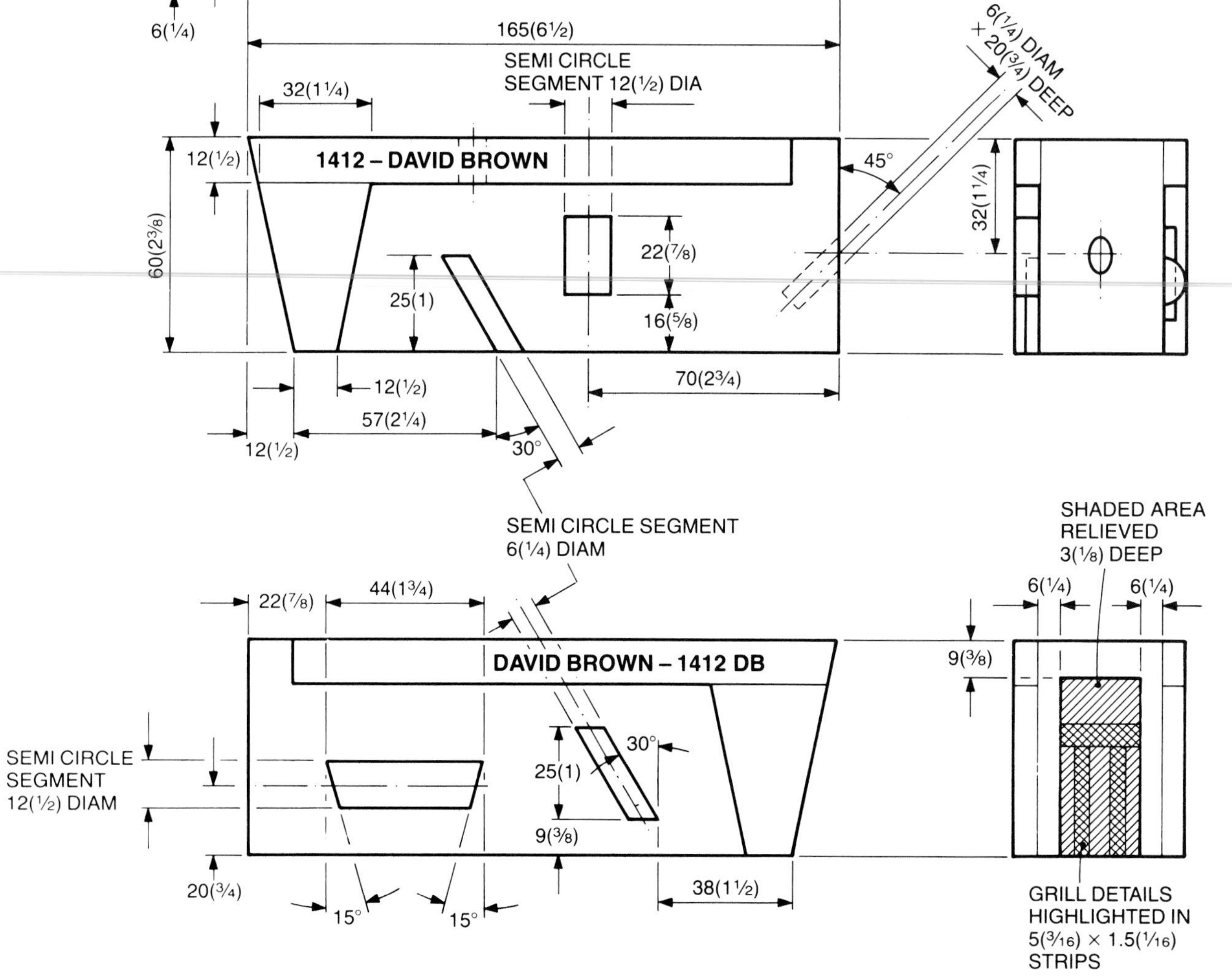
165(6 1/2)
SEMI CIRCLE SEGMENT 12(1/2) DIA
32(1 1/4)
6(1/4) DIAM × 20(3/4) DEEP
12(1/2)
1412 – DAVID BROWN
45°
60(2 3/8)
22(7/8)
32(1 1/4)
25(1)
16(5/8)
12(1/2)
70(2 3/4)
57(2 1/4)
12(1/2)
30°
SEMI CIRCLE SEGMENT 6(1/4) DIAM
SHADED AREA RELIEVED 3(1/8) DEEP
22(7/8)
44(1 3/4)
6(1/4)
6(1/4)
DAVID BROWN – 1412 DB
9(3/8)
SEMI CIRCLE SEGMENT 12(1/2) DIAM
30°
25(1)
9(3/8)
20(3/4)
15°
15°
38(1 1/2)
GRILL DETAILS HIGHLIGHTED IN 5(3/16) × 1.5(1/16) STRIPS

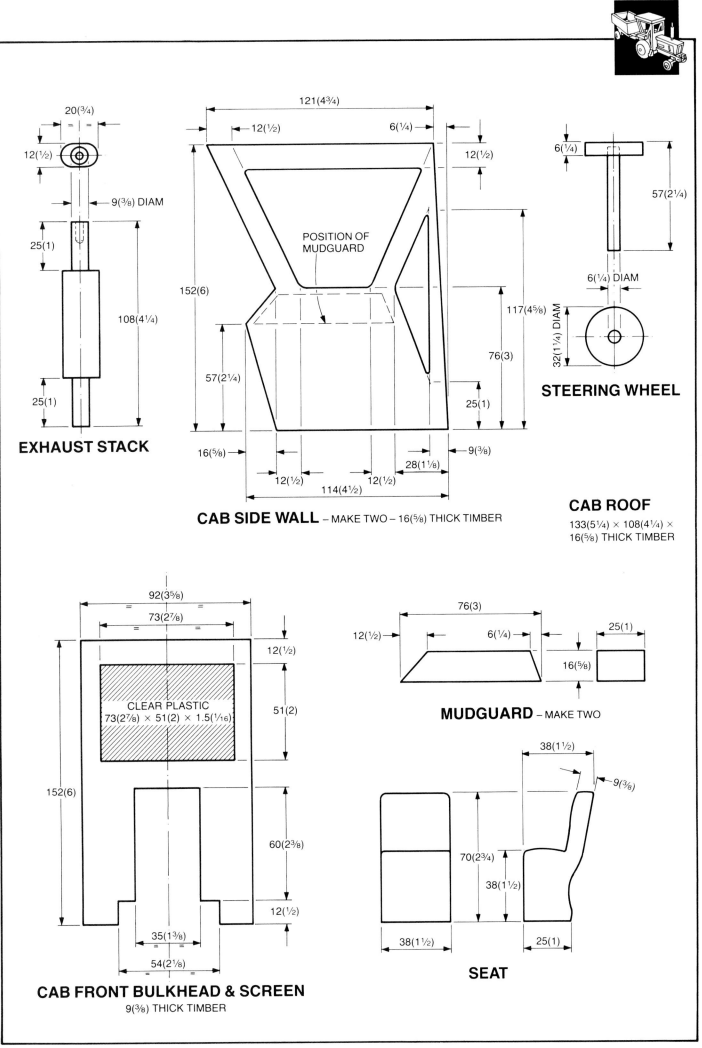

EXHAUST STACK

20(¾)
12(½)
9(⅜) DIAM
25(1)
108(4¼)
25(1)

121(4¾)
12(½)
6(¼)
12(½)
POSITION OF MUDGUARD
152(6)
117(4⅝)
76(3)
57(2¼)
25(1)
16(⅝)
12(½)
12(½)
28(1⅛)
9(⅜)
114(4½)

CAB SIDE WALL – MAKE TWO – 16(⅝) THICK TIMBER

6(¼)
57(2¼)
6(¼) DIAM
32(1¼) DIAM

STEERING WHEEL

CAB ROOF

133(5¼) × 108(4¼) ×
16(⅝) THICK TIMBER

92(3⅝)
73(2⅞)
12(½)
CLEAR PLASTIC
73(2⅞) × 51(2) × 1.5(1/16)
51(2)
152(6)
60(2⅜)
12(½)
35(1⅜)
54(2⅛)

CAB FRONT BULKHEAD & SCREEN
9(⅜) THICK TIMBER

76(3)
12(½)
6(¼)
25(1)
16(⅝)

MUDGUARD – MAKE TWO

38(1½)
9(⅜)
70(2¾)
38(1½)
38(1½)
25(1)

SEAT

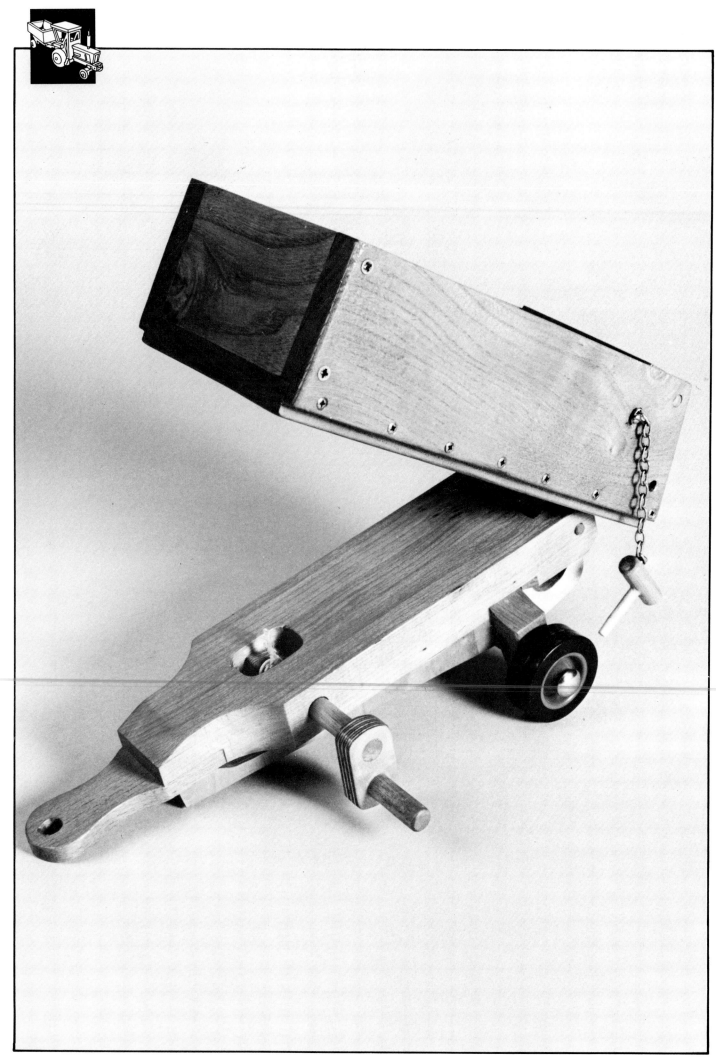

DAVID BROWN TRAILER

The tractor is incomplete and would lose a great deal of its play value if you didn't go on to make this fairly simple trailer.

1 Start by carefully marking and cutting out the trailer chassis. Cut the recess on the underside to take the axle unit and the recess for the tow hitch at the front. Now drill the hole at the back to take the pivot pin for the tipping mechanism and the hole that takes the winch handle.

In order to make room for the nylon cord to 'wind on' as the trailer is being tipped it is also necessary to cut a hole and a groove in the chassis. When the winding mechanism is finally assembled this hole allows you to tie the nylon cord to the rod, and to position and glue on to the winding rod 2 spacers that prevent the rod coming out. The groove prevents the cord rubbing on the underside of the chassis.

2 Now mark and cut out the axle block. I found it easier to drill the axle hole right through the axle before cutting out the centre recess. Once this is done, countersink the holes for the screws that will secure the axle to the chassis.

3 Cut out and shape the trailer hitch, drill the hole for the hitch pin and glue the hitch to the chassis.

4 Glue the forward and rear under chassis members onto the underside of the chassis to represent the underframe strengthening. Actually they are only there for decoration as without them the chassis looks very uninteresting.

5 Now make the trailer container. Cut out the front, sides, tailgate and floor. Cut the rebates in the sides and drill the holes for the tailgate dowels and the lock pin in both the sides and tailgate. Glue the tailgate dowels into the holes in the tailgate.

6 Slot the protruding ends of the dowels into the holes in the sides. The tailgate should swing freely so that when the container is winched up, its contents tip out easily.

7 Glue the front and floor onto the container sides.

8 Make the tailgate lock pin and attach it with a length of cord or chain and a screwed eye to the container. When the lock pin is inserted into the tailgate through the container side the flap will remain closed. When the trailer is raised and the lock pin is withdrawn the flap should open automatically.

9 Cut out the block of wood that fits onto the underside of the container floor and drill the dowel rod hole. Glue the block in place. Assemble the container and the chassis by inserting the trailer floor dowel right through the holes in the chassis and the floor block. This joint needs to be carefully checked as the dowel rod needs to move easily in the trailer floor block. When you are satisfied with the fit, glue the ends of the dowel into the chassis.

10 The tipping mechanism is very simple. Screw a hook eye into the trailer floor block. Knot a piece of nylon cord through this eye and pass one end through the hole in the axle and tie it onto the shaft of the winding handle. You will now find out how useful the large hole is that you cut earlier in the chassis, as the cord has to be knotted onto the shaft of the winch handle while it is in place. It is a good idea to 'set' the handle at a convenient place for the winding since it is very positive and only ¾ of a turn should raise the container completely. I found the best position for the handle to be at '1 o'clock' so that you press down to start the container lifting.

11 The little winch handle on the end of the winding shaft is easily made, but as it will have to do a great deal of work it's a good idea not only to glue the dowel rods in, but also to drive in a small panel pin – this will lock the handles securely in place.

12 Now fit the steel axle into the axle block and, after chamfering the ends of the steel rod, fit on the wheels and spring caps.

Cutting list

Chassis	1 off	270 × 79 × 28mm (10⅝ × 3⅛ × 1⅛in)	Timber
Hitch	1 off	102 × 41 × 9mm (4 × 1⅝ × ⅜in)	Timber
Spacer block	2 off	20 × 20 × 9mm (¾ × ¾ × ⅜in)	Timber
Winch handle	1 off	51 × 25 × 12mm (2 × 1 × ½in)	Timber
	Make from 171mm (6¾in) × 12mm (½in) diam dowelling		
Forward under chassis member	2 off	191 × 22 × 9mm (7½ × ⅞ × ⅜in)	Timber
Rear under chassis member	2 off	41 × 22 × 9mm (1⅝ × ⅞ × ⅜in)	Timber
Axle block	1 off	105 × 47 × 22mm (4⅛ × 1⅞ × ⅞in)	Timber
Trailer floor	1 off	267 × 114 × 16mm (10½ × 4½ × ⅝in)	Timber
	1 off	49 × 38 × 32mm (1¹⁵⁄₁₆ × 1½ × 1¼in)	Timber
	1 off	79mm (3⅛in) × 6mm (¼in) diam dowelling	
Trailer front	1 off	102 × 67 × 16mm (4 × 2⅝ × ⅝in)	Timber
Trailer side	2 off	263 × 76 × 16mm (10⅜ × 3 × ⅝in)	Timber
Tailgate	1 off	102 × 70 × 16mm (4 × 2¾ × ⅝in)	Timber
	2 off	41mm (1⅝in) × 6mm (¼in) diam dowelling	
Tailgate lock pin	1 off	35mm (1⅜in) × 9mm (⅜in) diam dowelling	
	1 off	38mm (1½in) × 6mm (¼in) diam dowelling	

Ancillaries

	2 off	51mm (2in) diam road wheels
	1 off	159mm (6¼in) × 6mm (¼in) diam steel axle
	2 off	Spring dome caps to suit 6mm (¼in) diam axle
	4 off	6mm (¼in) washers
	1 off	Screwed eye
	1 off	305mm (12in) length of strong cord
	1 off	102mm (4in) length of chain for tailgate lock pin

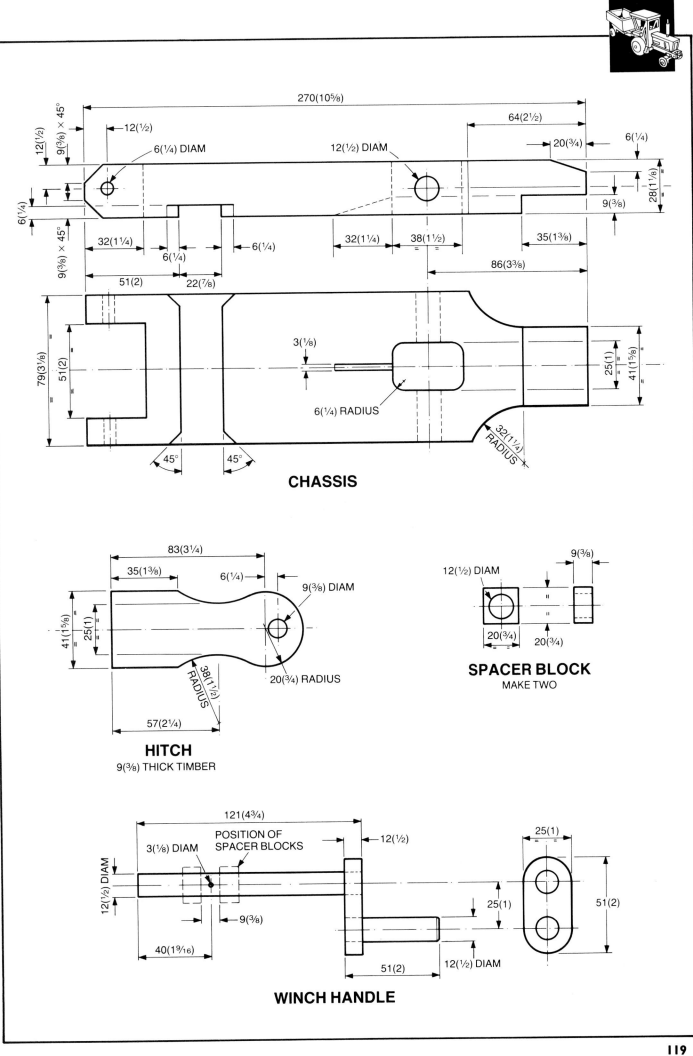

CHASSIS

HITCH

9(³⁄₈) THICK TIMBER

SPACER BLOCK

MAKE TWO

WINCH HANDLE

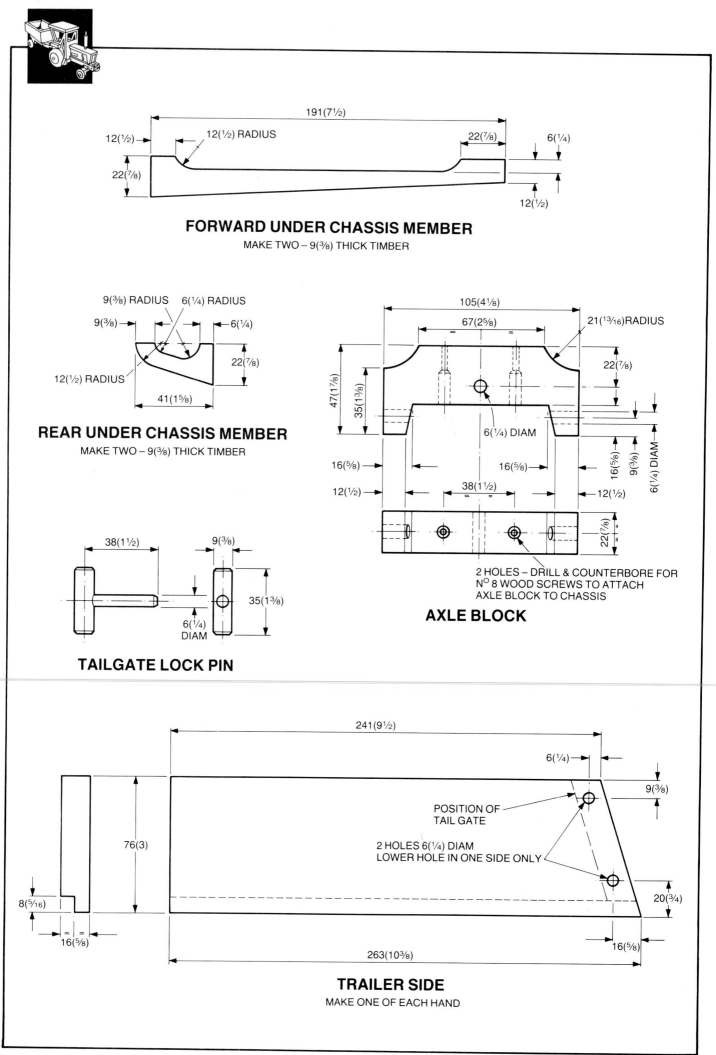

FORWARD UNDER CHASSIS MEMBER
MAKE TWO – 9(³⁄₈) THICK TIMBER

REAR UNDER CHASSIS MEMBER
MAKE TWO – 9(³⁄₈) THICK TIMBER

AXLE BLOCK

2 HOLES – DRILL & COUNTERBORE FOR
N⁰ 8 WOOD SCREWS TO ATTACH
AXLE BLOCK TO CHASSIS

TAILGATE LOCK PIN

POSITION OF
TAIL GATE

2 HOLES 6(¹⁄₄) DIAM
LOWER HOLE IN ONE SIDE ONLY

TRAILER SIDE
MAKE ONE OF EACH HAND

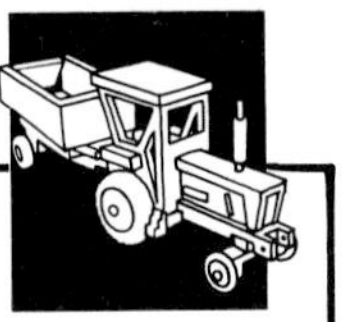

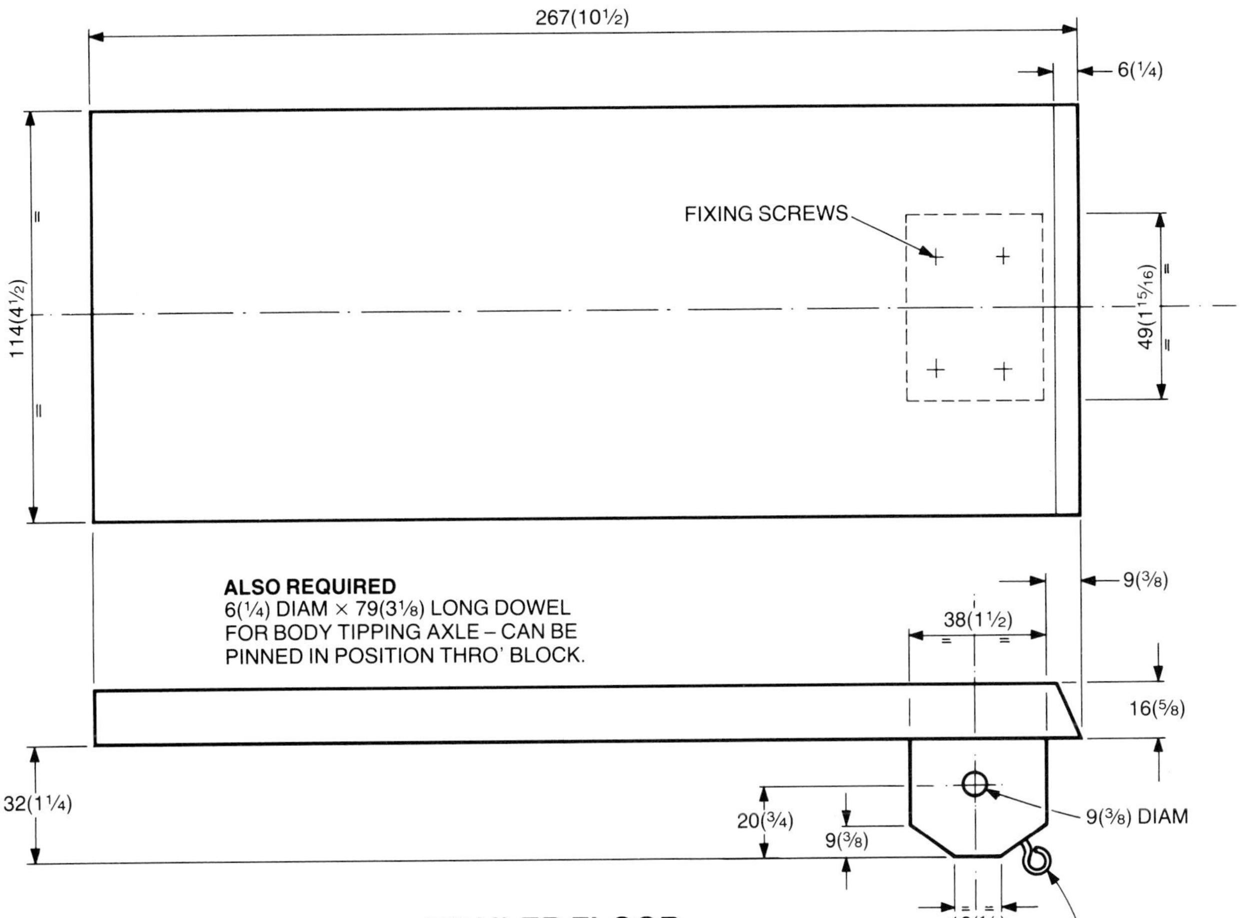
267(10½)
6(¼)
FIXING SCREWS
114(4½)
49(1 15/16)
9(⅜)
ALSO REQUIRED
6(¼) DIAM × 79(3⅛) LONG DOWEL
FOR BODY TIPPING AXLE – CAN BE
PINNED IN POSITION THRO' BLOCK.
38(1½)
16(⅝)
32(1¼)
20(¾)
9(⅜)
9(⅜) DIAM
12(½)
SCREWED EYE

TRAILER FLOOR

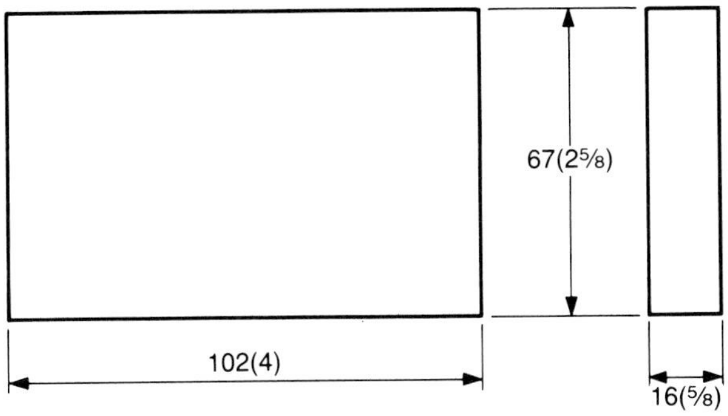
67(2⅝)
102(4)
16(⅝)

TRAILER FRONT

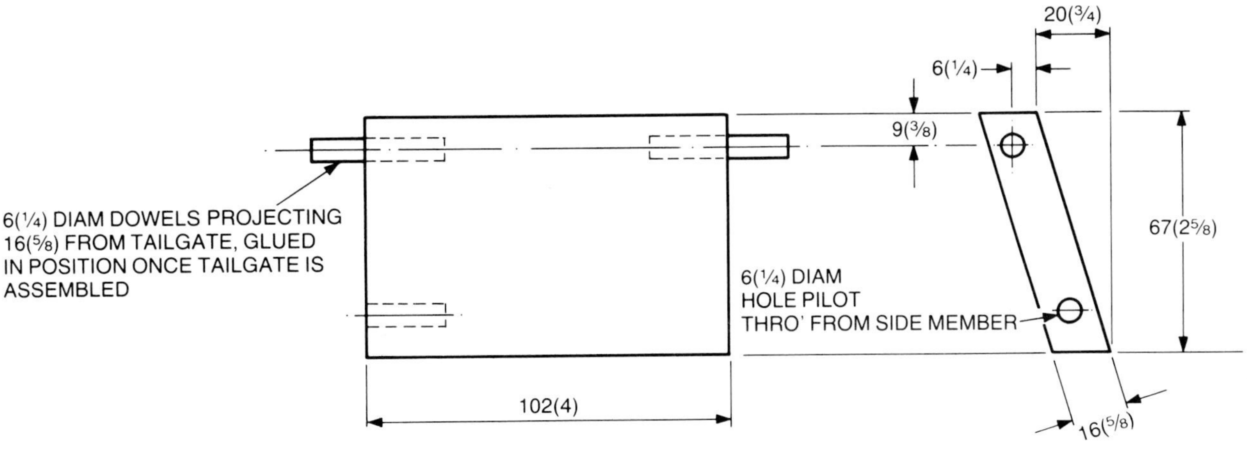
20(¾)
6(¼)
9(⅜)
67(2⅝)
6(¼) DIAM DOWELS PROJECTING
16(⅝) FROM TAILGATE, GLUED
IN POSITION ONCE TAILGATE IS
ASSEMBLED
6(¼) DIAM
HOLE PILOT
THRO' FROM SIDE MEMBER
102(4)
16(⅝)

TAILGATE

TRACTION ENGINE

The sight, sound and smell of one of these fine old traction engines puffing to a show never fails to fill me with a sense of wonder and a feeling that I was born too late! Perhaps that is why making this wooden version gave me so much pleasure. It is made from a combination of woods. I used oak for the road wheels, bulkheads, canopy etc. and elm for the boiler, but any hardwood is suitable. One essential tool for making this model is a wood-turning lathe. Now this is a fairly expensive piece of equipment, but there are drill-powered lathes available now which should be within the financial grasp of keen woodworkers.

1 Start by marking and cutting out the cab sides and rear wall. Now any corner joint will do to hold the pieces together, but I used through dovetails. The dovetail joint is my favourite joint and as this engine was made to be looked at as well as played with, I decided I would use the one I like best. If you have never cut a dovetail before then practise on a scrap piece of wood first. Basically the method is this:

i Make a template by marking out the shape and angle of the dovetail on hardboard and cutting it out.

ii Work out the required spacing of the tails and mark them in pencil on the edge of the piece of wood (in this case the cab side walls), using the template to draw round.

iii When you are sure that the dovetails you have marked are correctly spaced, mark with a knife and carefully cut them out with a fine-toothed saw (see page 210).

iv Place the cut-out tails against the end grain of the other piece of wood to be jointed (in this case the cab rear wall) and mark the pins, in between which the dovetails must fit. Cut out the pins. Ideally the pins and tails should fit together first time and no shavings should have to be pared off with a chisel, but you may need some practice to achieve this. Persevere though – the through dovetail joint is, I believe, one of the prettiest decorative joints in cabinet making and well worth the effort.

By the way, they have been arguing over the rights and wrongs of tails first or pins since Egyptian craftsmen (or was it the Chinese?) first cut the dovetail. I am a tail man.

2 Cut the housing joint in the cab side walls to take the cab front bulkhead. Cut the large diameter hole in the cab front bulkhead which will take the spigot end of the boiler. (This hole can be cut with a tank cutter.)

3 Cut the recess to take the towing hook in the cab rear wall. Cut out and assemble the towing hook.

4 Fit both cab side walls together, using tape to keep them in place, and drill the axle holes. Be careful **not** to drill the hole for the flywheel axle in the right-hand cab wall right through to the other side of the wood.

5 Now turn the flywheel and the rear and front wheels on the lathe. This sort of job is a good introduction to lathe work and you will soon gain confidence. I decided to decorate the front wheels and leave the rear wheels plain.

6 The next task is to turn the boiler, not a difficult shape, and, of course, it's a matter of personal choice what band decoration you add using a small chisel.

7 Now turn the chimney. I feel this definitely looks better with a few decorative lines around the top. The tapered shape of the chimney is best cut with a gouge, although when you become experienced at wood turning you can use a skew chisel. Don't forget to allow sufficient length on the bottom of the chimney to go into the boiler barrel.

8 Now return to the boiler and drill the large diameter hole for the chimney. This hole has to be carefully aligned at 90° in both planes. (A drill stand and a helper will be useful here!) It is important to make this a 'tidy hole' as you will have spent quite a bit of time making the boiler and it would be a shame to spoil it.

9 Mark out the front axle and then drill the axle hole from both ends. Once the hole has been drilled you can cut out the two semi-circles of the axle itself. Great care is necessary when cutting out the semi-circle that the bottom of the boiler rests on. If you find you have to make 'a little adjustment' here a useful tip is to wrap a piece of glasspaper around the boiler barrel and rub the front axle onto it.

10 The front canopy support frame is a little difficult as it is vital to bore the holes supporting the roof at a 15° angle. My method was to cut out from a piece of hardboard a large template with an angle of 15°. I then fixed the bottom of the support frame (the piece that fits onto the boiler) into a vice, lined up the template and drill at 15° and started drilling. It is always useful to have someone to watch while you do this since in the other 'plane' you still have to be drilling at 90°! You then have to repeat this procedure with the top piece of the canopy frame. Fortunately the rear canopy support frame presents no such difficulties.

11 Cut out the cab floor and the canopy. Drill the hole in the canopy that is to take the chimney, being careful to make it as tidy as possible to avoid spoiling the final look of the model.

12 Now for the final assembly. It is always an advantage only to glue all the parts together when all the major pieces have been cut out and finally shaped. You can always use elastic bands to hold the model together if you wish to gain some impression of the final object prior to this point. Use epoxy resin glue and matt polyurethane for the finish, although I

'polished' the wheels and boiler on the lathe and left them unvarnished (see Materials and Finishes, page 214).

Cutting list

Boiler	1 off	216mm (8½in) × 73mm (2⅞in) diam	Timber
Chimney stack	1 off	219mm (8⅝in) × 32mm (1¼in) diam	Timber
Canopy support frame (front)	1 off	178 × 22 × 16mm (7 × ⅞ × ⅝in)	Timber
	1 off	108 × 22 × 20mm (4¼ × ⅞ × ¾in)	Timber
	2 off	149mm (5⅞in) × 12mm (½in) diam dowelling	
Canopy support frame (rear)	1 off	178 × 22 × 16mm (7 × ⅞ × ⅝in)	Timber
	2 off	187mm (7⅜in) × 12mm (½in) diam dowelling	
Cab side wall	2 off	210 × 105 × 16mm (8¼ × 4⅛ × ⅝in)	Timber
Cab front bulkhead	1 off	137 × 89 × 12mm (5⅜ × 3½ × ½in)	Timber
Cab rear wall	1 off	108 × 70 × 12mm (4¼ × 2¾ × ½in)	Timber
Cab floor	1 off	146 × 108 × 6mm (5¾ × 4¼ × ¼in)	Timber
Canopy	1 off	419 × 188 × 12mm (16½ × 7½ × ½in)	Timber
Front axle	1 off	130 × 57 × 32mm (5⅛ × 2¼ × 1¼in)	Timber
Front wheel assembly	2 off	32mm (1¼in) × 76mm (3in) diam	Timber
	1 off	197mm (7¾in) × 12mm (½in) diam dowelling	
Rear wheel assembly	2 off	47mm (1⅞in) × 108mm (4¼in) diam	Timber
	1 off	243mm (9⅝in) × 12mm (½in) diam dowelling	
Flywheel assembly	1 off	16mm (⅝in) × 92mm (3⅝in) diam	Timber
	1 off	121mm (4¾in) × 12mm (½in) diam dowelling	
	2 off	20 × 20 × 16mm (¾ × ¾ × ⅝in)	Timber
Towing hook	1 off	44 × 20 × 12mm (1¾ × ¾ × ½in)	Timber
	1 off	70mm (2¾in) × 12mm (½in) diam dowelling	

Ancillaries

	1 off	12mm (½in) i/diam × 20mm (¾in) o/diam × 25mm (1in) tube spacer	
	1 off	12mm (½in) i/diam × 20mm (¾in) o/diam × 9mm (⅜in) tube spacer	

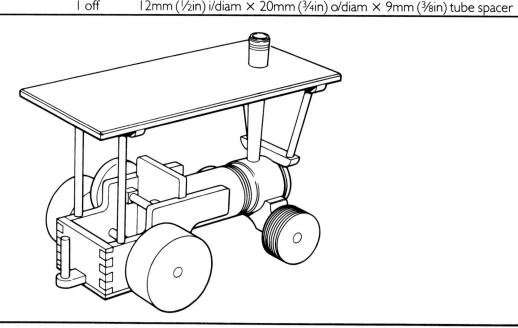

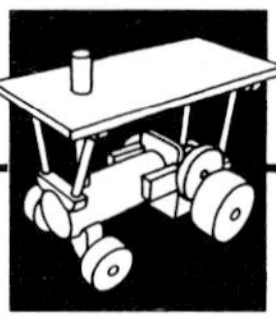

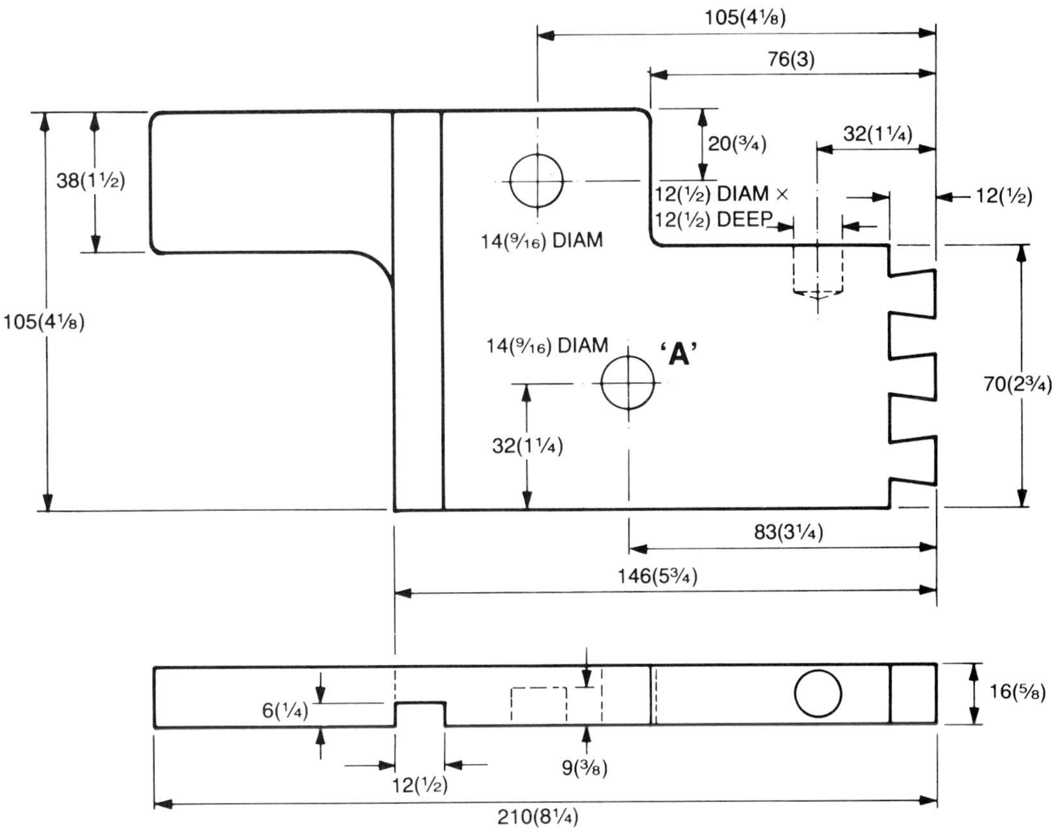
105(4⅛)
76(3)
32(1¼)
20(¾)
38(1½)
12(½) DIAM ×
12(½) DEEP
12(½)
14(9⁄16) DIAM
105(4⅛)
14(9⁄16) DIAM
'A'
70(2¾)
32(1¼)
83(3¼)
146(5¾)
6(¼)
16(⅝)
9(⅜)
12(½)
210(8¼)

CAB SIDE WALL MAKE TWO

GROOVE MUST BE ON OPPOSITE FACE ON FLYWHEEL SIDE WALL AND HOLE 'A' MUST BE DRILLED THROUGH.

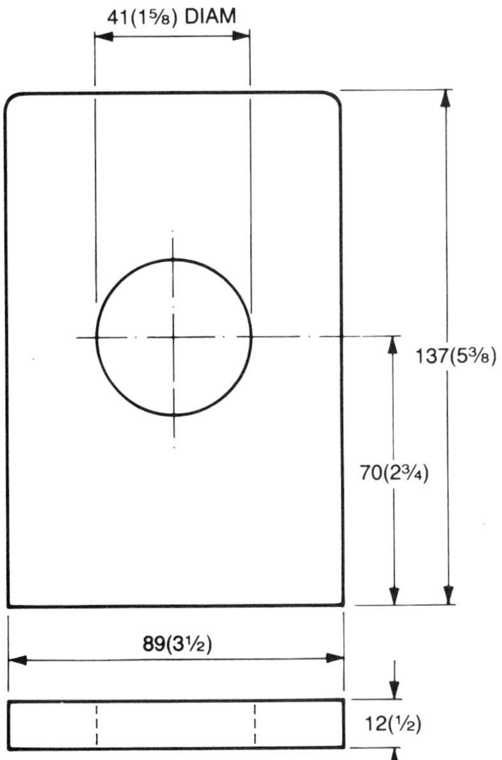
41(1⅝) DIAM
137(5⅜)
70(2¾)
89(3½)
12(½)

CAB FRONT BULKHEAD

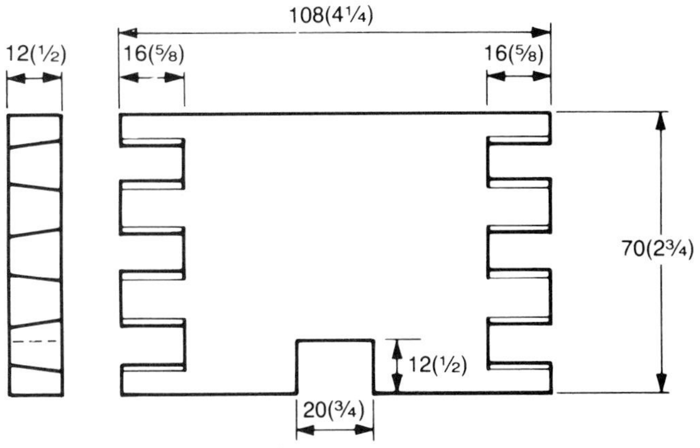
108(4¼)
12(½)
16(⅝)
16(⅝)
70(2¾)
12(½)
20(¾)

CAB REAR WALL

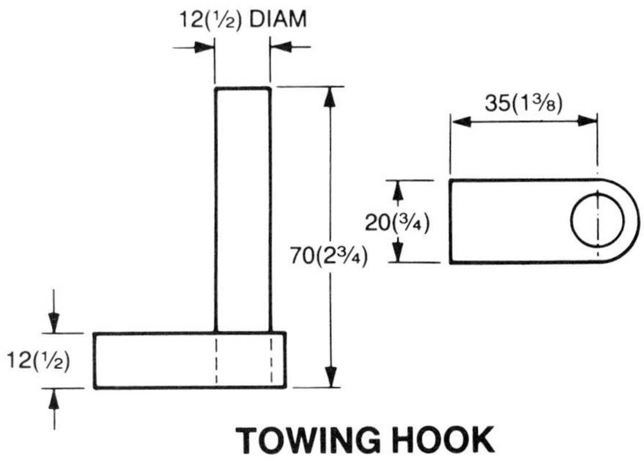
12(½) DIAM
35(1⅜)
20(¾)
70(2¾)
12(½)

TOWING HOOK

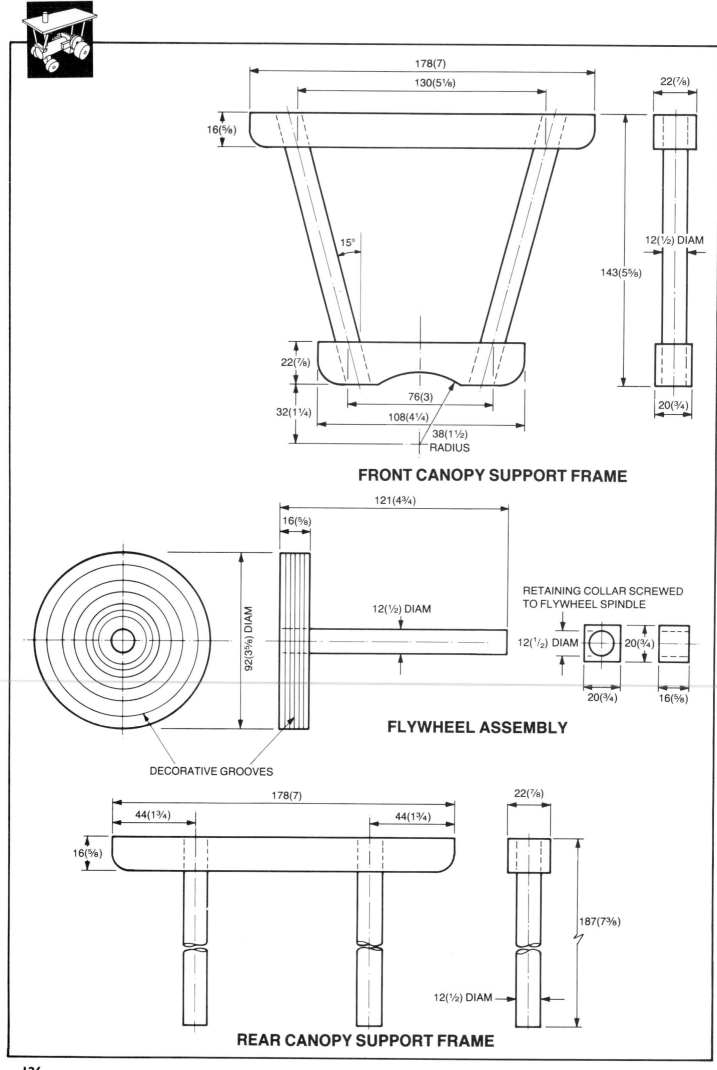

178(7)

130(5⅛)

16(⅝)

22(⅞)

15°

143(5⅝)

12(½) DIAM

22(⅞)

32(1¼)

76(3)

108(4¼)

20(¾)

38(1½)
RADIUS

FRONT CANOPY SUPPORT FRAME

121(4¾)

16(⅝)

92(3⅝) DIAM

12(½) DIAM

RETAINING COLLAR SCREWED
TO FLYWHEEL SPINDLE

12(½) DIAM

20(¾)

20(¾)

16(⅝)

DECORATIVE GROOVES

FLYWHEEL ASSEMBLY

178(7)

44(1¾)

44(1¾)

22(⅞)

16(⅝)

187(7⅜)

12(½) DIAM

REAR CANOPY SUPPORT FRAME

126

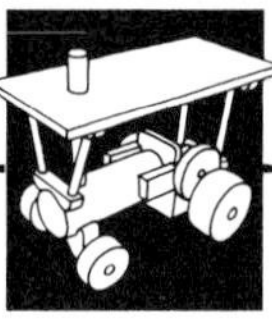

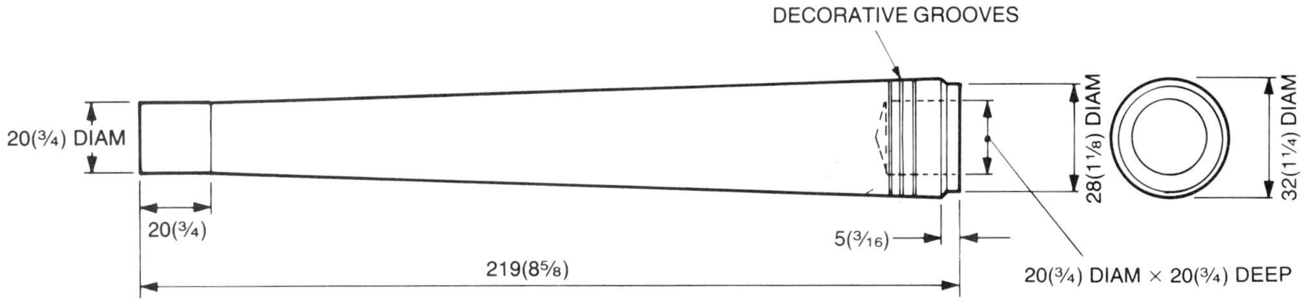
DECORATIVE GROOVES
20(3/4) DIAM
20(3/4)
219(8 5/8)
5(3/16)
28(1 1/8) DIAM
32(1 1/4) DIAM
20(3/4) DIAM × 20(3/4) DEEP

CHIMNEY STACK

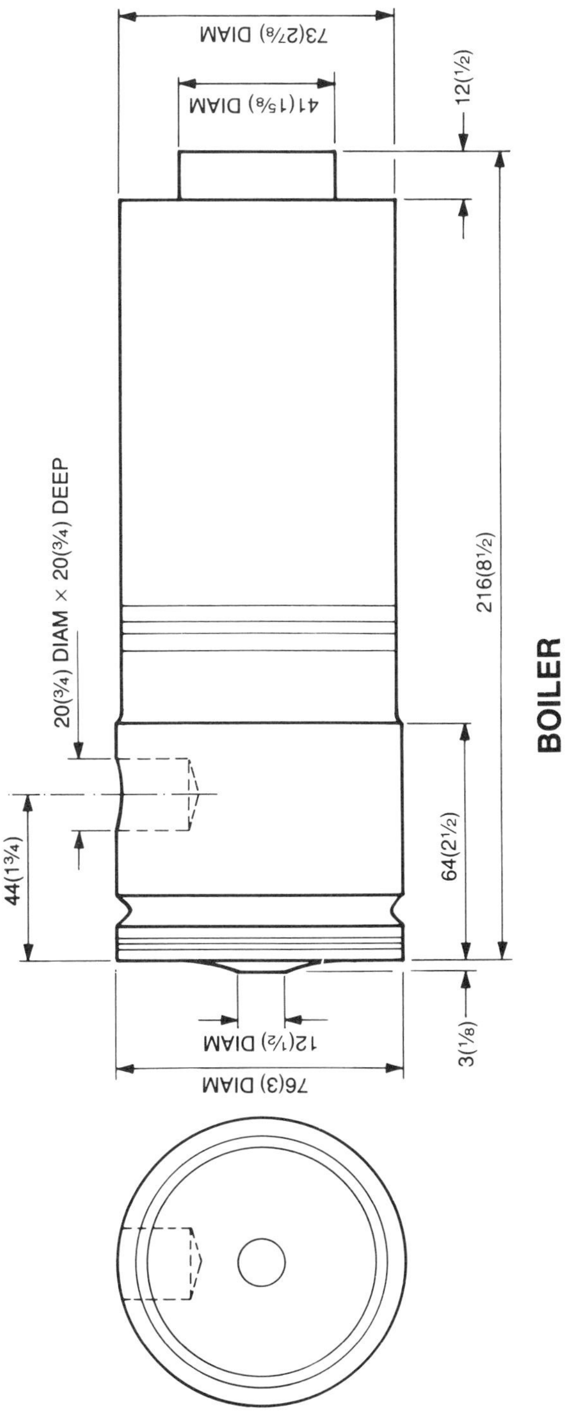
73(2 7/8) DIAM
41(1 5/8) DIAM
12(1/2)
216(8 1/2)
20(3/4) DIAM × 20(3/4) DEEP
44(1 3/4)
64(2 1/2)
3(1/8)
12(1/2) DIAM
76(3) DIAM

BOILER

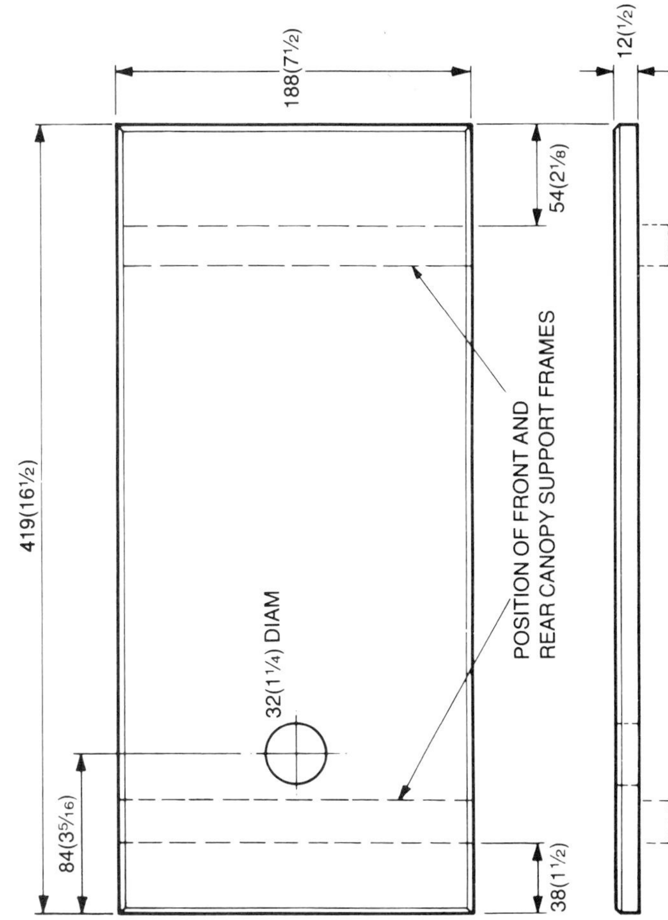
188(7 1/2)
12(1/2)
54(2 1/8)
419(16 1/2)
POSITION OF FRONT AND
REAR CANOPY SUPPORT FRAMES
32(1 1/4) DIAM
84(3 5/16)
38(1 1/2)

CANOPY

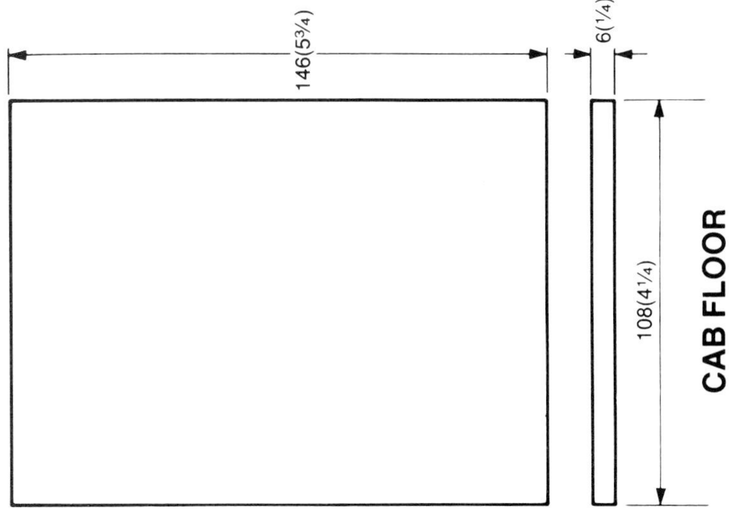
146(5 3/4)
6(1/4)
108(4 1/4)

CAB FLOOR

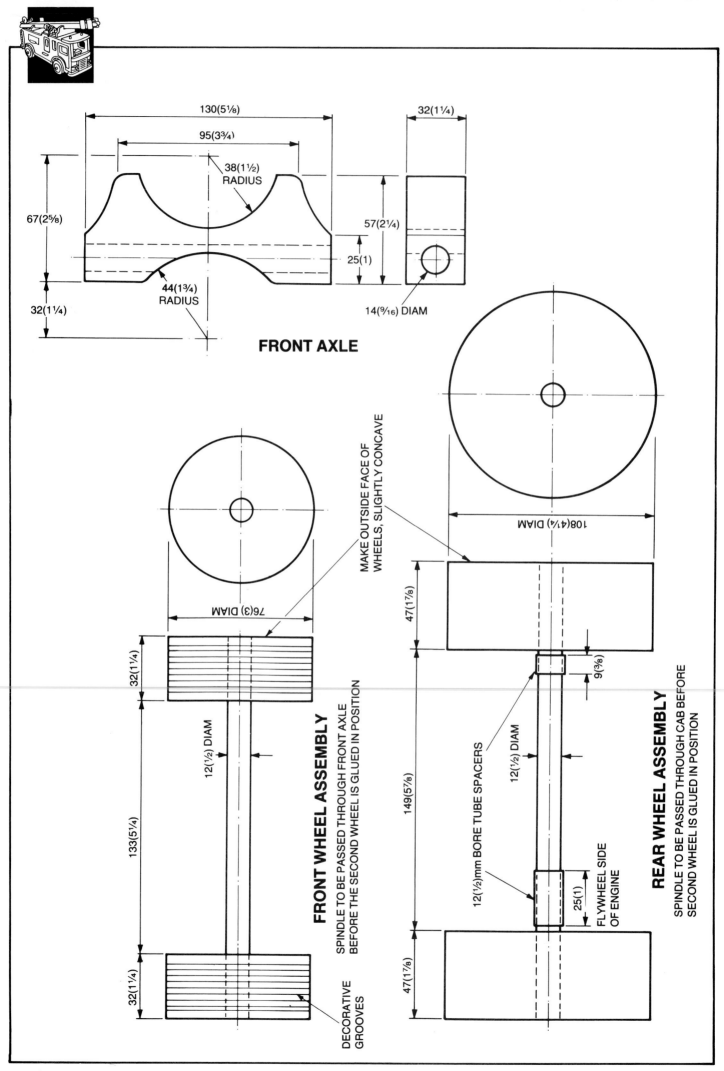

130(5⅛)

95(3¾)

38(1½)
RADIUS

67(2⅝)

32(1¼)

44(1¾)
RADIUS

32(1¼)

57(2¼)

25(1)

14(9/16) DIAM

FRONT AXLE

MAKE OUTSIDE FACE OF
WHEELS, SLIGHTLY CONCAVE

76(3) DIAM

32(1¼)

12(½) DIAM

133(5¼)

32(1¼)

DECORATIVE
GROOVES

FRONT WHEEL ASSEMBLY

SPINDLE TO BE PASSED THROUGH FRONT AXLE
BEFORE THE SECOND WHEEL IS GLUED IN POSITION

108(4¼) DIAM

47(1⅞)

9(3/8)

12(½) DIAM

149(5⅞)

12(½)mm BORE TUBE SPACERS

25(1)

FLYWHEEL SIDE
OF ENGINE

47(1⅞)

REAR WHEEL ASSEMBLY

SPINDLE TO BE PASSED THROUGH CAB BEFORE
SECOND WHEEL IS GLUED IN POSITION

DENNIS FIRE ENGINE

The sight and sound of a fire engine rushing to the scene of a fire is always exciting and since my early years I have been fascinated by the great variety of fire tenders that are to be found in most city fire stations. Gleaming paintwork, polished chrome, nicely blacked tyres all point to the pride with which the crews cherish their engines.

This is not the simplest of models to make, but the final result is well worth the effort. I made the engine in parana pine as I wanted to get a reddish effect without using paint. However, beech or any of the African mahoganies would be equally suitable. Fittings such as pumps, lights and so on can sometimes be difficult to get. I have a ready supply of pumps (please see Accessories, page 215), but the electric lights, spot lamp, etc, can all be found in model shops or even car accessory shops. It really is a case of hunting for the bits and pieces. Some model railway shops stock light-emitting diodes – these make ideal headlights.

1   Start by cutting out the vehicle under chassis panel and glueing the two rear wheel arches in place. Note the notches that have to be cut out of the arches to support the rear bulkhead.

2   Make the two side panels, but be careful not to confuse the right- and left-hand sides when marking and cutting out.

3   The two side panels are held together by four plywood panels which have to be rebated and eventually glued into place. The rebates should be cut in the side panels with a router, of which two kinds are available, the hand router and the electric router. The latter has become very popular in the last five years and is an extremely versatile machine. Using a router ensures that the bottom of the rebate is uniform throughout its length – this is extremely difficult to achieve with a hand-held chisel.

4   After you have cut all the rebates on the inner sides of the side panels you can start work on the outer sides. In order to get some realism into the outside shape, I cut grooves around the doors and windows and cut locker shapes on the nearside panel. This does require skill if you are using hand tools, but with an electric router it's a simple matter of choosing a small grooving bit and off you go.

5   Now glue and panel pin the wheel arches and running board trim onto the sides. Once the glue has set, careful shaping with a small chisel and gouge is necessary to form a rounded edge. This is quite a time-consuming operation, but it does look most effective when done carefully. I also glued and pinned a piece of trim onto each driver door and a step below each crew door for extra authenticity.

6   Cut out the hatch, fit on the hatch handle with screws, then fix the hatch onto the offside panel with hinges. This hides the switch panel from view but allows easy access to it.

7   Cut and shape the front cab roof and rear cabin roof. Cut rebates on the undersides so that they will fit snugly onto the side panels. Cut and fit the front ladder support into a rebate cut in the top of the rear cabin roof. As the water

pump unit is housed in this section it is advisable to use small brass screws to fix the rear cabin roof to the sides rather than glue, since from time to time maintenance may need to be carried out to the pump and tubes. The fitting of the pump will vary according to which pump unit you buy.

The front cab roof also has a rebate cut on the front of the underside to hold the perspex windscreen at the top edge.

8   Cut out and assemble the extension hose mounting with its handle and spindle. This carries an extra length of hose and should be attached to the rear cabin roof with a screw.

9   Access to the water reservoir (small plastic box) and batteries in the back of the engine is through the hinged cover, onto which you must glue the rear ladder support. It is advisable to buy the accessories before fitting any container supports in this compartment. When you come to fit the cover, the hinge must be screwed to a hinge block which in turn is screwed to the central plywood cross panel.

10   I made the search light by 'cannibalising' an old torch complete with lens, etc. and fitting this into a shaped wooden block. I then drilled a hole in the base of the block and into the top edge of the nearside panel at the back to take a dowel rod to hold the searchlight. At the back of the search light unit I also fixed a small block to act as a clamp for the wire. Wind the twin flex wire tightly round a small piece of dowel rod from the clamp to the point where it goes into the engine. When you withdraw the rod the wire will remain neatly coiled.

11   Now cut out the cab front panel and glue on the four pieces of timber to make the radiator. The radiator grill can be made to look even more realistic if you obtain a piece of aluminium mesh and fit this into a rebate instead of cutting radiator grooves as shown. If you decide to fit electric lights they should be incorporated into the grill at this stage of construction. The front panel is rebated to fit onto the cab side panels.

12   Make the driver's and crew seats next and make and fit the steering wheel.

Many small details can now be added to the inside of the cab. You could cut out dials, for instance, from card, paint them and glue them in position.

13 Make the two small ladders and pin one on each side panel. These allow the crew to climb onto the roof.

14 Fit the hinge block for the main ladder onto the rear bulkhead, which should also be drilled with holes for the search light wire and hose and fitted with the search light switch. Assemble all the pieces of timber for the rear staging and fix the ladder clips in position.

15 Now for the ladder itself. The easiest way to construct this is to cut all the dowel rods to exactly the same length. (If you make a small blockwood jig it will make accurate cutting easier.) The sides of the main ladder and extension ladder should be treated as pairs and taped together with masking tape. Mark on one side the position of the rung holes and drill them right through the two sides. Then separate them and carefully glue all

the dowels into the holes of one side, tapping them firmly home with a hammer.

Before trying to fit the other half of the ladder onto the projecting dowels, countersink the rung holes on the inside of that half. The countersink will help the rungs to locate into the holes. Before you apply any pressure it is vital to line *all* the rungs (dowels) up with the holes. Once the rungs are all in the holes put the ladder in a vice and use the pressure of the vice jaws to squeeze the ladder sides together. Once the dowel rods are through they will touch the vice jaws. By this method it is easy to get the sides of the ladder parallel. (To have parallel sides for the ladders is very important as one 'telescopes' inside the other and any tapering of the sides would prevent this happening.) Both the main and extension ladders are made by the same method.

Fit the guide plates onto the main ladder sides.

16 Cut and shape the winding block, winding handle ratchet and ratchet arm

and assemble them on the ladder. The inner extension ladder is raised by a cord that is tied to the bottom rung of the extension ladder, taken to the top of the main ladder and passed over the top rung. It is then threaded back to the shaft of the winding block. When the handle is turned, the bottom of the extension ladder is pulled to the top of the main ladder where it is prevented from coming out by two dowels fitted in the top of the main ladder.

Fit the complete ladder assembly onto the mounting block on the rear bulkhead with brass hinges.

17 Secure the wheels to the under chassis panel using blocks of wood. Fit two wheels to the front axle and four wheels to the back axle.

18 Before assembling all the different parts it is best to complete the varnishing process (see page 214) which is really quite extensive for this complicated model.

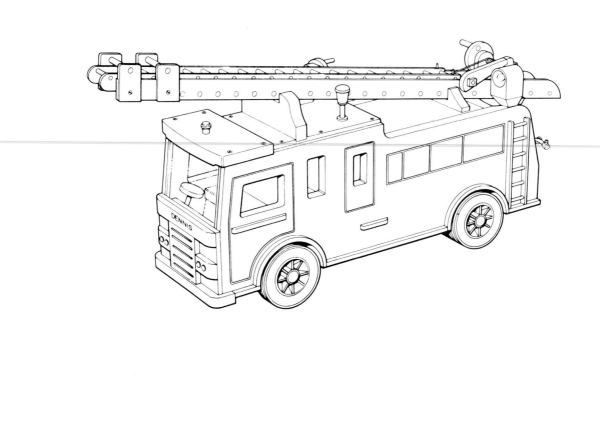

Cutting list

Part	Quantity	Dimensions	Material
Side panel	2 off	610 × 203 × 22mm (24 × 8 × ⅞in)	Timber
Lower trim	Make from 686 × 9 × 9mm (27 × ⅜ × ⅜in)		Timber
Wheel arch trim	Make from 279 × 70 × 9mm (11 × 2¾ × ⅜in)		Timber
Crew door step	Make from 76 × 6 × 6mm (3 × ¼ × ¼in)		Timber
Door trim	Make from 191 × 6 × 3mm (7½ × ¼ × ⅛in)		Timber
Front wheel arch	2 off	127 × 64 × 9mm (5 × 2½ × ⅜in)	Timber
Hatch	1 off	152 × 51 × 9mm (6 × 2 × ⅜in)	Plywood
Hatch handle	1 off	76 × 6 × 6mm (3 × ¼ × ¼in)	Timber
Switch panel	1 off	171 × 70 × 6mm (6¾ × 2¾ × ¼in)	Timber
Switch panel packing	Make from 445 × 9 × 9mm (17½ × ⅜ × ⅜in)		Timber
Chassis panel	1 off	610 × 152 × 9mm (24 × 6 × ⅜in)	Plywood
Rear wheel arch	2 off	121 × 60 × 9mm (4¾ × 2⅜ × ⅜in)	Plywood
Front axle block	1 off	152 × 51 × 32mm (6 × 2 × 1¼in)	Timber
Rear axle block	1 off	92 × 51 × 32mm (3⅝ × 2 × 1¼in)	Timber
Crew area floor	1 off	229 × 146 × 9mm (9 × 5¾ × ⅜in)	Plywood
Cab floor	1 off	146 × 64 × 9mm (5¾ × 2½ × ⅜in)	Plywood
Crew area rear wall	1 off	159 × 146 × 9mm (6¼ × 5¾ × ⅜in)	Plywood
Rear bulkhead	1 off	146 × 121 × 9mm (5¾ × 4¾ × ⅜in)	Plywood
Driver's bench seat	1 off	133 × 70 × 16mm (5¼ × 2¾ × ⅝in)	Timber
Driver's bench back	1 off	133 × 57 × 16mm (5¼ × 2¼ × ⅝in)	Timber
Crew bench seat	1 off	133 × 51 × 9mm (5¼ × 2 × ⅜in)	Plywood
Crew bench back	1 off	133 × 57 × 22mm (5¼ × 2¼ × ⅞in)	Timber
Crew bench support	1 off	133 × 22 × 16mm (5¼ × ⅞ × ⅝in)	Timber
Rear cabin roof	1 off	219 × 159 × 22mm (8⅝ × 6¼ × ⅞in)	Timber
Front cab roof	1 off	184 × 86 × 22mm (7¼ × 3⅜ × ⅞in)	Timber
Hinged cover	1 off	221 × 133 × 9mm (8¹¹⁄₁₆ × 5¼ × ⅜in)	Plywood
Forward hinge block	1 off	133 × 25 × 12mm (5¼ × 1 × ½in)	Timber
Rear hinge block	1 off	133 × 38 × 22mm (5¼ × 1½ × ⅞in)	Timber
Rear staging	1 off	133 × 35 × 9mm (5¼ × 1⅜ × ⅜in)	Plywood
	1 off	133 × 51 × 9mm (5¼ × 2 × ⅜in)	Plywood
	1 off	76 × 32 × 9mm (3 × 1¼ × ⅜in)	Plywood
	1 off	76 × 57 × 9mm (3 × 2¼ × ⅜in)	Plywood
	2 off	60 × 44 × 9mm (2⅜ × 1¾ × ⅜in)	Plywood
	1 off	76 × 9 × 9mm (3 × ⅜ × ⅜in)	Timber
Battery support	1 off	133 × 41 × 9mm (5¼ × 1⅝ × ⅜in)	Plywood
Container support	1 off	133 × 76 × 9mm (5¼ × 3 × ⅜in)	Plywood
Cab front panel	1 off	178 × 102 × 20mm (7 × 4 × ¾in)	Timber
Radiator grill	Make from 286 × 22 × 12mm (11¼ × ⅞ × ½in)		Timber
	1 off	79 × 76 × 12mm (3⅛ × 3 × ½in)	Timber
Steering wheel	1 off	32 × 32 × 6mm (1¼ × 1¼ × ¼in)	Timber
Steering column	1 off	95mm (3¾in) × 6mm (¼in) diam dowelling	
Bumper	1 off	203 × 38 × 25mm (8 × 1½ × 1in)	Timber
Step	1 off	51 × 25 × 6mm (2 × 1 × ¼in)	Timber
Fixed ladder stringers	4 off	152 × 9 × 5mm (6 × ⅜ × ³⁄₁₆in)	Timber
Fixed ladder rungs	12 off	25mm (1in) × 6mm (¼in) diam dowelling	
Front ladder support	1 off	159 × 70 × 22mm (6¼ × 2¾ × ⅞in)	Timber
Rear ladder support	1 off	133 × 32 × 16mm (5¼ × 1¼ × ⅝in)	Timber
Main ladder stringers	2 off	851 × 32 × 8mm (33½ × 1¼ × ⁵⁄₁₆in)	Timber
Main ladder rungs	22 off	57mm (2¼in) × 8mm (⁵⁄₁₆in) diam dowelling	
Main ladder guide plates	4 off	64 × 32 × 8mm (2½ × 1¼ × ⁵⁄₁₆in)	Timber

Main ladder guide pins	2 off	64mm (2½in) × 6mm (¼in) diam dowelling	
Extension ladder stringers	2 off	673 × 25 × 8mm (26½in × 1 × ⁵⁄₁₆in)	Timber
Extension ladder rungs	18 off	38mm (1½in) × 6mm (¼in) diam dowelling	
Extension ladder stops	2 off	20mm (¾in) × 3mm (⅛in) diam dowelling	
Main ladder hinge block	1 off	41 × 32 × 12mm (1⅝ × 1¼ × ½in)	Timber
Ratchet arm	1 off	95 × 24 × 9mm (3¾ × ¹⁵⁄₁₆ × ⅜in)	Plywood
Ratchet arm spindle	1 off	76mm (3in) × 8mm (⁵⁄₁₆in) diam dowelling	
	1 off	16 × 16 × 9mm (⅝ × ⅝ × ⅜in)	Timber
Winding handle	1 off	57 × 57 × 9mm (2¼ × 2¼ × ⅜in)	Timber
	Make from	124mm (4⅞in) × 9mm (⅜in) diam dowelling	
Ratchet	1 off	38 × 38 × 9mm (1½ × 1½ × ⅜in)	Plywood
Winding block	1 off	70 × 57 × 25mm (2¾ × 2¼ × 1in)	Timber
Extension hose mounting	1 off	114 × 51 × 22mm (4½ × 2 × ⅞in)	Timber
Extension hose handle	1 off	44 × 44 × 9mm (1¾ × 1¾ × ⅜in)	Timber
	Make from	178mm (7in) × 8mm (⁵⁄₁₆in) diam dowelling	
Extension hose end stop	1 off	9mm (⅜in) × 20mm (¾in) diam dowelling	
Search light	1 off	64 × 38 × 38mm (2½ × 1½ × 1½in)	Timber
	1 off	25 × 6 × 6mm (1 × ¼ × ¼in)	Timber
	1 off	38mm (1½in) × 8mm (⁵⁄₁₆in) diam dowelling	

Ancillaries

	6 off	102mm (4in) road wheels
	2 off	229mm (9in) × 6mm (¼in) diam steel axles
	4 off	Spring dome caps to suit 6mm (¼in) diam axles
	6 off	25mm (1in) brass hinges
	1 off	140 × 111 × 3mm (5½ × 4⅜ × ⅛in) clear plastic
	1 off	Manual car windscreen washer pump
	1 off	Non-return valve
	2 off	Nozzles
	1 off	1220mm (48in) × 3mm (⅛in) bore plastic tube
	1 off	Water container
	1 off	Lamp and holder for search light
	1 off	Search light switch
	2 off	Flashing lights
	1 off	Flashing light switch
		Batteries to suit
	2 off	Terry clips for 8mm (⁵⁄₁₆in) diam dowelling
	1 off	457mm (18in) length twin flex wire
	2 off	Screwed eyes to retain stowed hoses

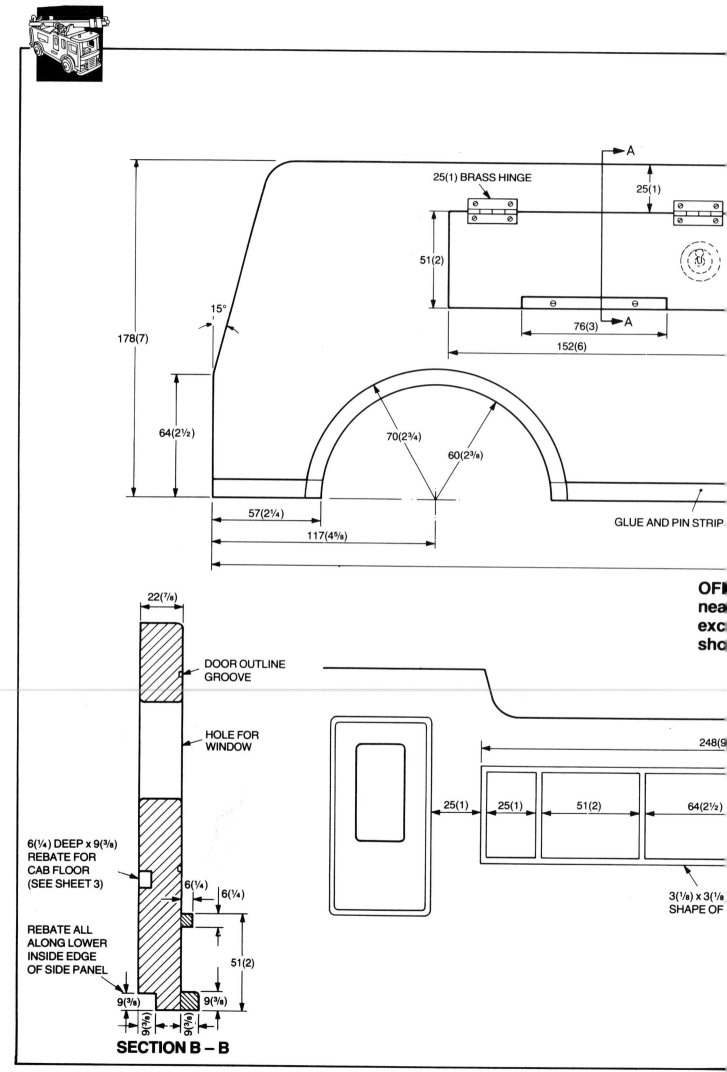

25(1) BRASS HINGE

25(1)

51(2)

178(7)

15°

64(2½)

76(3)

152(6)

70(2¾)

60(2⅜)

57(2¼)

117(4⁵⁄₈)

GLUE AND PIN STRIP

OF
nea
exc
sho

22(⁷⁄₈)

DOOR OUTLINE
GROOVE

HOLE FOR
WINDOW

248(9

6(¼) DEEP x 9(³⁄₈)
REBATE FOR
CAB FLOOR
(SEE SHEET 3)

6(¼)

6(¼)

25(1)

25(1)

51(2)

64(2½)

REBATE ALL
ALONG LOWER
INSIDE EDGE
OF SIDE PANEL

51(2)

3(⅛) x 3(⅛
SHAPE OF

9(³⁄₈)

9(³⁄₈)

9(³⁄₈)

9(³⁄₈)

SECTION B – B

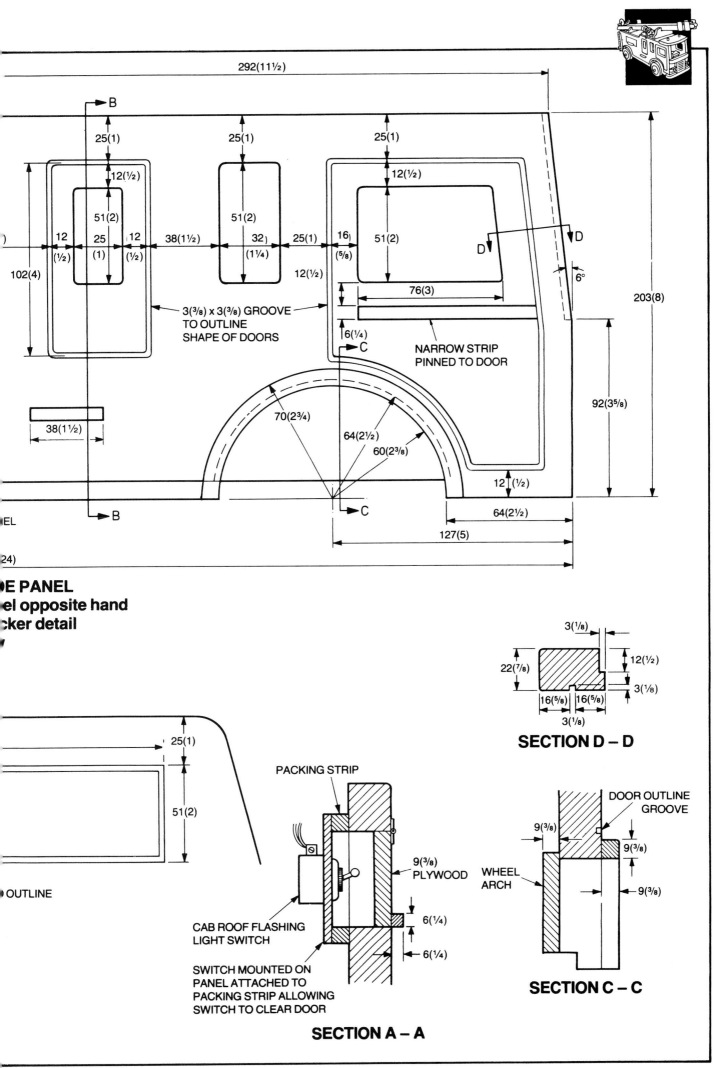

292(11½)

B

25(1)   25(1)   25(1)

12(½)   12(½)

51(2)   51(2)   51(2)

12   25   12   38(1½)   32)   25(1)   16   76(3)   D   D
(½)   (1)   (½)   (1¼)   (⅝)   6°

102(4)   12(½)   203(8)

3(⅜) x 3(⅜) GROOVE
TO OUTLINE
SHAPE OF DOORS

6(¼)   NARROW STRIP
PINNED TO DOOR

C   C

92(3⅝)

38(1½)   70(2¾)   64(2½)   60(2⅜)

12   (½)

B   64(2½)

EL

127(5)

24)

E PANEL
el opposite hand
ker detail

25(1)

22(⅞)   3(⅛)   12(½)   3(⅛)
16(⅝)   16(⅝)
3(⅛)

SECTION D – D

51(2)

PACKING STRIP

OUTLINE

CAB ROOF FLASHING
LIGHT SWITCH

SWITCH MOUNTED ON
PANEL ATTACHED TO
PACKING STRIP ALLOWING
SWITCH TO CLEAR DOOR

9(⅜)
PLYWOOD

6(¼)

6(¼)

SECTION A – A

DOOR OUTLINE
GROOVE

9(⅜)   9(⅜)

WHEEL
ARCH

9(⅜)

SECTION C – C

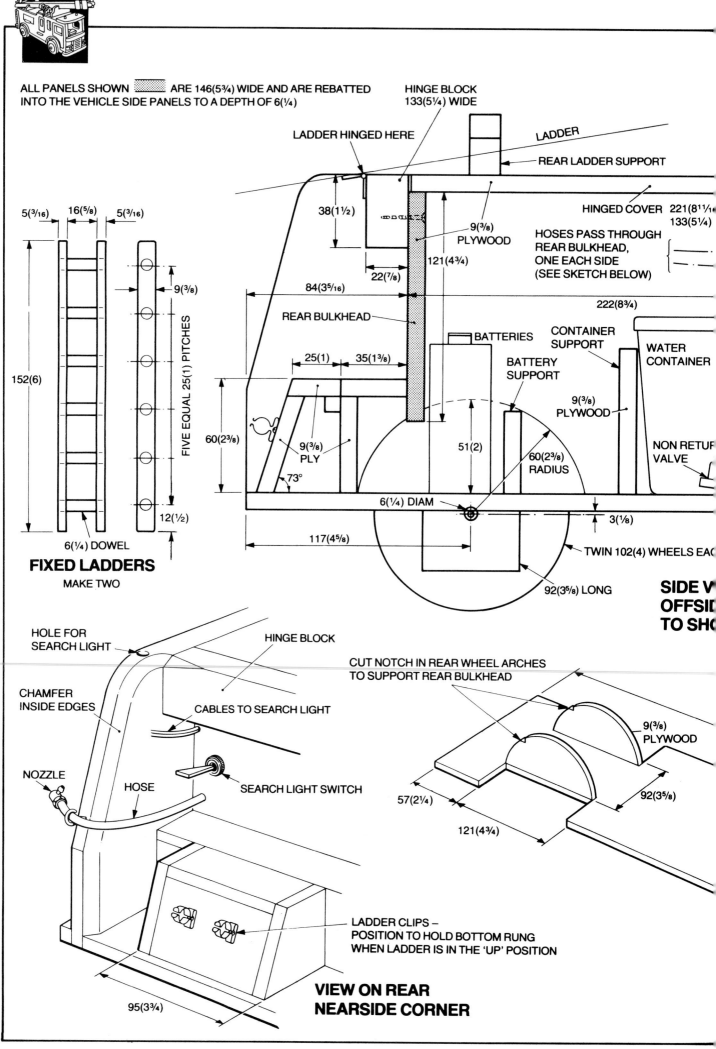

ALL PANELS SHOWN ▨ ARE 146(5¾) WIDE AND ARE REBATTED
INTO THE VEHICLE SIDE PANELS TO A DEPTH OF 6(¼)

HINGE BLOCK
133(5¼) WIDE

LADDER HINGED HERE

LADDER

REAR LADDER SUPPORT

38(1½)

9(⅜)
PLYWOOD

HINGED COVER 221(8¹¹/₁₆
133(5¼)

HOSES PASS THROUGH
REAR BULKHEAD,
ONE EACH SIDE
(SEE SKETCH BELOW)

121(4¾)

22(⅞)

84(3⁵/₁₆)

REAR BULKHEAD

222(8¾)

25(1)   35(1⅜)

BATTERIES

CONTAINER
SUPPORT

WATER
CONTAINER

BATTERY
SUPPORT

9(⅜)
PLY

9(⅜)
PLYWOOD

60(2⅜)

73°

51(2)

60(2⅜)
RADIUS

NON RETUR
VALVE

6(¼) DIAM

3(⅛)

117(4⁵/₈)

TWIN 102(4) WHEELS EAC

92(3⁵/₈) LONG

SIDE V
OFFSID
TO SH⊙

5(³/₁₆)   16(⁵/₈)   5(³/₁₆)

9(⅜)

152(6)

FIVE EQUAL 25(1) PITCHES

12(½)

6(¼) DOWEL

FIXED LADDERS
MAKE TWO

HOLE FOR
SEARCH LIGHT

HINGE BLOCK

CUT NOTCH IN REAR WHEEL ARCHES
TO SUPPORT REAR BULKHEAD

CHAMFER
INSIDE EDGES

CABLES TO SEARCH LIGHT

9(⅜)
PLYWOOD

NOZZLE

HOSE

SEARCH LIGHT SWITCH

57(2¼)

92(3⁵/₈)

121(4¾)

LADDER CLIPS –
POSITION TO HOLD BOTTOM RUNG
WHEN LADDER IS IN THE 'UP' POSITION

95(3¾)

VIEW ON REAR
NEARSIDE CORNER

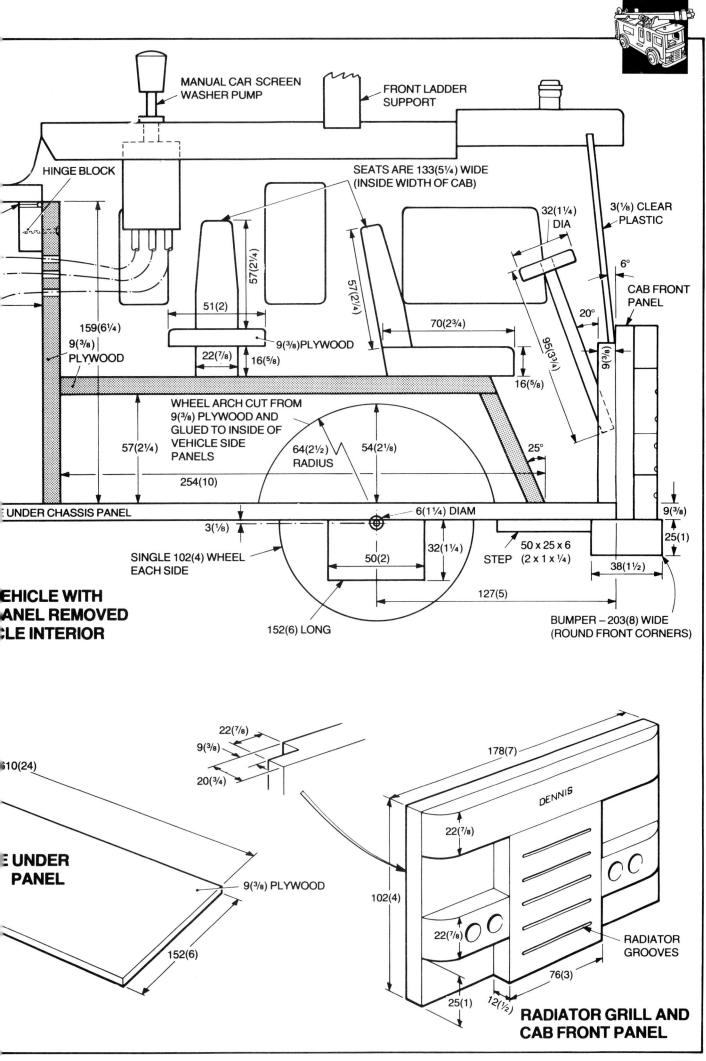

MANUAL CAR SCREEN WASHER PUMP

FRONT LADDER SUPPORT

HINGE BLOCK

SEATS ARE 133(5¼) WIDE
(INSIDE WIDTH OF CAB)

32(1¼) DIA

3(⅛) CLEAR PLASTIC

6°

CAB FRONT PANEL

159(6¼)

9(⅜) PLYWOOD

57(2¼)

51(2)

57(2¼)

70(2¾)

95(3¾)

20°

9(⅜)

9(⅜)PLYWOOD

22(⅞)

16(⅝)

16(⅝)

WHEEL ARCH CUT FROM
9(⅜) PLYWOOD AND
GLUED TO INSIDE OF
VEHICLE SIDE
PANELS

64(2½)
RADIUS

54(2⅛)

25°

57(2¼)

254(10)

UNDER CHASSIS PANEL

6(1¼) DIAM

9(⅜)

3(⅛)

32(1¼)

50 x 25 x 6
STEP   (2 x 1 x ¼)

25(1)

SINGLE 102(4) WHEEL
EACH SIDE

50(2)

127(5)

38(1½)

EHICLE WITH
ANEL REMOVED
CLE INTERIOR

152(6) LONG

BUMPER – 203(8) WIDE
(ROUND FRONT CORNERS)

22(⅞)

9(⅜)

20(¾)

178(7)

610(24)

DENNIS

22(⅞)

E UNDER
PANEL

102(4)

9(⅜) PLYWOOD

22(⅞)

RADIATOR GROOVES

152(6)

25(1)

12(½)

76(3)

**RADIATOR GRILL AND
CAB FRONT PANEL**

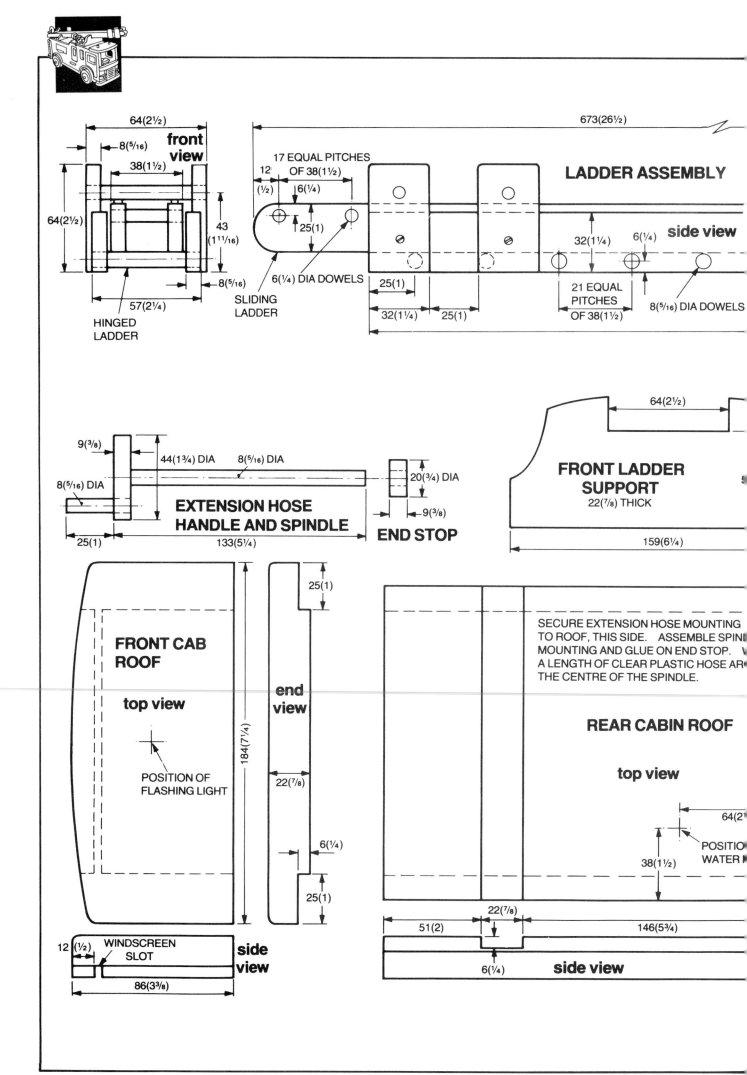

front view

64(2½)

8(⁵⁄₁₆)

38(1½)

64(2½)

43 (1¹¹⁄₁₆)

57(2¼)

8(⁵⁄₁₆)

HINGED LADDER

SLIDING LADDER

6(¼) DIA DOWELS

673(26½)

LADDER ASSEMBLY

17 EQUAL PITCHES OF 38(1½)

12 (½)

6(¼)

25(1)

side view

32(1¼)

6(¼)

25(1)

32(1¼)

25(1)

21 EQUAL PITCHES OF 38(1½)

8(⁵⁄₁₆) DIA DOWELS

9(³⁄₈)

44(1¾) DIA

8(⁵⁄₁₆) DIA

8(⁵⁄₁₆) DIA

20(¾) DIA

9(³⁄₈)

EXTENSION HOSE HANDLE AND SPINDLE

END STOP

25(1)

133(5¼)

64(2½)

FRONT LADDER SUPPORT
22(⁷⁄₈) THICK

159(6¼)

FRONT CAB ROOF

top view

POSITION OF FLASHING LIGHT

end view

25(1)

184(7¼)

22(⁷⁄₈)

6(¼)

25(1)

SECURE EXTENSION HOSE MOUNTING TO ROOF, THIS SIDE.   ASSEMBLE SPIN MOUNTING AND GLUE ON END STOP.   A LENGTH OF CLEAR PLASTIC HOSE AR THE CENTRE OF THE SPINDLE.

REAR CABIN ROOF

top view

64(2

POSITIO WATER

38(1½)

12 (½)

WINDSCREEN SLOT

side view

86(3³⁄₈)

22(⁷⁄₈)

51(2)

146(5¾)

6(¼)

side view

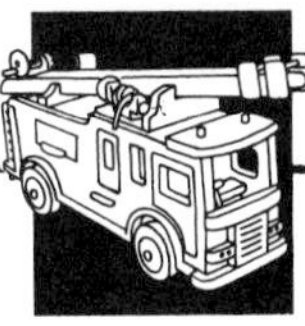

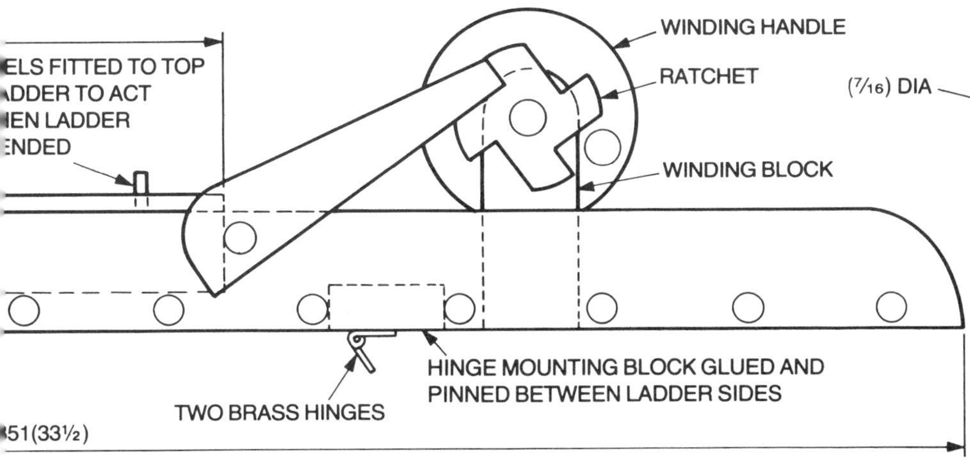
ELS FITTED TO TOP
DDER TO ACT
IEN LADDER
ENDED
WINDING HANDLE
RATCHET
WINDING BLOCK
HINGE MOUNTING BLOCK GLUED AND
PINNED BETWEEN LADDER SIDES
TWO BRASS HINGES
51(33½)

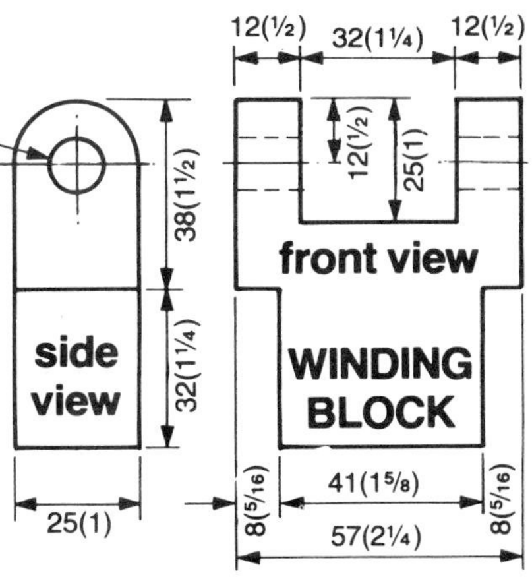
(7/16) DIA
38(1½)
32(1¼)
side view
25(1)
12(½)
32(1¼)
12(½)
12(½)
25(1)
front view
WINDING BLOCK
8(5/16)
41(1⅝)
57(2¼)
8(5/16)

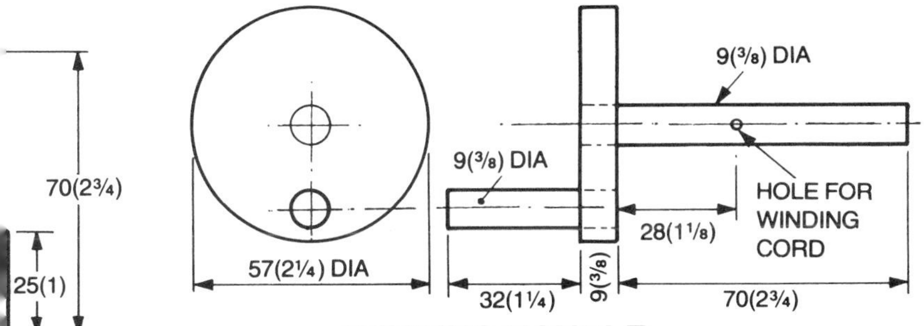
70(2¾)
25(1)
9(⅜) DIA
9(⅜) DIA
HOLE FOR WINDING CORD
28(1⅛)
57(2¼) DIA
32(1¼)
9(⅜)
70(2¾)

WINDING HANDLE

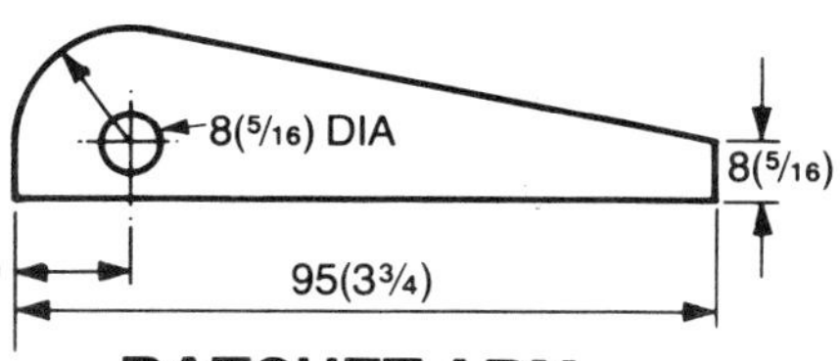
16(⅝) RADIUS
8(5/16) DIA
8(5/16)
16(⅝)
95(3¾)

RATCHET ARM
9(⅜) PLYWOOD

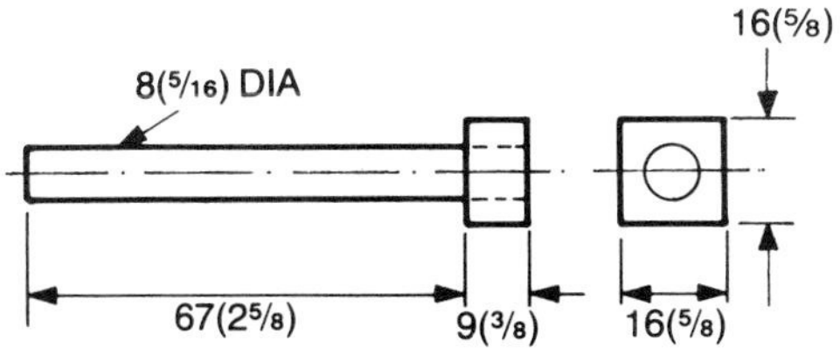
8(5/16) DIA
16(⅝)
67(2⅝)
9(⅜)
16(⅝)

RATCHET ARM SPINDLE

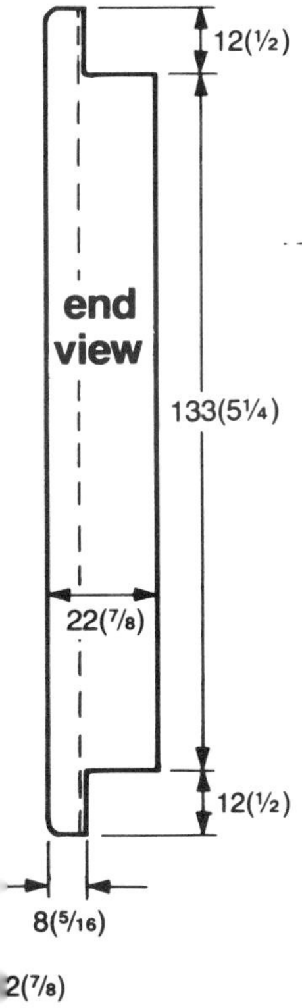
12(½)
end view
133(5¼)
22(⅞)
12(½)
8(5/16)
2(⅞)

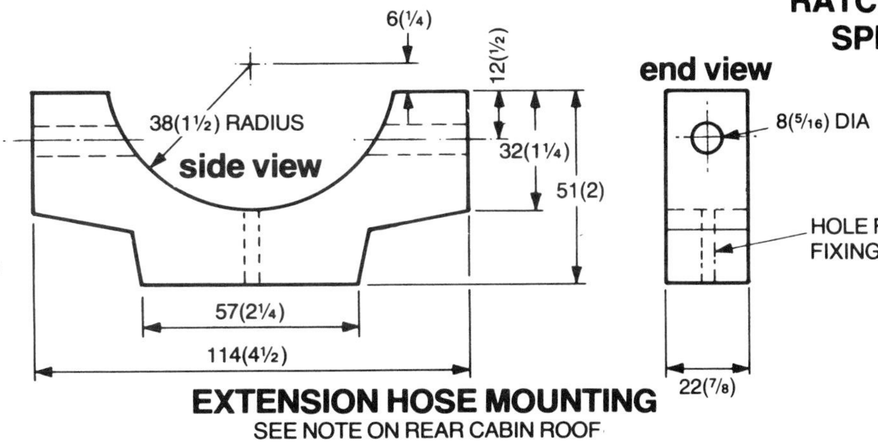
6(¼)
12(½)
38(1½) RADIUS
side view
32(1¼)
51(2)
57(2¼)
114(4½)
end view
8(5/16) DIA
HOLE FOR FIXING SCREW
22(⅞)

EXTENSION HOSE MOUNTING
SEE NOTE ON REAR CABIN ROOF

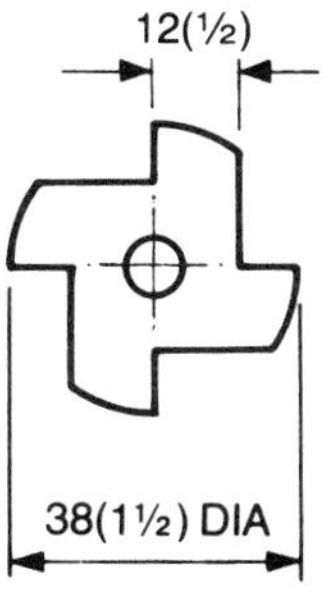
12(½)
38(1½) DIA

RATCHET
9(⅜) PLYWOOD

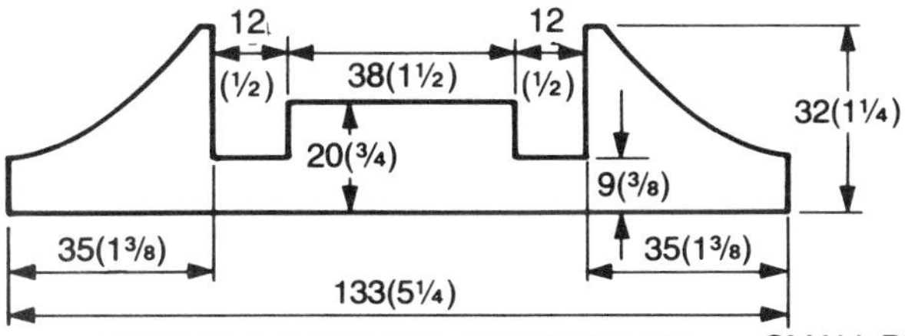
12
(½)
38(1½)
12
(½)
20(¾)
9(⅜)
32(1¼)
35(1⅜)
35(1⅜)
133(5¼)

REAR LADDER SUPPORT
16(⅝) THICK

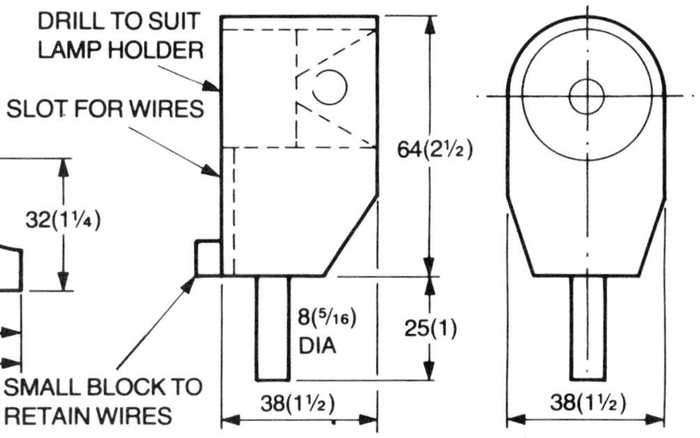
DRILL TO SUIT
LAMP HOLDER
SLOT FOR WIRES
64(2½)
8(5/16)
DIA
25(1)
SMALL BLOCK TO
RETAIN WIRES
38(1½)
38(1½)

SEARCH LIGHT

LEYLAND LORRY

Although I am very much aware of the great success of the large articulated truck models I have designed previously, I am equally aware of the parking problems that they make! This little lorry is designed for the junior trucker and will take up a lot less room. It can work in unison with the Hyster fork lift truck (page 147).

The chassis was made from mahogany, but as it is quite difficult to get mahogany of the thinness required for the cab, I felt that the use of mahogany-faced plywood was justified here. A particular feature of the design is a demountable bed. I have designed one bed for pallet loading and the other has sides for filling with sand or gravel.

1 The chassis is quite straightforward. Tape together the two main chassis members, then mark out, drill and cut the necessary halving joints.

2 Now mark out the four cross members, remembering that the front one is different from the other three. Cut out the notches for the chassis members. Assemble all the cross members onto the chassis and fix with glue. Cut out the front and rear bumpers.

3 Now for the cab – this requires quite a bit of time spent in getting the pieces cut carefully and tidied up. First cut out the two cab side walls, front bulkhead, windscreen and cab rear upper panel. It is essential to use a fine-toothed saw blade when working on plywood, otherwise huge ugly 'spilches' will result.

The windows in all these panels can be cut out with a coping saw. The technique is to drill a hole, preferably in a corner of your window-to-be, detach the blade from one end of the coping saw frame and thread it through the drilled hole; then re-attach it to the frame. As the cutting procedure continues you will have to move both plywood and the back of the saw frame to get all the way round. When these pieces are completed, cut out the cab rear lower panel and cab roof. Great patience has to be exercised when working with plywood otherwise the various pieces can look very tattered and spoil the appearance of the toy.

4 When all the windows have been cut out, lightly glasspaper all the edges. (One of the features of this Leyland truck is the little window on the passenger side. Assemble with glue the individual pieces for the cab front bulkhead, windscreen assembly, cab side walls and steering wheel, and cut out the dashboard. Glue the dashboard and steering wheel to the front bulkhead.

NB It is best to glue the clear plastic windows in place after you have varnished the finished pieces (see Materials and Finishes, page 214).

5 The bed plates for both body configurations are identical. The 'tongue' shape at the front is designed as a 'friction fit' under the cab rear panel and when in place forms part of the cab floor. It is therefore best to leave the final assembly until all the parts have been made. Glue onto the bedplate the four sides, or head and tail boards according to whether you wish to make the low-sided or flatbed version respectively.

6 Cut out the mudguards and glue them onto the cab side walls. I made wing mirrors as a small detail but if the lorry is for a young child then I suggest that this feature is left out. If you are making and fitting wing mirrors then the wire should be fitted into pre-drilled pilot holes with epoxy resin glue.

7 The use of plywood means that you are going to get a 'stripe' around the edges of the wood. This can be coloured using mahogany wood stain. The lorry was finished with clear polyurethane varnish (see page 214).

Cutting list

Main chassis member	2 off	378 × 28 × 12mm (14⅞ × 1⅛ × ½in)	Timber
Front chassis member	1 off	121 × 28 × 12mm (4¾ × 1⅛ × ½in)	Timber
Other cross members	3 off	133 × 28 × 9mm (5¼ × 1⅛ × ⅜in)	Timber
Front bumper	1 off	146 × 18 × 9mm (5¾ × ¹¹⁄₁₆ × ⅜in)	Timber
Rear bumper assembly	1 off	133 × 12 × 5mm (5¼ × ½ × ³⁄₁₆in)	Timber
	2 off	25 × 12 × 6mm (1 × ½ × ¼in)	Timber
Spare wheel arm	1 off	47 × 12 × 6mm (1⅞ × ½ × ¼in)	Timber
Fuel tank	1 off	38mm (1½in) × 25mm (1in) diam dowelling	
Cab front floor	1 off	121 × 28 × 6mm (4¾ × 1⅛ × ¼in)	Plywood
Cab side wall	2 off	140 × 117 × 6mm (5½ × 4⅝ × ¼in)	Plywood
	2 off	20 × 12 × 6mm (¾ × ½ × ¼in)	Plywood
Cab mudguard	2 off	117 × 47 × 6mm (4⅝ × 1⅞ × ¼in)	Plywood
Wing mirror	2 off	25 × 20 × 6mm (1 × ¾ × ¼in)	Plywood
Cab front bulkhead	1 off	133 × 64 × 6mm (5¼ × 2½ × ¼in)	Plywood
	1 off	127 × 16 × 6mm (5 × ⅝ × ¼in)	Plywood
Windscreen assembly	1 off	133 × 67 × 6mm (5¼ × 2⅝ × ¼in)	Plywood
	1 off	127 × 9 × 3mm (5 × ⅜ × ⅛in)	Plywood
Cab rear upper panel	1 off	133 × 54 × 6mm (5¼ × 2⅛ × ¼in)	Plywood
Cab rear lower panel	1 off	133 × 38 × 6mm (5¼ × 1½ × ¼in)	Plywood
Cab roof	1 off	133 × 89 × 6mm (5¼ × 3½ × ¼in)	Plywood
Dashboard	1 off	121 × 25 × 6mm (4¾ × 1 × ¼in)	Plywood
Steering wheel assembly	1 off	6mm (¼in) × 25mm (1in) diam dowelling	
	1 off	25mm (1in) × 6mm (¼in) diam dowelling	
Common body bed plate	1 off	350 × 146 × 6mm (13¾ × 5¾ × ¼in)	Plywood
Open sided flatbed body 　　　Head and tail board	2 off	159 × 28 × 12mm (6¼ × 1⅛ × ½in)	Timber
Low sided body 　　　Side	2 off	263 × 41 × 12mm (10⅜ × 1⅝ × ½in)	Timber
Head board	1 off	159 × 41 × 12mm (6¼ × 1⅝ × ½in)	Timber
Tail board	1 off	133 × 35 × 12mm (5¼ × 1⅜ × ½in)	Timber

Ancillaries

	7 off	51mm (2in) diam road wheels
	2 off	171mm (6¾in) long × 6mm (¼in) diam steel axles
	2 off	9mm (⅜in) o/diam × 6mm (¼in) i/diam × 22mm (⅞in) long spacers
	4 off	Spring dome caps to suit 6mm (¼in) diam axles
	2 off	102mm (4in) long × 1·5mm (¹⁄₁₆in) diam steel wires for wing mirrors
	2 off	98 × 64 × 1·5mm (3⅞ × 2½ × ¹⁄₁₆in) clear plastic
	1 off	54 × 32 × 1·5mm (2⅛ × 1¼ × ¹⁄₁₆in) clear plastic
	1 off	121 × 60 × 1·5mm (4¾ × 2⅜ × ¹⁄₁₆in) clear plastic
	1 off	121 × 51 × 1·5mm (4¾ × 2 × ¹⁄₁₆in) clear plastic

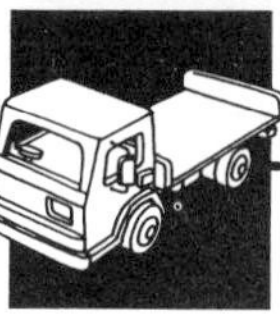

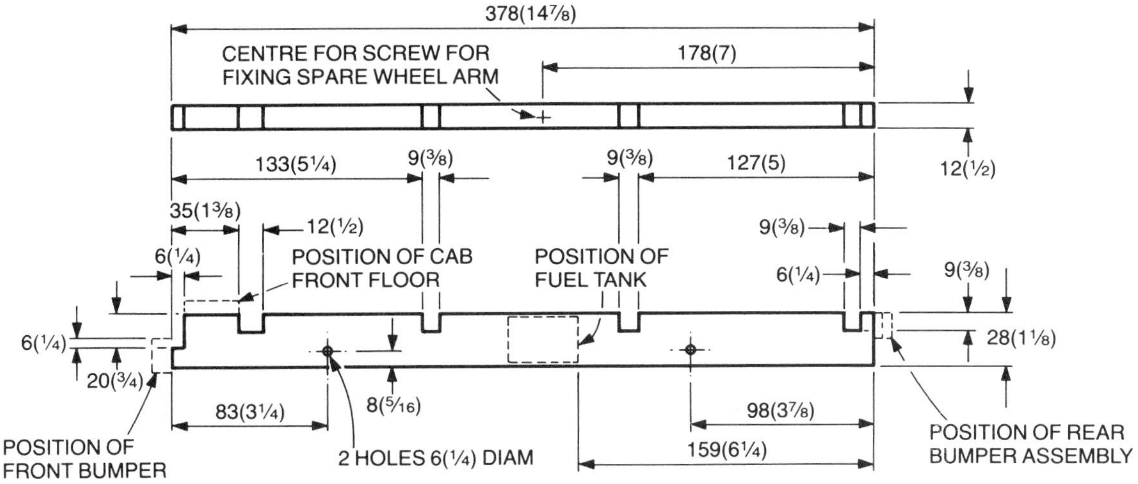

378(14 7/8)
CENTRE FOR SCREW FOR
FIXING SPARE WHEEL ARM
178(7)
12(1/2)
133(5 1/4)
9(3/8)
9(3/8)
127(5)
35(1 3/8)
12(1/2)
9(3/8)
6(1/4)
POSITION OF CAB
FRONT FLOOR
POSITION OF
FUEL TANK
6(1/4)
9(3/8)
6(1/4)
28(1 1/8)
20(3/4)
8(5/16)
83(3 1/4)
98(3 7/8)
POSITION OF
FRONT BUMPER
2 HOLES 6(1/4) DIAM
159(6 1/4)
POSITION OF REAR
BUMPER ASSEMBLY

MAIN CHASSIS MEMBER – MAKE TWO

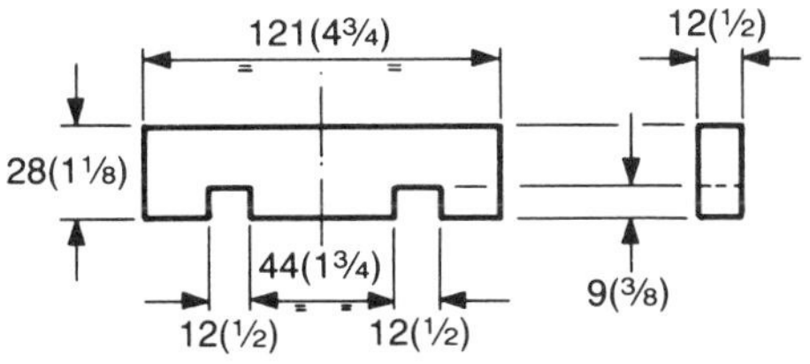

121(4 3/4)
12(1/2)
28(1 1/8)
44(1 3/4)
9(3/8)
12(1/2)
12(1/2)

FRONT CROSS MEMBER

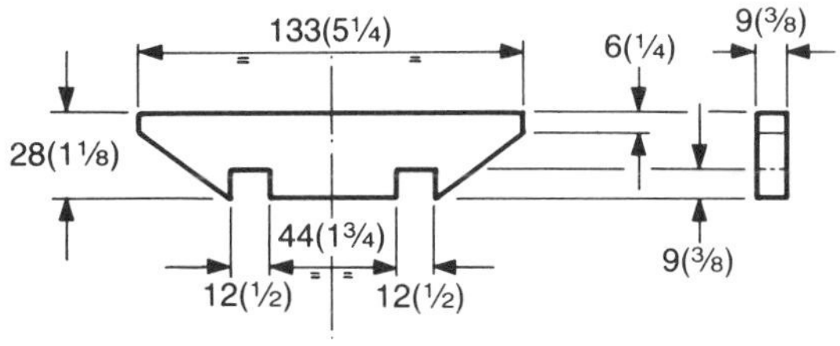

133(5 1/4)
9(3/8)
6(1/4)
28(1 1/8)
44(1 3/4)
9(3/8)
12(1/2)
12(1/2)

REMAINING CROSS MEMBERS

MAKE THREE

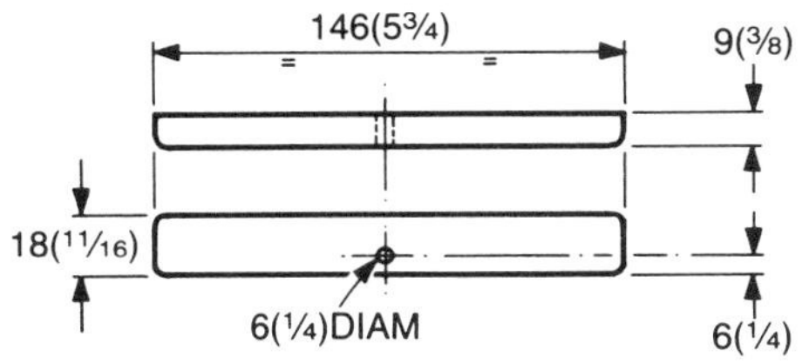

146(5 3/4)
9(3/8)
18(11/16)
6(1/4)DIAM
6(1/4)

FRONT BUMPER

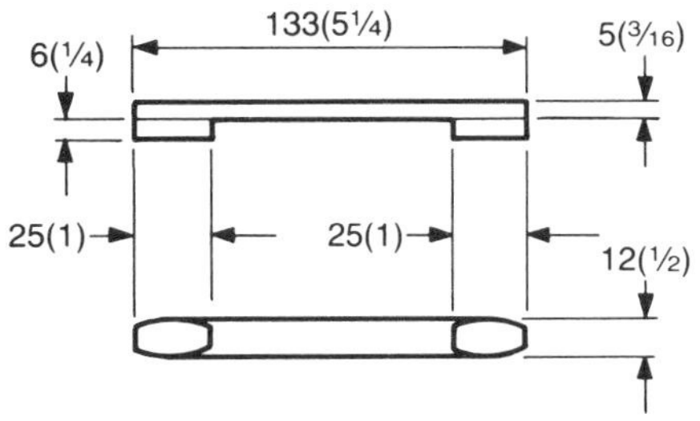

133(5 1/4)
6(1/4)
5(3/16)
25(1)
25(1)
12(1/2)

REAR BUMPER ASSEMBLY

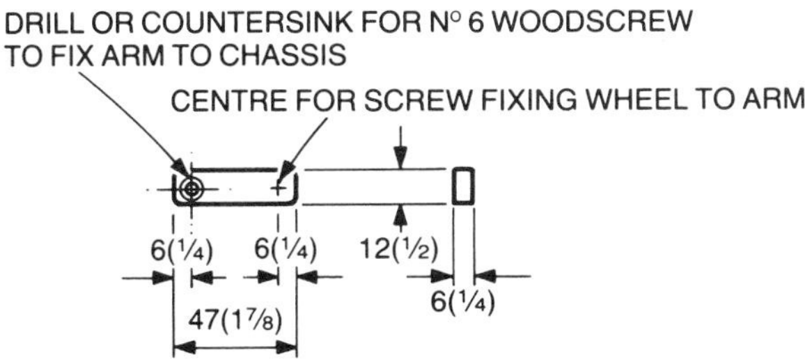

DRILL OR COUNTERSINK FOR Nº 6 WOODSCREW
TO FIX ARM TO CHASSIS
CENTRE FOR SCREW FIXING WHEEL TO ARM
6(1/4)
6(1/4)
12(1/2)
6(1/4)
47(1 7/8)

SPARE WHEEL SUPPORT ARM

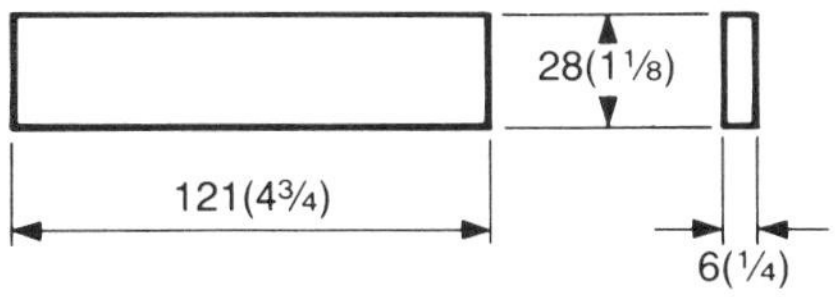

28(1 1/8)
121(4 3/4)
6(1/4)

CAB FRONT FLOOR

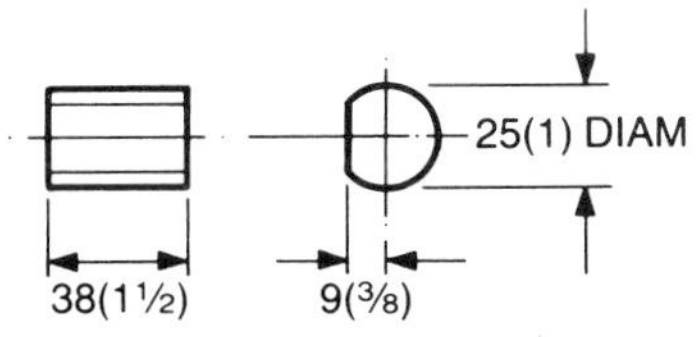

25(1) DIAM
38(1 1/2)
9(3/8)

FUEL TANK

MODELS

Instructions for 'Models' are on pages III to 209

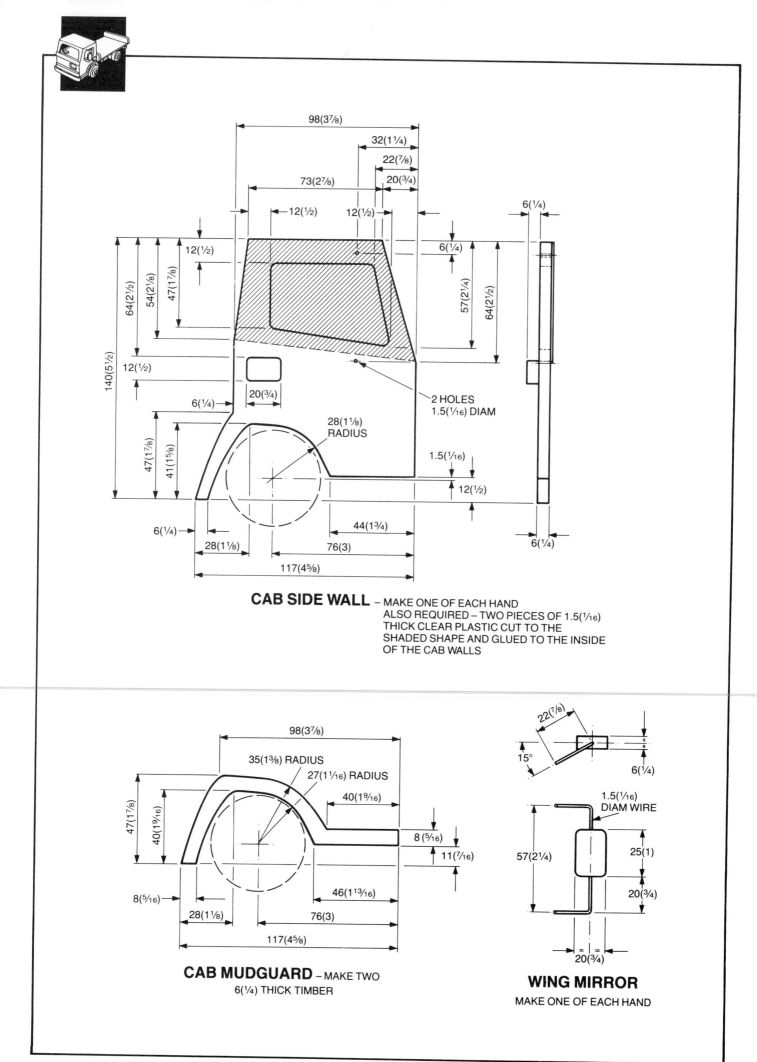

CAB SIDE WALL – MAKE ONE OF EACH HAND
ALSO REQUIRED – TWO PIECES OF 1.5(¹⁄₁₆)
THICK CLEAR PLASTIC CUT TO THE
SHADED SHAPE AND GLUED TO THE INSIDE
OF THE CAB WALLS

2 HOLES
1.5(¹⁄₁₆) DIAM

CAB MUDGUARD – MAKE TWO
6(¼) THICK TIMBER

WING MIRROR
MAKE ONE OF EACH HAND

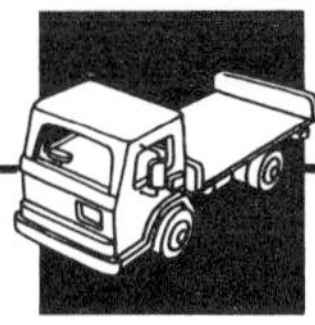

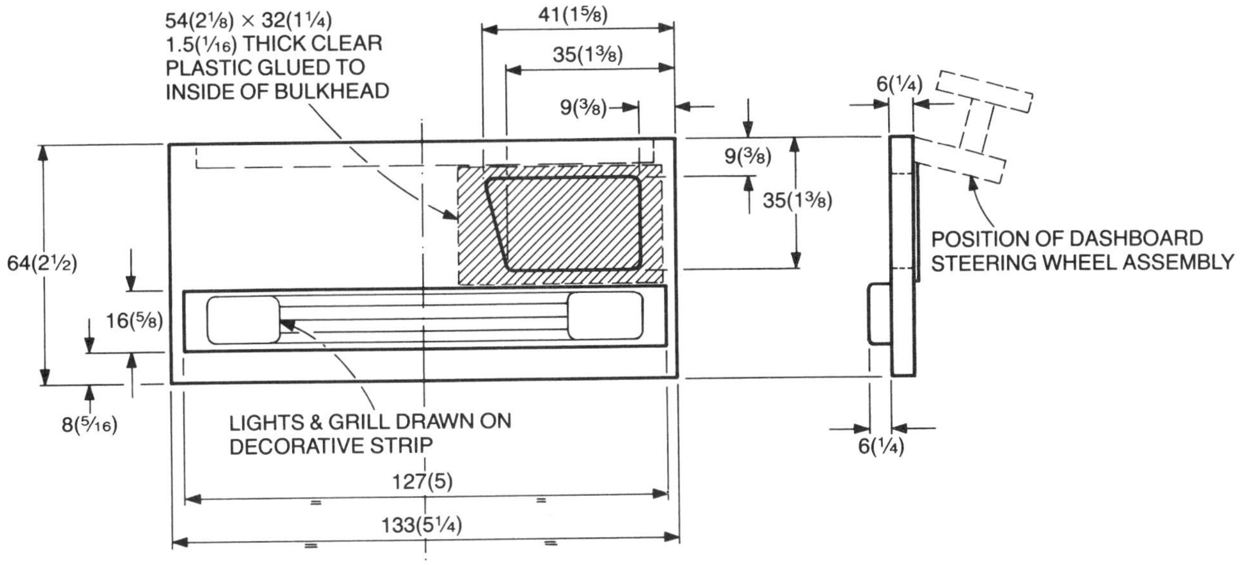
54(2 1/8) × 32(1 1/4)
1.5(1/16) THICK CLEAR
PLASTIC GLUED TO
INSIDE OF BULKHEAD
41(1 5/8)
35(1 3/8)
9(3/8)
6(1/4)
9(3/8)
35(1 3/8)
POSITION OF DASHBOARD
STEERING WHEEL ASSEMBLY
64(2 1/2)
16(5/8)
8(5/16)
LIGHTS & GRILL DRAWN ON
DECORATIVE STRIP
6(1/4)
127(5)
133(5 1/4)

CAB FRONT BULKHEAD

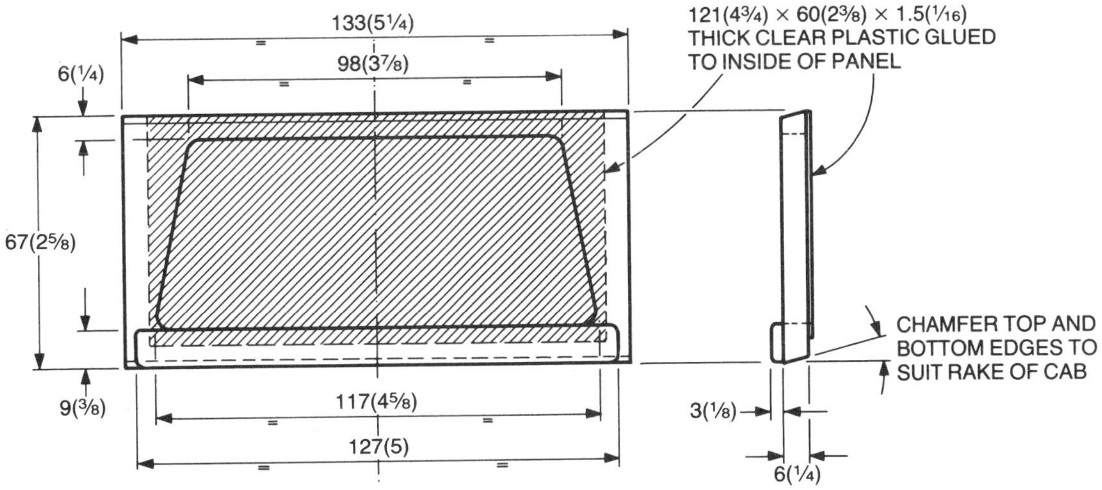
133(5 1/4)
121(4 3/4) × 60(2 3/8) × 1.5(1/16)
THICK CLEAR PLASTIC GLUED
TO INSIDE OF PANEL
98(3 7/8)
6(1/4)
67(2 5/8)
CHAMFER TOP AND
BOTTOM EDGES TO
SUIT RAKE OF CAB
9(3/8)
117(4 5/8)
3(1/8)
127(5)
6(1/4)

WINDSCREEN ASSEMBLY

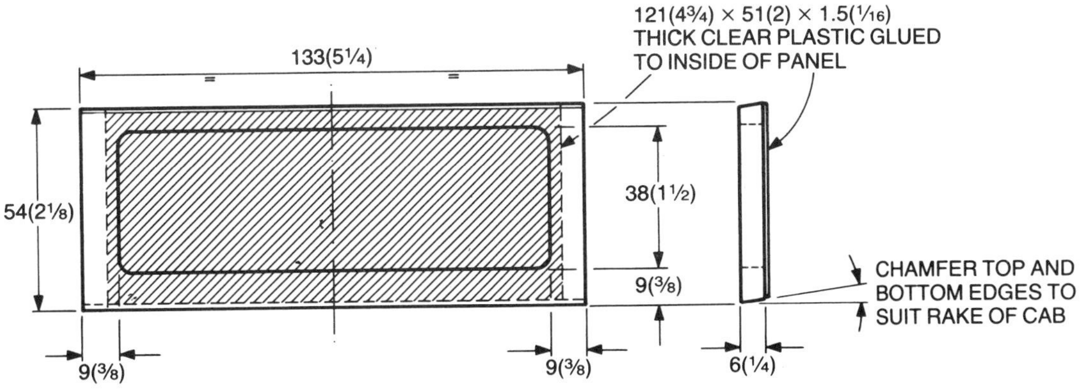
121(4 3/4) × 51(2) × 1.5(1/16)
THICK CLEAR PLASTIC GLUED
TO INSIDE OF PANEL
133(5 1/4)
54(2 1/8)
38(1 1/2)
9(3/8)
CHAMFER TOP AND
BOTTOM EDGES TO
SUIT RAKE OF CAB
9(3/8)
9(3/8)
6(1/4)

CAB REAR UPPER PANEL

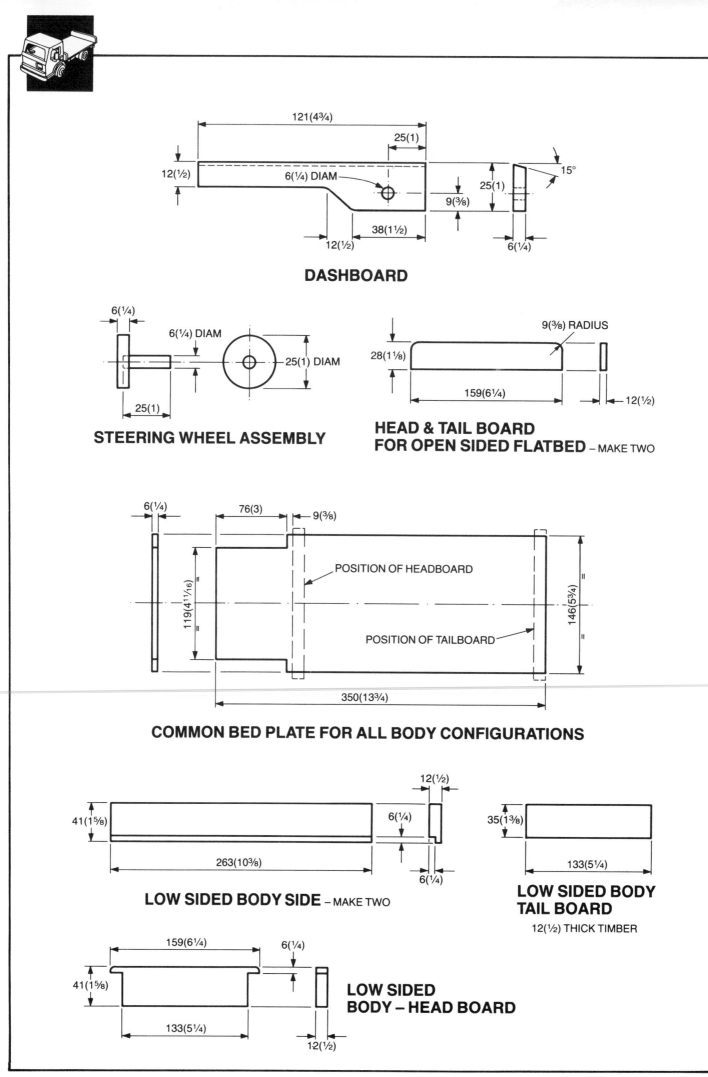

DASHBOARD

STEERING WHEEL ASSEMBLY

**HEAD & TAIL BOARD
FOR OPEN SIDED FLATBED** – MAKE TWO

COMMON BED PLATE FOR ALL BODY CONFIGURATIONS

LOW SIDED BODY SIDE – MAKE TWO

**LOW SIDED BODY
TAIL BOARD**

12(½) THICK TIMBER

**LOW SIDED
BODY – HEAD BOARD**

HYSTER FORK LIFT

Children have a fascination for copying the work of the world around them. This small Hyster fork lift is a hard-working jack of all trades, capable of stacking building blocks, Lego, sand, and so on. Ideally it should be teamed up with the Leyland flatbed lorry which will give any youngster hours of pleasure. The body was made from mahogany, the masts from beech, and dowel rods were used for the forks.

1　The main body is cut from a solid piece of mahogany (or one of the red hardwoods). It is important that you use well seasoned wood otherwise it may distort when large amounts of shaping are carried out on it. As you can see from the plans the forks are lifted up the masts by a cord that is activated by a winding handle at the back. This arrangement adds to the realism but does require the use of pulleys for the cord to run round on. The order of cutting things out on the body is quite important:

i　Drill the two axle holes, the hole for the winding handle and the large counterbored hole that takes the winding cord. A small hole should also be drilled at the front to take the cord from the mast onto the pulley on the front axle.

ii　Now cut a deep trench on the underside to accommodate the two pulleys that run on the axles.

iii　Chisel out the wheel recesses by cutting deeply into the body as detailed in the plans. This is best done by removing a small quantity of waste wood at a time and not attempting to remove it all at once. When you are getting close to the final shape, it will be essential to have a very sharp chisel as you will be cutting through end grain and it is important to cut the fibres cleanly to get a good finish.

iv　Now plane off the dashboard and cut the recess on the top to accommodate the driver's feet. Drill the hole for the steering wheel and glue it in place.

2　Select two pieces of straight-grained beech for the mast and tape both pieces together. Drill holes for the fixing screws and for the rod at the top of the mast on which the top pulley wheel rotates.

3　Cut the sliding block which has to be done with great care because it is essential that it slides easily up and down the mast. Too slack and it will jam as it comes down, too tight and it will stick. When the mast is attached to the body it is vital that the arms of the mast are kept parallel otherwise, again, the sliding block will stick.

4　Making the fork assembly is not difficult but it does require a great deal of accuracy in the drilling process. Drill all

the holes for the dowels and fixing screws. Chamfer the ends of the dowel rods, then glue them all in place and screw the fork assembly onto the sliding block on the mast.

5　Cut and assemble the fork raising handle. The small hole in the dowel shaft must be drilled with great care. Cut the ratchet wheel and pawl. The ratchet cogs need very careful working as they are so small and there is the problem of end grain and the small teeth being broken off.

6　Shape all the pieces for the cab carefully and then glue them together. When the glue is dry, glue the cab onto the body.

7　The guide pulleys (see Accessories, page 215) are not available with grooves cut in them so it is necessary to shape them. An easy method is to fit a small bolt head in the jaws of an electric drill, fit the pulley wheel onto the bolt and tighten it up with a nut to prevent it rotating. With a small sharp chisel or gouge it is then fairly easy to form a groove in the wheel.

8　Fit the fork raising handle in the body, thread a length of nylon cord through the small pre-drilled hole and knot it. Now fit the nylon cord around the guide pulleys and finally attach it to the fork assembly through a small screw eye.

9　All that remains is to cut out and shape the driver's seat, and to glue it in place.

10　The model was finished in clear polyurethane (see Materials and Finishes, page 214).

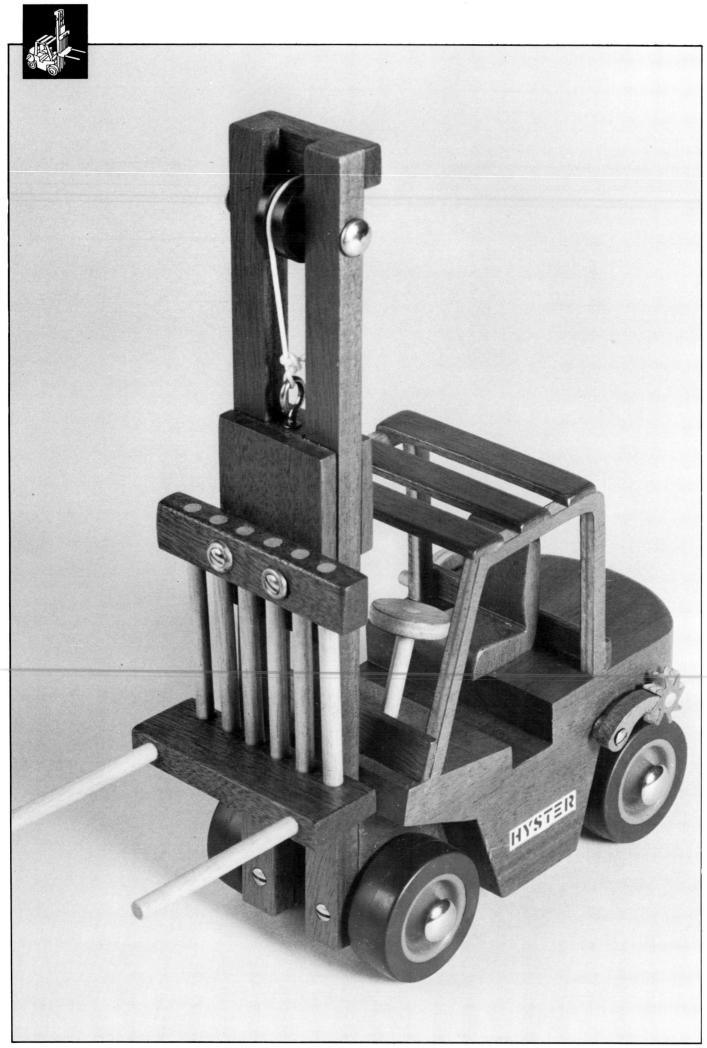

Cutting list

Body	1 off	171 × 89 × 70mm (6¾ × 3½ × 2¾in)	Timber
Steering wheel	1 off	6mm (¼in) × 32mm (1¼in) diam dowelling	
	1 off	51mm (2in) × 6mm (¼in) diam dowelling	
Fork raising handle	1 off	6mm (¼in) × 41mm (1⅝in) diam dowelling	
	1 off	38mm (1½in) × 6mm (¼in) diam dowelling	
	1 off	111mm (4⅜in) × 6mm (¼in) diam dowelling	
Ratchet wheel	1 off	6mm (¼in) × 22mm (⅞in) diam dowelling	
Ratchet pawl	1 off	25 × 20 × 6mm (1 × ¾ × ¼in)	Timber
Seat	1 off	44 × 32 × 32mm (1¾ × 1¼ × 1¼in)	Timber
Cab frame assembly	2 off	92 × 76 × 6mm (3⅝ × 3 × ¼in)	Timber
	4 off	89 × 16 × 3mm (3½ × ⅝ × ⅛in)	Timber
	1 off	89 × 12 × 3mm (3½ × ½ × ⅛in)	Timber
Mast	2 off	292 × 16 × 11mm (11½ × ⅝ × ⁷⁄₁₆in)	Timber
	1 off	47 × 12 × 11mm (1⅞ × ½ × ⁷⁄₁₆in)	Timber
Sliding block	1 off	70 × 47 × 24mm (2¾ × 1⅞ × ¹⁵⁄₁₆in)	Timber
Fork assembly	1 off	89 × 20 × 11mm (3½ × ¾ × ⁷⁄₁₆in)	Timber
	1 off	89 × 28 × 11mm (3½ × 1⅛ × ⁷⁄₁₆in)	Timber
	6 off	89mm (3½in) × 6mm (¼in) diam dowelling	
	2 off	76mm (3in) × 6mm (¼in) diam dowelling	

Ancillaries

	4 off	51mm (2in) diam road wheels
	2 off	98mm (3⅞in) × 6mm (¼in) diam steel axles
	4 off	Spring dome caps to suit 6mm (¼in) diam axles
	3 off	Grooved 25mm (1in) diam pulley wheels
	1 off	54mm (2⅛in) × 5mm (³⁄₁₆in) diam steel pin
	4 off	6mm (¼in) washers
	1 off	9mm (⅜in) screwed eye
	1 off	610mm (24in) long nylon cord

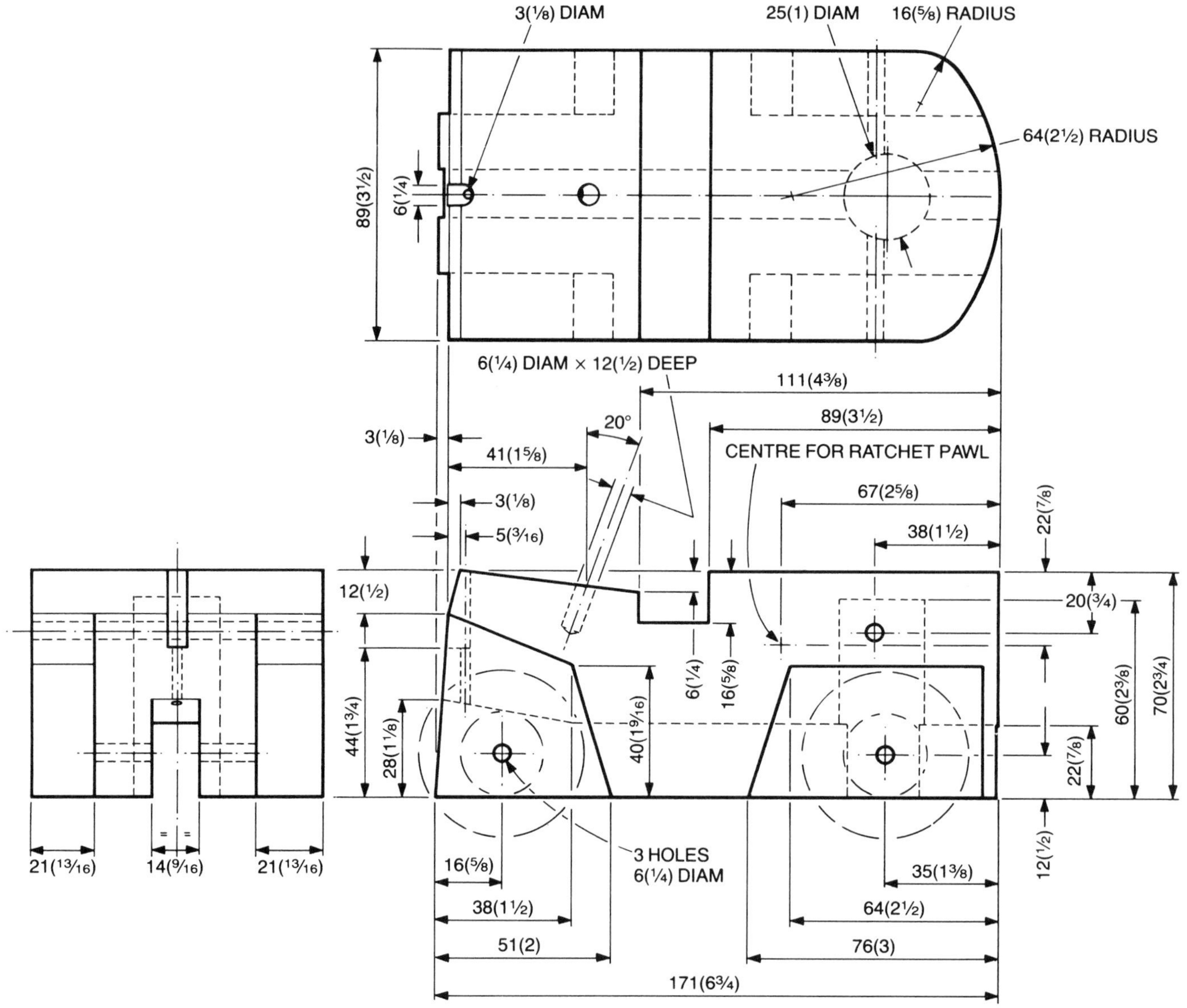
3(1/8) DIAM
25(1) DIAM
16(5/8) RADIUS
64(2 1/2) RADIUS
89(3 1/2)
6(1/4)
6(1/4) DIAM × 12(1/2) DEEP
111(4 3/8)
20°
89(3 1/2)
3(1/8)
41(1 5/8)
CENTRE FOR RATCHET PAWL
3(1/8)
67(2 5/8)
5(3/16)
38(1 1/2)
22(7/8)
12(1/2)
20(3/4)
6(1/4)
16(5/8)
44(1 3/4)
28(1 1/8)
40(1 9/16)
60(2 3/8)
70(2 3/4)
22(7/8)
21(13/16)
14(9/16)
21(13/16)
16(5/8)
3 HOLES
6(1/4) DIAM
35(1 3/8)
12(1/2)
38(1 1/2)
64(2 1/2)
51(2)
76(3)
171(6 3/4)

BODY

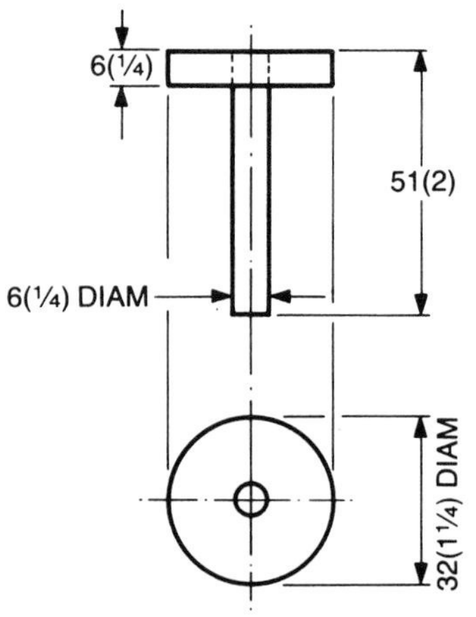
6(1/4)
51(2)
6(1/4) DIAM
32(1 1/4) DIAM

STEERING WHEEL

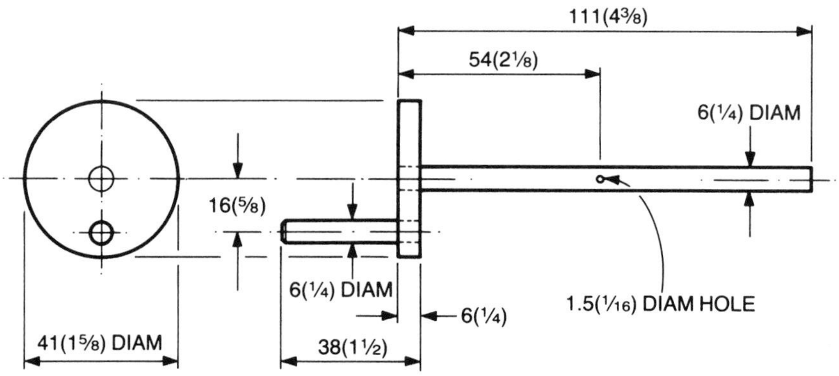
111(4 3/8)
54(2 1/8)
6(1/4) DIAM
16(5/8)
6(1/4) DIAM
6(1/4)
1.5(1/16) DIAM HOLE
41(1 5/8) DIAM
38(1 1/2)

FORK RAISING HANDLE

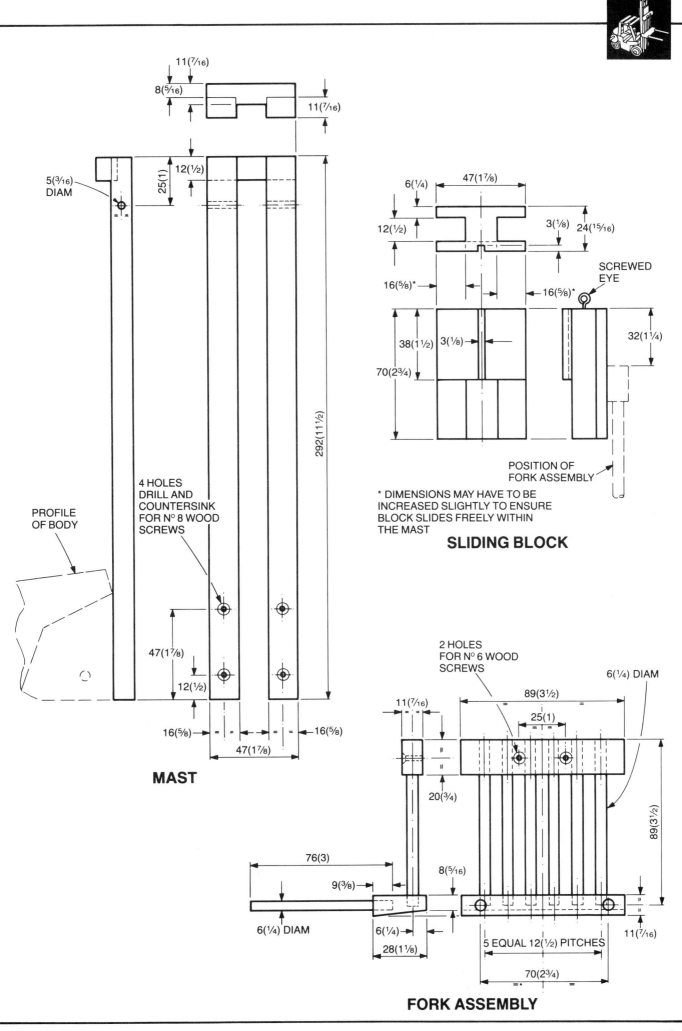

11(7/16)

8(5/16)

11(7/16)

5(3/16)
DIAM

25(1)

12(1/2)

292(11 1/2)

PROFILE
OF BODY

4 HOLES
DRILL AND
COUNTERSINK
FOR N° 8 WOOD
SCREWS

47(1 7/8)

12(1/2)

16(5/8)

16(5/8)

47(1 7/8)

MAST

6(1/4)

47(1 7/8)

12(1/2)

3(1/8)

24(15/16)

16(5/8)*

16(5/8)*

SCREWED
EYE

38(1 1/2)

3(1/8)

32(1 1/4)

70(2 3/4)

POSITION OF
FORK ASSEMBLY

* DIMENSIONS MAY HAVE TO BE
INCREASED SLIGHTLY TO ENSURE
BLOCK SLIDES FREELY WITHIN
THE MAST

SLIDING BLOCK

2 HOLES
FOR N° 6 WOOD
SCREWS

11(7/16)

20(3/4)

89(3 1/2)

25(1)

6(1/4) DIAM

89(3 1/2)

76(3)

9(3/8)

8(5/16)

6(1/4) DIAM

6(1/4)

28(1 1/8)

5 EQUAL 12(1/2) PITCHES

11(7/16)

70(2 3/4)

FORK ASSEMBLY

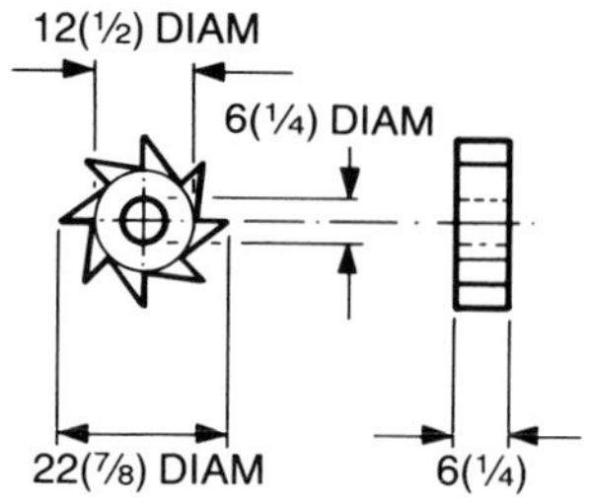
12(½) DIAM
6(¼) DIAM
22(⅞) DIAM
6(¼)

RATCHET WHEEL

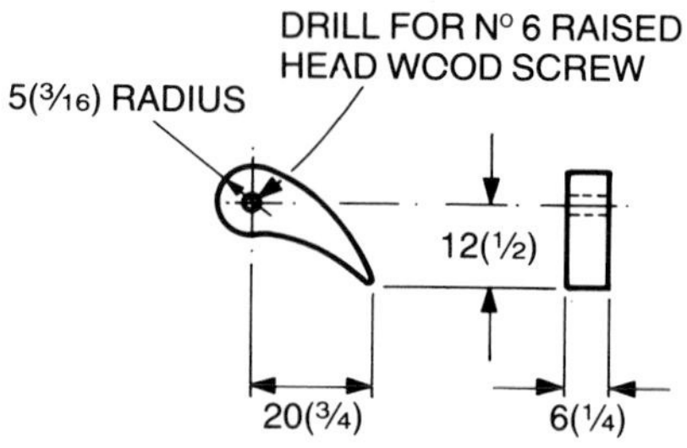
DRILL FOR Nº 6 RAISED HEAD WOOD SCREW
5(³⁄₁₆) RADIUS
12(½)
20(¾)
6(¼)

RATCHET PAWL

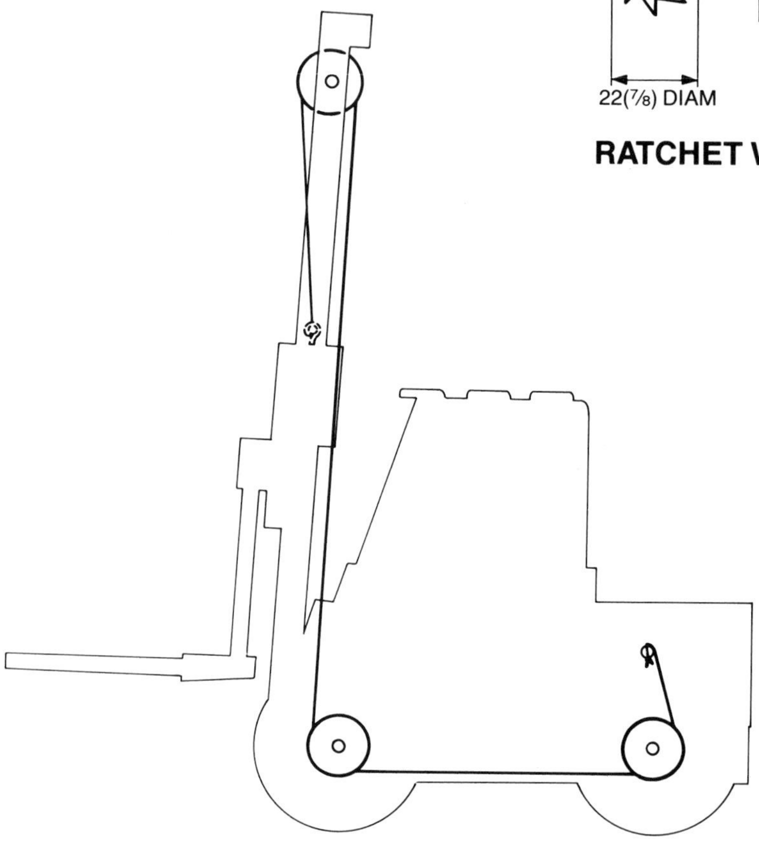

ARRANGEMENT OF GUIDE PULLEYS AND FORK RAISING CORD

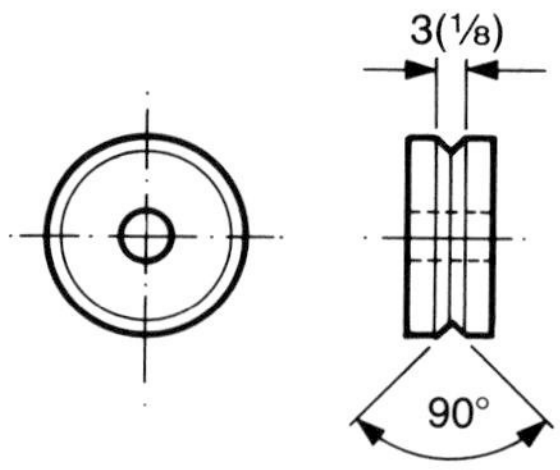
3(⅛)
90°

GUIDE PULLEY – THREE REQUIRED
TWO WITH 6(¼) BORE AND ONE 5(³⁄₁₆) BORE

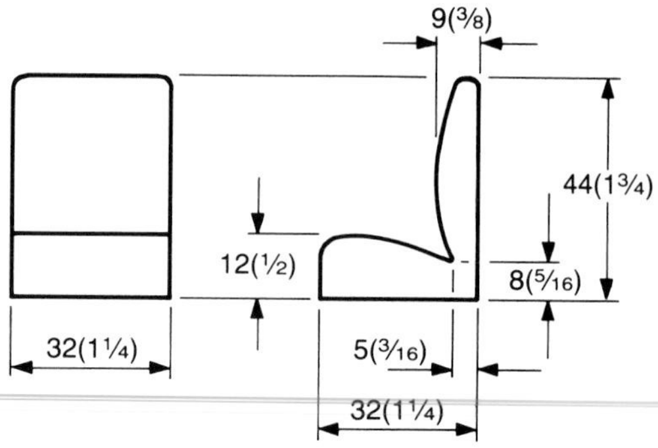
9(⅜)
44(1¾)
12(½)
8(⁵⁄₁₆)
32(1¼)
5(³⁄₁₆)
32(1¼)

SEAT

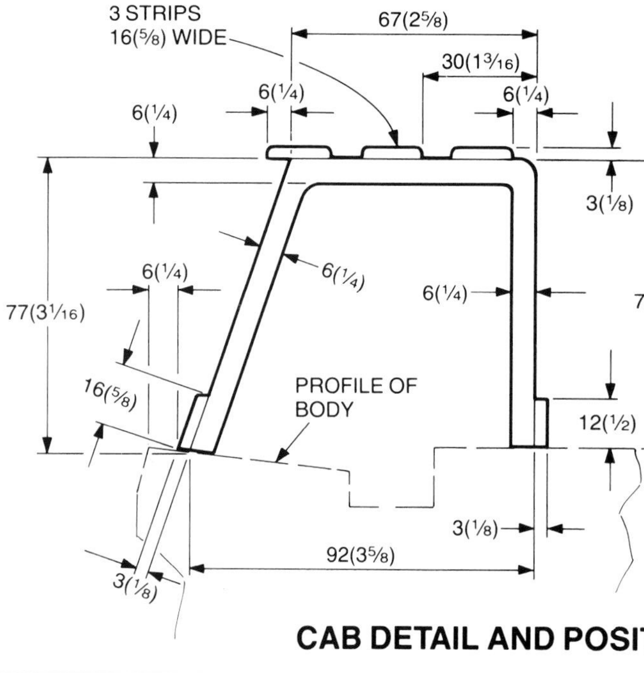
3 STRIPS 16(⅝) WIDE
67(2⅝)
30(1³⁄₁₆)
6(¼)
6(¼)
6(¼)
3(⅛)
6(¼)
6(¼)
6(¼)
77(3¹⁄₁₆)
76(3)
16(⅝)
PROFILE OF BODY
12(½)
3(⅛)
92(3⅝)
3(⅛)

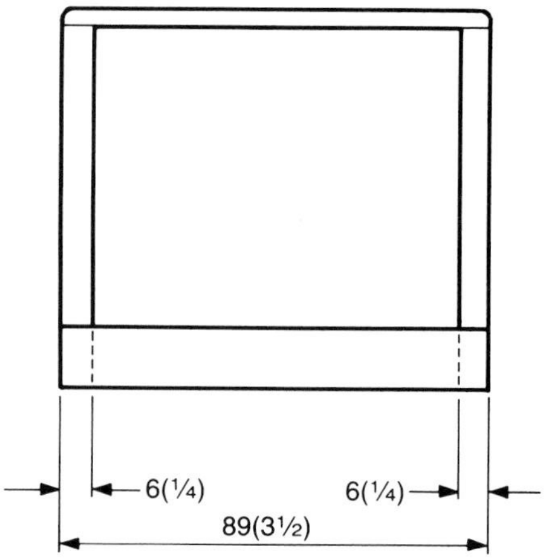
6(¼)
6(¼)
89(3½)

CAB DETAIL AND POSITION ON BODY

MACK SUPERLINER

The first Mack truck was designed in 1914 and the AC Model was first built in 1915. The trucks were used by the British in the First World War and, because of their dependability and rugged quality, were nicknamed 'Bulldog Macks'. Today the bulldog mascot carried proudly on the bonnet of all Macks is a symbol of quality and excellence in both design and engineering.

The Superliner II is a fine example of the manufacturing company's ability to produce 'the best on wheels'. After visiting the USA I was determined to try to re-create this 'monster' Mack which is so much a part of the North American trucking scene.

My truck is built from a number of different hardwoods. I used beech for the chassis and mahogany for the superstructure and other parts. It is not essential to use these timbers, but the truck looks better in the darker-coloured hardwoods.

Chassis

1 As with all vehicles it is best to start by constructing the chassis. As the chassis is the foundation and strength of the whole truck, it must be rigid. To achieve this, you will need to cut stopped mortice and tenon joints to hold the chassis together. Select the two main chassis members with care and, if possible, make sure that they are straight-grained. Tape the two members together and, using a pencil, mark them out as a pair, thus ensuring that both sides are identical. Drill the holes, separate them and cut out the stopped mortice holes.

2 Now cut the six chassis cross members which will hold the two main members together and cut the tenons.

3 Cut the front bumper (fender) and cut stopped mortice holes for the chassis members to fit into.

4 The front axle cross bar fits into the 'cut out' section at the front of the chassis and it is important to cut this before fitting the chassis together. The fuel tanks are held in place by dowel rods that pass through the chassis; drill the holes for these rods before assembling the chassis.

5 Assemble the chassis dry (without glue) and check that all joints fit well and that the six chassis cross members are all at 90° to the two main chassis members.

6 Now mark out the rear axle mounting blocks and cut them to shape. I find that it is best to use a drill mounted in a stand for all hole-drilling operations, otherwise it is very difficult to drill holes accurately at 90° in both planes. Screw both rear axle mounting blocks onto the main chassis members.

7 To give the sense of the massive power of this machine, it is vital to make a convincing rear bogie unit. Using my method a realistic suspension is created which allows one wheel to be raised while the others are all on the ground. Make two rear axle suspension units. Drill slightly elongated holes for the axles and an oval centre hole. Careful working of these holes is essential, otherwise they may well become too large and the axle fit will be loose and sloppy.

Now cut the rear springs from spring steel. To hold the leaves together, cut two small pieces of steel to form spring clips and simply 'wrap' them around the leaves. The best way to form these spring clips is by actually working them into shape on the spring itself – mild steel is easily bent. However, a word of warning: don't leave any sharp edges – finish off everything with a smooth cut file.

Drill holes in the ends of the leaves and screw them onto the rear axle suspension unit. The springs don't actually work but they do look very effective.

8 Work can now begin on the front axle steering assembly. Start by preparing the front axle block, marking out and cutting recesses in the ends. Cut chamfers in the recesses to allow the stub axles to rotate freely when fitted. Mark out and cut a pair of stub axles. The stub axles fit into the recesses cut in the front axle block. Place the stub axles on a flat surface with a sheet of glasspaper underneath and rub them carefully over it until a smooth fit is achieved in the front axle block. Now drill the axle holes in both stub axle blocks and fit the axle rods to take the front wheels. Also drill the pin holes for the steering tie bar. Assemble the stub axles in the axle block and, after careful positioning and lining up, drill holes right through the axle block and stub axles. This method ensures that the holes in both components line up.

Perhaps the most difficult part of this task is clamping the various pieces firmly so that they don't move while drilling. I have found adhesive tape very helpful in keeping items stable as it doesn't get in the way of the drilling operation as much as a 'G' cramp would. A good deal of care is required over this part of the work.

Cut and shape the steering tie bar. Drill the pin holes for the stub axles. Assemble the steering tie bar, front axle block and stub axles using steel rods and spring caps. Now cut and shape the front axle cross bar and glue it onto the front axle block.

9 Cut the battery boxes to shape and plane a taper onto the sides. Turn the air cylinders on the lathe and plane a small 'flat' on the top of each in order to give extra 'glueing surface'. After glueing the air cylinders onto the battery boxes, screw the units onto the chassis.

10 Turn the two massive fuel tanks (filling them with fuel would make a hole in anybody's credit card!) on the lathe. After turning, bore two holes in each tank to take dowel rods that pass through the chassis and hold the tanks in place on each side of the model. Create a flat area on the top of each tank by planing. All the edges should be carefully rounded off and the end grain finished well, otherwise the tanks will not look authentic. Access is gained to the cab by a step fitted on the side of each tank. To achieve a realistic appearance I suggest cutting a piece of fine aluminium mesh to wrap around each of two small pre-shaped blocks of wood and glueing these onto the sides of the tanks.

11 Cut out the rear bumper and cut two 'notches' in it so that it will fit into the back of the chassis. To form mudflaps, attach two pieces of stiff thick black plastic to the bumper bar with cup screw washers and raised-head wood screws. Then glue two small lengths of reflector tape onto the bottom of the mudflaps.

12 Shape the trailer hitch (in Britain this is called a fifth wheel) from a piece of beech and recess it to assist the coupling of the trailer hitch pin. Screw the hitch firmly to the chassis.

13 Now you can carry out the final shaping on the front bumper (fender). I cut out the recessed shaped areas with a bevel-edged chisel. Care is necessary when removing wood chips from the bottom of the recess as the finished recess must be flat. The secret is to take only light cuts.

14 Once all the chassis pieces have been cut and shaped as described above, assemble the whole job dry. At this stage it is easy to make slight adjustments and get the entire thing right. Check the squareness of all joints and, with a cabinet scraper, 'clean up' all surfaces in preparation for glueing. However, it is advisable to build the superstructure before finally glueing the chassis together.

Superstructure

1 Start by preparing the engine/cab side panel. The engine compartment walls are set at an angle so it's a good idea to draw a full-size plan on a sheet of paper first. From the drawing you will be able to mark off accurately the angle required for the forward and rear bonnet spacers. With a marking gauge mark out the positions for the stopped mortice holes and tenons. The two spacers fit into the mortices at the bottom of the side panel.

To compensate for the angled 'off-set' of the side panel walls it is necessary to plane the cab side on the outside edge to the correct angle.

Now cut out the cab rear wall. I always chamfer off the window edges as I think this gives a more 'finished' appearance to the model. Glue on the seat support.

2 Quite a lot of work is required to make the enormous radiator. Start by carefully marking out the basic shape. To make sure of a clean cut, use a marking knife across the grain at the top and a marking gauge down the sides. The recess is best cut out with a router – if you don't have one, very careful chiselling is the only alternative.

Now glue small wooden strips (six in all) across the radiator. Cut strips of fine aluminium mesh and fit these between the wooden strips. Cut a piece of aluminium mesh large enough to cover the entire grill and, using panel pins, fix it to the wooden slats. Using mesh in this way gives a three-dimensional effect to the radiator grill. Glue a small strip of wood onto the base of the radiator and another across the top. Fit the name board bearing the letters 'MACK' onto the radiator front. (A number of firms make 'dry print' suitable for making the name board.)

3 The bonnet and dashboard are formed from one piece of timber. Make the dashboard by planing an angle and then shaping with a coping saw.

The steering wheel takes quite a bit of care. Mark it out and, using a series of drill holes, remove most of the wood to form the centre boss and two spokes. Carry out the final shaping with a set of small fine-cut wood rasps. Now drill a hole in the dashboard to take the steering column.

4 Shape the cab seats from solid blocks of wood. After shaping, it is worth covering the seats in a soft felt material, preferably red. The use of fabric in the cab will add a touch of luxury – just like the real thing.

5 Make the cab side walls (really the side window frames), remembering to chamfer the inside edges slightly. Cut the two side screen sills ready for assembly, but do not fit these until after the clear plastic side screens themselves are in place.

6 The front windscreen of the Superliner II is curved. Shaping thick plastic to make this can present problems. You can try the hazardous

method of heating it in a mould in an ordinary oven, but I arrived at a safer compromise. Glue the plastic screen onto the front edges of the cab walls and fit a chamfered windscreen frame over the top of this. The slight curvature of the frame is sufficient to give the illusion of a curved windscreen – and anything is better than cleaning melted plastic from the walls of your oven! The frame itself needs careful shaping and, until it has been glued onto the plastic screen, is quite fragile.

7 Shape the cab roof and drill small holes for the air horns and spot lamps. I turned all the horns and spot lamps on the lathe. Glue a small piece of brass wire into each horn and spot lamp and mount these fittings on the roof.

8 Once all the cab parts have been cut and shaped, fit them together dry and test for a good fit.

Use soft wire to form windscreen wipers and black electric flex rubber for the blades. Shape door handles from scrap wood and glue them onto the cab sides.

9 All driving mirror and aerial assemblies on Mack trucks are pretty impressive and to capture the looks of the real-life versions it is necessary to do a little metalwork (sorry, purists!). Using soft wire and small soldering iron it is quite easy to make the mirror assemblies. Use a small drill to bore a hole right through each mirror to take the upright aerial wire. Paint the wires silver and, once the paint is dry, bore small holes in the cab side wall and glue each mirror/aerial into place.

10 Shape the exhaust stacks on the lathe and insert a dowel spigot at the top to take a length of black plastic pipe. Cover the stacks with fine aluminium mesh fixed on with panel pins at the back. Use raised-head chrome-plated screws, cup washers and spacers to fit the exhaust stacks to the cab rear wall

A word of warning: if you intend to let a youngster play with this model be sure to fit flexible plastic tube to the tops of the exhaust boxes – do not use any material which could break and cause injury. If you intend just to display the truck on a shelf, well polished aluminium tube would look very impressive.

11 Cut the mudguards from solid blocks of wood. Do the inside shaping first as it is easier to hold the wood in the vice to remove the saw marks. Once you are satisfied with the inside shaping, cut the outside to shape. The outside edges of the mudguards should be chamfered. Headlights can be made from a contrasting-coloured timber.

12 No Mack truck would be complete without its bulldog bonnet mascot. Because of its miniature size, this requires careful working. I cut out the basic shape with a coping saw and then completed the carving with a variety of small chisels, gouges and wood rasps. I am sure that other craftsmen will be able to fashion a far more bullish dog than I have managed.

Sleeping cabin
One of the most prominent features of this vehicle is the high specification of driver comfort and accommodation.

1 Cut out the front and rear walls of the sleeping cabin and cut rebates to take the roof and floor. Assemble the whole cabin dry and then glue, checking for squareness. Glue the upper bunk floor between the two sides and then fit the lower partition.

2 Provide a small ladder to assist the driver into his bunk and also fit ladders outside on both sides of the cabin. The easiest way to make these ladders is to tape two long lengths of wood together, marking the position of the rungs. Now drill holes to take the dowel rods which will form the rungs right through the two uprights. Separate them and lightly countersink the holes on the inside edges. Make a small jig to cut all the dowel rods to the same length. Glue all the dowel rods into one upright first, then guide the 'free' ends into the other side using a small hammer and block of wood. Once all the dowels are 'started', put the ladder in the vice and squeeze the sides together. Now cut off the lengths of ladder you need.

3 Cut out and fix the sleeping cabin doors using small brass hinges and either magnetic catches or brass latches as fasteners. Glue small oblong pieces of wood onto the outside of the doors to represent air vents and shape handles from small offcuts of wood.

General construction notes
It helps to cut all joints first and then carry out the shaping. Glue nothing together until the end. You will always find that parts are easier to work on flat on the bench than on a partly assembled cab or chassis. With a complex model like the Mack Superliner II, some parts need finishing completely before final assembly. For example, certain internal parts — in this case, the cab interior — will need to be varnished before the plastic screens are fitted. Always plan ahead and think the job carefully through before starting work.

The sleeping cabin, battery boxes, front axle and engine/cab assembly are all secured to the chassis by screws that pass through from the underside.

Aluminium mesh used for the Mack truck is of the type sold for repairing small holes in car bodywork and is available in most car accessory shops. When building this sort of model you will find that there are all sorts of bits and pieces that come in useful for detailing different parts — for example, reflector tape for mudflaps.

This model was finished with polyurethane varnish. Apply the first coat with a lint-free cloth and allow at least twenty-four hours to dry. Using very fine glasspaper, work over the job and, after removing all particles of dust and so on, 'cloth on' another coat of polyurethane varnish. I repeat this operation four times and then finish off with wax polish. 'Clothing on' the varnish gives a better finish than brushing for this particular sort of job.

Wheels, axles and spring caps
The wheels used on this model are 102mm (4in) in diameter and take a 6mm (¼in) mild steel rod. The wheels are held onto the axles with chrome-plated spring caps. I know that model-makers in USA experience difficulty in obtaining this sort of wheel. If you are unable to buy the wheels, steel axles and spring caps, I can supply the complete wheel kit by mail order, either via surface mail (taking six weeks in transit) or via air mail (taking two weeks in transit). Write to the address given on page 215.

Cutting list

Item	Qty	Dimensions	Material
Main chassis member	2 off	680 × 38 × 20mm (26¾ × 1½ × ¾in)	Timber
Chassis cross member	6 off	89 × 25 × 20mm (3½ × 1 × ¾in)	Timber
Rear axle mounting block	2 off	127 × 25 × 20mm (5 × 1 × ¾in)	Timber
Rear axle suspension unit	2 off	206 × 44 × 16mm (8⅛ × 1¾ × ⅝in)	Timber
Rear bumper	1 off	267 × 20 × 16mm (10½ × ¾ × ⅝in)	Timber
Front bumper	1 off	241 × 41 × 25mm (9½ × 1⅝ × 1in)	Timber
Fifth wheel	1 off	108 × 95 × 20mm (4¼ × 3¾ × ¾in)	Timber
Fuel tank assembly	2 off	121mm (4¾in) × 64mm (2½in) diam	Timber
	2 off	197mm (7¾in) × 12mm (½in) diam dowel	
Front axle block	1 off	197 × 51 × 20mm (7¾ × 2 × ¾in)	Timber
Front axle cross bar	1 off	197 × 25 × 9mm (7¾ × 1 × ⅜in)	Timber
Stub axle block	2 off	76 × 32 × 20mm (3 × 1¼ × ¾in)	Timber
Steering tie bar	1 off	197 × 28 × 6mm (7¾ × 1⅛ × ¼in)	Timber
Battery box	2 off	89 × 44 × 41mm (3½ × 1¾ × 1⅝in)	Timber
Air cylinders	3 off	28mm (1⅛in) × 22mm (⅞in) diam dowel	
Engine/cab side panel	2 off	264 × 95 × 16mm (10⅜ × 3¾ × ⅝in)	Timber
Forward bonnet spacer	1 off	137 × 35 × 16mm (5⅜ × 1⅜ × ⅝in)	Timber
Rear bonnet spacer	1 off	152 × 35 × 16mm (6 × 1⅜ × ⅝in)	Timber
Radiator	1 off	149 × 114 × 20mm (5⅞ × 4½ × ¾in)	Timber
	1 off	149 × 20 × 9mm (5⅞ × ¾ × ⅜in)	Timber
Radiator trim	1 off	51 × 16 × 3mm (2 × ⅝ × ⅛in)	Timber
	1 off	149 × 3 × 15mm (5⅞ × ⅛ × 1⁄16in)	Timber
	6 off	137 × 3 × 3mm (5⅜ × ⅛ × ⅛in)	Timber
Bonnet/dash board	1 off	213 × 168 × 20mm (8⅜ × 6⅝ × ¾in)	Timber
Cab side wall	2 off	105 × 86 × 12mm (4⅛ × 3⅜ × ½in)	Timber
Side screen sill	2 off	86mm (3⅜in) × 6mm (¼in) segment	Timber
Cab roof	1 off	171 × 127 × 16mm (6¾ × 5 × ⅝in)	Timber
Steering wheel	1 off	9mm (⅜in) × 38mm (1½in) diam	Timber
	1 off	38mm (1½in) × 6mm (¼in) diam dowel	
Air horn	2 off	70mm (2¾in) × 6mm (¼in) diam dowel	
Spot lamp	3 off	25mm (1in) × 16mm (⅝in) diam dowel	
Windscreen frame	1 off	168 × 73 × 12mm (6⅝ × 2⅞ × ½in)	Timber
Exhaust	1 off	152mm (6in) × 22mm (⅞in) diam dowel	
	1 off	25mm (1in) × 11mm (7⁄16in) diam dowel	
Door handle	5 off	22 × 9 × 6mm (⅞ × ⅜ × ¼in)	Timber
Cab seat	2 off	67 × 54 × 44mm (2⅝ × 2⅛ × 1¾in)	Timber
Cab rear wall	1 off	181 × 168 × 12mm (7⅛ × 6⅝ × ½in)	Timber
	1 off	140 × 35 × 12mm (5½ × 1⅜ × ½in)	Timber
Front mudguard	2 off	143 × 79 × 44mm (5⅝ × 3⅛ × 1¾in)	Timber
	2 off	35 × 12 × 9mm (1⅜ × ½ × ⅜in)	Timber
Sleeping cabin front wall	1 off	229 × 210 × 12mm (9 × 8¼ × ½in)	Timber
Sleeping cabin rear wall	1 off	229 × 210 × 12mm (9 × 8¼ × ½in)	Timber
Sleeping cabin roof	1 off	210 × 79 × 16mm (8¼ × 3⅛ × ⅝in)	Timber
	1 off	83 × 41 × 3mm (3¼ × 1⅝ × ⅛in)	Timber
Sleeping cabin floor	1 off	210 × 79 × 16mm (8¼ × 3⅛ × ⅝in)	Timber
Sleeping cabin driver's side door	1 off	229 × 92 × 12mm (9 × 3⅝ × ½in)	Timber
	2 off	32 × 20 × 3mm (1¼ × ¾ × ⅛in)	Timber
Sleeping cabin upper passenger's side door	1 off	130 × 92 × 12mm (5⅛ × 3⅝ × ½in)	Timber
	1 off	32 × 20 × 3mm (1¼ × ¾ × ⅛in)	Timber
Sleeping cabin lower passenger's side door	1 off	98 × 92 × 12mm (3⅞ × 3⅝ × ½in)	Timber

	1 off	32 × 20 × 3mm (1¼ × ¾ × ⅛in)	Timber
Mudguard and sleeping cabin access ladder	2 off	83 × 16 × 6mm (3¼ × ⅝ × ¼in)	Timber
	4 off	76 × 11 × 5mm (3 × ⁷⁄₁₆ × ³⁄₁₆in)	Timber
	8 off	25mm (1in) × 6mm (¼in) diam dowel	
Sleeping cabin upper bunk floor	1 off	197 × 67 × 12mm (7¾ × 2⅝ × ½in)	Timber
Sleeping cabin partition	1 off	76 × 67 × 12mm (3 × 2⅝ × ½in)	Timber
Sleeping cabin upper bunk access ladder	2 off	95 × 11 × 5mm (3¾ × ⁷⁄₁₆ × ³⁄₁₆in)	Timber
	5 off	25mm (1in) × 6mm (¼in) diam dowel	

Ancillaries

	10 off	102mm (4in) diam road wheels
	2 off	267mm (10½in) × 6mm (¼in) diam steel axles (rear)
	2 off	76mm (3in) × 6mm (¼in) diam steel axles (front)
	2 off	Spring dome caps to suit 9mm (⅜in) diam rod
	12 off	Spring dome caps to suit 6mm (¼in) diam rod
	2 off	Spring dome caps to suit 5mm (³⁄₁₆in) diam rod
	1 off	152mm (6in) × 9mm (⅜in) diam steel rear axle pivot pin
	2 off	149mm (5⅞in) × 6mm (¼in) diam steel rear axle tie bars
	2 off	108mm (4¼in) × 14mm (⁹⁄₁₆in) o/diam × 11mm (⁷⁄₁₆in) i/diam plastic tube – rear axle spacer
	2 off	5mm (³⁄₁₆in × 14mm (⁹⁄₁₆in) o/diam × 11mm (⁷⁄₁₆in i/diam spacer for rear axle pivot pin
	2 off	159mm (6¼in) × 14mm (⁹⁄₁₆in) o/diam × 11mm (⁷⁄₁₆in) i/diam plastic tube exhaust extension
	2 off	54mm (2⅛in) × 6mm (¼in) diam steel stub axle block pivot pin
	2 off	32mm (1¼in) × 5mm (³⁄₁₆in) diam steel steering tie bar pin
	Made from 1778mm (70in) × 16mm (⅝in) × 1.5mm (¹⁄₁₆in) thick spring steel
	1 off	305mm (12in) × 152mm (6in) aluminium mesh
	4 off	95mm (3¾in) × 76mm (3in) × 1mm (¹⁄₃₂in) thick stiff black plastic
	2 off	57mm (2¼in) × 9mm (⅜in) reflective tape
	Made from 1270mm (50in) × 1.5mm (¹⁄₁₆in) diam soft wire
	1 off	143mm (5⅝in) × 67mm (2⅝in) × 1.5mm (¹⁄₁₆in) thick clear plastic
	2 off	102mm (4in) × 86mm (3⅜in) × 1.5mm (¹⁄₁₆in) thick clear plastic
	1 off	143mm (5⅝in) × 89mm × (3½in) × 1.5mm (¹⁄₁₆in) thick clear plastic
	4 off	6mm (¼in) × 6mm (¼in) o/diam × 5mm (³⁄₁₆in) i/diam aluminium tube spacer – exhaust
	2 off	44mm (1¾in) × 3mm (⅛in) o/diam × 1.5mm (¹⁄₁₆in) i/diam rubber tube – windscreen wiper blade
	2 off	127mm (5in) × 44mm (1¾in) red felt to cover seats
	6 off	25mm (1in) × 25mm (1in) brass hinges

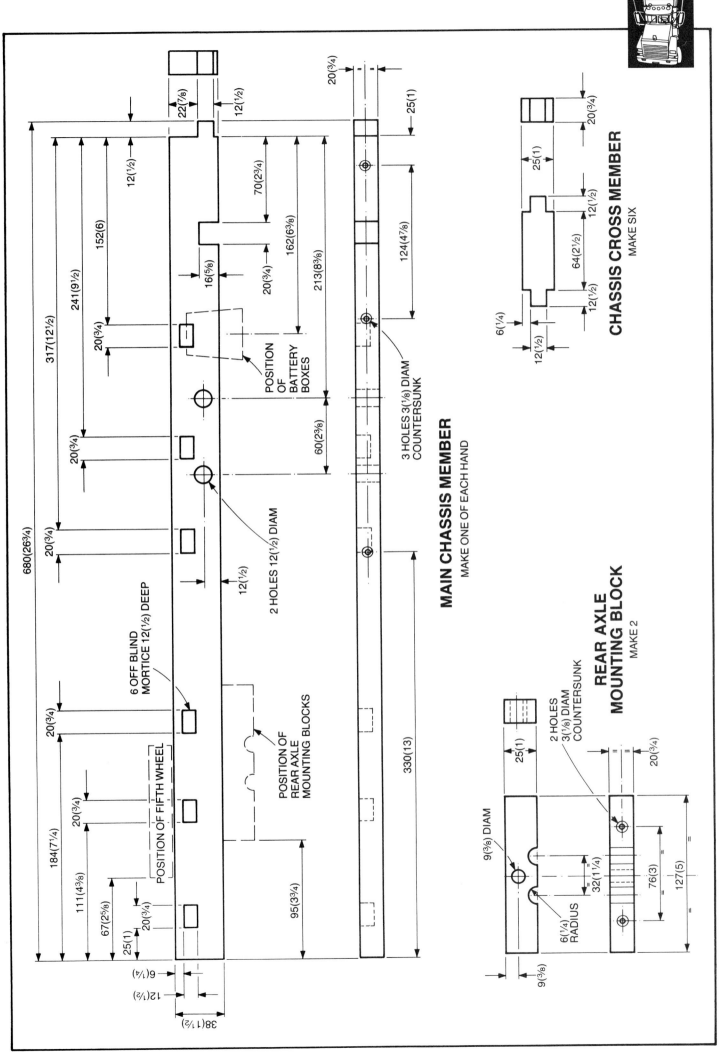

MAIN CHASSIS MEMBER
MAKE ONE OF EACH HAND

CHASSIS CROSS MEMBER
MAKE SIX

REAR AXLE MOUNTING BLOCK
MAKE 2

POSITION OF BATTERY BOXES

3 HOLES 3(1/8) DIAM COUNTERSUNK

2 HOLES 12(1/2) DIAM

6 OFF BLIND MORTICE 12(1/2) DEEP

POSITION OF REAR AXLE MOUNTING BLOCKS

POSITION OF FIFTH WHEEL

2 HOLES 3(1/8) DIAM COUNTERSUNK

9(3/8) DIAM

6(1/4) RADIUS

159

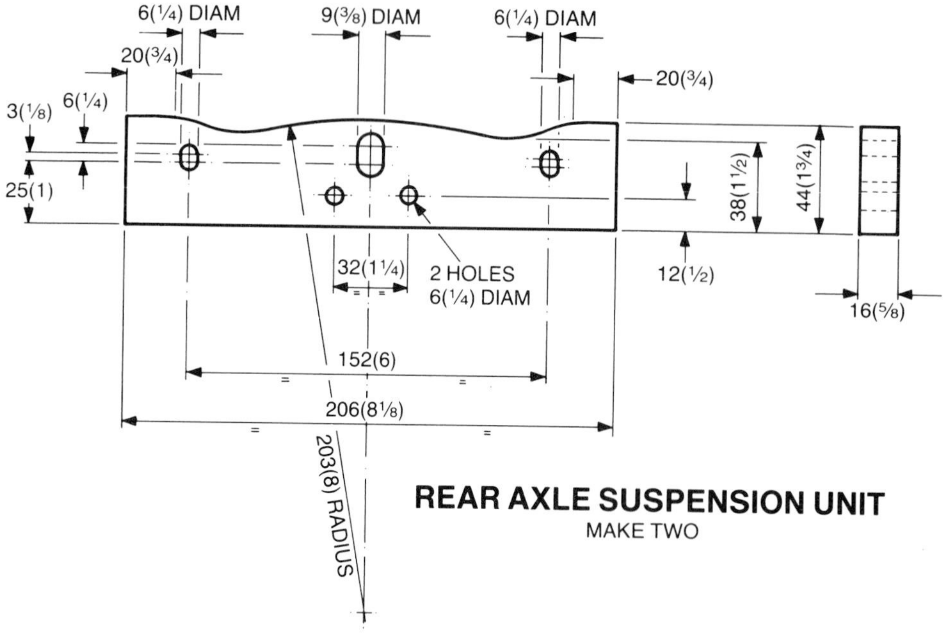
6(1/4) DIAM
9(3/8) DIAM
6(1/4) DIAM
20(3/4)
20(3/4)
3(1/8)
6(1/4)
25(1)
38(1 1/2)
44(1 3/4)
12(1/2)
16(5/8)
32(1 1/4)
2 HOLES
6(1/4) DIAM
152(6)
206(8 1/8)
203(8) RADIUS

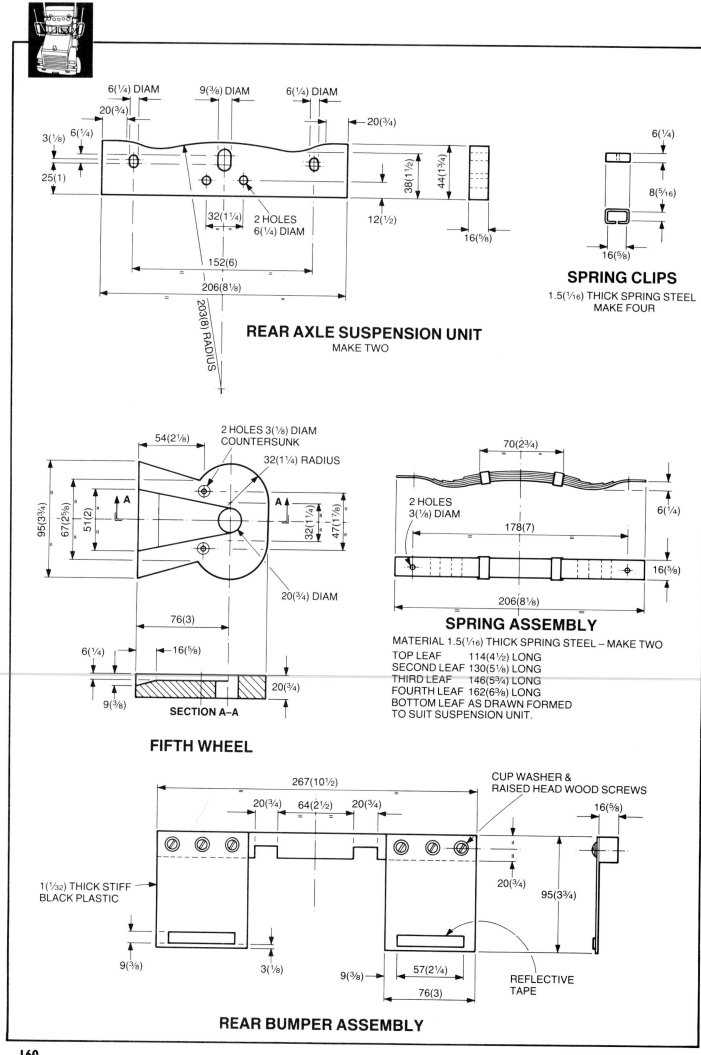

REAR AXLE SUSPENSION UNIT
MAKE TWO

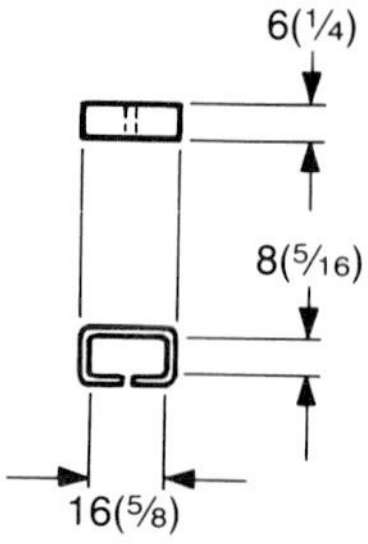
6(1/4)
8(5/16)
16(5/8)

SPRING CLIPS
1.5(1/16) THICK SPRING STEEL
MAKE FOUR

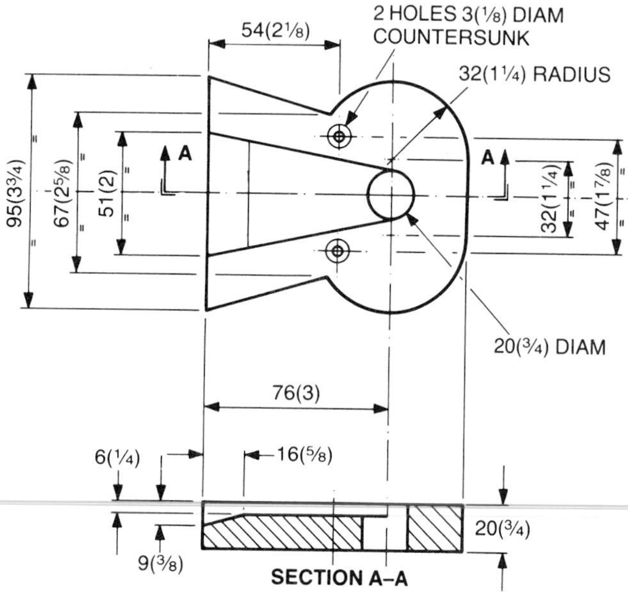
54(2 1/8)
2 HOLES 3(1/8) DIAM
COUNTERSUNK
32(1 1/4) RADIUS
95(3 3/4)
67(2 5/8)
51(2)
A
A
32(1 1/4)
47(1 7/8)
20(3/4) DIAM
76(3)
6(1/4)
16(5/8)
20(3/4)
9(3/8)
SECTION A–A

FIFTH WHEEL

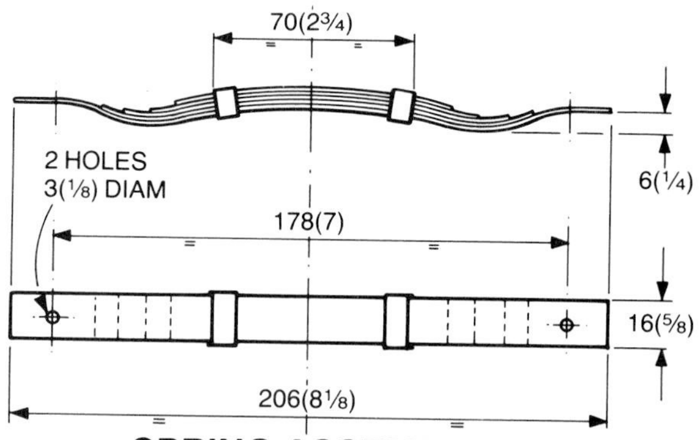
70(2 3/4)
2 HOLES
3(1/8) DIAM
178(7)
6(1/4)
16(5/8)
206(8 1/8)

SPRING ASSEMBLY

MATERIAL 1.5(1/16) THICK SPRING STEEL – MAKE TWO

TOP LEAF	114(4 1/2) LONG
SECOND LEAF	130(5 1/8) LONG
THIRD LEAF	146(5 3/4) LONG
FOURTH LEAF	162(6 3/8) LONG
BOTTOM LEAF	AS DRAWN FORMED TO SUIT SUSPENSION UNIT.

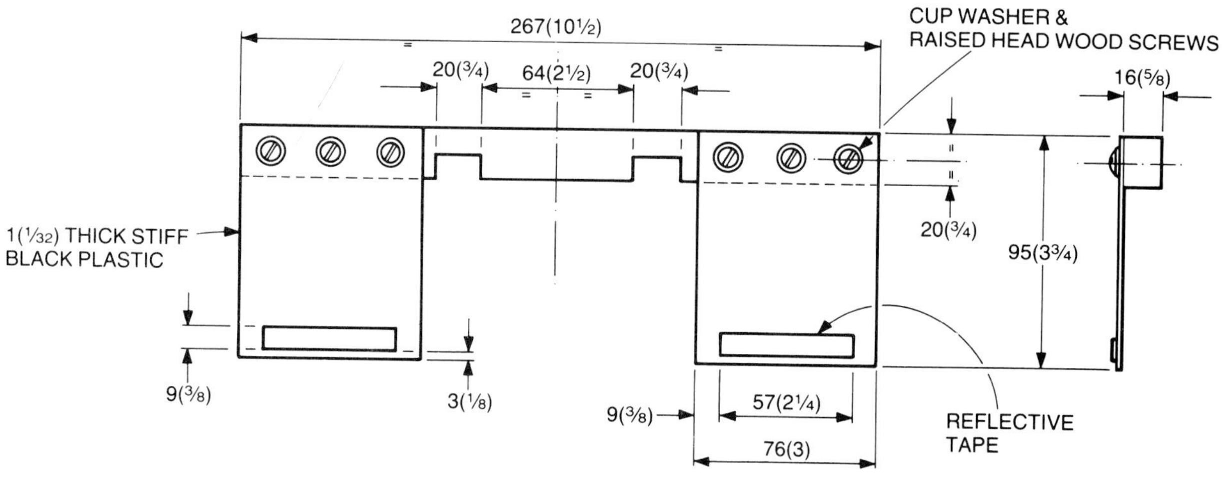
267(10 1/2)
CUP WASHER &
RAISED HEAD WOOD SCREWS
20(3/4)
64(2 1/2)
20(3/4)
16(5/8)
1(1/32) THICK STIFF
BLACK PLASTIC
20(3/4)
95(3 3/4)
9(3/8)
3(1/8)
9(3/8)
57(2 1/4)
76(3)
REFLECTIVE
TAPE

REAR BUMPER ASSEMBLY

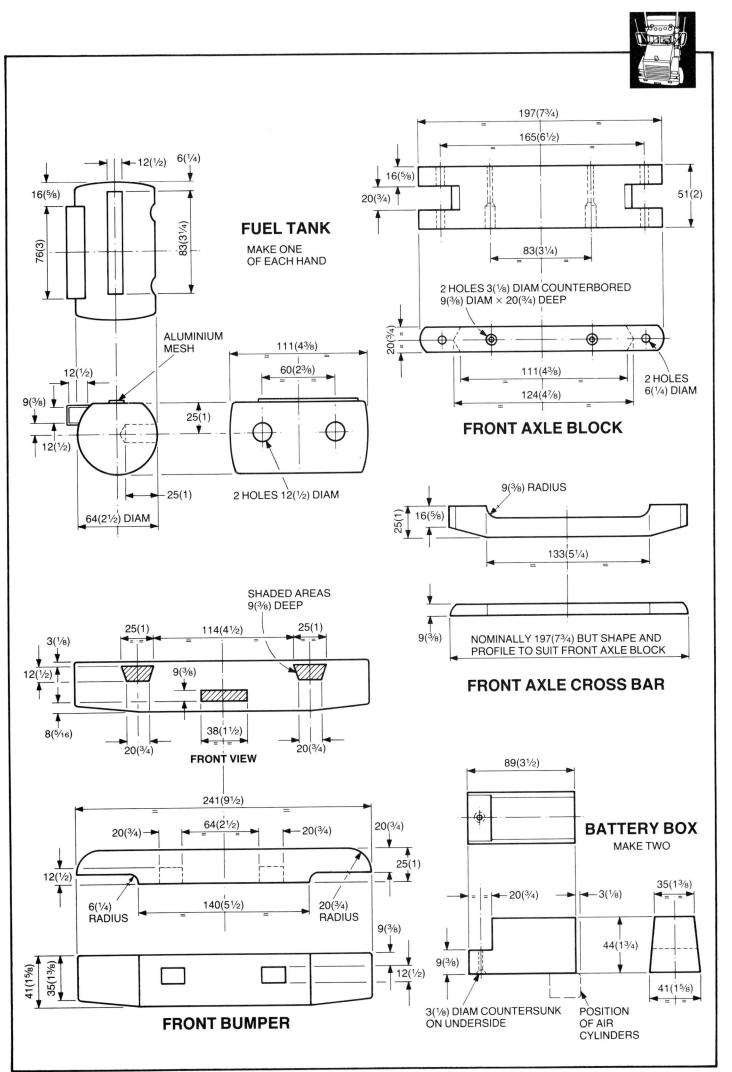

FUEL TANK

MAKE ONE
OF EACH HAND

ALUMINIUM MESH

2 HOLES 12(½) DIAM

FRONT AXLE BLOCK

2 HOLES 3(⅛) DIAM COUNTERBORED
9(⅜) DIAM × 20(¾) DEEP

2 HOLES
6(¼) DIAM

9(⅜) RADIUS

FRONT AXLE CROSS BAR

NOMINALLY 197(7¾) BUT SHAPE AND
PROFILE TO SUIT FRONT AXLE BLOCK

SHADED AREAS
9(⅜) DEEP

FRONT VIEW

6(¼) RADIUS

20(¾) RADIUS

FRONT BUMPER

BATTERY BOX

MAKE TWO

3(⅛) DIAM COUNTERSUNK
ON UNDERSIDE

POSITION
OF AIR
CYLINDERS

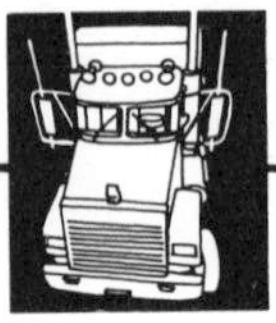

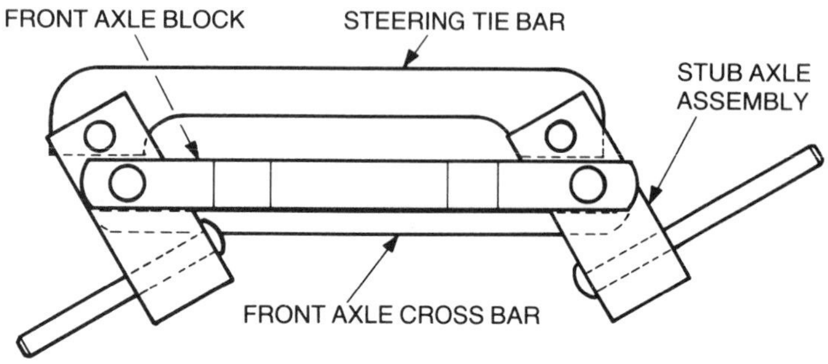
FRONT AXLE BLOCK
STEERING TIE BAR
STUB AXLE ASSEMBLY
FRONT AXLE CROSS BAR

FRONT AXLE STEERING ASSEMBLY

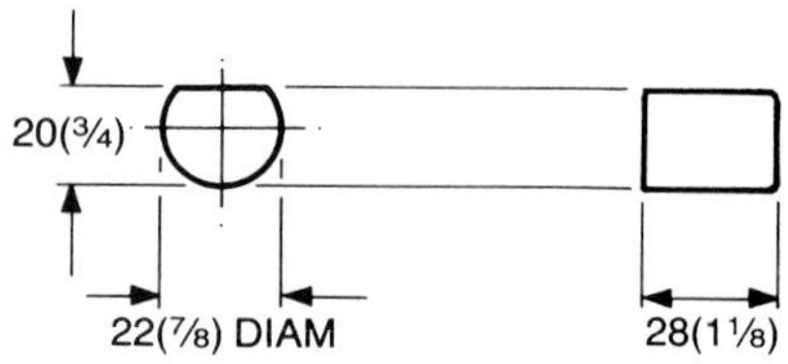
20(3/4)
22(7/8) DIAM
28(1 1/8)

AIR CYLINDERS

MAKE THREE

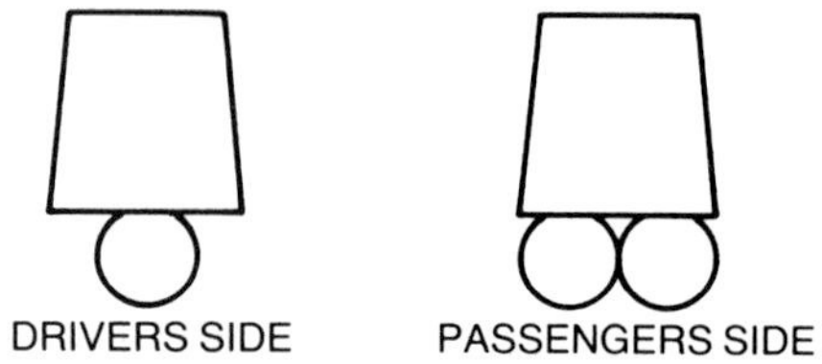
DRIVERS SIDE
PASSENGERS SIDE

AIR CYLINDER/BATTERY BOX ARRANGEMENT

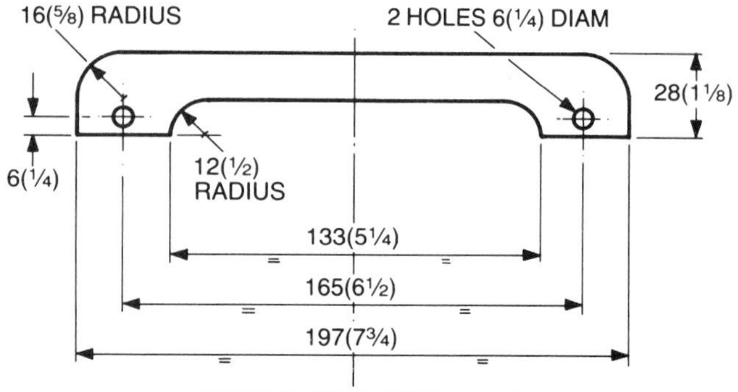
16(5/8) RADIUS
2 HOLES 6(1/4) DIAM
28(1 1/8)
6(1/4)
12(1/2) RADIUS
133(5 1/4)
165(6 1/2)
197(7 3/4)

STEERING TIE BAR

6(1/4) THICK

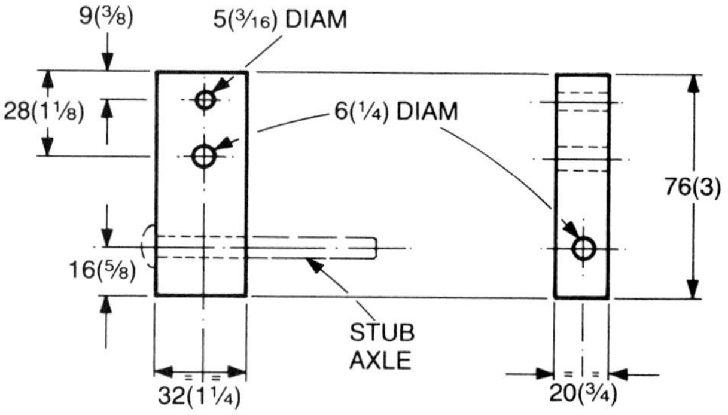
9(3/8)
5(3/16) DIAM
28(1 1/8)
6(1/4) DIAM
76(3)
16(5/8)
STUB AXLE
32(1 1/4)
20(3/4)

STUB AXLE ASSEMBLY

MAKE TWO

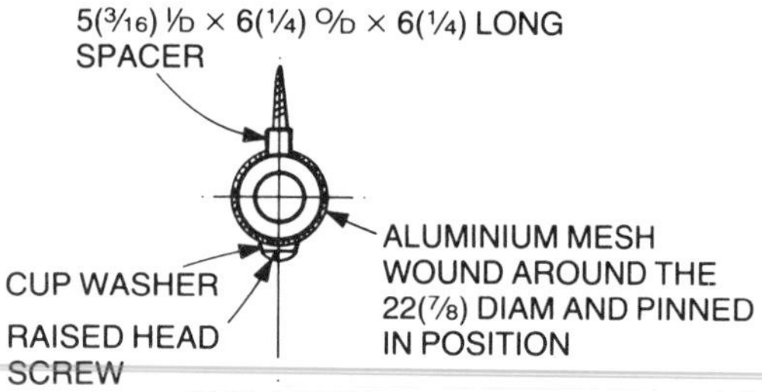
5(3/16) I/D × 6(1/4) O/D × 6(1/4) LONG SPACER
ALUMINIUM MESH WOUND AROUND THE 22(7/8) DIAM AND PINNED IN POSITION
CUP WASHER
RAISED HEAD SCREW

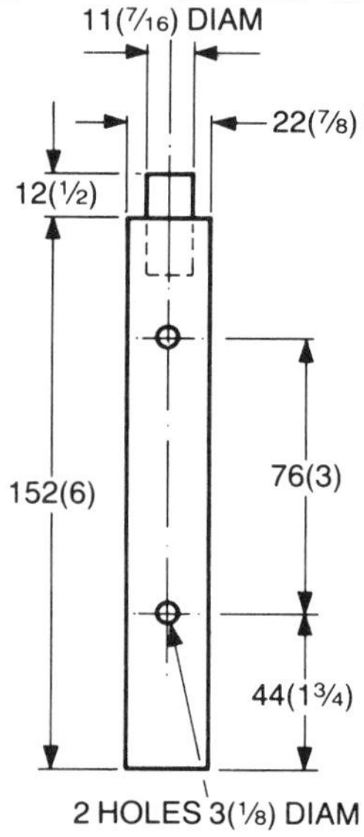
11(7/16) DIAM
22(7/8) DIAM
12(1/2)
152(6)
76(3)
44(1 3/4)
2 HOLES 3(1/8) DIAM

EXHAUST

MAKE TWO

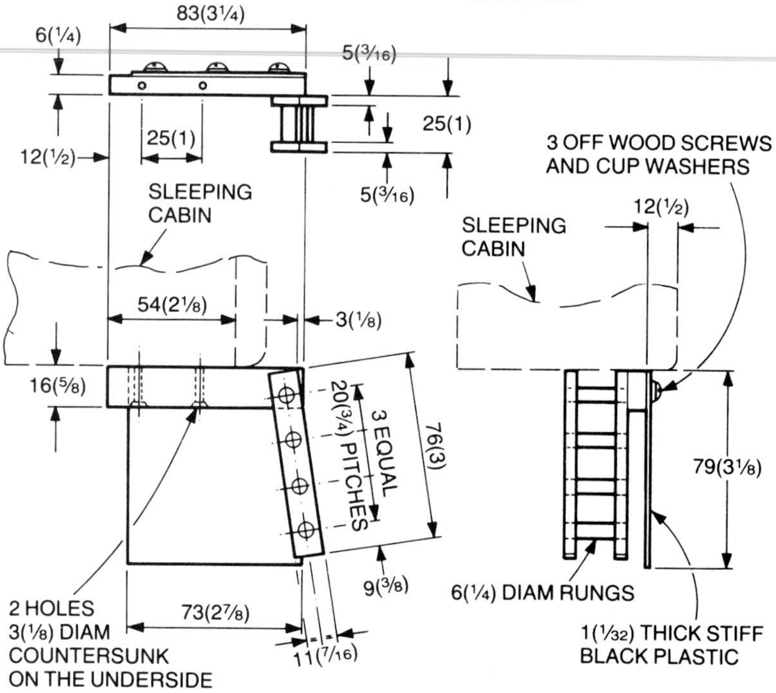
83(3 1/4)
6(1/4)
5(3/16)
25(1)
25(1)
12(1/2)
5(3/16)
SLEEPING CABIN
54(2 1/8)
3(1/8)
16(5/8)
20(3/4) 3 EQUAL PITCHES
76(3)
9(3/8)
2 HOLES 3(1/8) DIAM COUNTERSUNK ON THE UNDERSIDE
73(2 7/8)
11(7/16)
3 OFF WOOD SCREWS AND CUP WASHERS
12(1/2)
SLEEPING CABIN
79(3 1/8)
6(1/4) DIAM RUNGS
1(1/32) THICK STIFF BLACK PLASTIC

MUDFLAP & SLEEPING CABIN ACCESS LADDER

MAKE ONE OF EACH HAND

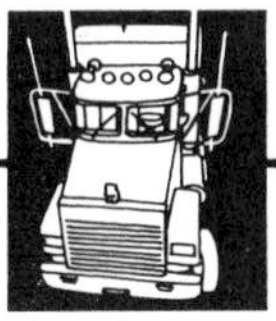

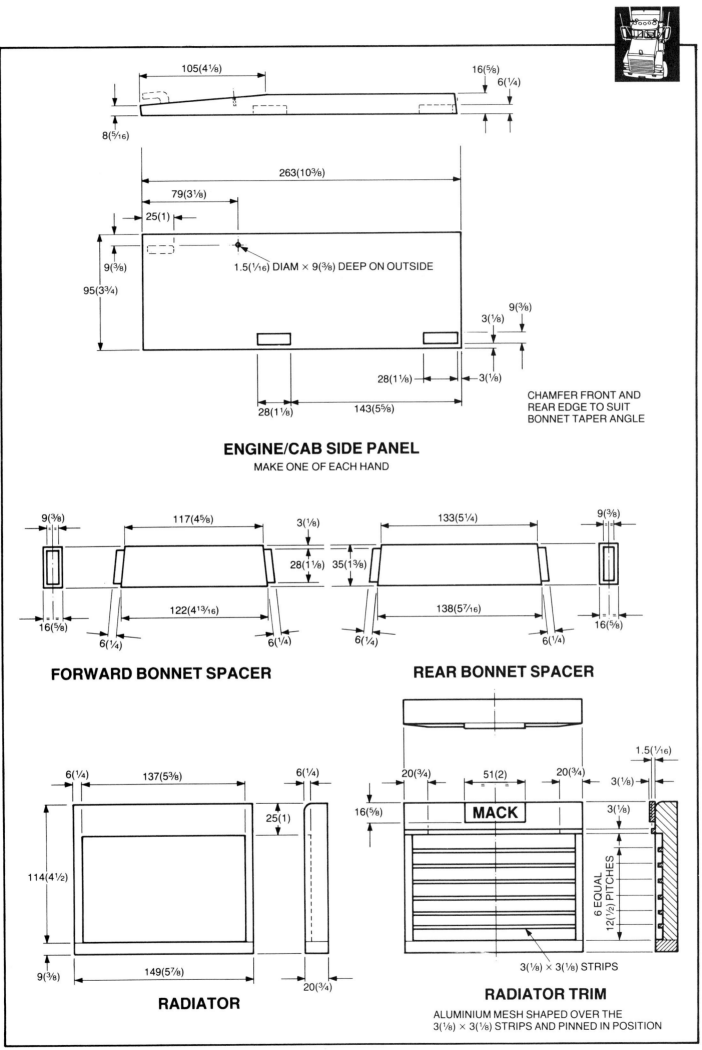

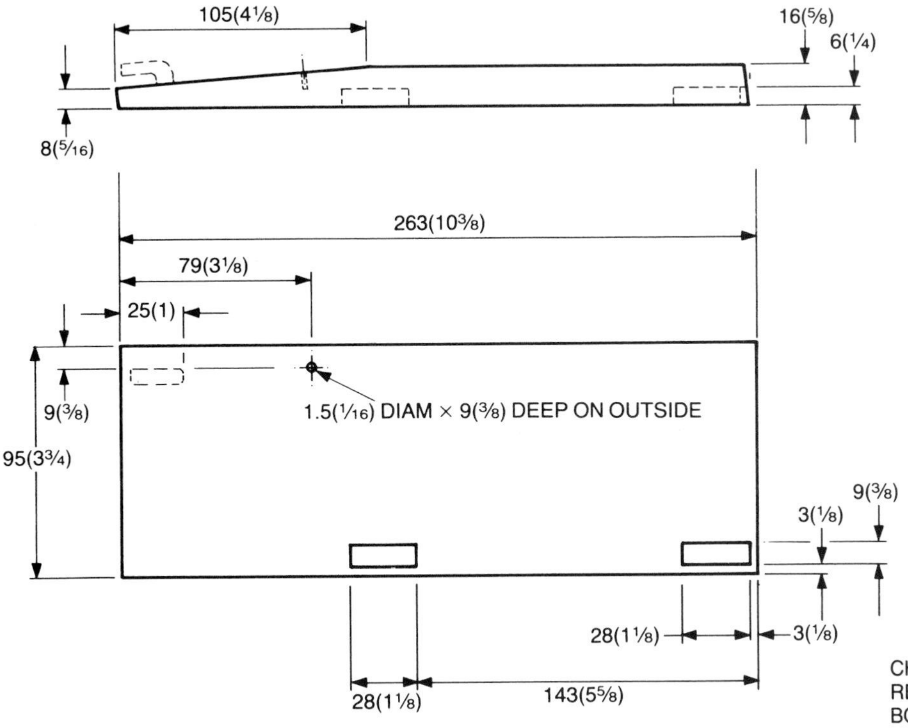
105(4 1/8)
16(5/8)
6(1/4)
8(5/16)
263(10 3/8)
79(3 1/8)
25(1)
9(3/8)
1.5(1/16) DIAM × 9(3/8) DEEP ON OUTSIDE
95(3 3/4)
9(3/8)
3(1/8)
28(1 1/8)
3(1/8)
28(1 1/8)
143(5 5/8)

CHAMFER FRONT AND
REAR EDGE TO SUIT
BONNET TAPER ANGLE

ENGINE/CAB SIDE PANEL

MAKE ONE OF EACH HAND

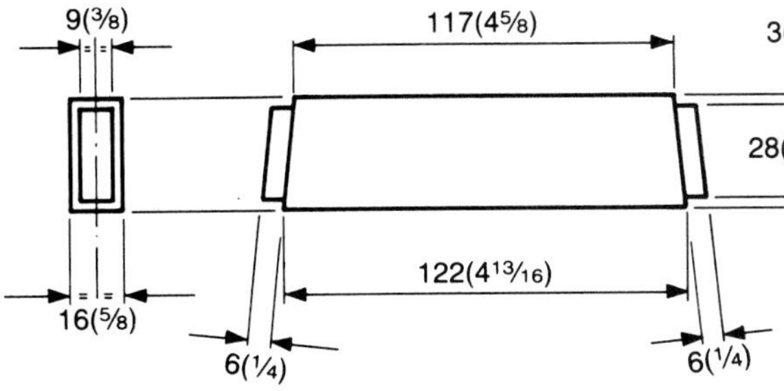
9(3/8)
117(4 5/8)
3(1/8)
28(1 1/8)
16(5/8)
122(4 13/16)
6(1/4)
6(1/4)

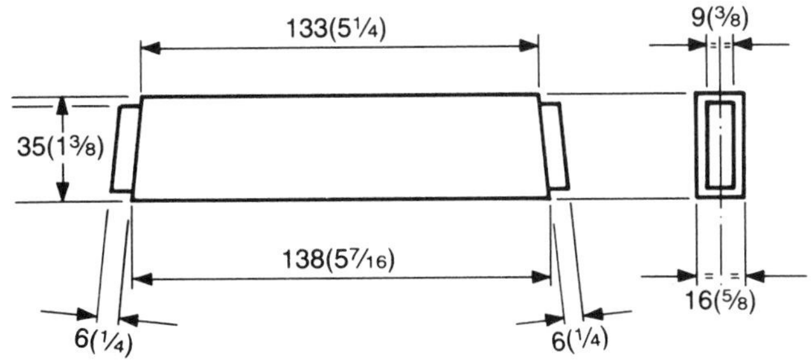
35(1 3/8)
133(5 1/4)
9(3/8)
138(5 7/16)
16(5/8)
6(1/4)
6(1/4)

FORWARD BONNET SPACER

REAR BONNET SPACER

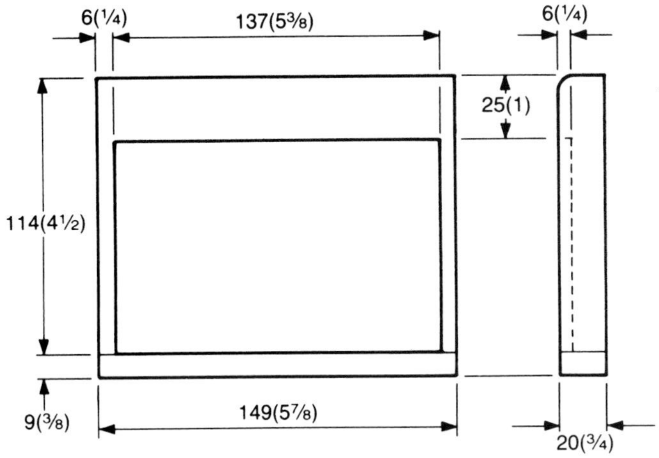
6(1/4)
137(5 3/8)
6(1/4)
25(1)
114(4 1/2)
9(3/8)
149(5 7/8)
20(3/4)

RADIATOR

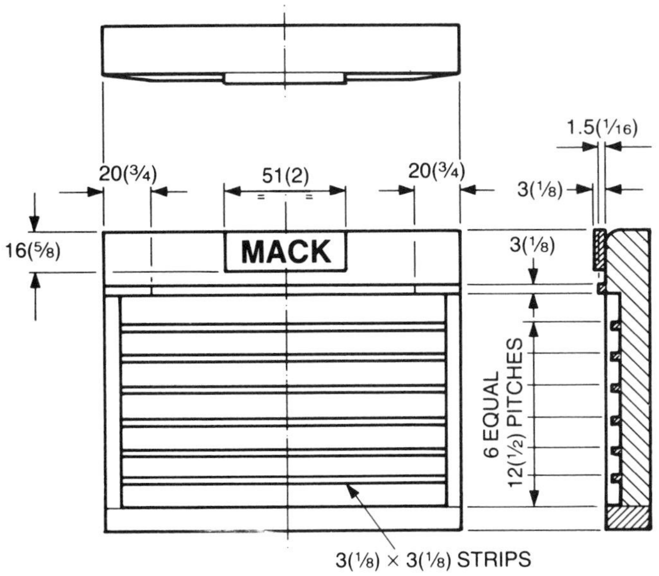
1.5(1/16)
20(3/4)
51(2)
20(3/4)
3(1/8)
16(5/8)
MACK
3(1/8)
6 EQUAL
12(1/2) PITCHES
3(1/8) × 3(1/8) STRIPS

RADIATOR TRIM

ALUMINIUM MESH SHAPED OVER THE
3(1/8) × 3(1/8) STRIPS AND PINNED IN POSITION

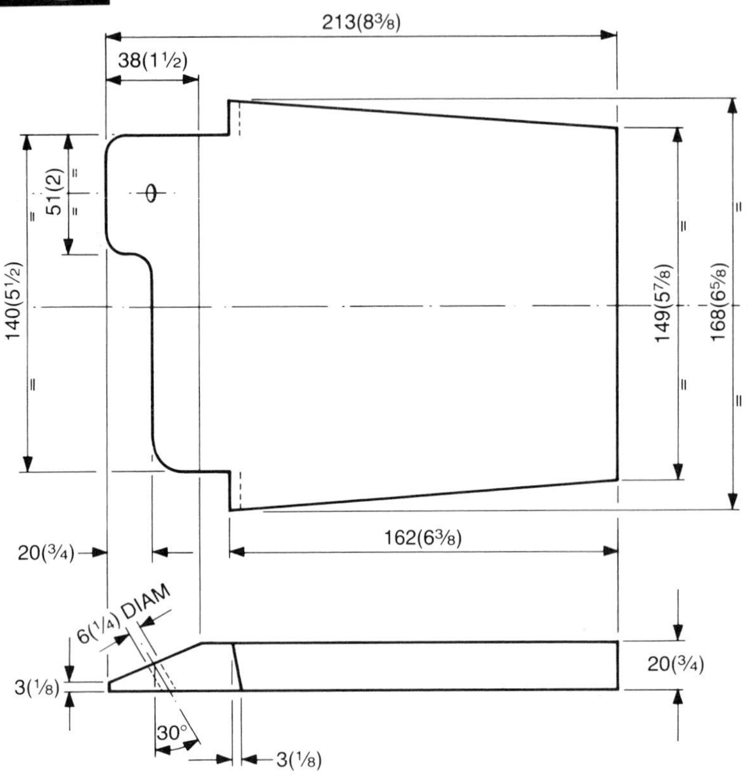

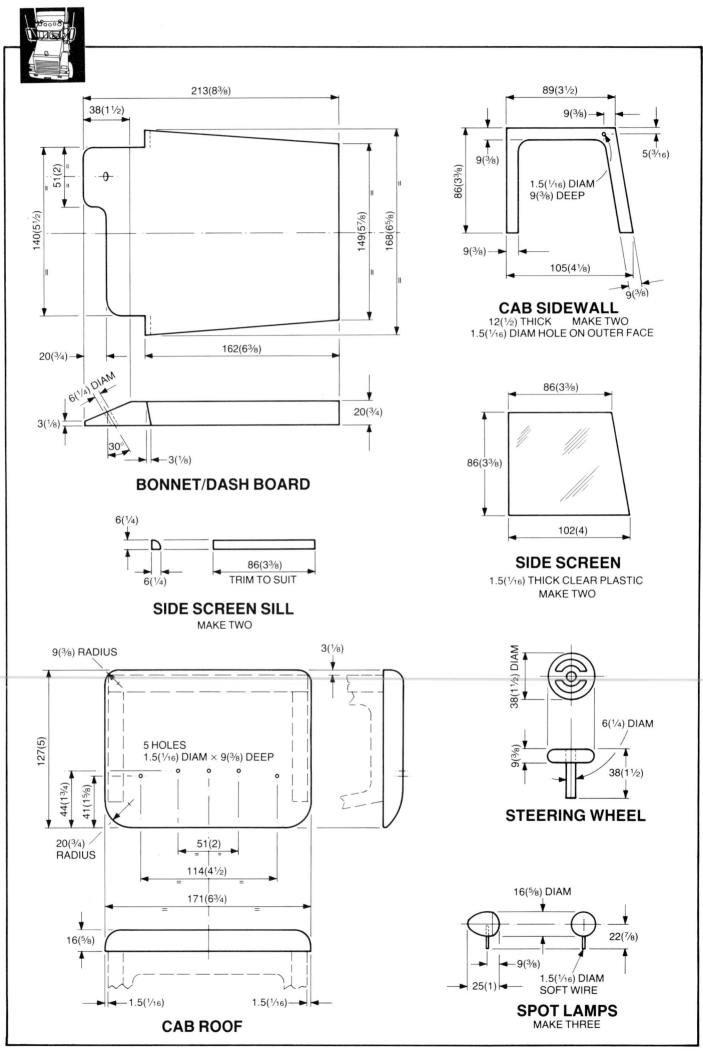

213(8 3/8)
38(1 1/2)
51(2)
140(5 1/2)
149(5 7/8)
168(6 5/8)
20(3/4)
162(6 3/8)
6(1/4) DIAM
3(1/8)
20(3/4)
30°
3(1/8)

BONNET/DASH BOARD

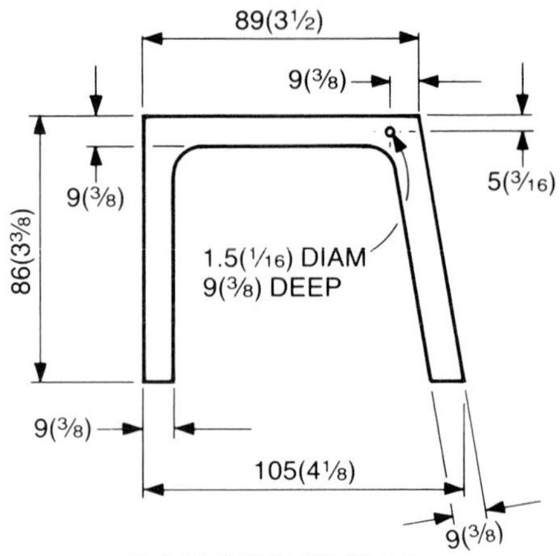

89(3 1/2)
9(3/8)
5(3/16)
86(3 3/8)
9(3/8)
1.5(1/16) DIAM
9(3/8) DEEP
9(3/8)
105(4 1/8)
9(3/8)

CAB SIDEWALL

12(1/2) THICK MAKE TWO
1.5(1/16) DIAM HOLE ON OUTER FACE

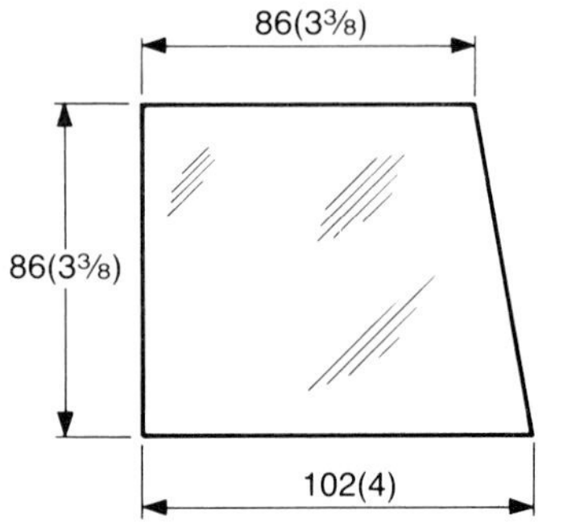

86(3 3/8)
86(3 3/8)
102(4)

SIDE SCREEN

1.5(1/16) THICK CLEAR PLASTIC
MAKE TWO

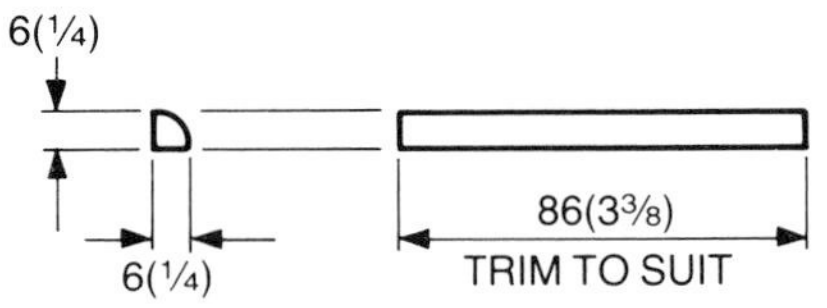

6(1/4)
6(1/4)
86(3 3/8)
TRIM TO SUIT

SIDE SCREEN SILL

MAKE TWO

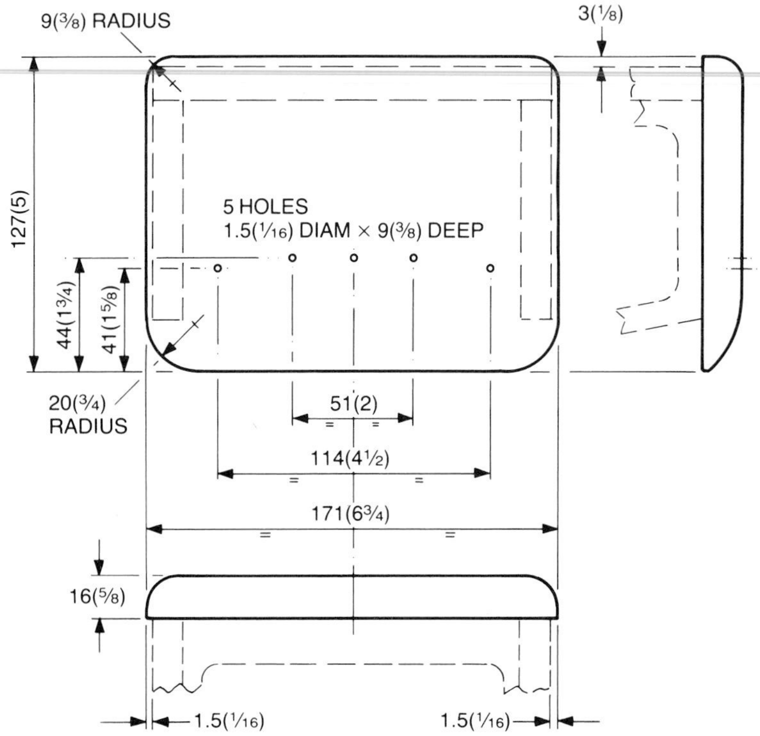

9(3/8) RADIUS
3(1/8)
127(5)
5 HOLES
1.5(1/16) DIAM × 9(3/8) DEEP
44(1 3/4)
41(1 5/8)
20(3/4)
RADIUS
51(2)
114(4 1/2)
171(6 3/4)
16(5/8)
1.5(1/16)
1.5(1/16)

CAB ROOF

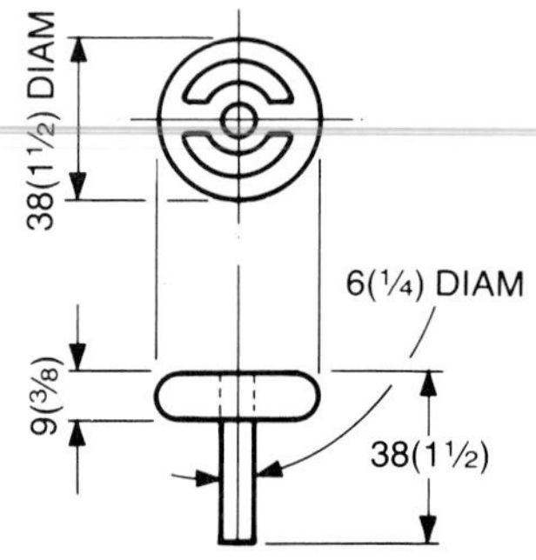

38(1 1/2) DIAM
6(1/4) DIAM
9(3/8)
38(1 1/2)

STEERING WHEEL

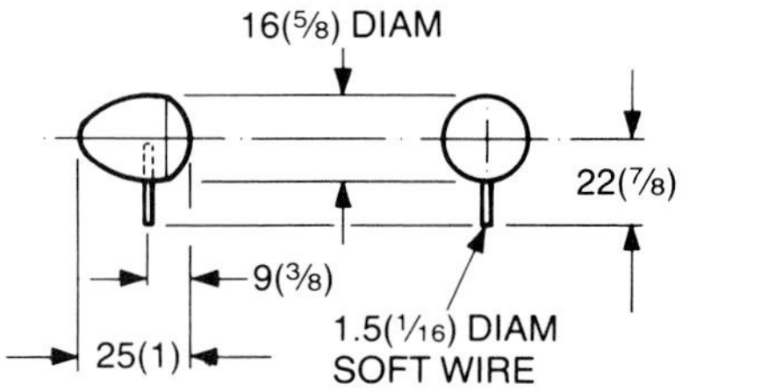

16(5/8) DIAM
22(7/8)
9(3/8)
1.5(1/16) DIAM
SOFT WIRE
25(1)

SPOT LAMPS

MAKE THREE

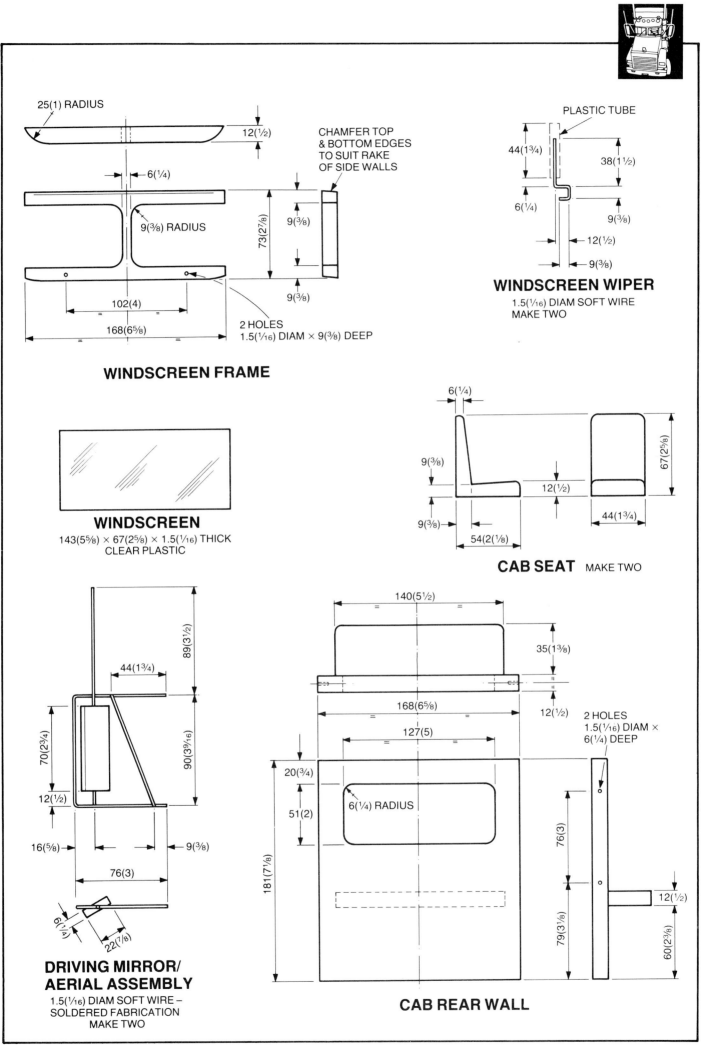

25(1) RADIUS

12(½)

6(¼)

9(⅜) RADIUS

73(2⅞)

CHAMFER TOP
& BOTTOM EDGES
TO SUIT RAKE
OF SIDE WALLS

9(⅜)

9(⅜)

102(4)

168(6⅝)

2 HOLES
1.5(¹⁄₁₆) DIAM × 9(⅜) DEEP

WINDSCREEN FRAME

PLASTIC TUBE

44(1¾)

38(1½)

6(¼)

9(⅜)

12(½)

9(⅜)

WINDSCREEN WIPER

1.5(¹⁄₁₆) DIAM SOFT WIRE
MAKE TWO

WINDSCREEN

143(5⅝) × 67(2⅝) × 1.5(¹⁄₁₆) THICK
CLEAR PLASTIC

6(¼)

9(⅜)

12(½)

67(2⅝)

9(⅜)

54(2⅛)

44(1¾)

CAB SEAT   MAKE TWO

89(3½)

44(1¾)

70(2¾)

90(3⁹⁄₁₆)

12(½)

16(⅝)

9(⅜)

76(3)

6(¼)

22(⅞)

DRIVING MIRROR/
AERIAL ASSEMBLY

1.5(¹⁄₁₆) DIAM SOFT WIRE –
SOLDERED FABRICATION
MAKE TWO

140(5½)

35(1⅜)

168(6⅝)

12(½)

2 HOLES
1.5(¹⁄₁₆) DIAM ×
6(¼) DEEP

127(5)

20(¾)

6(¼) RADIUS

51(2)

181(7⅛)

76(3)

79(3⅛)

12(½)

60(2⅜)

CAB REAR WALL

165

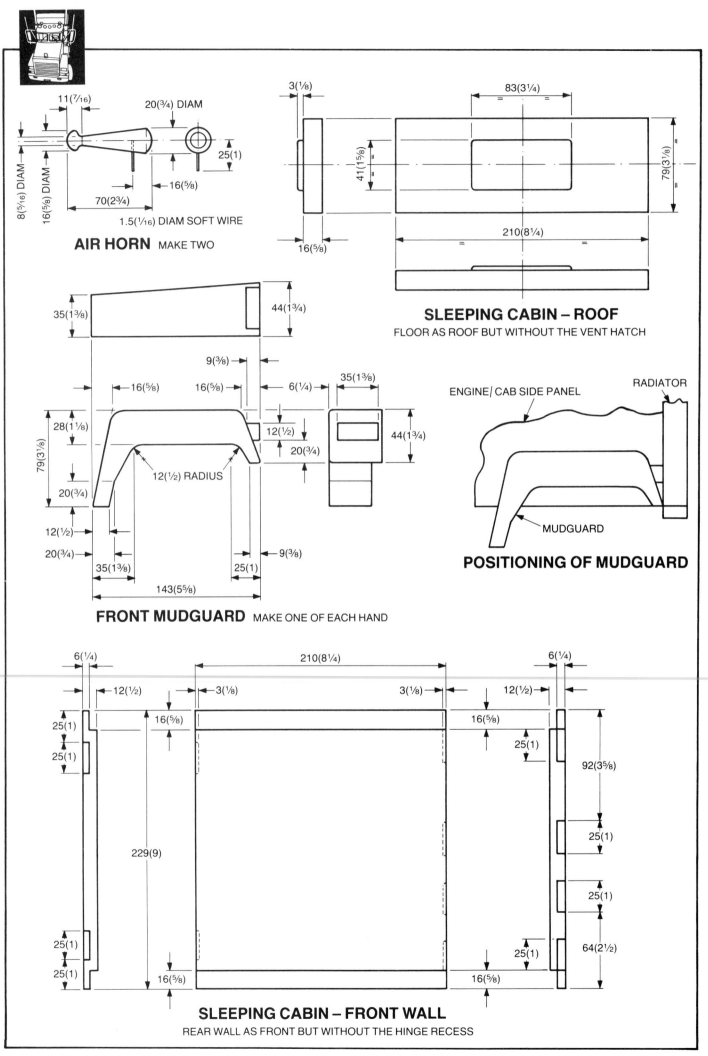

AIR HORN MAKE TWO

11(7/16)
20(3/4) DIAM
8(5/16) DIAM
16(5/8) DIAM
25(1)
16(5/8)
70(2 3/4)
1.5(1/16) DIAM SOFT WIRE

3(1/8)
83(3 1/4)
41(1 5/8)
79(3 1/8)
210(8 1/4)
16(5/8)

SLEEPING CABIN – ROOF
FLOOR AS ROOF BUT WITHOUT THE VENT HATCH

35(1 3/8)
44(1 3/4)
9(3/8)
16(5/8)
16(5/8)
6(1/4)
35(1 3/8)
28(1 1/8)
12(1/2)
20(3/4)
44(1 3/4)
79(3 1/8)
12(1/2) RADIUS
20(3/4)
12(1/2)
20(3/4)
35(1 3/8)
25(1)
9(3/8)
143(5 5/8)

FRONT MUDGUARD MAKE ONE OF EACH HAND

ENGINE/ CAB SIDE PANEL
RADIATOR
MUDGUARD

POSITIONING OF MUDGUARD

6(1/4)
210(8 1/4)
6(1/4)
12(1/2)
3(1/8)
3(1/8)
12(1/2)
25(1)
16(5/8)
16(5/8)
25(1)
25(1)
25(1)
92(3 5/8)
25(1)
229(9)
25(1)
25(1)
64(2 1/2)
25(1)
25(1)
16(5/8)
25(1)
16(5/8)

SLEEPING CABIN – FRONT WALL
REAR WALL AS FRONT BUT WITHOUT THE HINGE RECESS

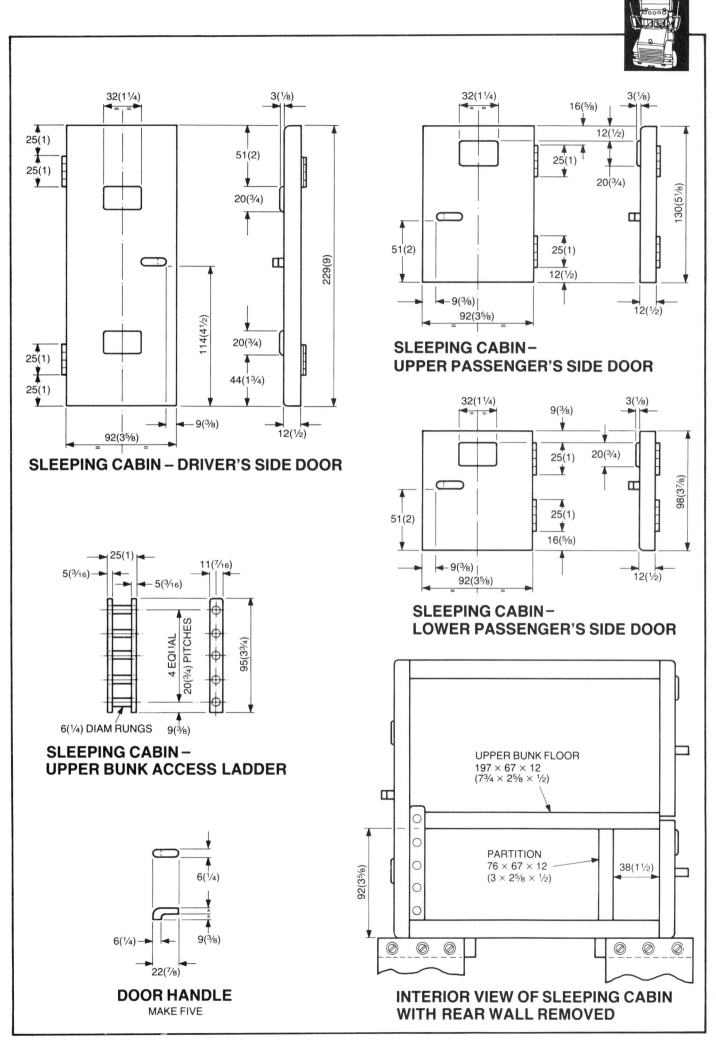

SLEEPING CABIN – DRIVER'S SIDE DOOR

SLEEPING CABIN –
UPPER PASSENGER'S SIDE DOOR

SLEEPING CABIN –
LOWER PASSENGER'S SIDE DOOR

6(¼) DIAM RUNGS

SLEEPING CABIN –
UPPER BUNK ACCESS LADDER

4 EQUAL
20(¾) PITCHES

UPPER BUNK FLOOR
197 × 67 × 12
(7¾ × 2⅝ × ½)

PARTITION
76 × 67 × 12
(3 × 2⅝ × ½)

DOOR HANDLE
MAKE FIVE

INTERIOR VIEW OF SLEEPING CABIN
WITH REAR WALL REMOVED

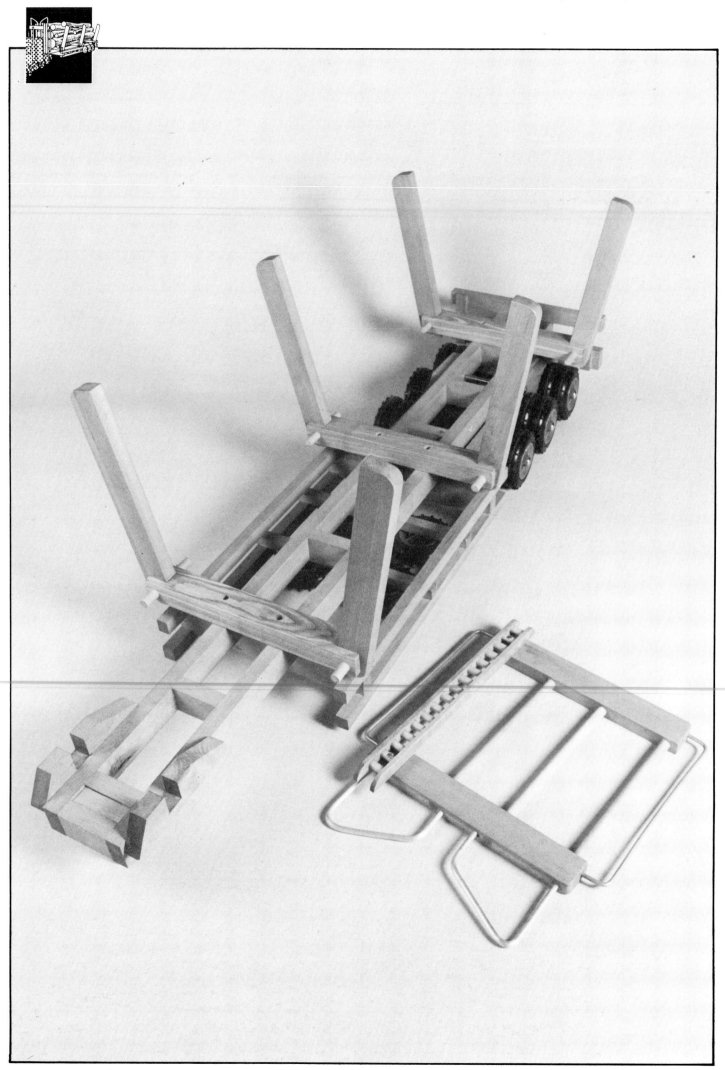

MACK TRAILER

It's not until you have built the trailer for the Mack that you appreciate just how large these North America 'rigs' really are. If you can find some logs for the trailer, it looks very impressive.

1 Select the two longitudinal chassis members. Try to find two lengths that are straight-grained and knot-free. Now tape both together and mark out the stopped mortice holes. Cut out the holes.

2 Cut to length eight chassis cross members, tape them together and mark out the tenons. It is vital that all marking out is done while the pieces are held together. Cut out the tenons. Note that you also need two cross members without tenons for the ends.

3 Make the front hitch pin block and glue the dowel rod into place. Now cut out the front safety bar mounting blocks.

4 Mark out a pair of bogie side plates and drill the axle holes and central pivot pin hole before shaping starts. Once the holes have been accurately bored, the bogie side plates can be shaped.

5 Make the rear bumper assembly and the subframe assembly which carries the spare wheels. Logging trailers are purpose-built for their operators and really give the model-maker a great deal of scope for improvising his or her own details. I have given the vehicle four spare wheels, but there is no reason why it shouldn't just have two.

6 Mark out the six cradle arms. I always find that identical pieces are best marked out together. Bore the holes on the ends of the arms to take the cradle arm pins.

7 Now make the cradle cross members. Drill holes to take the cradle arm pins and then, with a coping saw, cut out the slots to take the cradle arms. To enhance the appearance of the trailer attach short lengths of chain to each cradle pin and fix the end of the chain to the cradle cross member with a brass panel pin – it makes the whole unit look

very workmanlike. The cradle cross arms are fixed to the chassis by countersunk screws.

8 The front safety bar assembly is the genuine North American version – copied from a picture supplied by Mack Trucks. Start by making the top and bottom safety bars. Tape them together and mark the position of the dowel rods and the holes for the aluminium bars. Drill the holes. Aluminium is very easy to bend, and once the dowels have been glued into the safety bars, the aluminium tube can be fitted.

If you have not bent aluminium tube before, try experimenting with a short length. It is essential to have a vice (a woodworking vice will do) to hold one end while you are bending the other. Wood and metal complement each other rather well in this particular job and make the front safety bar look very realistic. The assembly simply slots onto the chassis and does not need to be glued on.

9 To make the ladder tape two pieces of prepared wood together (these will form the uprights) and drill holes right through them for the dowel rods which will form the rungs. Make up a small jig for cutting the dowel rods to length. On the inside edges of both ladder uprights, countersink each hole very slightly to help the rungs to locate easily. Glue all the rungs into one upright first, then manoeuvre the 'free' ends into the corresponding holes in the other upright. You will appreciate the advantage of the countersunk holes at this stage. For the final assembly, put the ladder in the vice and gently tighten it up. This has the effect of pushing the sides together parallel with each other.

The ladder is held to the safety bar by two small screws.

Cutting list

Main chassis member	2 off	1264 × 38 × 20mm (49¾ × 1½ × ¾in)	Timber
Front hitch pin block	1 off	64 × 38 × 20mm (2½ × 1½ × ¾in)	Timber
	1 off	76mm (3in) × 16mm (⅝in) diam dowelling	
Chassis cross member	8 off	89 × 38 × 20mm (3½ × 1½ × ¾in)	Timber
	2 off	64 × 38 × 20mm (2½ × 1½ × ¾in)	Timber
Front safety bar mounting block	2 off	152 × 38 × 20mm (6 × 1½ × ¾in)	Timber
Rear wheel bogie side plate	2 off	413 × 98 × 20mm (16¼ × 3⅞ × ¾in)	Timber
Rear bumper assembly	1 off	305 × 25 × 20mm (12 × 1 × ¾in)	Timber
	1 off	305 × 38 × 20mm (12 × 1½ × ¾in)	Timber
	2 off	102 × 20 × 9mm (4 × ¾ × ⅜in)	Timber
Subframe assembly	4 off	508 × 20 × 16mm (20 × ¾ × ⅝in)	Timber
	2 off	283 × 38 × 20mm (11⅛ × 1½ × ¾in)	Timber
	2 off	283 × 16 × 16mm (11⅛ × ⅝ × ⅝in)	Timber
Front safety bar assembly	2 off	279 × 38 × 20mm (11 × 1½ × ¾in)	Timber
	4 off	241mm (9½in) × 12mm (½in) diam dowelling	
Safety bar assembly ladder	2 off	330 × 16 × 6mm (13 × ⅝ × ¼in)	Timber
	16 off	32mm (1¼in) × 9mm (⅜in) diam dowelling	
Cradle cross member	1 off	311 × 38 × 32mm (12¼ × 1½ × 1¼in)	Timber
Cradle arm	6 off	308 × 38 × 20mm (12⅛ × 1½ × ¾in)	Timber
Cradle arm pin	6 off	89mm (3½in) × 12mm (½in) diam dowelling	

Ancillaries

	16 off	102mm (4in) diam road wheels
	3 off	273mm (10¾in) × 6mm (¼in) diam steel axles
	1 off	9mm (⅜in) o/diam × 6mm (¼in) i/diam × 111mm (4⅜in) long plastic tube
	1 off	162mm (6⅜in) × 9mm (⅜in) diam steel pin
	6 off	6mm (¼in) diam spring dome caps
	2 off	9mm (⅜in) diam spring dome caps
	2 off	12mm (½in) o/diam × 9mm (⅜in) i/diam × 3mm (⅛in) long plastic tube
	Make from 1320mm (52in) × 6mm (¼in) o/diam aluminium tube	
	6 off	89mm (3½in) lengths of lightweight chain
	Assorted woodscrews, cup washers and panel pins	

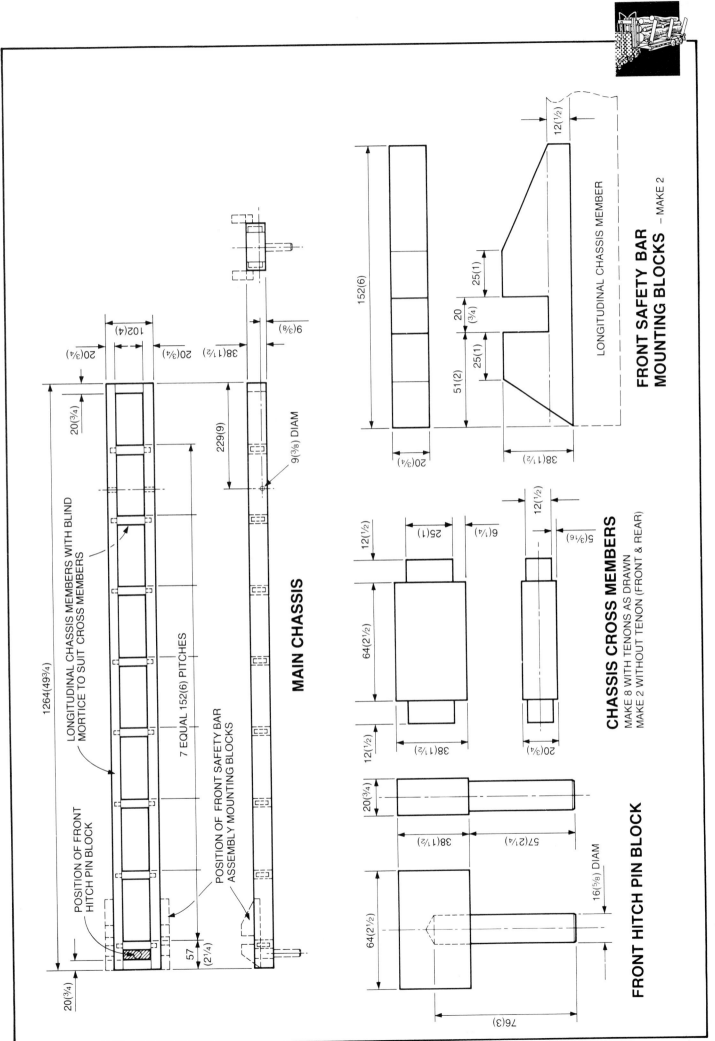

MAIN CHASSIS

1264(49¾)

LONGITUDINAL CHASSIS MEMBERS WITH BLIND MORTICE TO SUIT CROSS MEMBERS

7 EQUAL 152(6) PITCHES

POSITION OF FRONT HITCH PIN BLOCK

POSITION OF FRONT SAFETY BAR ASSEMBLY MOUNTING BLOCKS

20(¾)

102(4)

20(¾)

20(¾)

38(1½)

9(⅜)

229(9)

9(⅜) DIAM

57(2¼)

20(¾)

FRONT SAFETY BAR MOUNTING BLOCKS – MAKE 2

152(6)

20(¾)

25(1)

20(¾)

25(1)

51(2)

12(½)

38(1½)

LONGITUDINAL CHASSIS MEMBER

CHASSIS CROSS MEMBERS

MAKE 8 WITH TENONS AS DRAWN
MAKE 2 WITHOUT TENON (FRONT & REAR)

12(½)

25(1)

6(¼)

64(2½)

12(½)

38(1½)

12(½)

5(3/16)

20(¾)

FRONT HITCH PIN BLOCK

20(¾)

38(1½)

57(2¼)

64(2½)

16(⅝) DIAM

76(3)

171

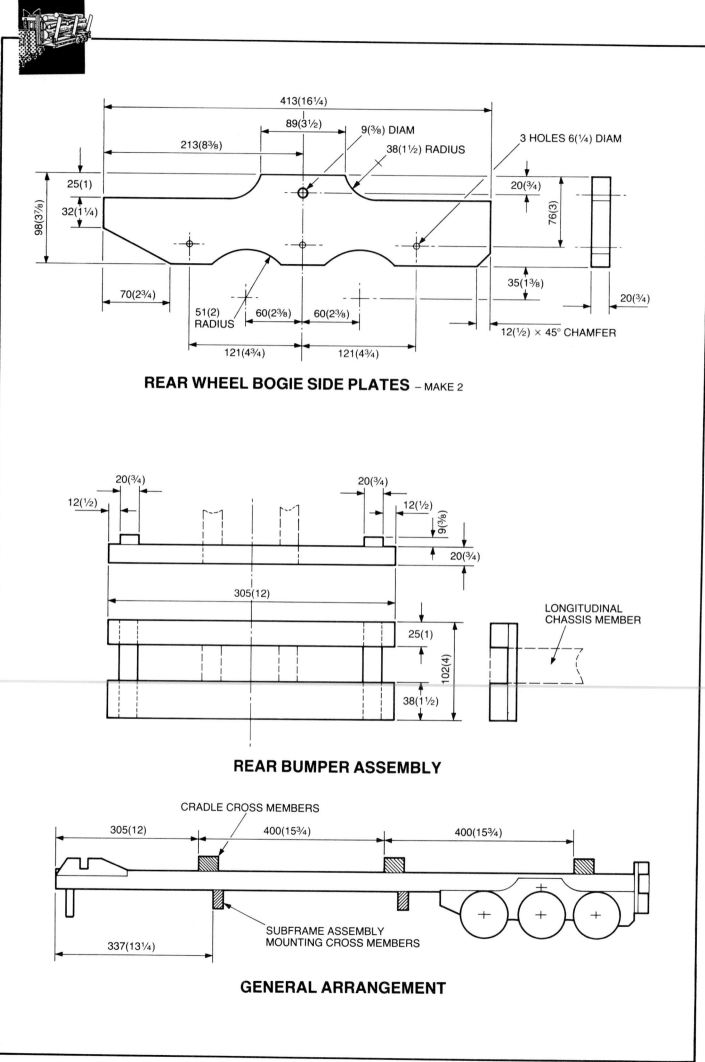

REAR WHEEL BOGIE SIDE PLATES – MAKE 2

413(16¼)
89(3½)
9(⅜) DIAM
38(1½) RADIUS
3 HOLES 6(¼) DIAM
213(8⅜)
25(1)
20(¾)
98(3⅞)
32(1¼)
76(3)
70(2¾)
35(1⅜)
20(¾)
51(2) RADIUS
60(2⅜) 60(2⅜)
12(½) × 45° CHAMFER
121(4¾) 121(4¾)

REAR BUMPER ASSEMBLY

20(¾)
20(¾)
12(½)
12(½)
9(⅜)
20(¾)
305(12)
LONGITUDINAL CHASSIS MEMBER
25(1)
102(4)
38(1½)

GENERAL ARRANGEMENT

CRADLE CROSS MEMBERS
305(12)
400(15¾)
400(15¾)
SUBFRAME ASSEMBLY MOUNTING CROSS MEMBERS
337(13¼)

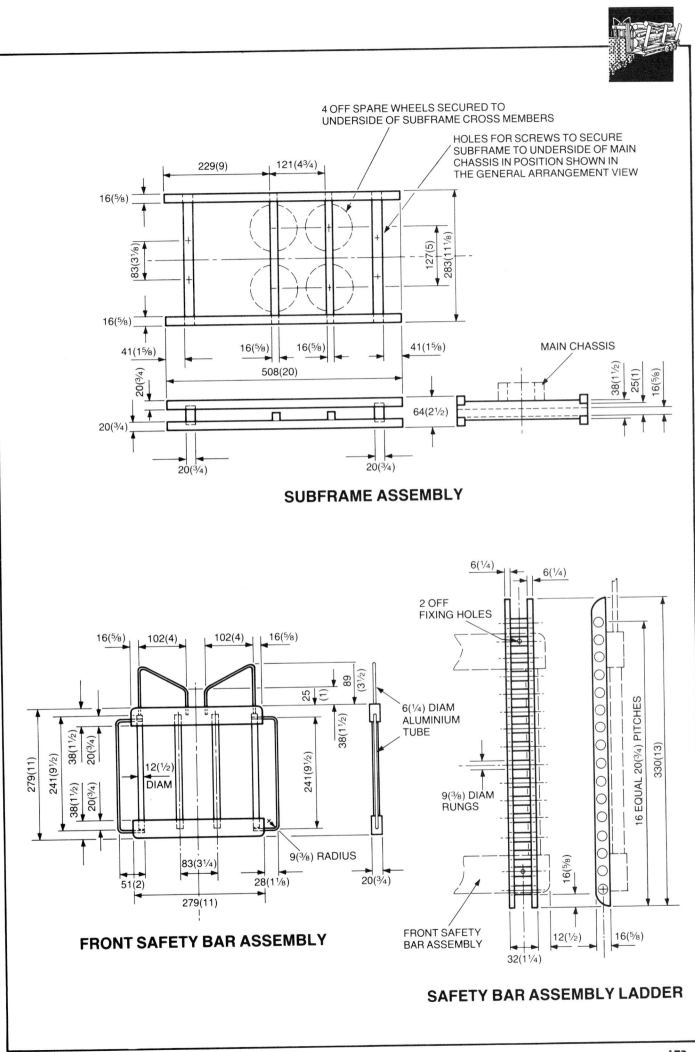

4 OFF SPARE WHEELS SECURED TO
UNDERSIDE OF SUBFRAME CROSS MEMBERS

HOLES FOR SCREWS TO SECURE
SUBFRAME TO UNDERSIDE OF MAIN
CHASSIS IN POSITION SHOWN IN
THE GENERAL ARRANGEMENT VIEW

229(9)　121(4¾)

16(⅝)

83(3⅛)

127(5)

283(11⅛)

16(⅝)

41(1⅝)　16(⅝)　16(⅝)　41(1⅝)

508(20)

MAIN CHASSIS

20(¾)

20(¾)

64(2½)

38(1½)

25(1)

16(⅝)

20(¾)　20(¾)

SUBFRAME ASSEMBLY

16(⅝)　102(4)　102(4)　16(⅝)

89(3½)

25(1)

6(¼) DIAM
ALUMINIUM
TUBE

279(11)

241(9½)

38(1½)

20(¾)

12(½)
DIAM

38(1½)

20(¾)

241(9½)

38(1½)

9(⅜) RADIUS

83(3¼)

51(2)

28(1⅛)

20(¾)

279(11)

FRONT SAFETY BAR ASSEMBLY

6(¼)　6(¼)

2 OFF
FIXING HOLES

9(⅜) DIAM
RUNGS

16(⅝)

16 EQUAL 20(¾) PITCHES

330(13)

FRONT SAFETY
BAR ASSEMBLY

32(1¼)　12(½)　16(⅝)

SAFETY BAR ASSEMBLY LADDER

173

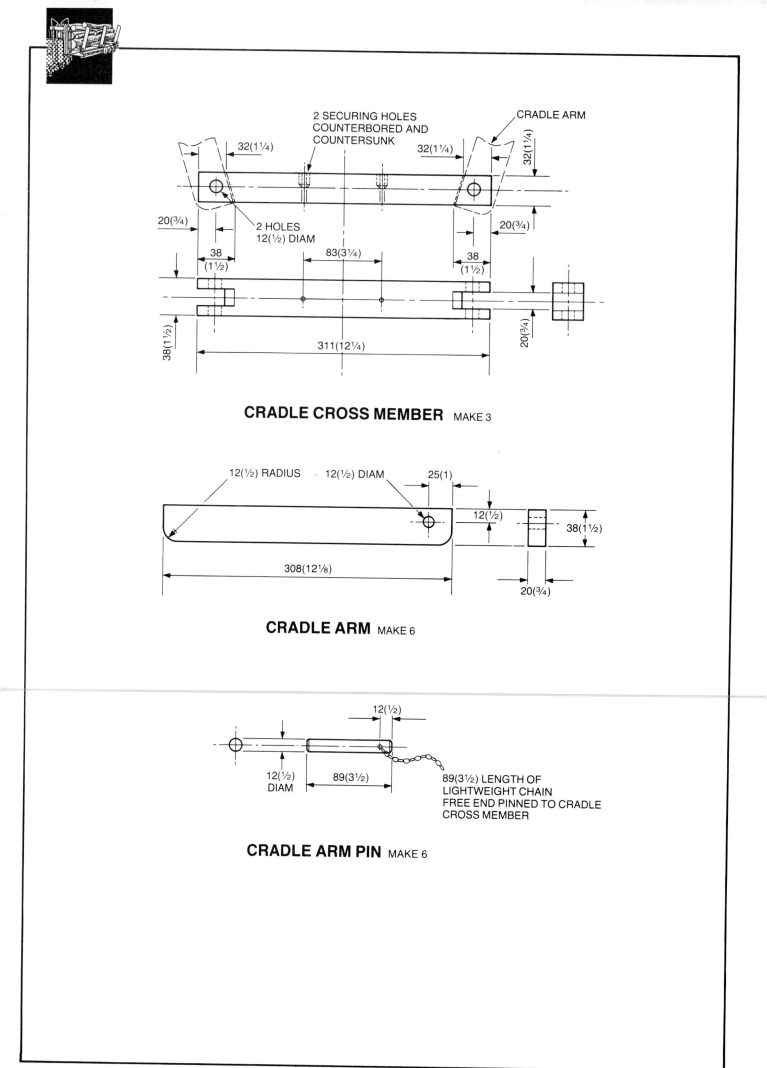

2 SECURING HOLES COUNTERBORED AND COUNTERSUNK

CRADLE ARM

32(1¼)

32(1¼)

32(1¼)

20(¾)

2 HOLES
12(½) DIAM

20(¾)

38
(1½)

83(3¼)

38
(1½)

38(1½)

20(¾)

311(12¼)

CRADLE CROSS MEMBER MAKE 3

12(½) RADIUS   12(½) DIAM

25(1)

12(½)

38(1½)

308(12⅛)

20(¾)

CRADLE ARM MAKE 6

12(½)

12(½)
DIAM

89(3½)

89(3½) LENGTH OF
LIGHTWEIGHT CHAIN
FREE END PINNED TO CRADLE
CROSS MEMBER

CRADLE ARM PIN MAKE 6

It was while visiting a National Construction Exhibition some years ago that I first became acquainted with this large chunky Volvo truck. The bright yellow paintwork is set off by the huge black tyres. The truck is designed to work in quarries and in all heavy construction work, but, in spite of its strength and sheer size, it is a very pleasing piece of functional machinery to look at.

Before starting work on this model, study the drawings and make sure that you can identify all the pieces. It is complicated to build, but the rewards are well worth all the effort. I used a combination of woods – beech (chassis and main members) and mahogany (smaller parts such as the steps and mudguards) – and I feel that this does make the machine look rather special.

1 Start by marking and cutting out the two main chassis members. It is important to tape the two pieces of wood together and treat them as a pair. Drill the holes with great care, ideally using a drill that is fitted in a drill stand. Cut out the recess for the front axle while both pieces are still taped together. Then separate the two chassis members and mark the stopped mortice holes that will accommodate the central and rear chassis cross members.

Cut out the cross members and assemble the entire chassis dry. It is vital that the main chassis members and cross members fit well and 'square', so that the two main members are held parallel over their entire length. As in the case of every vehicle, the chassis is the foundation for all the other components, so accuracy at the start is essential.

2 The front bulkhead requires careful shaping. Form the recess in the front that takes the radiator grill by carefully marking the sides with a marking knife and cutting out the recess with a very sharp chisel. Those who have an electric router will be able to do this part of the work very speedily.

3 Cut two elongated recesses in the front bulkhead to house the two pairs of headlamps. The easiest method of cutting these is to mark them out very accurately and then drill a shallow hole where the top and bottom of each recess will fall. The diameter of the drill needs to be the same width as the recess. By using this method you form a semi-circle at either end of each recess and all that remains is to remove the centre portions with a chisel.

4 Recess the back of the bulkhead to take the ends of the chassis (see the three-dimensional illustration).

5 Once the basic bulkhead shape has been cut out and recessed, you can glue on the bumper, capping strip, steps and headlamps, but really these fine details should wait until more of the basic construction is done. (The very fine mesh used on the radiator is the type sold for repairing holes in car bodywork.)

6 Glue the two main chassis members and cross members together and glue the front bulkhead in place. Glue the two small towing eyes underneath the front bulkhead.

7 Now cut out the pieces for the front mudguards and glue them onto the sides of the chassis. Each mudguard is different and, for the purposes of this model, they are used as platforms onto which other things are mounted, namely the air reservoir on the right hand mudguard and the cab on the left hand side.

8 Once the mudguards are in place, cut out all the pieces for the cab. I recommend you cut out the cab windows with a coping saw, and be sure to cut accurately to the pencil line you have marked, otherwise a great deal of time is lost in trying to glasspaper out all the wavy lines. However careful you are, a very light glasspapering of the insides of the window edges will still be necessary: a small piece of dowel rod wrapped in glasspaper will make the job easier around the curves.

Rebate the outside face of the inner cab wall so that the cab will fit against the engine compartment.

9 Cut out the driver's seat, rub down with glasspaper and cover in green felt.

10 Cut out the console and the steering wheel and fit them onto the cab front bulkhead. Forming the steering wheel is a very delicate job. Use a tank cutter to make the basic shape and then, working with small drills, files and glasspaper, finish off the shaping.

11 Glue all the cab walls together and fit the clear plastic screens. It is best to fit these very tightly and then only a touch of glue is necessary to keep them in place. Line the bottom half of the inside in green felt. On the outside of the cab, mark the edge of the door with a dark pencil line and glue on the door handle and decorative strips of wood. Cut the cab front bulkhead, then glue the cab onto the mudguard.

12 The air cylinders behind the cab are formed from lengths of dowel rod which are glued onto a backing strip that is in turn glued at the top onto the back of the cab and at the bottom onto the mudguard. The air lines are made of lengths of coaxial cable (obtainable in

various sizes from good motor accessory shops). Glue the cables into pre-drilled holes with epoxy resin glue.

Glue the cab access steps onto the left hand mudguard and the decorative strips onto the cab side walls.

13 Now make the front axle block. When designing such a detailed truck, I felt that steering was essential. Obviously a much simpler model can be constructed if the stub axles are left out.

The front axle block is formed from beech and it is onto this block that the stub axles are all fitted. Mark out the stub axles and, before shaping, drill the holes for the axles and the steering track rod. Fit the stub axles into the axle block and hold them firmly in place with tape or a small G cramp, then drill pin holes through the axle block and stub axle in one operation. This method of working is essential for accuracy.

Now angle the inside edges of the stub axles to allow them to swivel on the front axle block: a push fit is essential. Cut lengths of steel axle rod and finally drive each one through the front axle block and into each stub axle, thus 'trapping' it in place. This steel rod acts as a 'king pin' and the stub axles rotate around it. Cut and fit the steering track rod, which is held in place with steel axle rods and small spring caps. Shape the tie beams in readiness for fitting later.

14 Shape the engine block from a block of wood, and make a small slotted disc of wood to form the cooling fan. Drill a hole in the back to take the prop shaft. The engine locates in the recess on the front axle.

15 Cut out the rear axle block and drill holes to take both the back axle and prop shaft. The back axle is not glued into the chassis but is held in position by the rear axle block and the prop shaft. The prop shaft itself is a length of dowel rod: fit this and the engine block at the same time.

16 Now fix the lower mounting lever between the main chassis members and to the left of the prop shaft using a piece of dowel rod. Place the cylinder barrel inside the lower mounting lever and hold it in position with a dowel rod. Fit the tipping cylinder rod inside the barrel. Fit the upper clevis inside the body chassis members that are in turn screwed to the tipper body. At the back of the truck the body chassis members pivot around a steel axle rod that is fitted through the main chassis members. To get the tipping mechanism to function smoothly, it is important to work on each piece

individually and then assemble the whole unit in the chassis. On the prototype model it took several hours to get the whole mechanism to function smoothly.

17 The body of the tipper unit is made from six major parts. First cut and shape the body floor assembly. Glue these two pieces together after cutting and planing the angles. Now cut the body front wall and the front overhang. The most exciting part of this construction is planing accurate angles on the ends. Don't be tempted to rush the job, but mark out the angle very carefully in pencil and then make sure your plane is very sharp before you start.

Cut out and shape the two body side panels. It is vital that the floor, front wall and overhang are exactly the same width as these are 'sandwiched' between the two side panels.

Make absolutely sure that all 'cleaning up' is done before you attempt to glue the body together. Glueing up is not easy as there are so many angles to watch at the same time. I found light clamping all that was necessary to hold the pieces together while the glue set – it is possible to use large elastic bands on awkward shapes.

18 Once the glue has dried, cut and fit all the reinforcing members. Glue the raised surround onto the front overhang and all the reinforcing members and overhang support brackets onto the outside of the tipper. Before fixing the cross members to the underside of the floor assembly, fit the two body chassis members by screwing them onto the body from inside the tipper. To disguise the screwheads, fit wooden plugs. Make sure that these two body chassis sections are fitted parallel and do not 'foul' the upper clevis when the body is flat. Now glue the cross members in place.

19 As a safety precaution on the real Volvo truck, there are two massive stone ejectors that fit between the rear wheels. If stones get trapped between the rear tyres, these stone ejector blades prevent them from flying out and injuring people. Make two ejector blades and mounting blocks and glue them onto the underside of the body.

20 Shape the fuel tank and glue the side support pieces and front dowel in place. To add a touch of realism, make a little filler cap from a piece of dowel rod, forming the screw cap from a piece of rubber tube. Glue the tank onto the main chassis.

21 Now for the right-hand mudguard assembly. Drill the holes to take the handrail posts with great care. Now drill small holes in the posts to take the fine soft wire that acts as a guard rail. Glue the posts in place and then thread the wire through the holes.

22 Fit the mirrors and all the guard rails. Drill the holes to take the rails a little over-size to allow room for the epoxy resin glue. Make the windscreen wiper from a piece of wire and the blade by stripping a length of insulated electric cable.

23 Make the air tanks. For those with a lathe this will be a simple task, but those without must laboriously plane each piece of wood very carefully all round and then finally glasspaper it – this takes a great deal of time. Mount the air tanks on their supports and glue these onto the truck. All the air lines are coaxial cable of a slightly larger size than that used for the air cylinders. For the purposes of this model, all the air lines are fed to the engine block. A removable engine cover is worth making to allow access to the engine.

24 Position the wheels exactly in the correct places by cutting and fitting pieces of plastic tube as spacers on both back and front axles.

25 Before fitting the wheels, treat the truck with polyurethane varnish. I found that the first coat is best applied with a lint-free cloth (a messy job when it comes to cleaning your hands), and should be left to dry for twenty-four hours. Using fine glasspaper, rub over the whole truck. Now repeat the whole operation a further four times. Finally, rub a good-quality wax polish well into the wood and, if you wish, add lettering strips to the tipper unit sides. Finishing is a fairly lengthy process but well worth all the effort as the final result does justice to the many hours that have gone into the model.

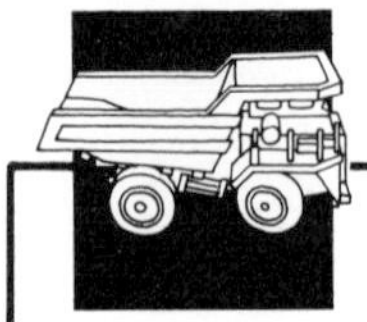

Cutting list

Part	Qty	Dimensions	Material
Main chassis member	2 off	365 × 111 × 22mm (14⅜ × 4⅜ × ⅞in)	Timber
Rear chassis cross member	1 off	70 × 25 × 22mm (2¾ × 1 × ⅞in)	Timber
Central chassis cross member	1 off	70 × 22 × 16mm (2¾ × ⅞ × ⅝in)	Timber
Front bulkhead	1 off	187 × 95 × 22mm (7⅜ × 3¾ × ⅞in)	Timber
Capping strip	1 off	130 × 12 × 6mm (5⅛ × ½ × ¼in)	Timber
Bumper	1 off	187 × 16 × 6mm (7⅜ × ⅝ × ¼in)	Timber
Steps	2 off	20 × 9 × 5mm (¾ × ⅜ × ³⁄₁₆in)	Timber
Towing eyes	2 off	22 × 20 × 16mm (⅞ × ¾ × ⅝in)	Timber
Headlamps	4 off	8mm (⁵⁄₁₆in) × 12mm (½in) diam dowelling	
Radiator grill verticals	Make from 127 × 6 × 5mm (5 × ¼ × ³⁄₁₆in)		Timber
horizontals	Make from 76 × 6 × 3mm (3 × ¼ × ⅛in)		Timber
centre plate	1 off	11 × 9 × 3mm (⁷⁄₁₆ × ⅜ × ⅛in)	Timber
diagonal	1 off	92 × 3 × 1.5mm (3⅝ × ⅛ × ¹⁄₁₆in)	Timber
Front axle block	1 off	152 × 51 × 20mm (6 × 2 × ¾in)	Timber
Stub axle assembly	2 off	64 × 32 × 20mm (2½ × 1¼ × ¾in)	Timber
	2 off	67mm (2⅝in) × 6mm (¼in) diam dowelling	
Steering track rod	1 off	152 × 22 × 6mm (6 × ⅞ × ¼in)	Timber
Tie beam	2 off	149 × 20 × 16mm (5⅞ × ¾ × ⅝in)	Timber
Engine block	1 off	143 × 73 × 35mm (5⅝ × 2⅞ × 1⅜in)	Timber
Dummy fan	1 off	9mm (⅜in) × 38mm (1½in) diam	Timber
Rear axle block	1 off	51 × 25 × 22mm (2 × 1 × ⅞in)	Timber
Prop shaft	1 off	152mm (6in) × 6mm (¼in) diam dowelling	
Engine cover	1 off	98 × 70 × 6mm (3⅞ × 2¾ × ¼in)	Timber
	2 off	89 × 12 × 6mm (3½ × ½ × ¼in)	Timber
Fuel tank	1 off	57 × 44 × 35mm (2¼ × 1¾ × 1⅜in)	Timber
	2 off	57 × 35 × 8mm (2¼ × 1⅜ × ⁵⁄₁₆in)	Timber
	Make from 95mm (3¾in) × 6mm (¼in) diam dowelling		
Right hand mudguard assembly	1 off	60 × 57 × 11mm (2⅜ × 2¼ × ⁷⁄₁₆in)	Timber
	1 off	146 × 60 × 11mm (5¾ × 2⅜ × ⁷⁄₁₆in)	Timber
	1 off	67 × 44 × 6mm (2⅝ × 1¾ × ¼in)	Timber
Platform rear guard	1 off	67 × 32 × 11mm (2⅝ × 1¼ × ⁷⁄₁₆in)	Timber
	1 off	32mm (1¼in) × 6mm (¼in) diam dowelling	
Battery box	1 off	41 × 20 × 18mm (1⅝ × ¾ × ¹¹⁄₁₆in)	Timber
Air reservoir	1 off	44 × 38 × 11mm (1¾ × 1½ × ⁷⁄₁₆in)	Timber
	1 off	25mm (1in) × 25mm (1in) diam dowelling	
Handrail posts	3 off	64mm (2½in) × 6mm (¼in) diam dowelling	
Wing mirrors	3 off	20 × 12 × 5mm (¾ × ½ × ³⁄₁₆in)	Timber
Air tank assembly	1 off	89 × 25 × 6mm (3½ × 1 × ¼in)	Timber
	2 off	47 × 32 × 6mm (1⅞ × 1¼ × ¼in)	Timber
	1 off	44mm (1¾in) × 38mm (1½in) diam	Timber
	1 off	25mm (1in) × 6mm (¼in) diam dowelling	
Cab front bulkhead	1 off	64 × 38 × 20mm (2½ × 1½ × ¾in)	Timber
Console/steering wheel assembly	1 off	44 × 20 × 9mm (1¾ × ¾ × ⅜in)	Timber
	1 off	28mm (1⅛in) × 6mm (¼in) diam dowelling	
	1 off	6mm (¼in) × 25mm (1in) diam dowelling	
Driver's seat	1 off	64 × 38 × 38mm (2½ × 1½ × 1½in)	Timber
Cab rear wall	1 off	89 × 64 × 9mm (3½ × 2½ × ⅜in)	Timber
Air cylinder rack assembly	1 off	64 × 38 × 6mm (2½ × 1½ × ¼in)	Timber
	3 off	44mm (1¾in) × 16mm (⅝in) diam dowelling	
Cab door handle	1 off	18 × 6 × 3mm (¹¹⁄₁₆ × ¼ × ⅛in)	Timber

Part	Quantity	Dimensions	Material
Left hand mudguard assembly	1 off	146 × 60 × 11mm (5¾ × 2⅜ × ⁷⁄₁₆in)	Timber
	1 off	60 × 57 × 11mm (2⅜ × 2¼ × ⁷⁄₁₆in)	Timber
Cab side wall	2 off	117 × 89 × 9mm (4⅝ × 3½ × ⅜in)	Timber
Cab front screen	1 off	64 × 54 × 9mm (2½ × 2⅛ × ⅜in)	Timber
Cab roof	1 off	143 × 64 × 9mm (5⅝ × 2½ × ⅜in)	Timber
Cab access steps assembly	1 off	67 × 6 × 6mm (2⅝ × ¼ × ¼in)	Timber
	1 off	67 × 41 × 6mm (2⅝ × 1⅝ × ¼in)	Timber
	1 off	73 × 25 × 6mm (2⅞ × 1 × ¼in)	Timber
	Make from 92 × 20 × 6mm (3⅝ × ¾ × ¼in)		Timber
Decorative strips on cab side wall	2 off	51 × 3 × 3mm (2 × ⅛ × ⅛in)	Timber
	Make from 98 × 6 × 6mm (3⅞ × ¼ × ¼in)		Timber
Lower mounting lever	1 off	64 × 20 × 20mm (2½ × ¾ × ¾in)	Timber
	1 off	25mm (1in) × 6mm (¼in) diam dowelling	
Stone ejector blade mounting block	2 off	25 × 20 × 18mm (1 × ¾ × ¹¹⁄₁₆in)	Timber
	2 off	25mm (1in) × 6mm (¼in) diam dowelling	
Stone ejector blade	2 off	86 × 20 × 6mm (3⅜ × ¾ × ¼in)	Timber
Tipping cylinder rod and upper clevis	1 off	58 × 30 × 22mm (2⁵⁄₁₆ × 1³⁄₁₆ × ⅞in)	Timber
	1 off	79mm (3⅛in) × 6mm (¼in) diam dowelling	
Body side panel	2 off	448 × 122 × 18mm (17⅝ × 4¹³⁄₁₆ × ¹¹⁄₁₆in)	Timber
Reinforcing members	Make from 1613 × 20 × 6mm (63½ × ¾ × ¼in)		Timber
Cross member 1	1 off	216 × 18 × 16mm (8½ × ¹¹⁄₁₆ × ⅝in)	Timber
Cross member 2	2 off	84 × 18 × 16mm (3⁵⁄₁₆ × ¹¹⁄₁₆ × ⅝in)	Timber
Cross member 3	1 off	216 × 18 × 16mm (8½ × ¹¹⁄₁₆ × ⅝in)	Timber
Body front overhang	1 off	181 × 162 × 12mm (7⅛ × 6⅜ × ½in)	Timber
Body front wall	1 off	181 × 106 × 12mm (7⅛ × 4³⁄₁₆ × ½in)	Timber
Raised surround	Make from 527 × 18 × 5mm (20¾ × ¹¹⁄₁₆ × ³⁄₁₆in)		Timber
Body floor assembly	1 off	213 × 181 × 12mm (8⅜ × 7⅛ × ½in)	Timber
	1 off	95 × 181 × 12mm (3¾ × 7⅛ × ½in)	Timber
Overhang support brackets	3 off	146 × 20 × 6mm (5¾ × ¾ × ¼in)	Timber
	2 off	44 × 20 × 6mm (1¾ × ¾ × ¼in)	Timber
Body chassis	2 off	165 × 54 × 16mm (6½ × 2⅛ × ⅝in)	Timber
	1 off	47mm (1⅞in) × 6mm (¼in) diam dowelling	
Ancillaries	6 off	102mm (4in) diam road wheels	
	4 off	Spring dome caps to suit 6mm (¼in) diam axles	
	1 off	248mm (9¾in) × 6mm (¼in) diam steel axle – rear axle	
	2 off	67mm (2⅝in) × 6mm (¼in) diam steel axles – front stub axles	
	1 off	95mm (3¾in) × 6mm (¼in) diam steel pin – tipping spindle	
	2 off	51mm (2in) × 5mm (³⁄₁₆in) diam steel pins – axle block pivot	
	2 off	28mm (1⅛in) × 5mm (³⁄₁₆in) diam steel pins – tie link pins	
	4 off	Spring dome caps to suit 5mm (³⁄₁₆in) diam pins	
	6 off	9mm (⅜in) o/diam × 6mm (¼in) i/diam × 6mm (¼in) long spacers	
	1 off	8mm (⁵⁄₁₆in) o/diam × 6mm (¼in) i/diam × 73mm (2⅞in) long chrome tube	
	Make from 1090mm (43in) × 1.5mm (¹⁄₁₆in) diam soft copper wire		
	2 off	54mm (2⅛in) × 44mm (1¾in) × 1.5mm (¹⁄₁₆in) thick clear plastic	
	2 off	54mm (2⅛in) × 111mm (4⅜in) × 1.5mm (¹⁄₁₆in) thick clear plastic	
	3 off	203mm (8in) × 3mm (⅛in) diam electric plastic-covered wire	
	3 off	178mm (7in) × 5mm (³⁄₁₆in) diam electric plastic-covered wire	
	Make from 9mm (⅜in) o/diam × 3mm (⅛in) i/diam × 114mm (4½in) rubber tube		
	1 off	229mm (9in) × 152mm (6in) green felt to line the cab and seat	
	1 off	76mm (3in) × 64mm (2½in) aluminium mesh for grill	

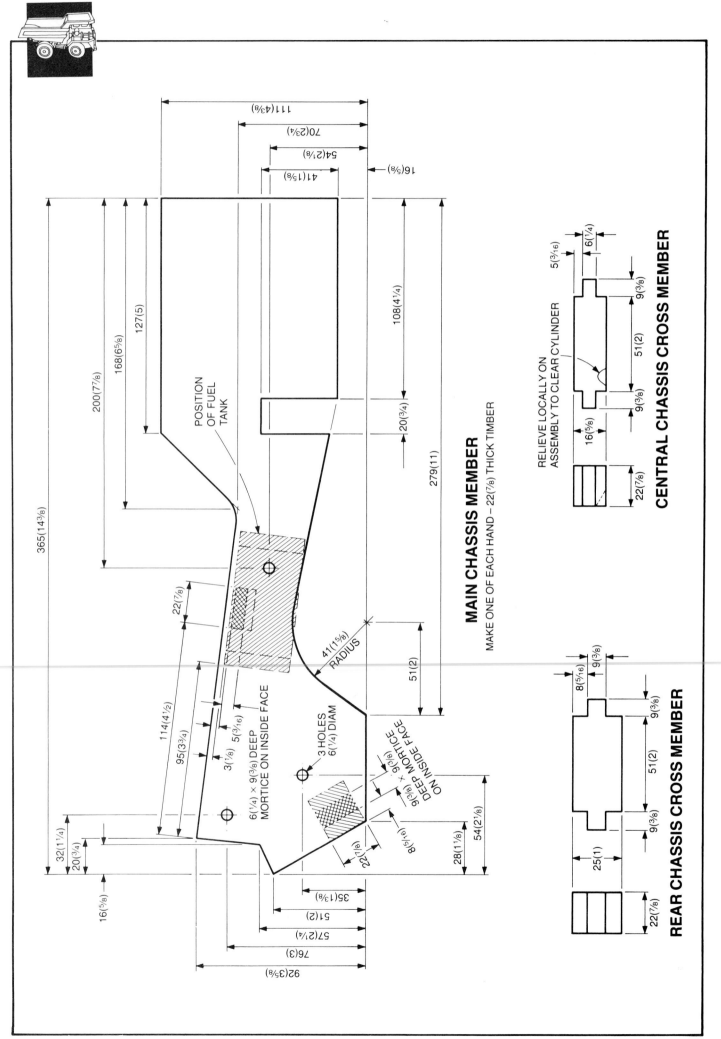

MAIN CHASSIS MEMBER

MAKE ONE OF EACH HAND – 22(⅞) THICK TIMBER

CENTRAL CHASSIS CROSS MEMBER

RELIEVE LOCALLY ON ASSEMBLY TO CLEAR CYLINDER

REAR CHASSIS CROSS MEMBER

POSITION OF FUEL TANK

6(¼) × 9(⅜) DEEP MORTICE ON INSIDE FACE

3 HOLES 6(¼) DIAM

9(⅜) × 9(⅜) DEEP MORTICE ON INSIDE FACE

41(1⅝) RADIUS

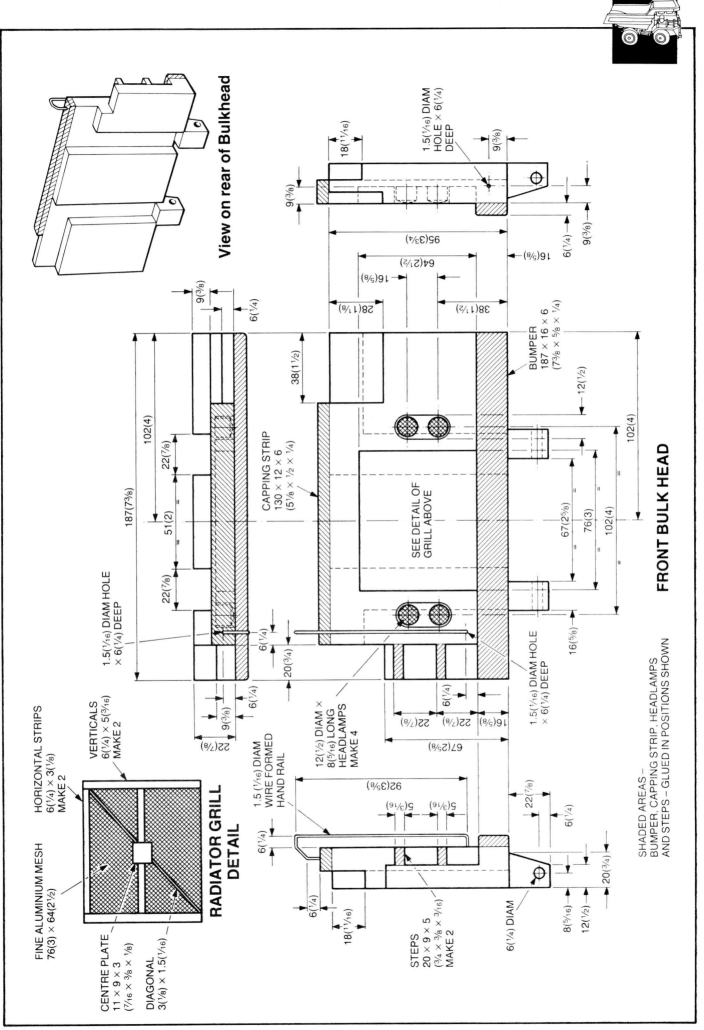

View on rear of Bulkhead

RADIATOR GRILL DETAIL

FINE ALUMINIUM MESH
76(3) × 64(2½)

CENTRE PLATE
11 × 9 × 3
(⁷⁄₁₆ × ³⁄₈ × ⅛)

DIAGONAL
3(⅛) × 1.5(¹⁄₁₆)

HORIZONTAL STRIPS
6(¼) × 3(⅛)
MAKE 2

VERTICALS
6(¼) × 5(³⁄₁₆)
MAKE 2

CAPPING STRIP
130 × 12 × 6
(5⅛ × ½ × ¼)

1.5(¹⁄₁₆) DIAM HOLE × 6(¼) DEEP

BUMPER
187 × 16 × 6
(7⅜ × ⁵⁄₈ × ¼)

SEE DETAIL OF GRILL ABOVE

1.5(¹⁄₁₆) DIAM HOLE × 6(¼) DEEP

1.5(¹⁄₁₆) DIAM HOLE × 6(¼) DEEP

1.5(¹⁄₁₆) DIAM WIRE FORMED HAND RAIL

12(½) DIAM × 8(⁵⁄₁₆) LONG HEADLAMPS MAKE 4

STEPS
20 × 9 × 5
(¾ × ³⁄₈ × ³⁄₁₆)
MAKE 2

6(¼) DIAM

FRONT BULK HEAD

SHADED AREAS –
BUMPER, CAPPING STRIP, HEADLAMPS
AND STEPS – GLUED IN POSITIONS SHOWN

18(¹¹⁄₁₆)
9(³⁄₈)
9(³⁄₈)
95(3¾)
16(⁵⁄₈)
6(¼)
9(³⁄₈)
64(2½)
16(⁵⁄₈)
28(1⅛)
38(1½)
38(1½)
102(4)
22(⅞)
51(2)
22(⅞)
187(7⅜)
9(³⁄₈)
6(¼)
9(³⁄₈)
22(⅞)
6(¼)
20(¾)
6(¼)
12(½)
102(4)
67(2⅝)
76(3)
102(4)
16(⁵⁄₈)
22(⅞)
22(⅞)
16(⁵⁄₈)
67(2⅝)
92(3⅝)
5(³⁄₁₆)
5(³⁄₁₆)
22(⅞)
6(¼)
6(¼)
18(¹¹⁄₁₆)
6(¼)
8(⁵⁄₁₆)
12(½)
20(¾)

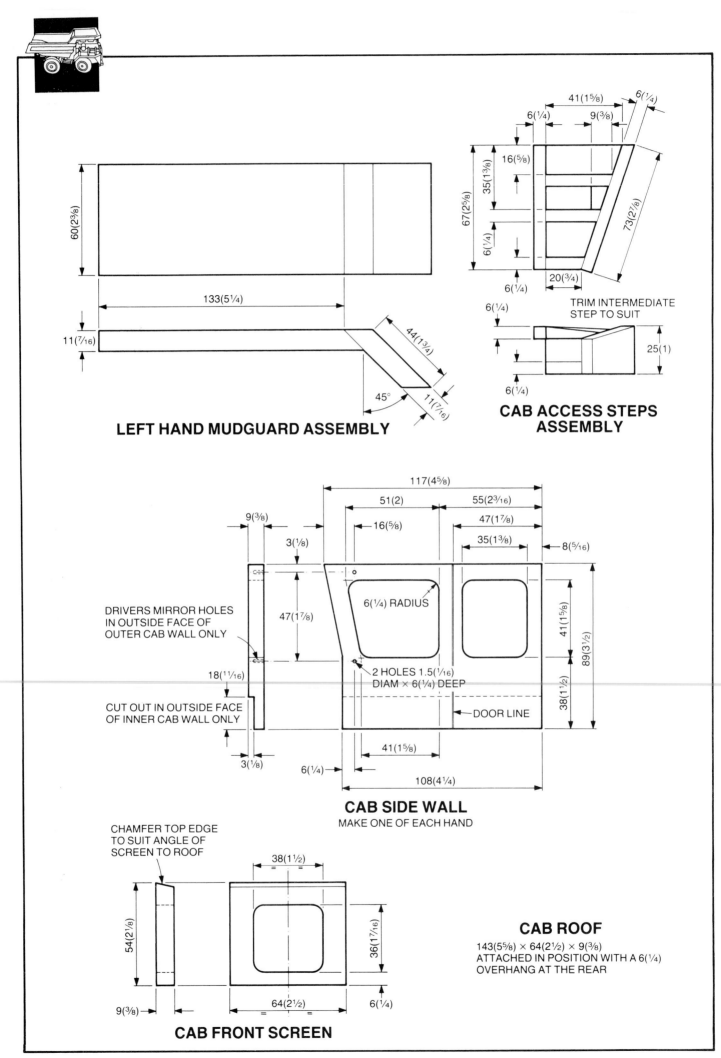

LEFT HAND MUDGUARD ASSEMBLY

**CAB ACCESS STEPS
ASSEMBLY**

TRIM INTERMEDIATE
STEP TO SUIT

DRIVERS MIRROR HOLES
IN OUTSIDE FACE OF
OUTER CAB WALL ONLY

CUT OUT IN OUTSIDE FACE
OF INNER CAB WALL ONLY

6(¼) RADIUS

2 HOLES 1.5(¹/₁₆)
DIAM × 6(¼) DEEP

DOOR LINE

CAB SIDE WALL
MAKE ONE OF EACH HAND

CHAMFER TOP EDGE
TO SUIT ANGLE OF
SCREEN TO ROOF

CAB ROOF

143(5⅝) × 64(2½) × 9(⅜)
ATTACHED IN POSITION WITH A 6(¼)
OVERHANG AT THE REAR

CAB FRONT SCREEN

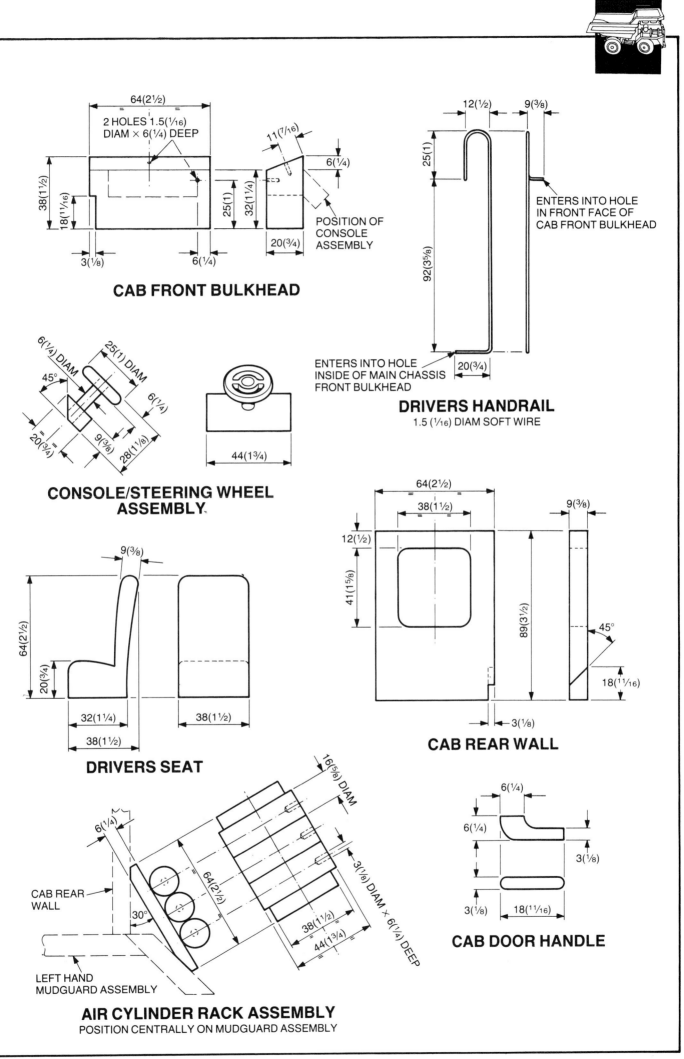

CAB FRONT BULKHEAD

64(2½)
2 HOLES 1.5(¹/₁₆) DIAM × 6(¼) DEEP
11(⁷/₁₆)
6(¼)
38(1½)
18(¹¹/₁₆)
25(1)
32(1¼)
POSITION OF CONSOLE ASSEMBLY
20(¾)
3(⅛)
6(¼)

CONSOLE/STEERING WHEEL ASSEMBLY

6(¼) DIAM
25(1) DIAM
45°
6(¼)
20(¾)
9(⅜)
28(1⅛)
44(1¾)

DRIVERS HANDRAIL
1.5 (¹/₁₆) DIAM SOFT WIRE

12(½)
9(⅜)
25(1)
ENTERS INTO HOLE IN FRONT FACE OF CAB FRONT BULKHEAD
92(3⅝)
ENTERS INTO HOLE INSIDE OF MAIN CHASSIS FRONT BULKHEAD
20(¾)

DRIVERS SEAT

9(⅜)
64(2½)
20(¾)
32(1¼)
38(1½)
38(1½)

CAB REAR WALL

64(2½)
38(1½)
12(½)
41(1⅝)
9(⅜)
89(3½)
45°
18(¹¹/₁₆)
3(⅛)

AIR CYLINDER RACK ASSEMBLY
POSITION CENTRALLY ON MUDGUARD ASSEMBLY

16(⅝) DIAM
6(¼)
CAB REAR WALL
64(2½)
3(⅛) DIAM × 6(¼) DEEP
30°
38(1½)
44(1¾)
LEFT HAND MUDGUARD ASSEMBLY

CAB DOOR HANDLE

6(¼)
6(¼)
3(⅛)
3(⅛)
18(¹¹/₁₆)

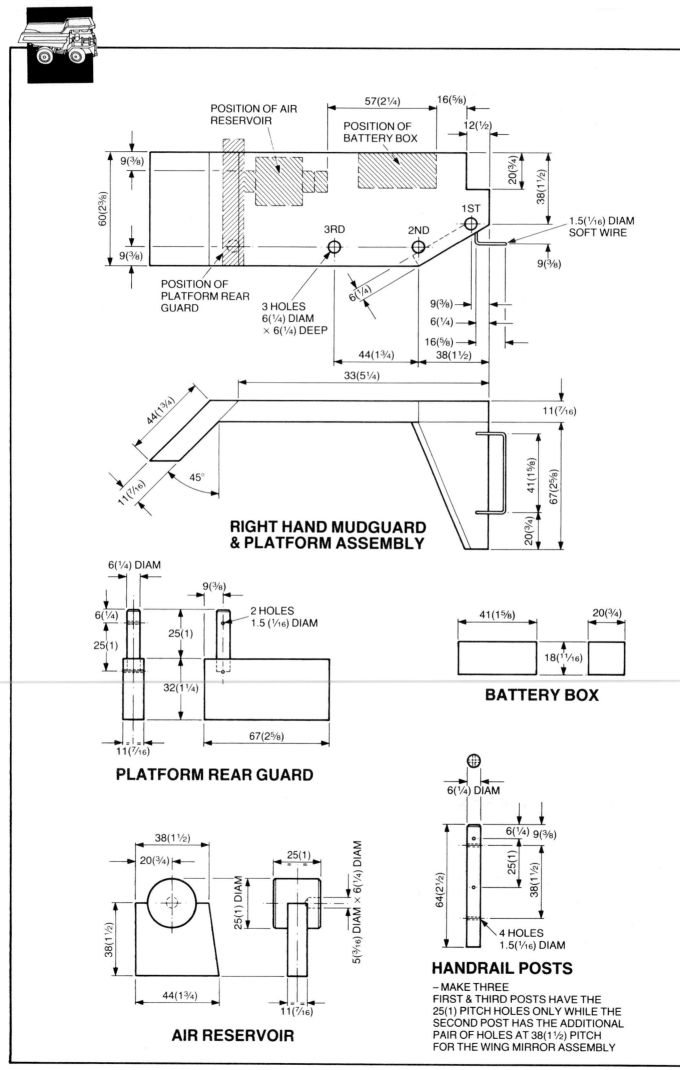

POSITION OF AIR RESERVOIR

POSITION OF BATTERY BOX

57(2¼) 16(⅝) 12(½)

9(⅜)

60(2⅜)

9(⅜)

20(¾)

38(1½)

1ST

1.5(¹⁄₁₆) DIAM SOFT WIRE

9(⅜)

3RD 2ND

POSITION OF PLATFORM REAR GUARD

3 HOLES 6(¼) DIAM × 6(¼) DEEP

6(¼)

9(⅜)

6(¼)

16(⅝)

44(1¾) 38(1½)

33(5¼)

44(1¾)

11(⁷⁄₁₆)

45°

11(⁷⁄₁₆)

11(⁷⁄₁₆)

41(1⅝)

67(2⅝)

20(¾)

RIGHT HAND MUDGUARD & PLATFORM ASSEMBLY

6(¼) DIAM

9(⅜)

6(¼)

2 HOLES 1.5 (¹⁄₁₆) DIAM

25(1)

25(1)

32(1¼)

67(2⅝)

11(⁷⁄₁₆)

PLATFORM REAR GUARD

41(1⅝) 20(¾)

18(¹¹⁄₁₆)

BATTERY BOX

6(¼) DIAM

6(¼) 9(⅜)

64(2½)

25(1)

38(1½)

4 HOLES 1.5(¹⁄₁₆) DIAM

HANDRAIL POSTS

– MAKE THREE
FIRST & THIRD POSTS HAVE THE
25(1) PITCH HOLES ONLY WHILE THE
SECOND POST HAS THE ADDITIONAL
PAIR OF HOLES AT 38(1½) PITCH
FOR THE WING MIRROR ASSEMBLY

38(1½)

20(¾)

25(1) DIAM

25(1)

5(³⁄₁₆) DIAM × 6(¼) DIAM

38(1½)

44(1¾)

11(⁷⁄₁₆)

AIR RESERVOIR

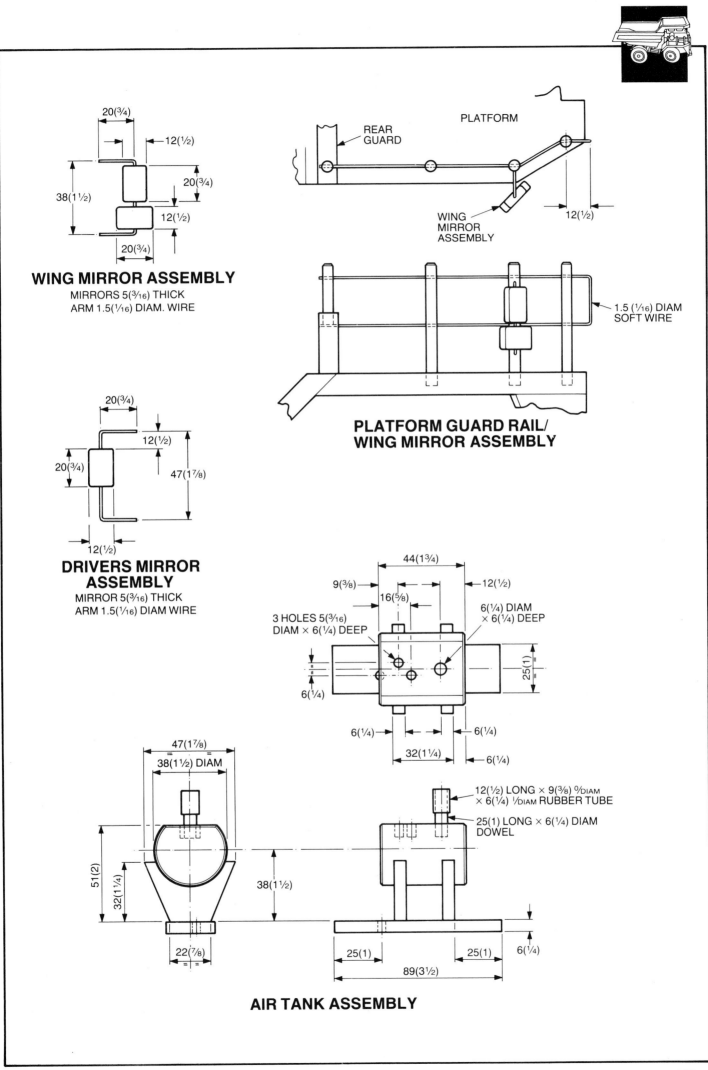

WING MIRROR ASSEMBLY

MIRRORS 5(³⁄₁₆) THICK
ARM 1.5(¹⁄₁₆) DIAM. WIRE

20(³⁄₄)
12(¹⁄₂)
38(1¹⁄₂)
20(³⁄₄)
12(¹⁄₂)
20(³⁄₄)

REAR
GUARD
PLATFORM
WING
MIRROR
ASSEMBLY
12(¹⁄₂)

1.5 (¹⁄₁₆) DIAM
SOFT WIRE

**PLATFORM GUARD RAIL/
WING MIRROR ASSEMBLY**

**DRIVERS MIRROR
ASSEMBLY**

MIRROR 5(³⁄₁₆) THICK
ARM 1.5(¹⁄₁₆) DIAM WIRE

20(³⁄₄)
12(¹⁄₂)
20(³⁄₄)
47(1⁷⁄₈)
12(¹⁄₂)

44(1³⁄₄)
9(³⁄₈)
16(⁵⁄₈)
12(¹⁄₂)
3 HOLES 5(³⁄₁₆)
DIAM × 6(¹⁄₄) DEEP
6(¹⁄₄) DIAM
× 6(¹⁄₄) DEEP
25(1)
6(¹⁄₄)
6(¹⁄₄)
6(¹⁄₄)
32(1¹⁄₄)
6(¹⁄₄)

47(1⁷⁄₈)
38(1¹⁄₂) DIAM
12(¹⁄₂) LONG × 9(³⁄₈) º/DIAM
× 6(¹⁄₄) ¹/DIAM RUBBER TUBE
25(1) LONG × 6(¹⁄₄) DIAM
DOWEL
51(2)
32(1¹⁄₄)
38(1¹⁄₂)
22(⁷⁄₈)
25(1)
25(1)
6(¹⁄₄)
89(3¹⁄₂)

AIR TANK ASSEMBLY

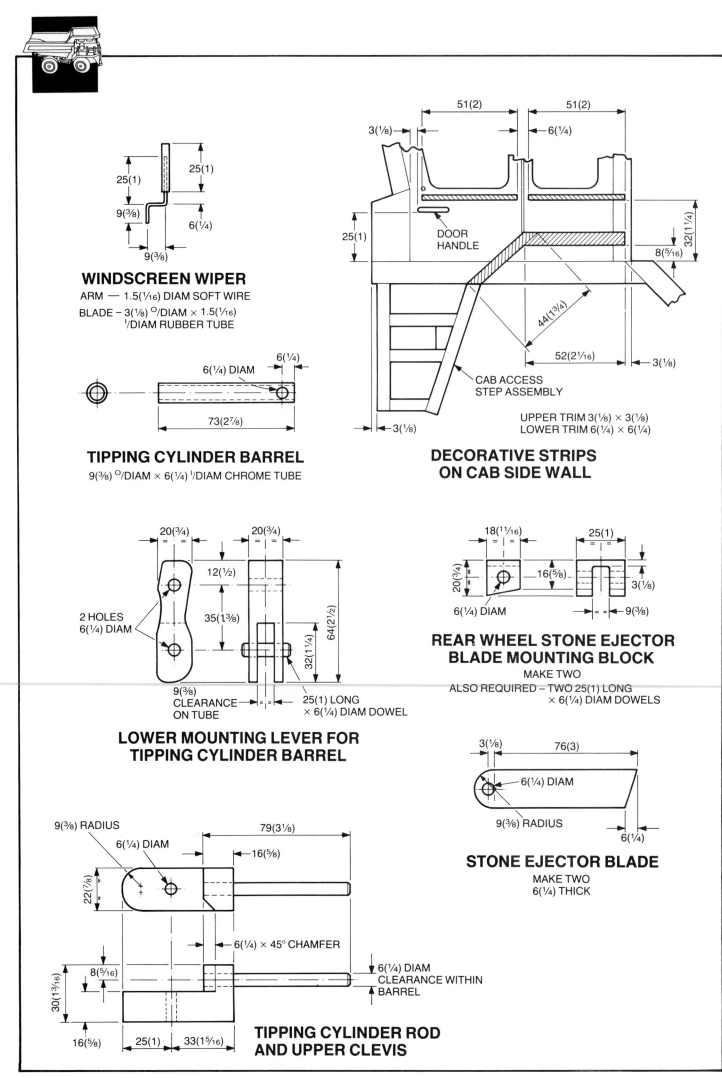

WINDSCREEN WIPER

ARM — 1.5($\frac{1}{16}$) DIAM SOFT WIRE

BLADE – 3($\frac{1}{8}$) ^{O}/DIAM × 1.5($\frac{1}{16}$)
^{I}/DIAM RUBBER TUBE

TIPPING CYLINDER BARREL

9($\frac{3}{8}$) ^{O}/DIAM × 6($\frac{1}{4}$) ^{I}/DIAM CHROME TUBE

DECORATIVE STRIPS
ON CAB SIDE WALL

DOOR HANDLE

CAB ACCESS
STEP ASSEMBLY

UPPER TRIM 3($\frac{1}{8}$) × 3($\frac{1}{8}$)
LOWER TRIM 6($\frac{1}{4}$) × 6($\frac{1}{4}$)

LOWER MOUNTING LEVER FOR
TIPPING CYLINDER BARREL

2 HOLES
6($\frac{1}{4}$) DIAM

9($\frac{3}{8}$)
CLEARANCE
ON TUBE

25(1) LONG
× 6($\frac{1}{4}$) DIAM DOWEL

REAR WHEEL STONE EJECTOR
BLADE MOUNTING BLOCK

MAKE TWO

ALSO REQUIRED – TWO 25(1) LONG
× 6($\frac{1}{4}$) DIAM DOWELS

6($\frac{1}{4}$) DIAM

STONE EJECTOR BLADE

MAKE TWO
6($\frac{1}{4}$) THICK

9($\frac{3}{8}$) RADIUS

6($\frac{1}{4}$) DIAM

TIPPING CYLINDER ROD
AND UPPER CLEVIS

9($\frac{3}{8}$) RADIUS

6($\frac{1}{4}$) DIAM

6($\frac{1}{4}$) × 45° CHAMFER

6($\frac{1}{4}$) DIAM
CLEARANCE WITHIN
BARREL

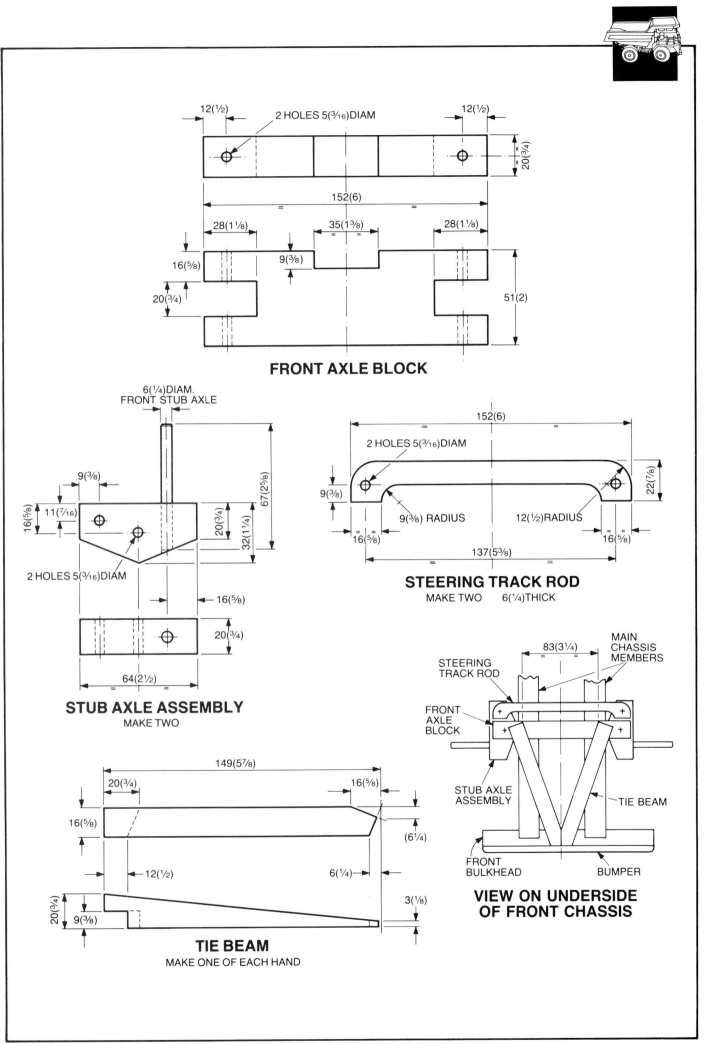

12(½)   2 HOLES 5(³⁄₁₆)DIAM   12(½)

20(¾)

152(6)

28(1⅛)   35(1³⁄₈)   28(1⅛)

16(⅝)   9(³⁄₈)

20(¾)   51(2)

FRONT AXLE BLOCK

6(¼)DIAM.
FRONT STUB AXLE

9(³⁄₈)

16(⅝)   11(⁷⁄₁₆)

67(2⅝)
20(¾)
32(1¼)

2 HOLES 5(³⁄₁₆)DIAM

16(⅝)

20(¾)

64(2½)

STUB AXLE ASSEMBLY
MAKE TWO

152(6)

2 HOLES 5(³⁄₁₆)DIAM

9(³⁄₈)
22(⁷⁄₈)

9(³⁄₈) RADIUS   12(½)RADIUS

16(⅝)   16(⅝)

137(5³⁄₈)

STEERING TRACK ROD
MAKE TWO   6(¼)THICK

MAIN
CHASSIS
MEMBERS

83(3¼)

STEERING
TRACK ROD

FRONT
AXLE
BLOCK

STUB AXLE
ASSEMBLY   TIE BEAM

FRONT
BULKHEAD   BUMPER

**VIEW ON UNDERSIDE
OF FRONT CHASSIS**

149(5⁷⁄₈)

20(¾)   16(⅝)

16(⅝)

(6¼)

12(½)   6(¼)

20(¾)
9(³⁄₈)   3(⅛)

TIE BEAM
MAKE ONE OF EACH HAND

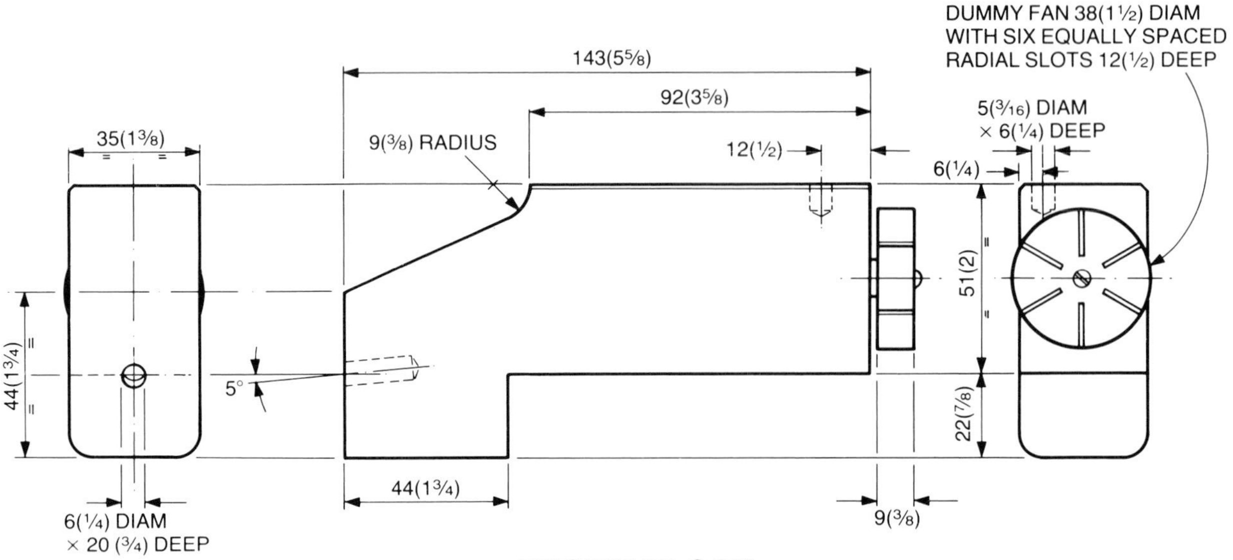

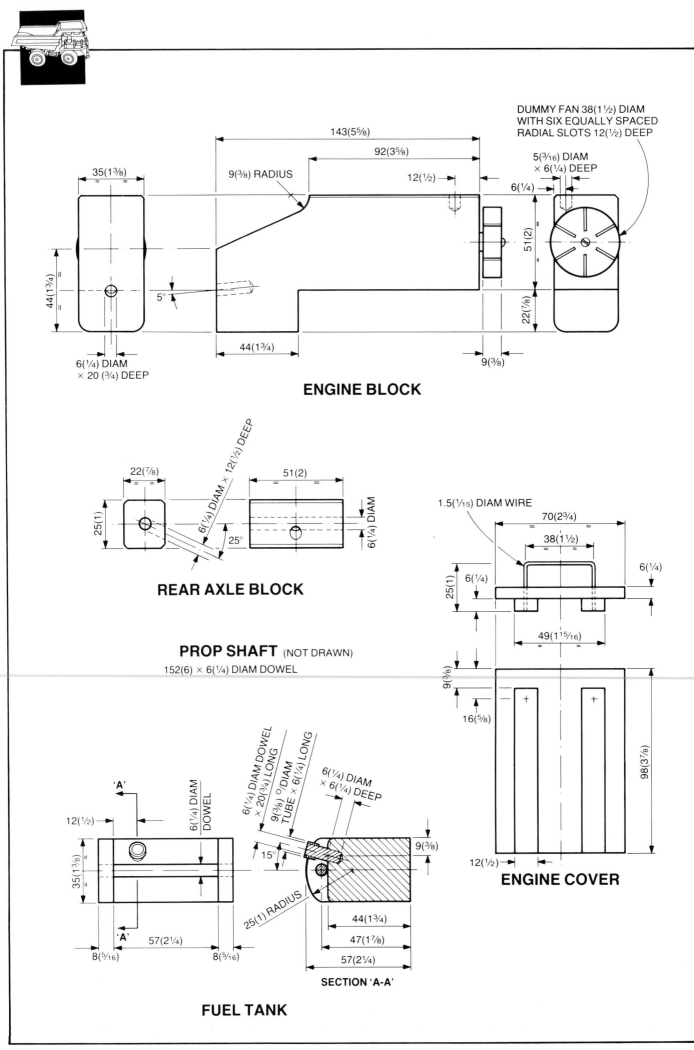

DUMMY FAN 38(1 1/2) DIAM
WITH SIX EQUALLY SPACED
RADIAL SLOTS 12(1/2) DEEP
143(5 5/8)
92(3 5/8)
35(1 3/8)
9(3/8) RADIUS
12(1/2)
5(3/16) DIAM
× 6(1/4) DEEP
6(1/4)
51(2)
44(1 3/4)
5°
22(7/8)
44(1 3/4)
6(1/4) DIAM
× 20 (3/4) DEEP
9(3/8)

ENGINE BLOCK

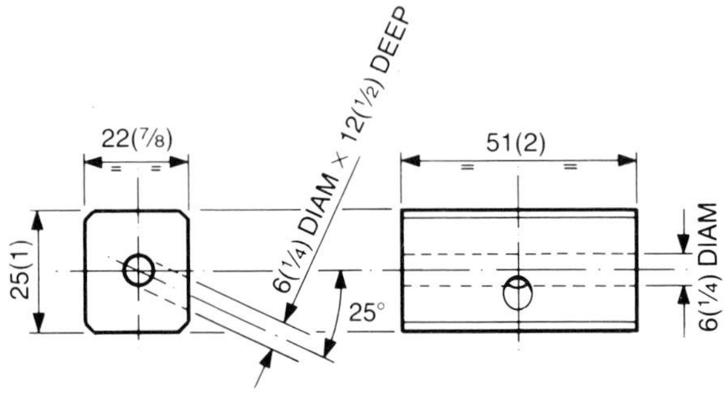

22(7/8)
6(1/4) DIAM × 12(1/2) DEEP
51(2)
25(1)
25°
6(1/4) DIAM

REAR AXLE BLOCK

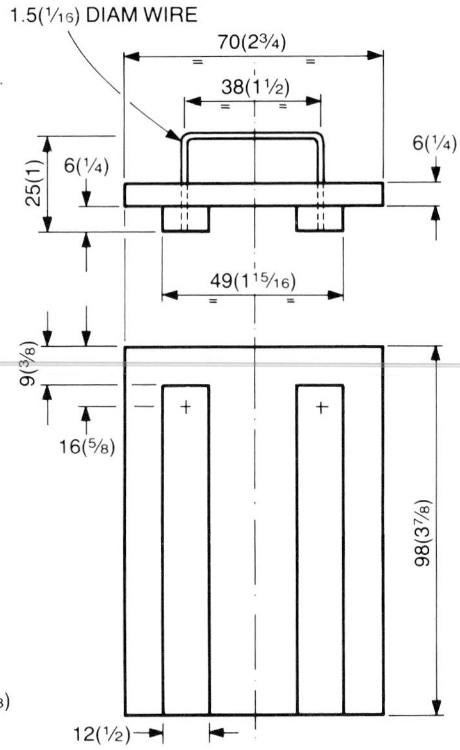

1.5(1/16) DIAM WIRE
70(2 3/4)
38(1 1/2)
6(1/4)
25(1)
6(1/4)
49(1 15/16)
9(3/8)
16(5/8)
98(3 7/8)
12(1/2)

ENGINE COVER

PROP SHAFT (NOT DRAWN)

152(6) × 6(1/4) DIAM DOWEL

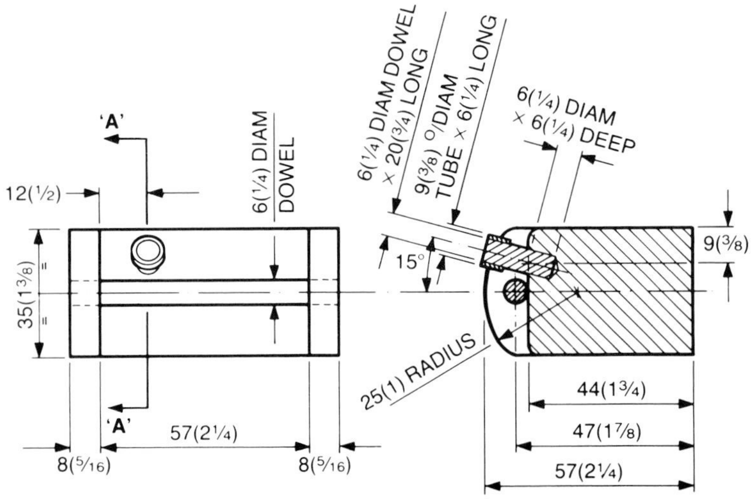

'A'
6(1/4) DIAM DOWEL
12(1/2)
35(1 3/8)
'A'
57(2 1/4)
8(5/16)
8(5/16)
6(1/4) DIAM DOWEL
× 20(3/4) LONG
9(3/8) O/DIAM
TUBE × 6(1/4) LONG
6(1/4) DIAM
× 6(1/4) DEEP
15°
9(3/8)
25(1) RADIUS
44(1 3/4)
47(1 7/8)
57(2 1/4)

SECTION 'A-A'

FUEL TANK

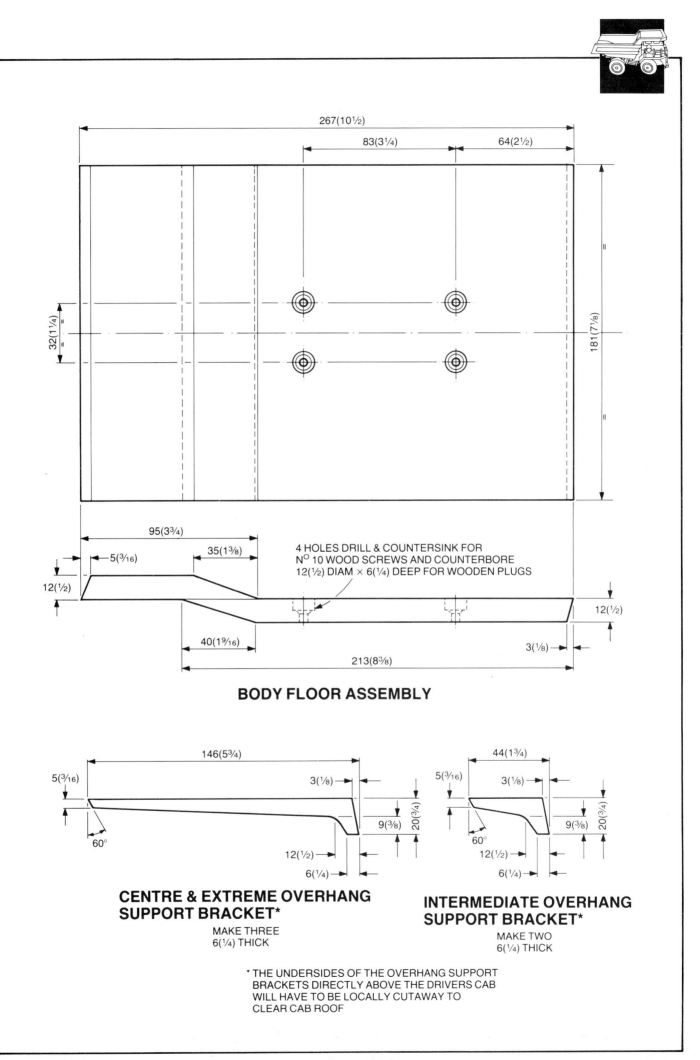

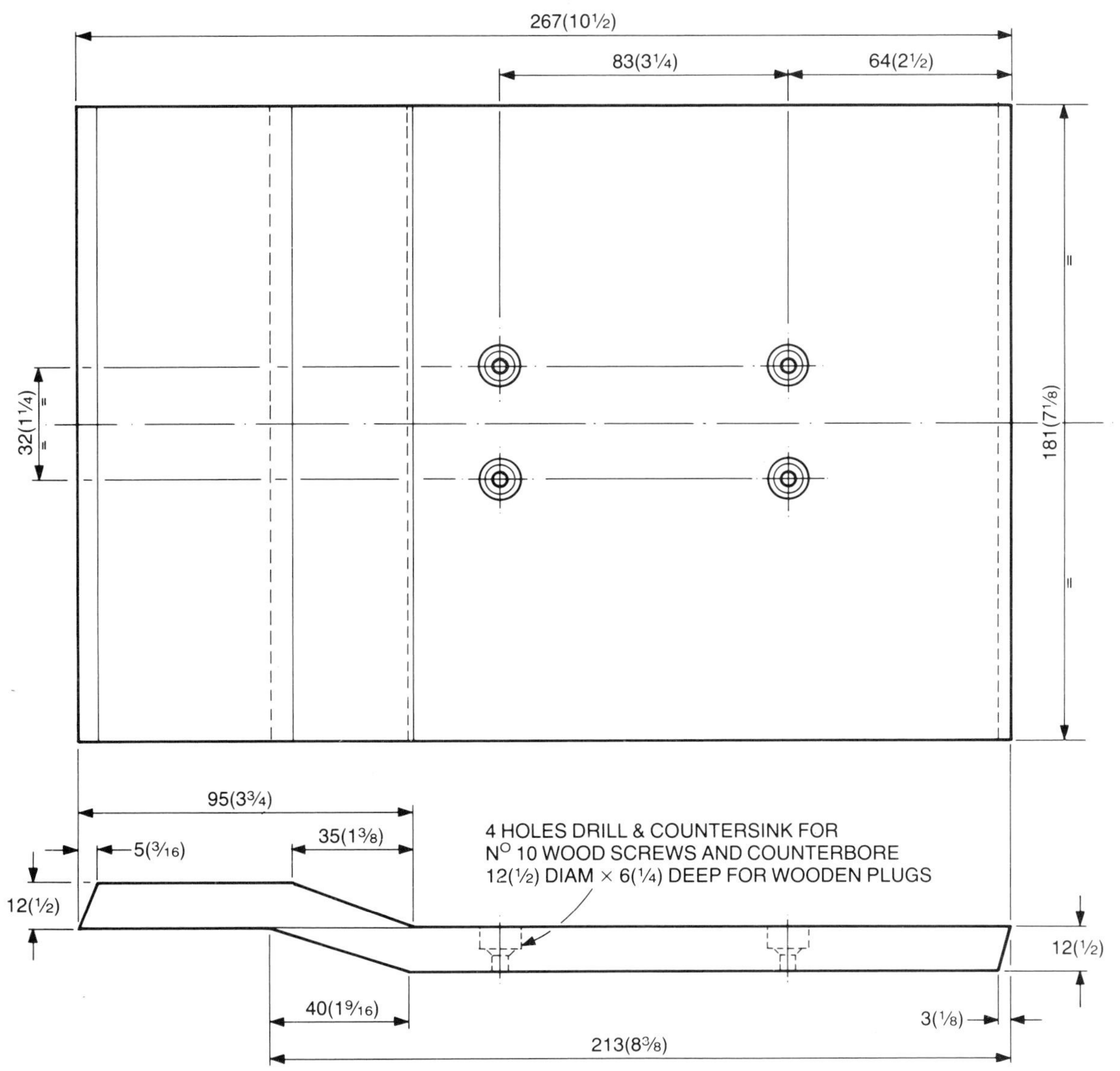
267(10½)
83(3¼)
64(2½)
181(7⅞)
32(1¼)
95(3¾)
35(1⅜)
5(3/16)
12(½)
4 HOLES DRILL & COUNTERSINK FOR
N° 10 WOOD SCREWS AND COUNTERBORE
12(½) DIAM × 6(¼) DEEP FOR WOODEN PLUGS
12(½)
40(1 9/16)
3(⅛)
213(8⅜)

BODY FLOOR ASSEMBLY

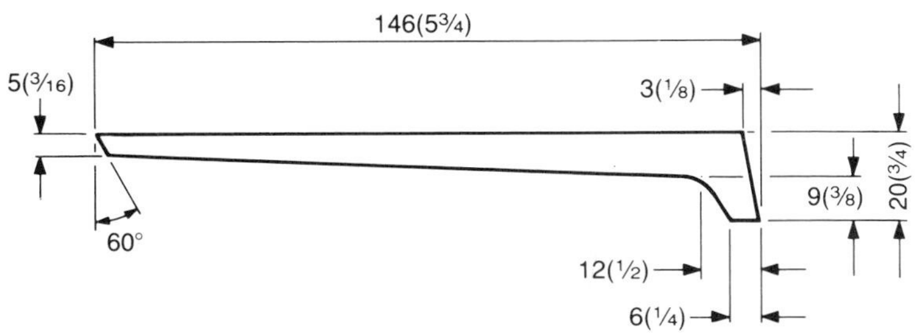
146(5¾)
5(3/16)
3(⅛)
20(¾)
9(⅜)
60°
12(½)
6(¼)

CENTRE & EXTREME OVERHANG SUPPORT BRACKET*

MAKE THREE
6(¼) THICK

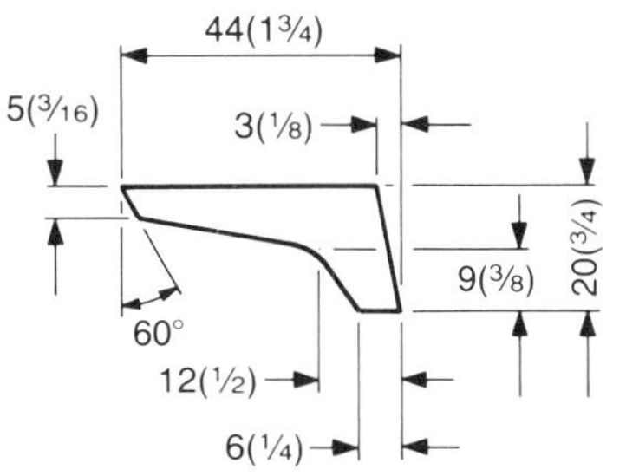
44(1¾)
5(3/16)
3(⅛)
20(¾)
9(⅜)
60°
12(½)
6(¼)

INTERMEDIATE OVERHANG SUPPORT BRACKET*

MAKE TWO
6(¼) THICK

* THE UNDERSIDES OF THE OVERHANG SUPPORT BRACKETS DIRECTLY ABOVE THE DRIVERS CAB WILL HAVE TO BE LOCALLY CUTAWAY TO CLEAR CAB ROOF

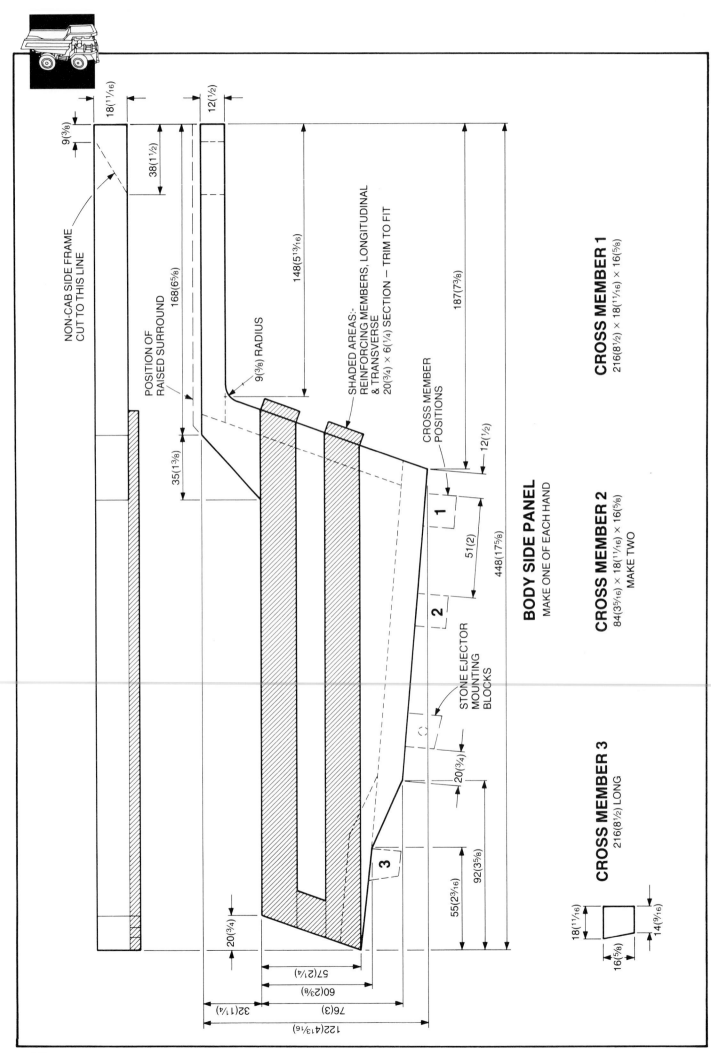

NON-CAB SIDE FRAME CUT TO THIS LINE

18(¹¹/₁₆)

9(³/₈)

12(¹/₂)

38(1½)

POSITION OF RAISED SURROUND

168(6⁵/₈)

35(1³/₈)

9(³/₈) RADIUS

148(5¹³/₁₆)

SHADED AREAS:- REINFORCING MEMBERS, LONGITUDINAL & TRANSVERSE 20(³/₄) × 6(¹/₄) SECTION – TRIM TO FIT

187(7³/₈)

CROSS MEMBER POSITIONS

12(1½)

1

51(2)

2

STONE EJECTOR MOUNTING BLOCKS

448(17⁵/₈)

20(³/₄)

92(3⁵/₈)

3

55(2³/₁₆)

20(³/₄)

57(2¼)

60(2³/₈)

32(1¼)

76(3)

122(4¹³/₁₆)

BODY SIDE PANEL

MAKE ONE OF EACH HAND

CROSS MEMBER 1

216(8½) × 18(1¹/₁₆) × 16(⁵/₈)

CROSS MEMBER 2

84(3⁵/₁₆) × 18(1¹/₁₆) × 16(⁵/₈)

MAKE TWO

CROSS MEMBER 3

216(8½) LONG

18(1¹/₁₆)

14(⁹/₁₆)

16(⁵/₈)

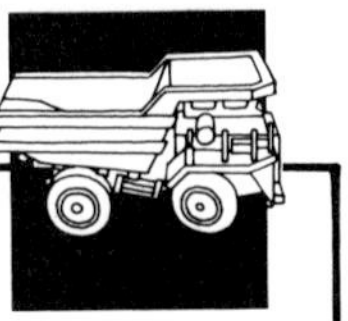

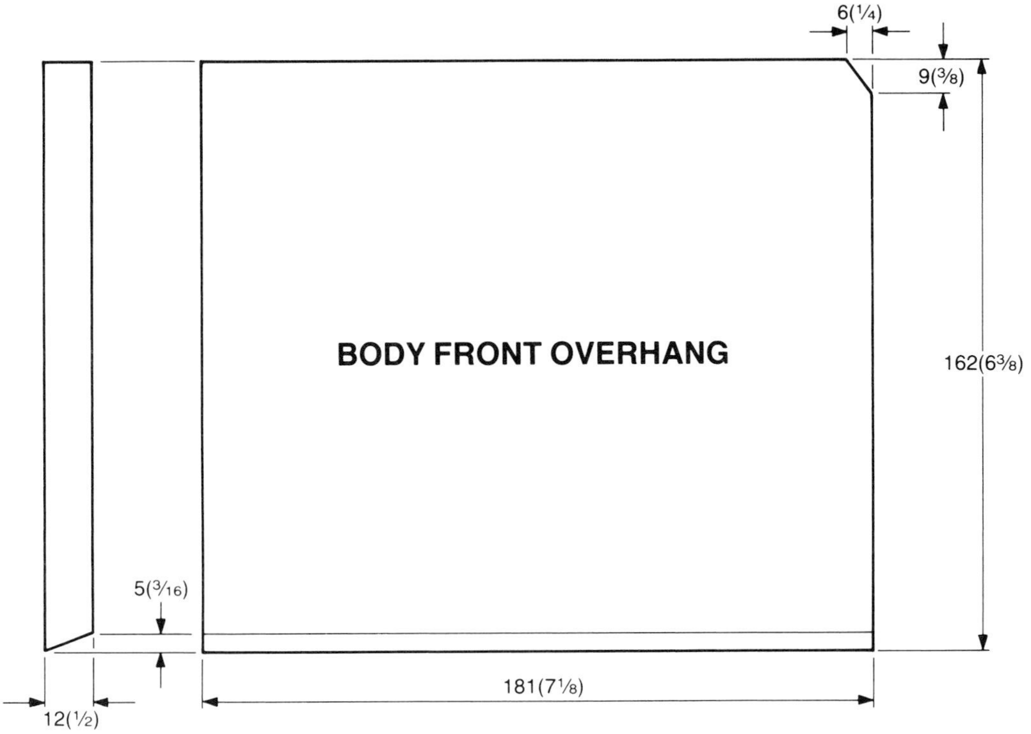
6(1/4)
9(3/8)
BODY FRONT OVERHANG
162(6 3/8)
5(3/16)
181(7 1/8)
12(1/2)

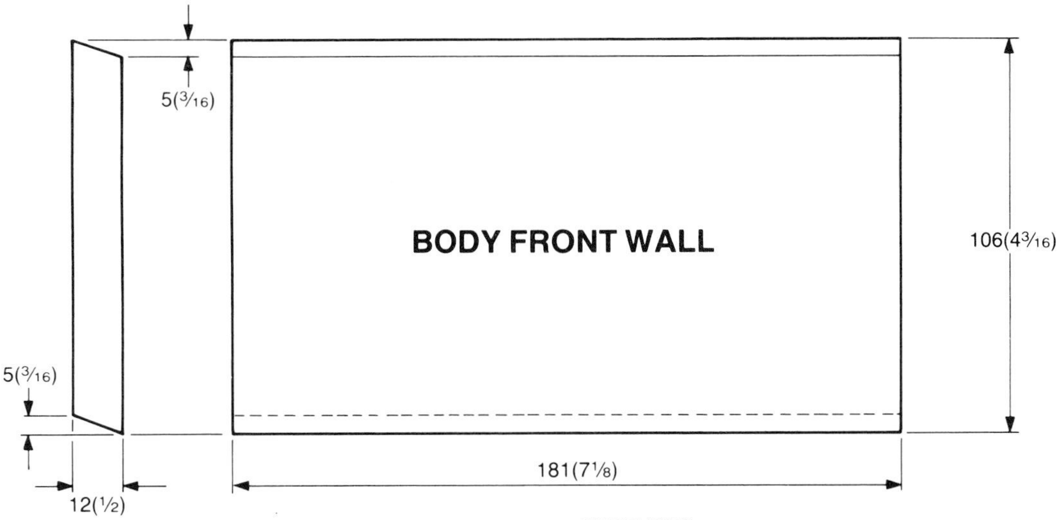
5(3/16)
BODY FRONT WALL
106(4 3/16)
5(3/16)
181(7 1/8)
12(1/2)

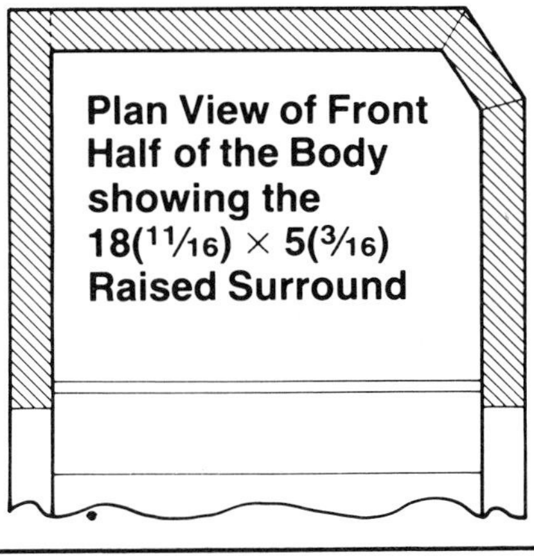

Plan View of Front Half of the Body showing the 18(11/16) × 5(3/16) Raised Surround

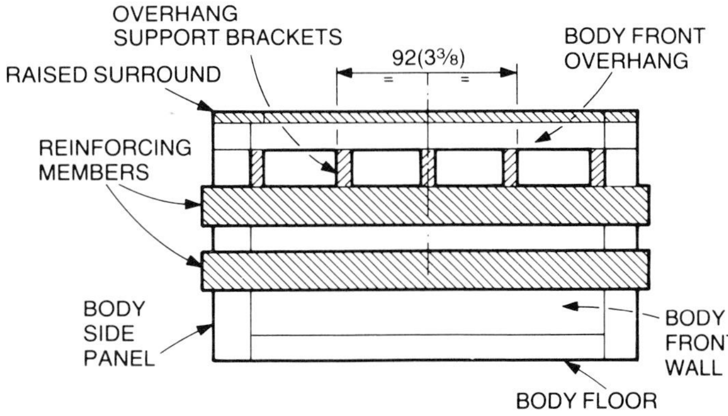
OVERHANG
SUPPORT BRACKETS
92(3 3/8)
BODY FRONT
OVERHANG
RAISED SURROUND
REINFORCING
MEMBERS
BODY
SIDE
PANEL
BODY
FRONT
WALL
BODY FLOOR

View on Front of Body

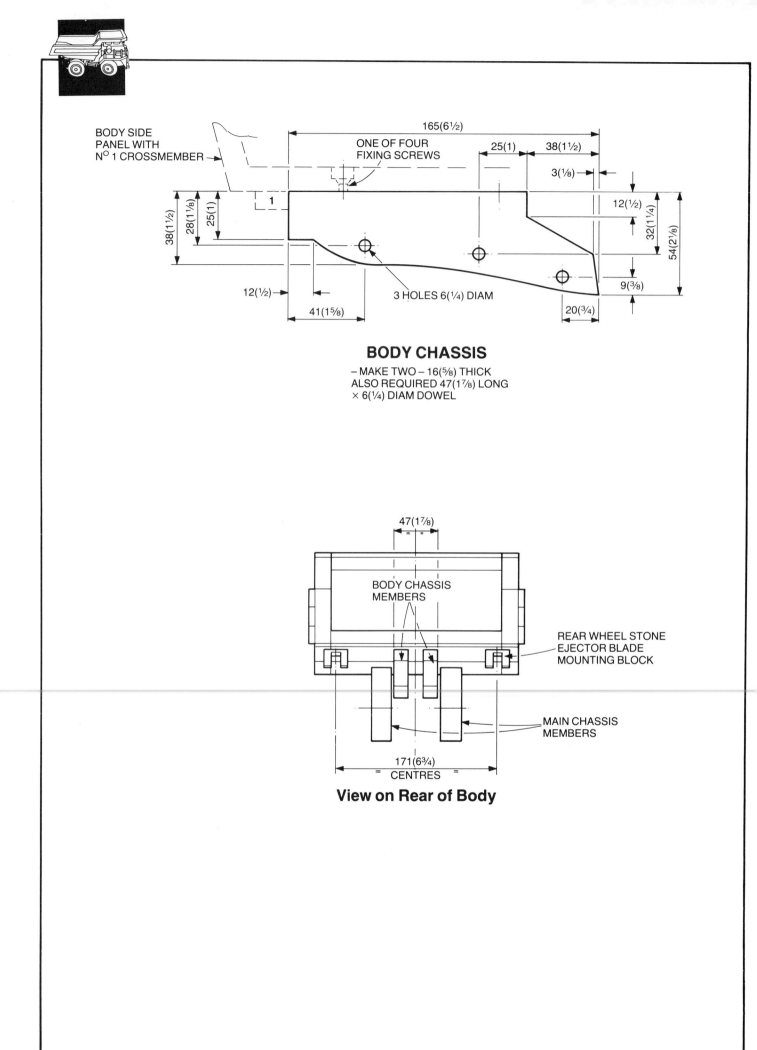

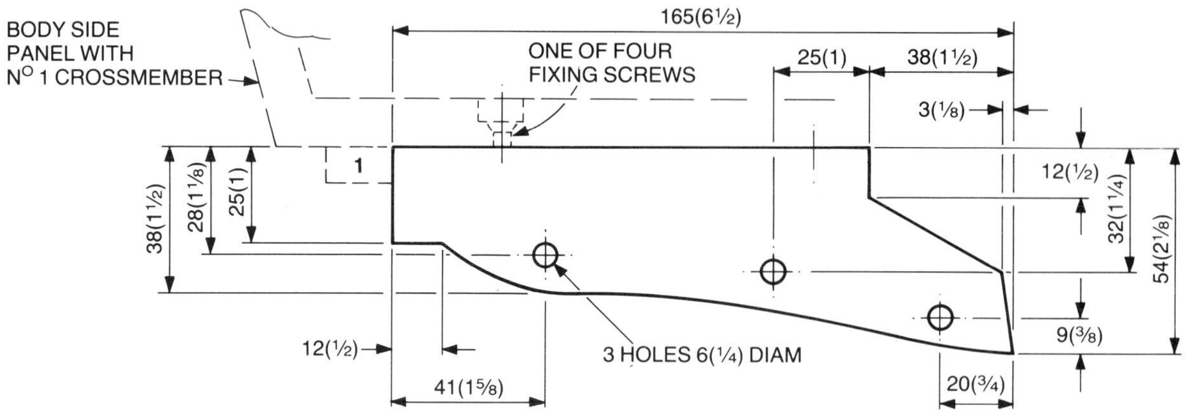
BODY SIDE PANEL WITH Nº 1 CROSSMEMBER
165(6½)
ONE OF FOUR FIXING SCREWS
25(1)
38(1½)
3(⅛)
1
38(1½)
28(1⅛)
25(1)
12(½)
32(1¼)
54(2⅛)
9(⅜)
12(½)
3 HOLES 6(¼) DIAM
41(1⅝)
20(¾)

BODY CHASSIS

– MAKE TWO – 16(⅝) THICK
ALSO REQUIRED 47(1⅞) LONG
× 6(¼) DIAM DOWEL

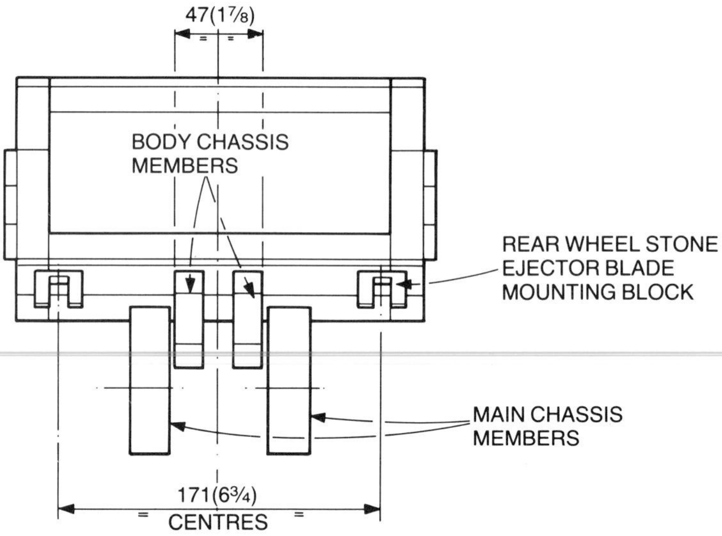
47(1⅞)
BODY CHASSIS MEMBERS
REAR WHEEL STONE EJECTOR BLADE MOUNTING BLOCK
MAIN CHASSIS MEMBERS
171(6¾)
CENTRES

View on Rear of Body

Cars today tend to have few endearing features and individual characteristics. We buy them new and trade them in within two years, barely even able to remember the registration number. As for giving them a name – well! The bright gleaming steel box with its fuel-efficient engine and go-faster spoilers and stripes does not seem to invite being christened, particularly as it was probably not assembled by human arms but by robot ones.

It is good to remember that things have not always been like this. Cars used to have names, were cherished by their makers and owners, and many are still around today as proof of the design and engineering qualities that went into their creation. A classic motor car is the combination of many skills, the finished product displaying both man's ingenuity and his craftsmanship.

On the morning of 14 April 1927 a new name in motoring history entered the lists when Volvo drove their first car off the production line. The car was an open tourer and the first models were all given affectionate names like 'The Mermaid', 'The Leprechaun' and so on. The most famous of all was called 'Jakob' and it was this name that stuck. Today any Volvo open tourer of this period (and they are rare) tends to be called a Jakob.

Making a model of a classic car gives particular pleasure because, as you work, you inevitably begin to understand more clearly the very real problems involved in drawing up and following through a complex design. So at the outset it is only fair to say that this is a very difficult woodworking project and really shouldn't be attempted until you have gained quite a bit of experience with easier models. Dimensions have been given wherever possible but there are a number of free-flowing curves (eg the mudguards) for which it is almost impossible to give full measurements and it will require the natural flair and skill of the woodworker to achieve success here. However, I am very confident that, as with the 1907 Rolls Royce Silver Ghost which appeared in *Blizzard's Wonderful Wooden Toys*, many of you will not only build the car but surpass the prototype that I have made.

1   Start by cutting out all the parts for the main chassis assembly. I used ash for these as it is both flexible and strong. You will probably find it useful to mark out on cardboard the side elevation before you assemble the chassis. To make it as strong as possible I advise you to cut stub mortice and tenon joints in the chassis sides though these are not actually detailed on the plan. You can use butt joints instead but if you do you will find it difficult to hold the chassis together when you come to glue it. Whichever jointing method you use, you will need to fit corner fillets, as shown, for extra strength.

2   From the plan view of the chassis you can see that there are some fairly tight 'bends' in it. In order to achieve this make small cuts on the *outside* face of the chassis side members just behind the front spring hangers, and again on the *inside* face just in front of the fourth cross member. Look at the plan view very carefully and it should be quite clear where the cuts have to be made. And don't forget to make them on the correct faces or you will waste a great deal of time and patience!

3   Assemble the stub tenons of the cross members into the mortices if you are using these joints and clamp the framework together to check for squareness and twists.

4   Before finally glueing the chassis together you must increase the width of the chassis members at the front and back to accommodate the steel springs. Glue pieces of ash (spacers) onto either side of each chassis member, shape them and drill the holes to take the shackle pins. Now glue all the spring hangers onto the chassis and drill the pin holes. Assemble the chassis again and, if all fits, glue it all together. When the glue is dry, glue all the corner fillets in place. The chassis should now be both strong and flexible.

5   Now shape and fit the running board support brackets. To get the front brackets at 90° to the chassis you will have to cut an angle on the bracket where it fits onto the inside of the chassis. The rear brackets fit between the rear spring hangers and the fourth set of cross members.

Front axle

1   The front wheels are made to steer, but to achieve this there is a considerable amount of work to do. Cut out a front axle beam and, following the drawings, shape the recessed part of the axle using small gouges. It is rather unorthodox to carry out shaping before cutting joints etc. but in this case it is difficult to hold the axle for shaping after the joints have been cut.

2   Cut recesses on the ends of the front axle to take the steering blocks. This should be done very carefully otherwise the steering blocks will be a sloppy fit. Chamfer off the back edge of the inside of the recesses to allow the steering blocks to pivot freely.

3   Carefully mark and cut out the steering blocks, then drill the axle holes and the pin holes that will secure them to the axle steering tie bar. Now fit the steering blocks into the front axle (a tight push fit is ideal), position them for drilling the king pin holes and tape them firmly in place. Drill the holes through the axle beam and each steering block in one operation so that the alignment of each king pin is exact.

4   Cut the front axle steering tie bar to shape and drill the pin holes.

5   Assemble the various pieces and work on each until all operates smoothly. When you are satisfied, fix the axle assembly together using steel pins which should be driven in tight. Fit spring caps over the pin heads.

Rear axle

1   Cut and shape the rear axle from solid timber. Drill the hole for the drive shaft.

2   Drill the rear axle holes in the ends, but note that these do not go all the way through. Cut recesses on the underside of the axle to take the springs. As there is very little clearance between the bottom of the spring recess and the axle it may be necessary to drill the spring fixing centres to one side of the axle since there is very little depth of wood here to hold a small screw securely.

Springs

The springs are made from nickel silver spring steel which has just the right flexibility for this job.

1   Make the 'eyes' of the springs through which the shackle pins pass using a pair of round-nosed pliers in conjunction with a 5 (3/16) diameter rod. Cut lengths of steel leaves and hold these in place with small spring clips. The spring clips are made by cutting the short off-cuts of nickel silver in half, then bending them to shape around the spring leaves.

2   Once you have made the springs, drill a hole right through each to take the screws that fix the springs to the axles. The rear springs only vary in one detail, and that is in the insertion of one mild steel (instead of spring steel) leaf to take the weight of the car. This leaf should be placed immediately under the leaf which carries the 'eyes' for the shackle pins.

Floor pan

1   Cut out the floor from a wide piece of beech.

2   Once this is done cut out the hole for the engine compartment and the two small niches where the floor meets the chassis members at the back.

3   Cut out two small strips of wood which will locate the bonnet at the base, but do not fix them in place until the model has progressed further.

Mudguards, running boards and inner wing

When the model is finished it is these three sections which give that smooth flowing line that is so pleasing to the eye.

1   The mudguard and running board pieces are not difficult to cut if you have the use of a fairly large band saw. (A visit to a local technical college may solve this problem.) Cut out the underside of each first. There is then sufficient waste wood on the top side to hold the wood firmly in the vice while you remove all the saw cuts with glasspaper. I always find that the insides of curved surfaces are more difficult to finish well than the outer curves, but do persevere. When you are satisfied with the inside curves, repeat the operation on the outside edge.

2   From the illustration of the car you will see that complete protection is given to the engine compartment by a curved inner wing. This wing is shaped up from a solid block and before starting this job you had best take a deep breath and be prepared to be patient because it is not easy, especially as you have to make a right-hand and left-hand wing, and

naturally they need to look alike. One of the biggest practical problems is how to hold the block in order to be able to work on it and once again I hollowed out the inside curve first. I also pencilled guidelines on the block first and carved both blocks simultaneously. Keep offering each wing up to the mudguard and then carving a little more. You will experience a great sense of achievement when you have finally finished this tricky job.

3   Glue the inner wings onto the mudguards. Later the whole unit has to be glued onto the floor pan and running board brackets – but not yet.

4   Make the infill panels which go behind the mudguard and beneath the floor.

Petrol tank and drive shaft

1   The petrol tank fits between the rear springs (it's a tight squeeze), but it's best to leave the final assembly until the model is nearer completion. Make the tank from a solid block of wood and shape the curve on the back using a smoothing plane and spokeshave. Drill the filler cap hole.

2   Glue a small strip of wood onto the top of the tank. It is this strip which should eventually be glued onto the back of the rear cross member.

3   Make the petrol filler cap and glue this into the tank.

4   Make the drive shaft from dowelling.

Bulkheads, bonnet and radiator

1   The chassis front bulkhead at the front of the car between the front springs is a most attractive feature and gives the front end of the car a sophisticated look. In reality it was probably put there as a protection for the sump. Cut and shape the piece of timber and drill a small hole to take the starting handle.

2   Make the headlamps from different thicknesses of dowel and the mounting blocks from timber. Make the reflectors from two aluminium discs and, if you have access to a lathe, as I did, you can add brass trims as well. It is details like this that make the car really come to life.

3   Shape up the engine block and drill the necessary holes. The recess at the back has to be cut so that the block will fit underneath the second chassis support member. I cut and fitted a cooling fan on the front and bent a piece of aluminium to represent the top radiator hose which fits into another piece of timber glued to the top of the main block. However, I know that there are those who will go to far

more trouble and not be content with the sparse fittings I have detailed here. Over to you!

4   Hollow out the engine compartment rear bulkhead. The first task when doing this is to remove most of the wood from the middle with a large firmer chisel. Then carry out final shaping using a spokeshave. If you leave a very thin piece at the bottom you will find it a great help when you come to assemble everything onto the floor pan.

The bulkhead slopes away down to the bonnet and the sides are tapered in. It's best to stop just before you carry out the final shaping and make the other two components that have a bearing on this one, namely the bonnet and the radiator.

5   Make the bonnet sides and glue on the thin strips of wood that represent the bonnet louvres. Shape the bonnet top roughly, then place the top, sides and rear bulkhead on the floor pan and begin the final shaping. As with all these shaping tasks it is a case of removing a shaving at a time and continuously 'offering up' the piece being worked on to the other parts to see how much more needs to be removed. Cut a groove along the length of the bonnet and insert a brass rod to simulate the bonnet hinge.

6   When I made the Rolls Royce Silver Ghost, one of the Rolls Royce craftsmen made me a stainless steel radiator and this feature really set the car off. I therefore decided that I must do the same for Jakob and had a radiator hand-made from copper plate and then chrome-plated to fit my model (see Accessories, page 215). I also commissioned a Volvo badge which I feel is an essential finishing touch. However, from the dimensions given on the plans it's not difficult to make a wooden radiator, if you prefer, and fit a mesh grill for realism.

7   Once the rear bulkhead, bonnet and radiator have been made they all have to be assembled on the floor pan and the final shaping and glasspapering carried out. It is quite impossible to make one piece in total isolation from the rest with this model and it is well worth spending the time getting the shaping just right.

Cab

1   First of all mark out the side panels full size on cardboard and use these templates to cut them out. The plan view will give you an indication of the amount of curvature you need to achieve. (I cut them from solid timber using a big bandsaw again.) Once you have cut out the basic right and left-hand panels there is a great deal of work to do using a sharp scraper to remove all the saw cuts.

2 Cut out the cab front bulkhead and the cab divider wall which fits into halving joints cut on the inside faces of the side panels. Assemble the whole job dry using elastic bands to hold the parts together. When making this sort of model assembly of half-finished parts is so valuable. You have time to stand back and assess your progress – thinking time in this sort of situation is most important.

3 Cut out the doors in the side panels using a coping saw. Very accurate work is necessary here as the sections being removed are going to be used as doors. Keep the removal of saw cuts to the very minimum. Fit brass hinges and hang the doors in the traditional way. Cut out handles from small off cuts of wood.

4 Glue the side panels, cab front bulkhead and cab divider wall together and, when the glue has dried, shape the rear cab wall to fit. Ideally this rear wall needs to be gently curved both around the sides and at the bottom. Cut a slight chamfer along the top edge of the side walls.

Dashboard, steering column support and steering wheel

1 Cut and shape the dashboard and cut out small discs of wood to represent instruments. Glue these in place.

2 The steering wheel is a small detail that is well worth taking time over. Cut out a complete wooden wheel (disc) and fit four small spokes inside the wheel. A tiny halving joint is necessary in the middle where the spokes cross. To take away the 'boxiness' chamfer each spoke very slightly. Drill a small hole through the centre to take the steering column.

3 Assemble the wheel and column and make the steering column support. Fit the support to the cab front bulkhead.

Windscreen assembly

This is quite a straightforward job but it does require skill and patience when it comes to glueing the clear plastic onto the wood. Nothing looks worse than long 'strings' of resin everywhere. The clear plastic adds great rigidity to an otherwise delicate structure.

1 Cut out the uprights and cross members. Glue them together and glue the frame onto the cab front bulkhead.

2 Glue on the plexiglass.

Seating and upholstery

One of the most prominent features of the early cars was their magnificent coach work and leather pleated seats. Now it is possible, with patience, to achieve leather pleating on a model's seats. First get a good supply of finely skived leather. This is available in some most surprising places, eg shoe repairers. Keep asking and looking through the Yellow Pages for your area. The leather needs to be soft and thin – almost as thin as chamois leather. Before you start cutting into the hide do experiment first, find out just how wide it is necessary to cut the grooves in the seats and how well the leather 'folds' into it. Once you have done a trial piece successfully you can begin.

1 Cut the wooden seats, backs etc to shape. Cut small grooves with a chisel or saw across the seats.

2 Cut the leather to size. Always remember each piece will need to be almost twice as long as the seat you are upholstering because of the amount that has to be pushed into the grooves. A fine leather is satisfying to work with and it is quite easy to tuck and fold the edges in at the corners etc.

3 Spread impact adhesive onto the wood and leather and after a short period (usually 10 minutes), place the leather onto the seat and press it into the seat with a wooden ruler. The leather will take on the contour of the wood beneath.

Suitable adhesive will usually be available from the place where you buy the leather but, if not, find a friendly shoe repairer and get him to sell you a small amount (about ½ pint) from the gallon drum he will probably use. I always find that in the majority of cases people are very helpful and even get quite enthusiastic when they know what you are trying to achieve.

4 Fit the seat pieces together.

Spare wheel

The spare wheel is carried on the back. Cut the spare wheel clamp to shape and screw this onto the back of the rear cab wall. As for other vehicles of this period new wheel rims were clamped onto the existing spokes, so you need to cut off the spokes on the wheel you buy and simply mount the rim and tyre.

The trimmings

The tops of the bodywork are trimmed with leather, and I used felt to line the bulkheads and 'carpet' the floor. You can, if you wish, shape up some pieces of wood and cover them in leather to form a hood as I did.

Assembly

It is difficult to be specific about how you assemble the various finished pieces. I have indicated that some components, eg the bonnet, bulkhead and radiator, have to be built as a complete unit. It is always better to make all the major pieces and use tape to attach them to the main chassis, rather than glue some pieces together only to find that they have to be taken apart (with great difficulty) because they are not quite right. I always find that the wheels are the very last items to be attached, and that varnishing and wax polishing are best done in sections. At the end I polish the whole job up.

Cutting list

Main chassis side members	2 off	800 × 54 × 10mm (31½ × 2⅛ × ¹³/₃₂in)	Timber
Front spacer	4 off	79 × 35 × 3mm (3⅛ × 1⅜ × ⅛in)	Timber
Rear spacer	2 off	35 × 25 × 6mm (1⅜ × 1 × ¼in)	Timber
Cross members	Make from 584 × 25 × 16mm (23 × 1 × ⅝in)		Timber
Cross member (rear)	1 off	183 × 25 × 20mm (7¼ × 1 × ¾in)	Timber
Fillets	Make from 152 × 25 × 9mm (6 × 1 × ⅜in)		Timber
Front spring hanger	4 off	35 × 18 × 8mm (1⅜ × ¹¹/₁₆ × ⁵/₁₆in)	Timber
Rear spring hanger (outer)	2 off	38 × 18 × 11mm (1½ × ¹¹/₁₆ × ⁷/₁₆in)	Timber
Rear spring hanger (inner)	2 off	38 × 18 × 5mm (1½ × ¹¹/₁₆ × ³/₁₆in)	Timber
Swinging spring hanger	8 off	32 × 16 × 5mm (1¼ × ⅝ × ³/₁₆in)	Timber
Running board support bracket (forward)	2 off	127 × 65 × 12mm (5 × 2⁹/₁₆ × ½in)	Timber
Running board support bracket (rear)	2 off	89 × 65 × 12mm (3½ × 2⁹/₁₆ × ½in)	Timber
Floor pan	1 off	521 × 241 × 8mm (20½ × 9½ × ⁵/₁₆in)	Timber
Bonnet stop strip	2 off	152 × 9 × 6mm (6 × ⅜ × ¼in)	Timber
Front axle	2 off	244 × 44 × 22mm (9⅝ × 1¾ × ⅞in)	Timber
Front axle steering tie bar	1 off	251 × 28 × 11mm (9⅞ × 1⅛ × ⁷/₁₆in)	Timber
Steering block	2 off	47 × 22 × 20mm (1⅞ × ⅞ × ¾in)	Timber
Rear axle	1 off	251 × 51 × 22mm (9⅞ × 2 × ⅞in)	Timber
Drive shaft	1 off	346mm (13⅝in) × 9mm (⅜in) diam dowelling	
	1 off	9mm (⅜in) × 38mm (1½in) diam dowelling	
Chassis infill side panel	2 off	374 × 49 × 9mm (14¾ × 1¹⁵/₁₆ × ⅜in)	Timber
Mudguards and running board	2 off	790 × 123 × 47mm (31⅛ × 4⅞ × 1⅞in)	Timber
Petrol tank	1 off	175 × 64 × 47mm (6⅞ × 2½ × 1⅞in)	Timber
	1 off	124 × 12 × 6mm (4⅞ × ½ × ¼in)	Timber
Filler cap	1 off	20mm (¾in) × 12mm (½in) diam dowelling	
Inner wing	2 off	197 × 67 × 44mm (7¾ × 2⅝ × 1¾in)	Timber
Chassis front bulkhead	1 off	110 × 54 × 44mm (4⁵/₁₆ × 2⅛ × 1¾in)	Timber
Head lamp	2 off	22mm (⅞in) × 35mm (1⅜in) diam dowelling	
	2 off	64mm (2½in) × 5mm (³/₁₆) diam dowelling	
Head lamp mounting block	2 off	38 × 22 × 16mm (1½ × ⅞ × ⅝in)	Timber
Engine block	1 off	197 × 114 × 54mm (7¾ × 4½ × 2⅛in)	Timber
	1 off	83 × 25 × 16mm (3¼ × 1 × ⅝in)	Timber
Cooling fan	1 off	76 × 76 × 9mm (3 × 3 × ⅜in)	Timber
Engine compartment rear bulkhead	1 off	210 × 137 × 75mm (8¼ × 5⅜ × 2¹⁵/₁₆in)	Timber
Radiator	1 off	129 × 105 × 24mm (5¹/₁₆ × 4⅛ × ¹³/₁₆in)	Timber
	1 off	127 × 98 × 3mm (5 × 3⅞ × ⅛in)	Timber
	1 off	12mm (½in) × 9mm (⅜in) diam dowelling	
	1 off	20 × 12 × 1.5mm (¾ × ½ × ¹/₁₆in)	Timber
Bonnet	1 off	178 × 140 × 27mm (7 × 5½ × 1¹/₁₆in)	Timber
	2 off	152 × 105 × 8mm (6 × 4⅛ × ⁵/₁₆in)	Timber
Bonnet louvres	14 off	64 × 6 × 5mm (2½ × ¼ × ³/₁₆in)	Timber
Cab front bulkhead	1 off	210 × 143 × 6mm (8¼ × 5⅝ × ¼in)	Timber
Dashboard	1 off	171 × 41 × 9mm (6¾ × 1⅝ × ⅜in)	Timber
Instruments	Make from 20mm (¾in) diam, 12mm (½in) diam and 11mm (⁷/₁₆in) diam dowelling offcuts		
Windscreen assembly	2 off	241 × 9 × 9mm (9½ × ⅜ × ⅜in)	Timber
	1 off	229 × 9 × 9mm (9 × ⅜ × ⅜in)	Timber
	1 off	229 × 9 × 6mm (9 × ⅜ × ¼in)	Timber
Steering wheel	1 off	89 × 89 × 6mm (3½ × 3½ × ¼in)	Timber
	Make from 137 × 9 × 6mm (5⅜ × ⅜ × ¼in)		Timber

Steering column	1 off	121mm (4¾in) × 5mm (³⁄₁₆) diam dowelling	
Steering column support	1 off	57 × 22 × 9mm (2¼ × ⅞ × ⅜in)	Timber
Side panel	2 off	445 × 116 × 32mm (17½ × 4⁹⁄₁₆ × 1¼in)	Timber
Door handles	Make from 89 × 8 × 6mm (3½ × ⁵⁄₁₆ × ¼in)		Timber
Cab divider wall	1 off	229 × 116 × 12mm (9 × 4⁹⁄₁₆ × ½in)	Timber
Rear cab wall	1 off	178 × 90 × 20mm (7 × 3⁹⁄₁₆ × ¾in)	Timber
Front seat	1 off	216 × 98 × 9mm (8½ × 3⅞ × ⅜in)	Timber
Front seat cushion	1 off	213 × 108 × 6mm (8⅜ × 4¼ × ¼in)	Timber
Front seat back cushion	1 off	213 × 76 × 6mm (8⅜ × 3 × ¼in)	Timber
Rear seat assembly	1 off	216 × 143 × 9mm (8½ × 5⅝ × ⅜in)	Timber
	1 off	216 × 51 × 9mm (8½ × 2 × ⅜in)	Timber
Rear seat cushion	1 off	213 × 159 × 6mm (8⅜ × 6¼ × ¼in)	Timber
Rear seat back cushion	1 off	213 × 86 × 6mm (8⅜ × 3⅜ × ¼in)	Timber
Spare wheel clamp	1 off	146 × 38 × 12mm (5¾ × 1½ × ½in)	Timber

Ancillaries

	5 off	165mm (6½in) diam road wheels	
Front axle assembly	2 off	9mm (⅜in) spring dome caps	
	2 off	35mm (1⅜in) × 5mm (³⁄₁₆in) diam steel pins	
	2 off	38mm (1½in) × 5mm (³⁄₁₆in) diam steel pins	
	6 off	5mm (³⁄₁₆in) spring dome caps	
	2 off	62mm (2⁷⁄₁₆in) × 9mm (⅜in) diam steel axles	
	2 off	12mm (½in) o/d × 9mm (⅜in) i/d × 9mm (⅜in) long spacers	
Rear axle assembly	2 off	9mm × (⅜in) spring dome caps	
	2 off	95mm (3¾in) × 9mm (⅜in) diam steel axles	
	2 off	12mm (½in) o/d × 9mm (⅜in) i/d × 12mm (½in) long spacers	
Running board mesh	Make from 964 × 6 × 1mm (38 × ¼ × ¹⁄₃₂in) brass strip		
	2 off	203 × 38 × 1.5mm (8 × 1½ × ¹⁄₁₆in) steel mesh	
Head lamp reflector	2 off	25mm (1in) diam × 1.5mm (¹⁄₁₆in) aluminium disc	
Radiator top hose	1 off	6mm (¼in) o/d × 5mm (³⁄₁₆in) i/d æ 102mm (4in) aluminium tube	
Radiator core	1 off	97 × 86 × 1.5mm (3¹³⁄₁₆ × 3⅜ × ¹⁄₁₆in) steel mesh	
Dummy bonnet hinge	1 off	143mm (5⅝in) × 1.5mm (¹⁄₁₆in) diam brass rod	
Front spring assembly	Make from 1570 × 16 × 1.5mm (62 × ⅝ × ¹⁄₁₆in) spring steel		
Rear spring assembly	Make from 2665 × 16 × 1.5mm (105 × ⅝ × ¹⁄₁₆in) spring steel		
Spring clips	Make from 930 × 16 × 1.5mm (36½ × ⅝ × ¹⁄₁₆in) spring steel		
Steering column tube	1 off	6mm (¼in) o/d × 5mm (³⁄₁₆in) i/d × 70mm (2¾in) brass tube	
Windscreen	1 off	210 × 128 × 1.5mm (8¼ × 5¹⁄₁₆ × ¹⁄₁₆in) clear plastic	
	8 off	25mm (1in) × 25mm (1in) brass hinges	
	1 off	1 metre (36in) length of cord to form ??ding	
	1 off	525mm (20in) × 240mm (9½in) soft leather for seat covering	
	1 off	380mm (15in) × 102mm (4in) canvas to form folded canopy	
	1 off	610mm (24in) × 380mm (15in) black felt to form carpets and line bulkheads	

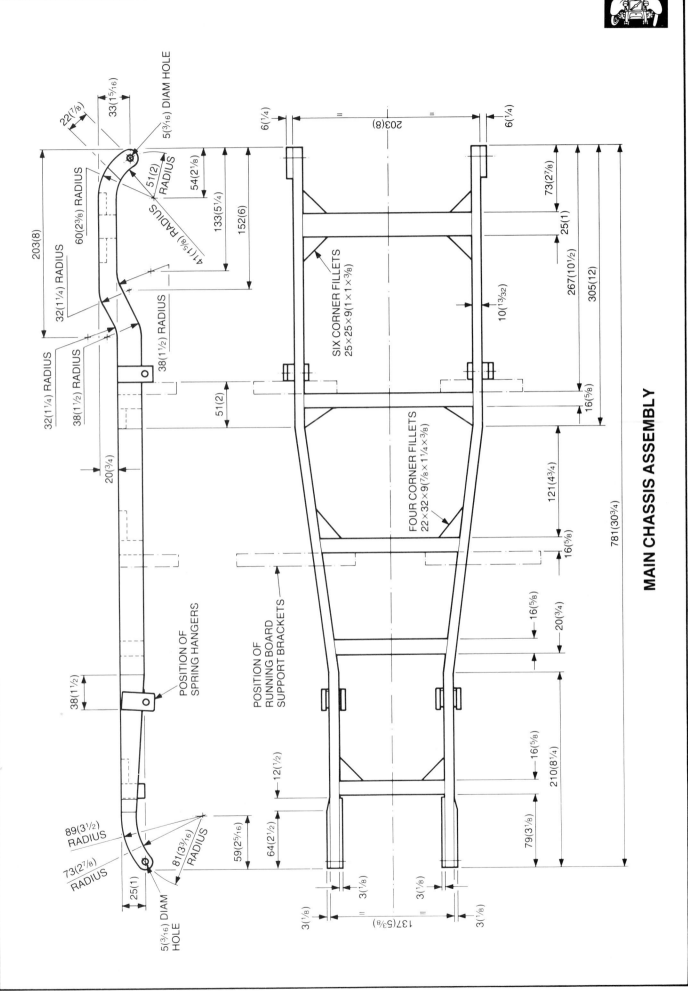

MAIN CHASSIS ASSEMBLY

33(1⁵/₁₆)

22(⁷/₈)

5(³/₁₆) DIAM HOLE

51(2) RADIUS

54(2¹/₈)

60(2³/₈) RADIUS

133(5¹/₄)

152(6)

41(1⁵/₈) RADIUS

203(8)

32(1¹/₄) RADIUS

32(1¹/₄) RADIUS

38(1¹/₂) RADIUS

38(1¹/₂) RADIUS

20(³/₄)

POSITION OF SPRING HANGERS

38(1¹/₂)

89(3¹/₂) RADIUS

73(2⁷/₈) RADIUS

81(3³/₁₆) RADIUS

25(1)

59(2⁵/₁₆)

64(2¹/₂)

12(¹/₂)

5(³/₁₆) DIAM HOLE

6(¹/₄)

203(8)

6(¹/₄)

73(2⁷/₈)

25(1)

267(10¹/₂)

305(12)

10(¹³/₃₂)

SIX CORNER FILLETS 25×25×9(1×1×³/₈)

16(⁵/₈)

FOUR CORNER FILLETS 22×32×9(⁷/₈×1¹/₄×³/₈)

121(4³/₄)

16(⁵/₈)

POSITION OF RUNNING BOARD SUPPORT BRACKETS

51(2)

16(⁵/₈)

20(³/₄)

16(⁵/₈)

210(8¹/₄)

79(3¹/₈)

781(30³/₄)

3(¹/₈)

3(¹/₈)

3(¹/₈)

3(¹/₈)

137(5³/₈)

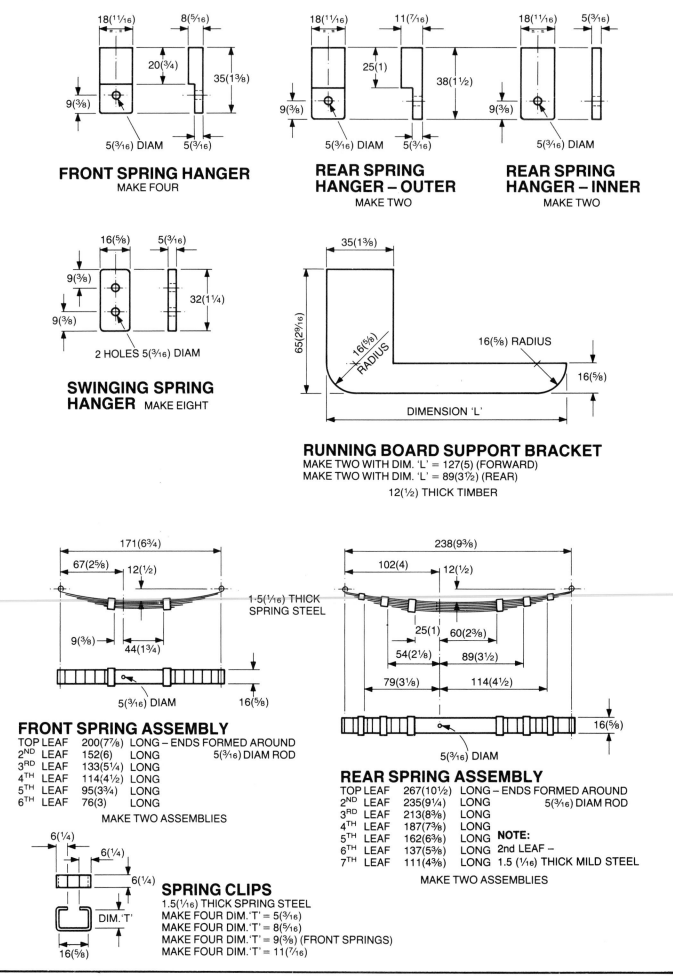

FRONT SPRING HANGER
MAKE FOUR

18(¹¹⁄₁₆) 8(⁵⁄₁₆)
20(³⁄₄) 35(1³⁄₈)
9(³⁄₈)
5(³⁄₁₆) DIAM 5(³⁄₁₆)

REAR SPRING HANGER – OUTER
MAKE TWO

18(¹¹⁄₁₆) 11(⁷⁄₁₆)
25(1) 38(1½)
9(³⁄₈)
5(³⁄₁₆) DIAM 5(³⁄₁₆)

REAR SPRING HANGER – INNER
MAKE TWO

18(¹¹⁄₁₆) 5(³⁄₁₆)
9(³⁄₈)
5(³⁄₁₆) DIAM

SWINGING SPRING HANGER MAKE EIGHT

16(⁵⁄₈) 5(³⁄₁₆)
9(³⁄₈)
9(³⁄₈) 32(1¼)
2 HOLES 5(³⁄₁₆) DIAM

RUNNING BOARD SUPPORT BRACKET
MAKE TWO WITH DIM. 'L' = 127(5) (FORWARD)
MAKE TWO WITH DIM. 'L' = 89(3½) (REAR)
12(½) THICK TIMBER

35(1³⁄₈)
65(2⁹⁄₁₆)
16(⁵⁄₈) RADIUS
16(⁵⁄₈) RADIUS
16(⁵⁄₈)
DIMENSION 'L'

FRONT SPRING ASSEMBLY

171(6¾)
67(2⁵⁄₈) 12(½)
9(³⁄₈) 44(1¾)
5(³⁄₁₆) DIAM 16(⁵⁄₈)
1·5(¹⁄₁₆) THICK SPRING STEEL

TOP LEAF	200(7⅞)	LONG – ENDS FORMED AROUND
2ND LEAF	152(6)	LONG 5(³⁄₁₆) DIAM ROD
3RD LEAF	133(5¼)	LONG
4TH LEAF	114(4½)	LONG
5TH LEAF	95(3¾)	LONG
6TH LEAF	76(3)	LONG

MAKE TWO ASSEMBLIES

REAR SPRING ASSEMBLY

238(9⅜)
102(4) 12(½)
25(1) 60(2³⁄₈)
54(2⅛) 89(3½)
79(3⅛) 114(4½)
5(³⁄₁₆) DIAM 16(⁵⁄₈)

TOP LEAF	267(10½)	LONG – ENDS FORMED AROUND
2ND LEAF	235(9¼)	LONG 5(³⁄₁₆) DIAM ROD
3RD LEAF	213(8⅜)	LONG
4TH LEAF	187(7⅜)	LONG **NOTE:**
5TH LEAF	162(6⅜)	LONG 2nd LEAF –
6TH LEAF	137(5⅜)	LONG 1.5 (¹⁄₁₆) THICK MILD STEEL
7TH LEAF	111(4⅜)	LONG

MAKE TWO ASSEMBLIES

SPRING CLIPS
1.5(¹⁄₁₆) THICK SPRING STEEL
MAKE FOUR DIM.'T' = 5(³⁄₁₆)
MAKE FOUR DIM.'T' = 8(⁵⁄₁₆)
MAKE FOUR DIM.'T' = 9(³⁄₈) (FRONT SPRINGS)
MAKE FOUR DIM.'T' = 11(⁷⁄₁₆)

6(¼) 6(¼)
6(¼)
DIM.'T'
16(⁵⁄₈)

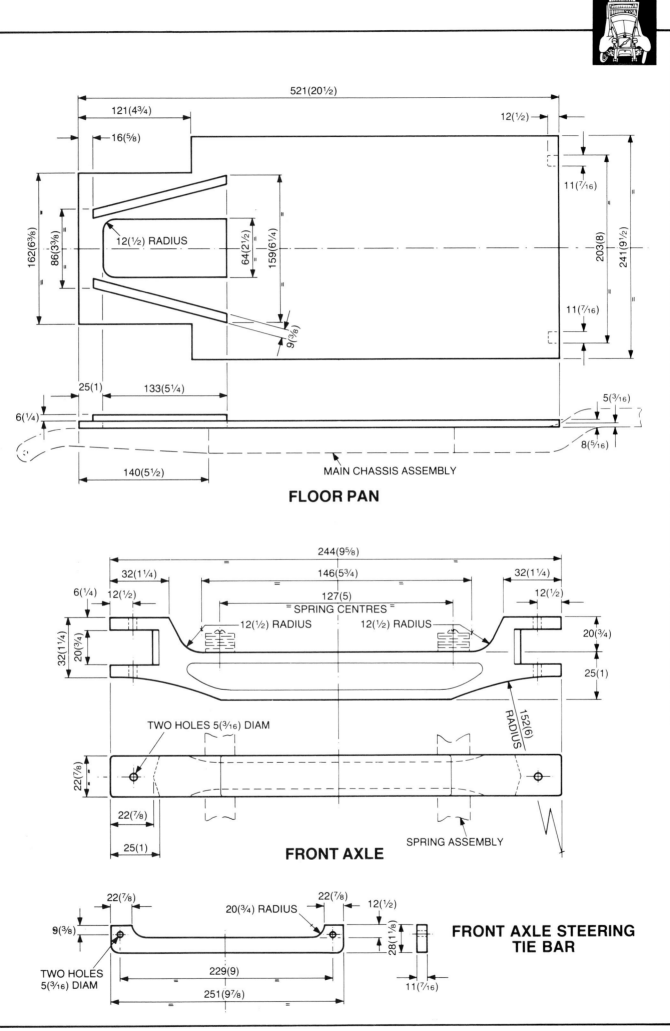

FLOOR PAN

FRONT AXLE

FRONT AXLE STEERING TIE BAR

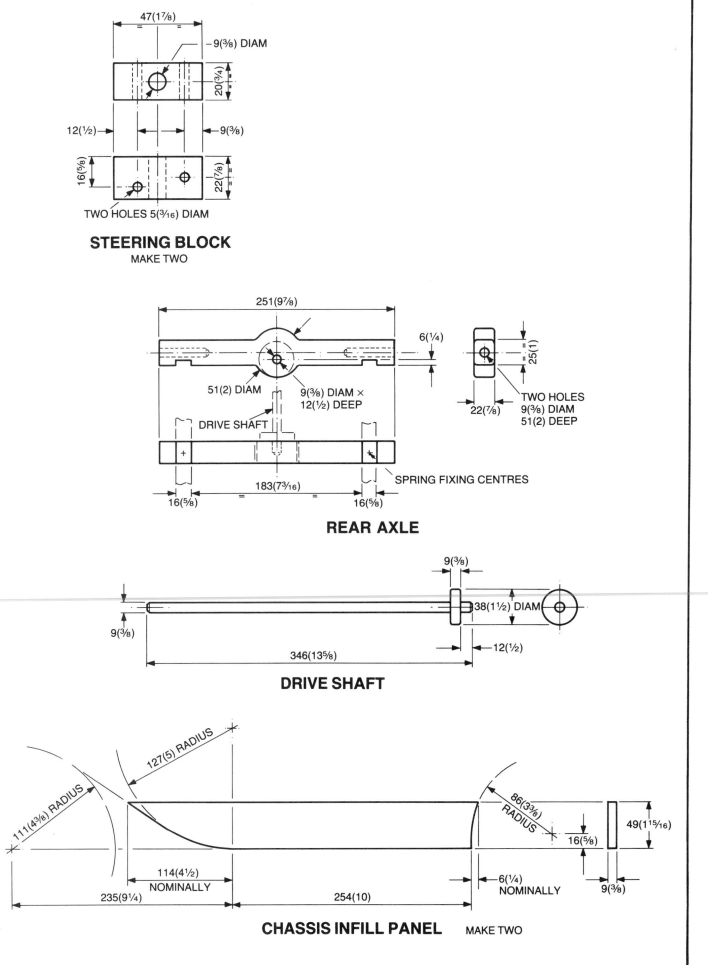

47(1⅞)

−9(⅜) DIAM

20(¾)

12(½)

9(⅜)

16(⅝)

22(⅞)

TWO HOLES 5(³⁄₁₆) DIAM

STEERING BLOCK
MAKE TWO

251(9⅞)

6(¼)

25(1)

51(2) DIAM

9(⅜) DIAM ×
12(½) DEEP

22(⅞)

TWO HOLES
9(⅜) DIAM
51(2) DEEP

DRIVE SHAFT

183(7³⁄₁₆)

16(⅝)

16(⅝)

SPRING FIXING CENTRES

REAR AXLE

9(⅜)

38(1½) DIAM

9(⅜)

346(13⅝)

12(½)

DRIVE SHAFT

127(5) RADIUS

111(4⅜) RADIUS

86(3⅜) RADIUS

49(1¹⁵⁄₁₆)

16(⅝)

114(4½)
NOMINALLY

6(¼)
NOMINALLY

9(⅜)

235(9¼)

254(10)

CHASSIS INFILL PANEL   MAKE TWO

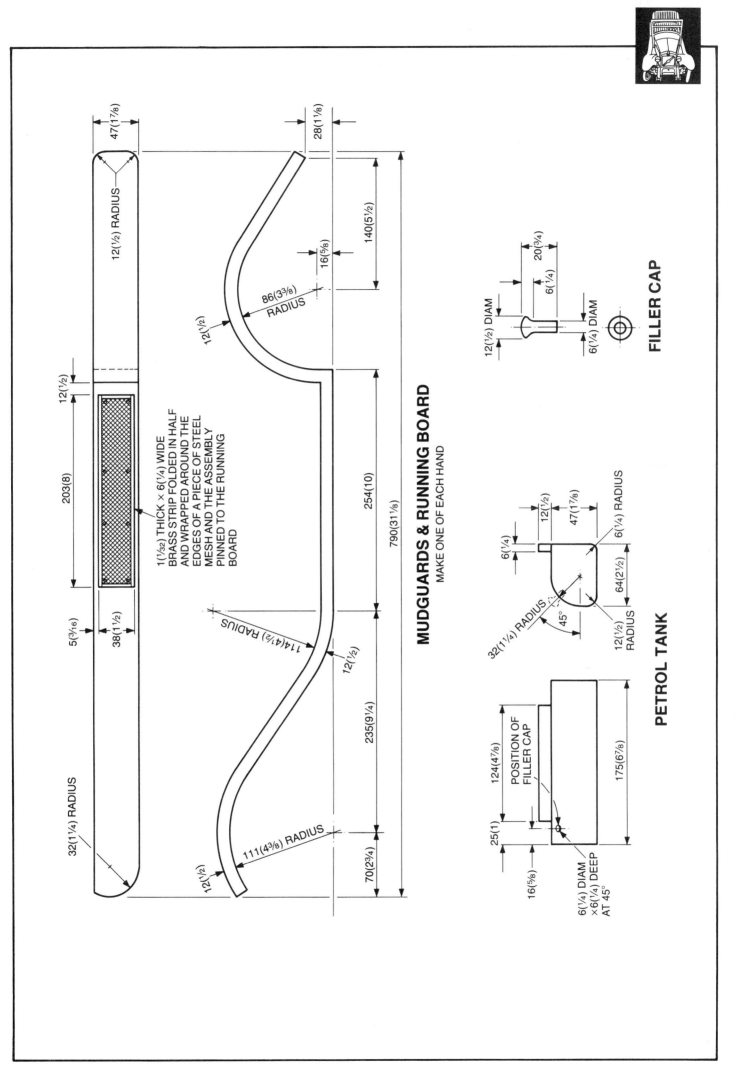

MUDGUARDS & RUNNING BOARD
MAKE ONE OF EACH HAND

47(1⅞)

28(1⅛)

12(½) RADIUS

12(½)

140(5½)

16(⅝)

86(3⅜) RADIUS

12(½)

12(½)

203(8)

1(¹⁄₃₂) THICK × 6(¼) WIDE BRASS STRIP FOLDED IN HALF AND WRAPPED AROUND THE EDGES OF A PIECE OF STEEL MESH AND THE ASSEMBLY PINNED TO THE RUNNING BOARD

254(10)

790(31⅛)

5(³⁄₁₆)

38(1½)

114(4½) RADIUS

12(½)

235(9¼)

32(1¼) RADIUS

12(½)

111(4⅜) RADIUS

70(2¾)

FILLER CAP

20(¾)

6(¼)

12(½) DIAM

6(¼) DIAM

PETROL TANK

12(½)

47(1⅞)

6(¼)

6(¼) RADIUS

64(2½)

32(1¼) RADIUS

45°

12(½) RADIUS

POSITION OF FILLER CAP

124(4⅞)

25(1)

16(⅝)

175(6⅞)

6(¼) DIAM × 6(¼) DEEP AT 45°

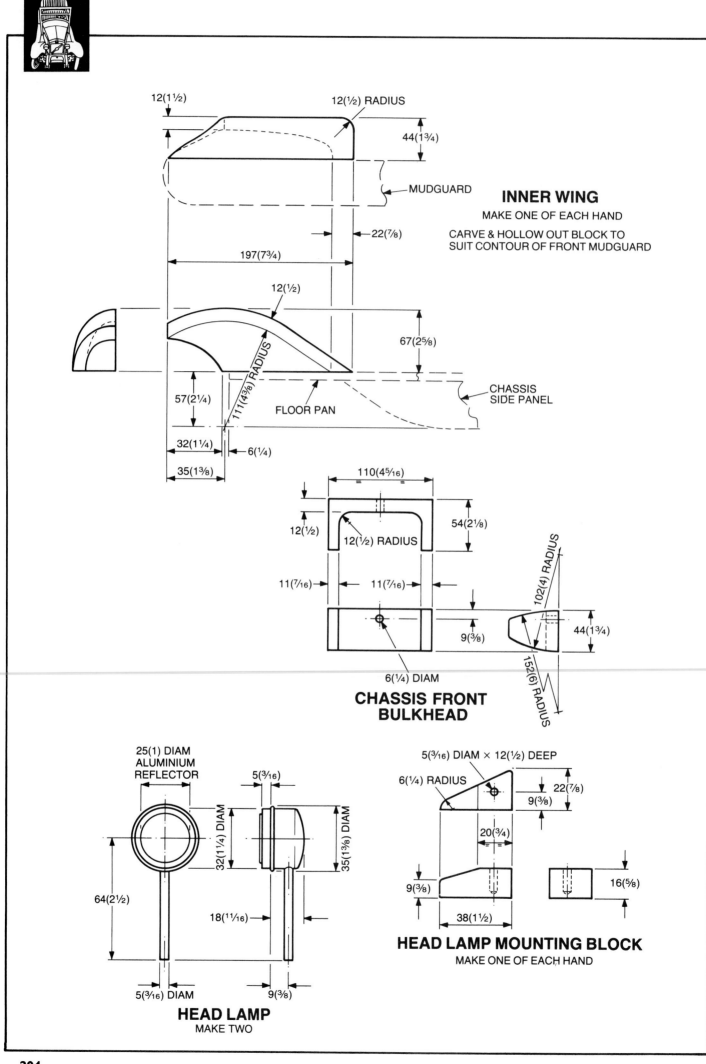

12(1½)

12(½) RADIUS

44(1¾)

MUDGUARD

INNER WING

MAKE ONE OF EACH HAND

CARVE & HOLLOW OUT BLOCK TO
SUIT CONTOUR OF FRONT MUDGUARD

22(⅞)

197(7¾)

12(½)

67(2⅝)

CHASSIS
SIDE PANEL

57(2¼)

111(4⅜) RADIUS

FLOOR PAN

32(1¼)

6(¼)

35(1⅜)

110(4⁵⁄₁₆)

12(½)

54(2⅛)

12(½) RADIUS

11(⁷⁄₁₆)

11(⁷⁄₁₆)

102(4) RADIUS

9(⅜)

44(1¾)

6(¼) DIAM

152(6) RADIUS

CHASSIS FRONT
BULKHEAD

25(1) DIAM
ALUMINIUM
REFLECTOR

5(³⁄₁₆)

32(1¼) DIAM

35(1⅜) DIAM

64(2½)

18(¹¹⁄₁₆)

5(³⁄₁₆) DIAM

9(⅜)

HEAD LAMP
MAKE TWO

5(³⁄₁₆) DIAM × 12(½) DEEP

6(¼) RADIUS

22(⅞)

9(⅜)

20(¾)

9(⅜)

38(1½)

16(⅝)

HEAD LAMP MOUNTING BLOCK
MAKE ONE OF EACH HAND

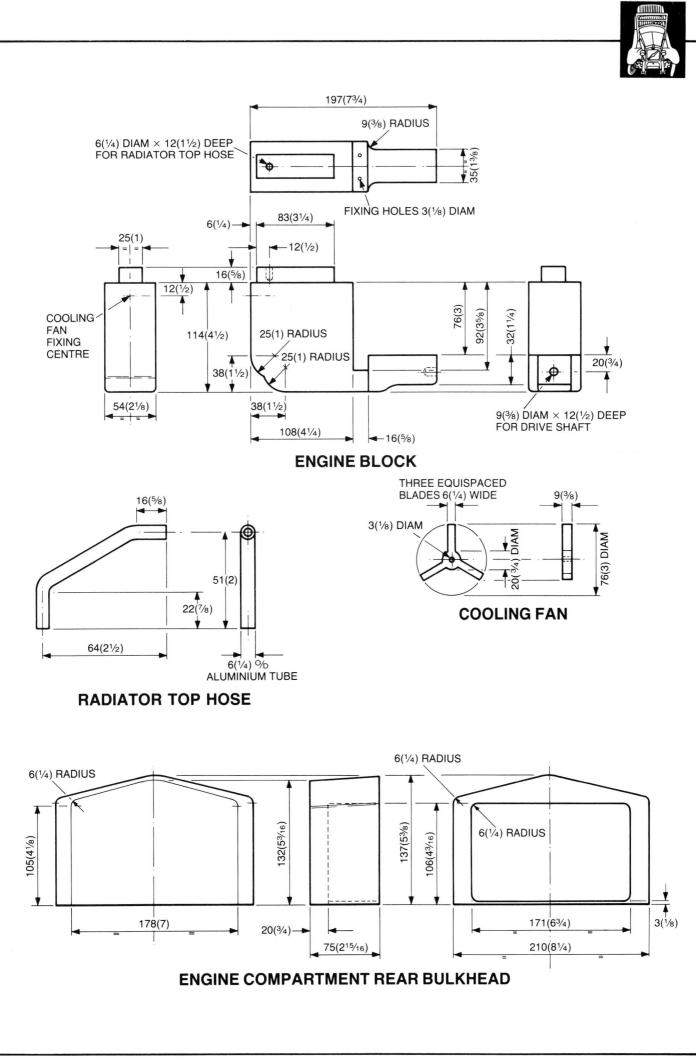

197(7¾)

9(⅜) RADIUS

6(¼) DIAM × 12(1½) DEEP
FOR RADIATOR TOP HOSE

35(1⅜)

FIXING HOLES 3(⅛) DIAM

6(¼)

83(3¼)

25(1)

12(½)

16(⅝)

COOLING
FAN
FIXING
CENTRE

12(½)

114(4½)

25(1) RADIUS

25(1) RADIUS

76(3)

92(3⅝)

32(1¼)

38(1½)

20(¾)

54(2⅛)

38(1½)

9(⅜) DIAM × 12(½) DEEP
FOR DRIVE SHAFT

108(4¼)

16(⅝)

ENGINE BLOCK

16(⅝)

51(2)

22(⅞)

64(2½)

6(¼) ⌀
ALUMINIUM TUBE

RADIATOR TOP HOSE

THREE EQUISPACED
BLADES 6(¼) WIDE

9(⅜)

3(⅛) DIAM

6(¾) DIAM

20(¾)

76(3) DIAM

COOLING FAN

6(¼) RADIUS

6(¼) RADIUS

6(¼) RADIUS

105(4⅛)

132(5³⁄₁₆)

137(5⅜)

106(4³⁄₁₆)

178(7)

20(¾)

75(2¹⁵⁄₁₆)

171(6¾)

210(8¼)

3(⅛)

ENGINE COMPARTMENT REAR BULKHEAD

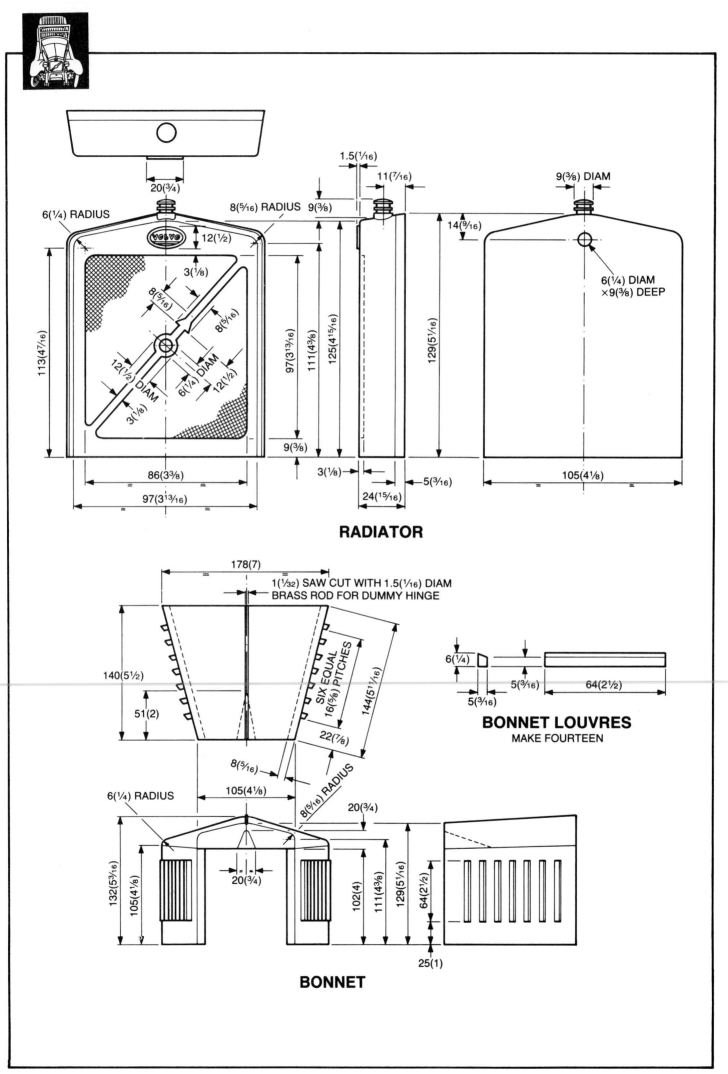

RADIATOR

1(1/32) SAW CUT WITH 1.5(1/16) DIAM BRASS ROD FOR DUMMY HINGE

BONNET LOUVRES
MAKE FOURTEEN

BONNET

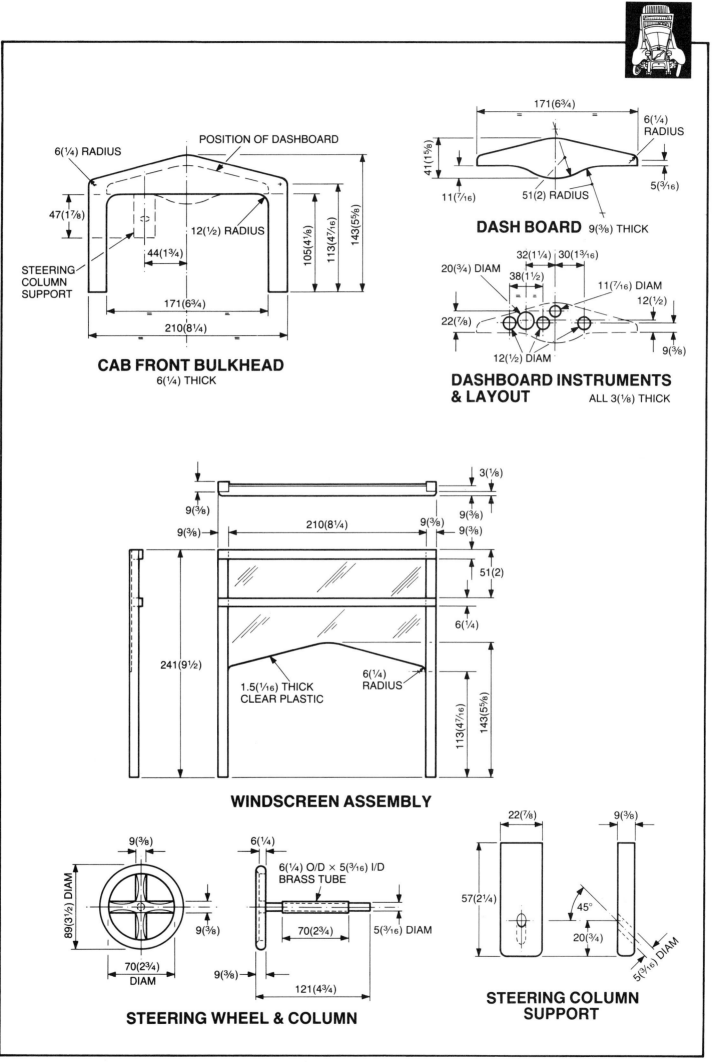

CAB FRONT BULKHEAD
6(¼) THICK

POSITION OF DASHBOARD

6(¼) RADIUS

47(1⅞)

STEERING
COLUMN
SUPPORT

12(½) RADIUS

44(1¾)

105(4⅛)

113(4⁷⁄₁₆)

143(5⅝)

171(6¾)

210(8¼)

DASH BOARD 9(⅜) THICK

171(6¾)

41(1⅝)

6(¼)
RADIUS

5(³⁄₁₆)

11(⁷⁄₁₆)

51(2) RADIUS

DASHBOARD INSTRUMENTS & LAYOUT   ALL 3(⅛) THICK

20(¾) DIAM

32(1¼)

30(1³⁄₁₆)

38(1½)

11(⁷⁄₁₆) DIAM

12(½)

22(⅞)

12(½) DIAM

9(⅜)

WINDSCREEN ASSEMBLY

3(⅛)

9(⅜)

9(⅜)

9(⅜)

9(⅜)

210(8¼)

9(⅜)

9(⅜)

51(2)

6(¼)

241(9½)

1.5(¹⁄₁₆) THICK
CLEAR PLASTIC

6(¼)
RADIUS

113(4⁷⁄₁₆)

143(5⅝)

STEERING WHEEL & COLUMN

9(⅜)

89(3½) DIAM

9(⅜)

70(2¾)
DIAM

6(¼)

6(¼) O/D × 5(³⁄₁₆) I/D
BRASS TUBE

70(2¾)

5(³⁄₁₆) DIAM

9(⅜)

121(4¾)

STEERING COLUMN SUPPORT

22(⅞)

9(⅜)

57(2¼)

45°

20(¾)

5(³⁄₁₆) DIAM

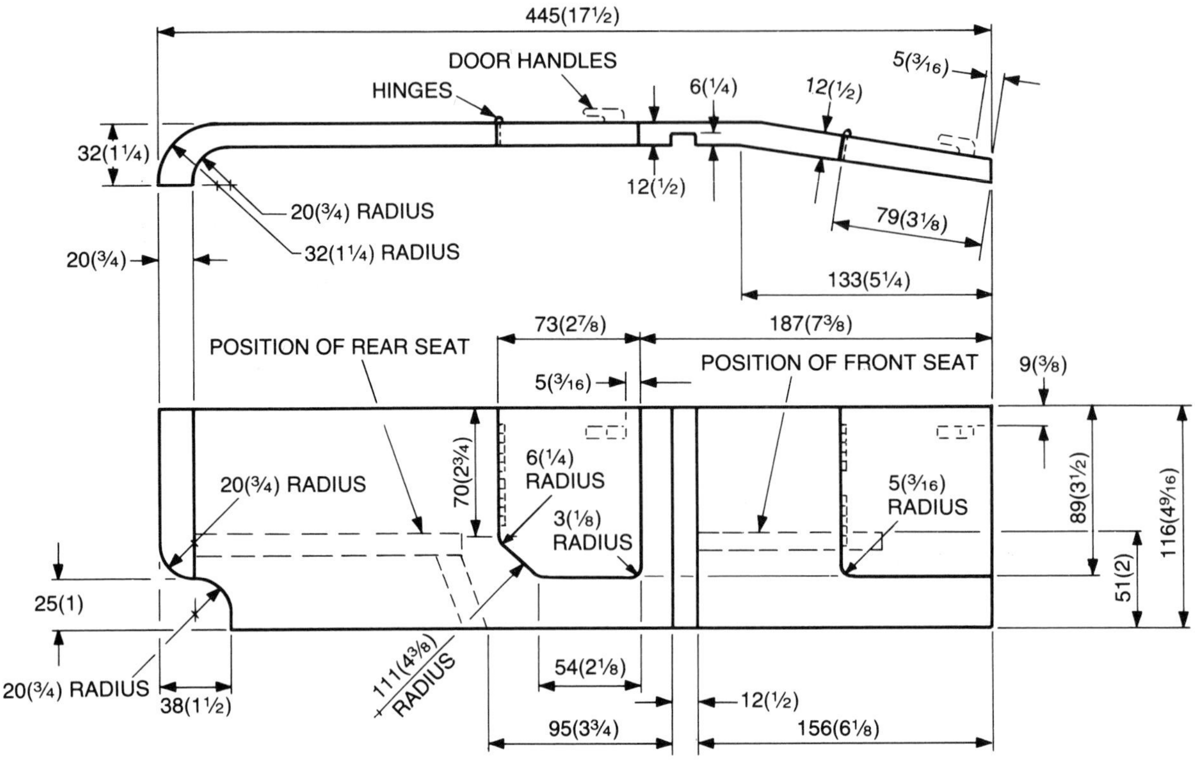
445(17½)
DOOR HANDLES
HINGES
6(¼)
12(½)
5(3/16)
32(1¼)
12(½)
20(¾) RADIUS
32(1¼) RADIUS
79(3⅛)
20(¾)
133(5¼)
73(2⅞)
187(7⅜)
POSITION OF REAR SEAT
POSITION OF FRONT SEAT
9(⅜)
5(3/16)
70(2¾)
6(¼) RADIUS
3(⅛) RADIUS
20(¾) RADIUS
5(3/16) RADIUS
89(3½)
116(4 9/16)
51(2)
25(1)
20(¾) RADIUS
38(1½)
111(4⅜) RADIUS
54(2⅛)
12(½)
95(3¾)
156(6⅛)

SIDE PANEL MAKE ONE OF EACH HAND

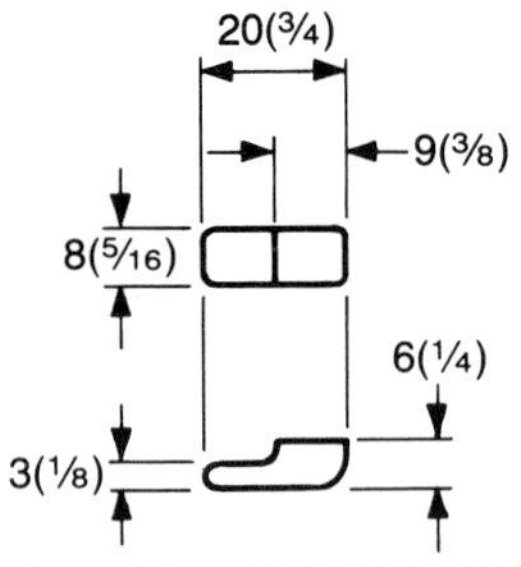
20(¾)
9(⅜)
8(5/16)
6(¼)
3(⅛)

DOOR HANDLE
MAKE FOUR

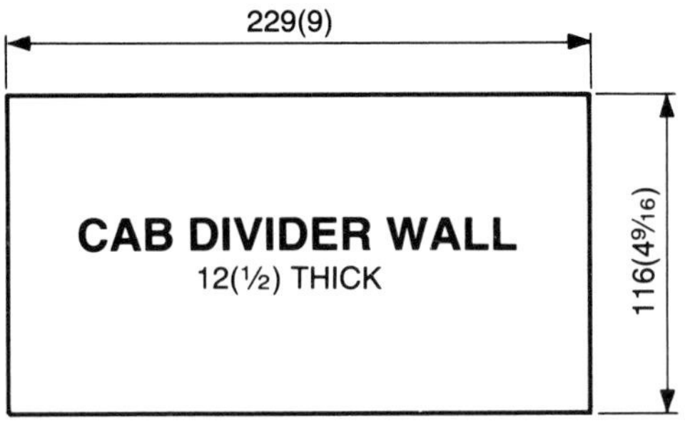
229(9)
CAB DIVIDER WALL
12(½) THICK
116(4 9/16)

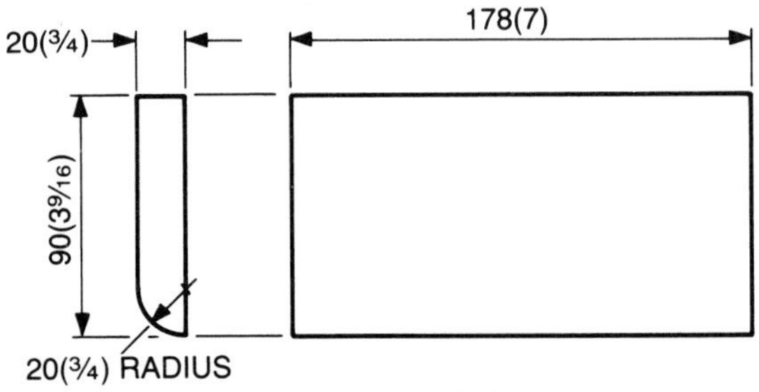
20(¾)
178(7)
90(3 9/16)
20(¾) RADIUS

REAR CAB WALL

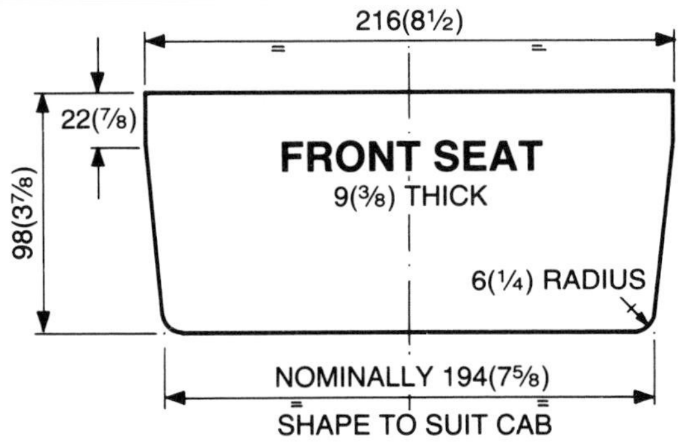
216(8½)
22(⅞)
FRONT SEAT
9(⅜) THICK
98(3⅞)
6(¼) RADIUS
NOMINALLY 194(7⅝)
SHAPE TO SUIT CAB

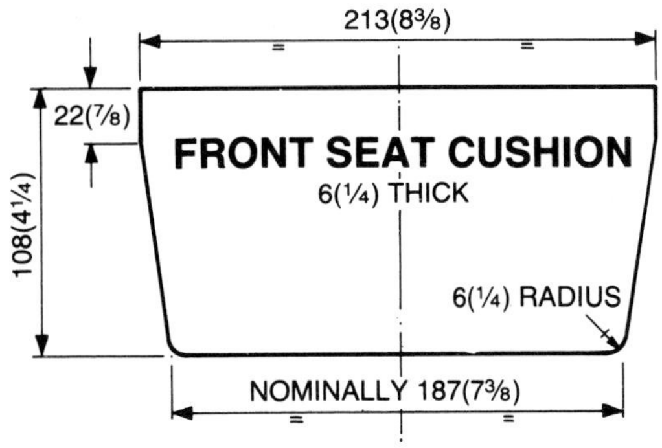
213(8⅜)
22(⅞)
FRONT SEAT CUSHION
6(¼) THICK
108(4¼)
6(¼) RADIUS
NOMINALLY 187(7⅜)

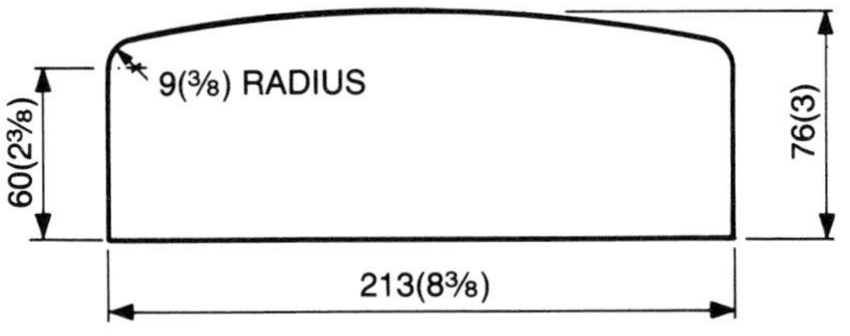
9(⅜) RADIUS
60(2⅜)
76(3)
213(8⅜)

FRONT SEAT BACK CUSHION
6(¼) THICK

CUSHIONS TO BE REEDED AND COVERED IN SOFT LEATHER AS DESCRIBED IN THE TEXT

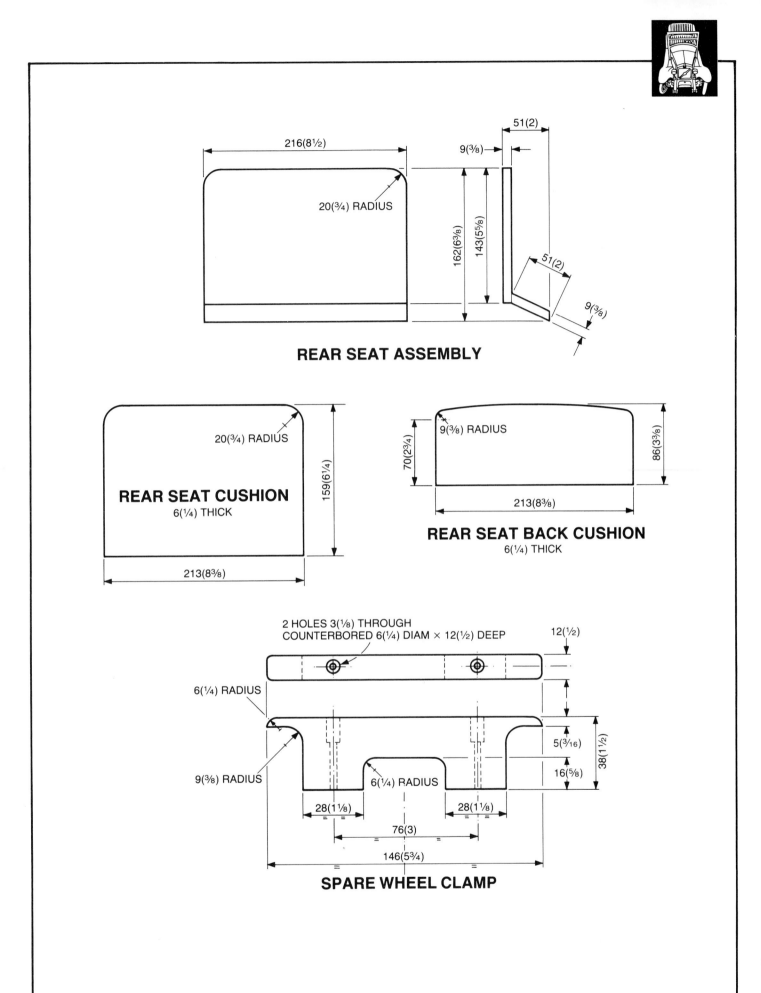

REAR SEAT ASSEMBLY

REAR SEAT CUSHION
6(¼) THICK

REAR SEAT BACK CUSHION
6(¼) THICK

SPARE WHEEL CLAMP

HAND TOOLS

There are a vast selection of these available from a number of most reputable tool makers. I believe you only get what you pay for so don't go for anything cheap; buy a good tool and, unlike your car, it will last you a lifetime.

If you are building up a tool kit for the first time, then on your shopping list must be a good set of, say, **4 bevel-edged wood chisels**. I prefer wooden handles because they improve as you use the chisels. The natural oils of your hands will polish the wood and after a number of years the tool will 'grow on you'. A **wood mallet** for use with these chisels is essential. You must never 'strike' a wooden-handled chisel with a hammer because after repeated blows the wood will split and totally ruin the handle. Plastic **chisel guards** are a good idea too as these prevent any damage to the cutting edge.

Chisels are usually blamed for accidents, as in the phrase 'The chisel slipped'. In reality what happens is that the chisel is allowed to become blunt, the user tries to force it, slips and so injures himself. Therefore a good **oilstone** is important to keep your chisels in good shape. It's also very well worth buying a **honing guide**. This tool holds chisels, plane blades, spokeshaves, and so on at the correct angle while you sharpen them on the oilstone. A variety of honing guides are available – look at them carefully before you buy.

A small set of **twist drills** is important as is a set of **flat bits** for boring large holes in wood. However, flat bits were designed for electric drills and really only work well when they are being rotated at high speed. Flat bits are essential for drilling large holes to take dowel rods, and if you intend to use countersunk screws then a **countersink bit** is another essential.

Cutting wood to length is one of the most basic operations yet unfortunately most DIY woodworkers use a **saw** that's 20 years old and is never sharpened! It's worth considering buying a saw with a 'hard point' label. This means that although the blade cannot be re-sharpened, the teeth on the saw will stay sharp for many many times longer than a traditional saw. However, if you intend to get serious about woodworking then buy a traditional saw – and learn to sharpen it!

The **coping saw** is really a most underestimated tool. It can perform many curved cutting operations very well because the 'back' is rotated around the handle, allowing it to get into many awkward corners. You will also find it most useful when cutting out plywood as its small teeth tend not to 'shatter' the wood.

In the last few years there have been a number of developments in **wood planes** and the traditional plane has seen some challengers. The new type of plane is really a sophisticated file set into a handle and it is very useful and effective. The traditional **smoothing plane** is nevertheless a good investment and, other than needing its blade replaced occasionally, will last longer than you!

A good **screwdriver** is obviously essential and there are some very attractive **ratchet screwdrivers** available that carry a set of different 'bits' in the handle. Check that the one you buy is not too big or heavy – a heavy clumsy screwdriver is a great nuisance.

Making toys often requires the woodworker to use plywood. Fixing plywood together with glue and panel pins will need the assistance of a **hammer**. Now don't think that the old hammer you use for breaking coal will do – it won't! Buy a lightweight **claw** or **warrington pattern hammer** and a **pin punch**. Panel pins are fine for toy-making provided that you punch the pin below the surface of the wood.

The success of any project relies heavily on marking out accurately. You therefore need a **carpenter's square**, and if you intend to get into cutting joints at a later stage then a **mortice gauge** is essential.

I know from many conversations and letters that most woodworkers carry on their craft in a small garden shed or on the kitchen table. It was for this reason that I designed and made the **workbench** featured in this book. You may have the best tools in the world but if the surface you are working on is not stable then your work will suffer. The bench can be fitted with any **vice** but do consider buying the biggest you can afford – it's always cheaper in the long term.

Wood chisel

Joiner's mallet

Oilstone and honing guide

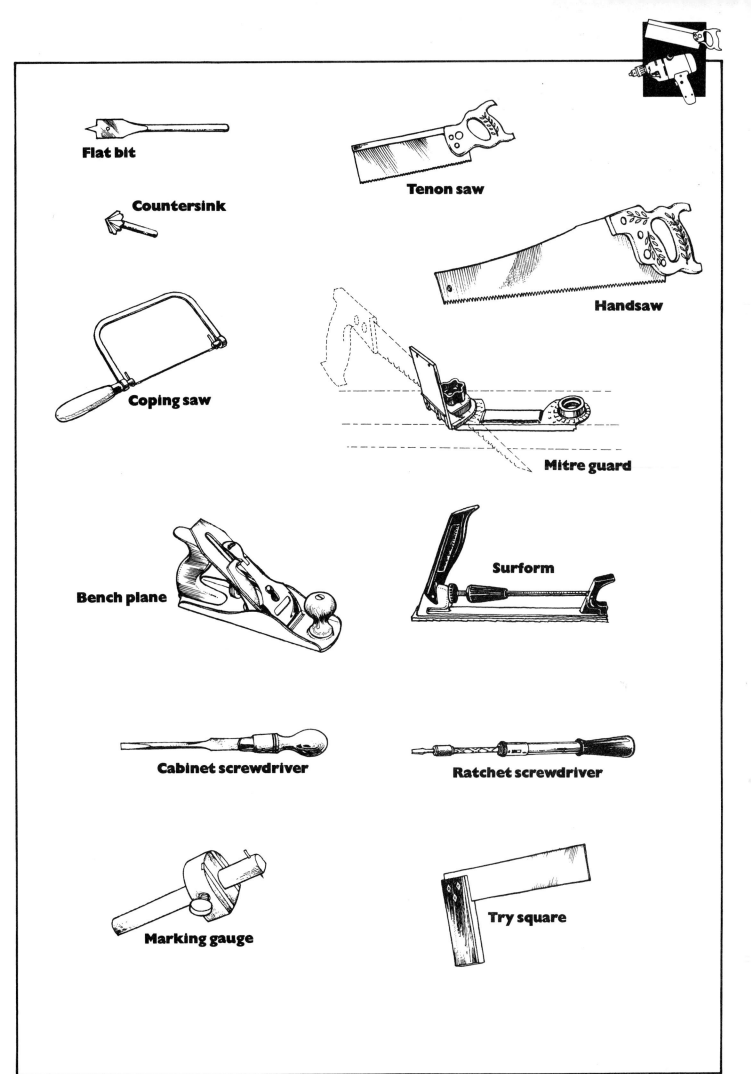

Flat bit

Countersink

Tenon saw

Handsaw

Coping saw

Mitre guard

Bench plane

Surform

Cabinet screwdriver

Ratchet screwdriver

Marking gauge

Try square

211

If you have no experience of power tools at all, don't buy anything until you have been to one of the woodworking shows and seen them demonstrated. I suggest that you also look very carefully through all the catalogues. Weigh up the advantages of each machine carefully and do go to a good shop to get the feel of a tool before you buy it. Most makers of power tools publish catalogues which make very interesting reading (see Useful Addresses, page 215).

Of all the power tools available it is perhaps the **jigsaw** that is most useful (after the electric drill, of course). It will cut almost anything that a conventional saw will – but faster. It is capable of cutting curves and shapes and is altogether a most versatile piece of equipment. One point to look for is a small roller wheel at the back of the blade. I feel this is essential – and the cheaper jigsaws don't have one.

There are also many small **bandsaws** available to the woodworker nowadays, some with very interesting built-in features such as a sanding disc. These machines really do speed up work and in most cases lead the woodworker on to tackle larger and larger jobs.

Bench-top circular saws are more expensive and if you are prepared to pay out this kind of money it's worth considering a 'universal' (a machine that has a saw, planer, spindle moulder and tennoner). These machines have become extremely popular in the last ten years as they are really a complete powered workshop in a small space. However, as I have said, get the catalogues first, watch them demonstrated at shows and really familiarise yourself with all the different makes available before you make your choice.

For small glueing operations such as are involved in making toys and models an electric **glue gun** is excellent. This gun has an electric element in the middle which brings the stick of glue to melting point. Pull the trigger and very hot glue (it really will burn) is ejected exactly to the right spot.

Note You can get some nasty cuts from hand tools and, of course, a bruised thumb from a hammer, but electric tools are far more dangerous. Remember – never wear a tie or scarf or have loose cuffs if you intend to operate an electric power tool.

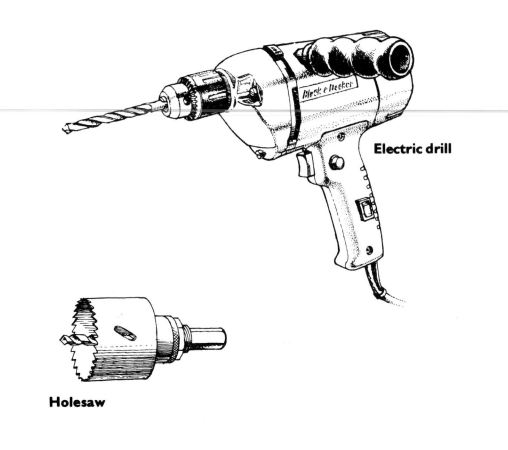

Electric drill

Holesaw

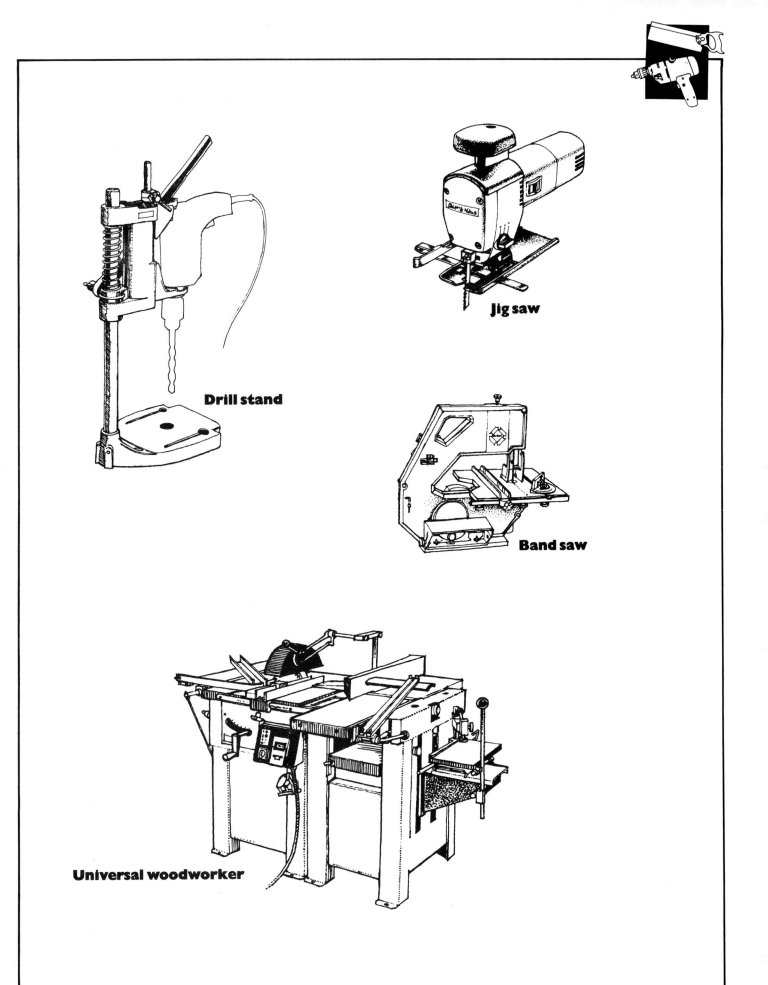

Drill stand

Jig saw

Band saw

Universal woodworker

MATERIALS

In my last toy book, *Blizzard's Wonderful Wooden Toys* (BBC Books, 1983), I used a great variety of woods and have continued to follow this method of enlivening my toys and models by combining different wood colours. I have tried to tell you what the woods I used are in the introductory text to each toy as I know that so many of you wish to use the same ones, but it is not always easy to get exactly what you want and a helpful timber merchant should be able to advise you on alternatives. I always find it worth investigating local companies to see if manufacture of their products results in much waste wood. Companies who specialise in double glazing and hardwood frames often have some prime toy-making offcuts!

Builders' merchants are usually good places to visit not only for tools and ancillaries, but also often joinery-quality softwoods which can be good for toy-making, though not as favoured as hardwoods. A useful softwood which comes in long, wide, straight, knot-free boards is parana pine – expensive but readily available.

In the past five years the number of hardwood suppliers has increased dramatically throughout the UK and I know of at least one supplier who is even prepared to select and make up a 'cutting list order' and post the wood to you. Obviously this is expensive as labour is involved, but it is a good service. Write to John Boddy Timber Ltd, Riverside Sawmills, Boroughbridge, North Yorkshire YO5 9LJ, or try your local Yellow Pages.

Many toy makers have written to me telling me of their visits to sale rooms and of the bargains they find there. This is a good source of supply, but you have to be prepared to dismantle the chest, cupboard or whatever, extract old tacks, panel pins, screws, etc. and maybe remove paint or varnish before work on the actual toy can start. However, oak and mahogany are valuable finds at such places, and I have seen some beautiful toys created from the most ugly pieces of furniture. Avoid using old plywood though; it has usually got weevil or some wood bug.

I am frequently asked about the non-standard sizes of timber I use in some of the complex models. When you are building a climbing frame, rocking horse, workbench, etc. the timber sizes are often not critical to the overall appearance of the finished item. However, when it is a model truck such as the Volvo 540 then the sizes of the timber are very important to the overall look of the finished vehicle. If you are going to build the models in this book successfully then you are going to have to plane timber to the thickness given. Obviously this is time-consuming, but to get the model to look right there is no easy way.

Paints and varnishes are a vital part of the finishing-off process, but do check on the can that the product you intend to use is non-toxic and quite safe for children (see Useful Addresses, opposite).

If you intend to leave any of the toys outdoors then it's advisable to use brass screws. If you use steel ones they will rust after only a very short period of time resulting in horrible marks on the wood.

USEFUL ADDRESSES

Because of the large number of specialty stores and catalogs that carry woodworking products, we suggest you consult your local Yellow Pages or look through the ads in many specialty magazines for the materials required in this book. However, accessories such as wheels and the go cart crank mechanism can be obtained from the author. Write to: R. Blizzard (Wheels), P.O. Box 5, Gloucester GL3 4RJ, U.K. Readers should please note that the Publisher cannot guarantee the supply of such parts. All queries should be directed to R. Blizzard.

INDEX